Mimetic Reflections

MIMETIC REFLECTIONS

A Study in
Hermeneutics, Theology, and Ethics

by

WILLIAM SCHWEIKER

FORDHAM UNIVERSITY PRESS
NEW YORK

Schweiker, William.
  Mimetic reflections: a study in hermeneutics, theology, and ethics.

  ISBN: 0–8232–1254–8

  1. Imitation. 2. Hermeneutics. 3. Theology. 4. Ethics. I. Title.

BH301.I55 S38 1995
190   LCCN: 89–85847

CONTENTS

ACKNOWLEDGMENTS

Like most books, this one has gone through many versions and formulations. Some of the material originally appeared in different form in a doctoral thesis written at The University of Chicago under the direction of James M. Gustafson, David Tracy, and Langdon B. Gilkey. I thank each of my mentors. My debt to them is obvious throughout the pages of this study even as I chart different directions of thought.

The argument of the book has been substantially rethought for its presentation in the current form. Bits of the argument have appeared in articles. I have noted these in the text. Throughout this process of rethinking, I have received insight and encouragement from C. Edward Arrington, Kristine Culp, Lois Daly, Julius J. Jackson, Jr., David E. Klemm, Terence J. Martin, Jr., Richard B. Miller, Douglas F. Ottati, Douglas Schuurman, Barry Stenger, and Michael Welker. My thanks to each of them. In and through these friendships the power of solidarity and of speaking has transformed and enhanced my thought.

Bringing a manuscript through revision and to publication is not an easy task. This work has been made easier for me through the care of Fordham University Press. I have also received considerable help with the text from Jane E. Jadlos, Beth Colleen Junker, Kelton Cobb, Peter Gerhard, and Steve McGuire. Each of them demanded clarity of me—a demand, I fear, I have not always met.

Along the way I received support from the Charlotte B. Newcombe Fellowship, the Dempster Graduate Award, the Institute for the Advanced Study of Religion at The University of Chicago, and an Old Gold Fellowship through the University of Iowa. My thanks to each of these institutions.

Finally, my deepest gratitude to my parents, William and Novello Schweiker, and my wife, Mary Ingberg Schweiker. Their lives have formed and refigured mine in ways too deep to express.

This book, like any other, is not the product of one person's imagination, insight, and labor. Yet for all of that, I alone remain responsible for its argument.

By Way of Introduction

The argument of this book is carried on at three interrelated levels. First, I contend that the problem of "mimesis" helps to unfold dimensions of hermeneutical reflection. In the exploring of it, the concerns and contributions of important theorists come to light. More specifically, I undertake a reading of the works of Hans-Georg Gadamer, Paul Ricoeur, and Søren Kierkegaard in two ways. First, I explore what I call the "mimetic strategies" of these thinkers relative to the classical and Enlightenment uses of imitation theory now under criticism. My claim is that any thinking beyond imitation requires undoing and reconstructing mimesis vis-à-vis the problems that imitation was used to conceptualize and address. These problems ranged from aesthetics to metaphysics, but they centered on understanding and language, truth claims, and the formation of the moral agent. Accordingly, I examine Gadamer's hermeneutic of understanding and language, Ricoeur's theory of narrative as a paradigmatic case of the mimetic power of language, and Kierkegaard's claims about human passion and existence relative to the *imitatio Christi*.

My concern in these chapters is to grasp the shape and texture of each position in relation to the problematic of mimesis. These readings are not extensive commentaries on the thinkers in question with respect to their dependency on and departure from other major figures, like Kant or Heidegger. That kind of scholarship is best left to works dedicated to an individual thinker. Yet I do argue that mimesis does open up a fruitful reading of the thinkers in question.

Second, the book attempts to reclaim the notion of mimesis as crucial for contemporary reflection. Of course, the very idea of critically reclaiming questions, problems, and ideas is suspect in much current philosophical and theological discourse, especially when such reclaiming is taken to mean repristinating past ideas and concepts. Thought cannot re-enact past modes of reflection untainted by its own historicity; ideas, concepts, and forms of discourse cannot simply be reduplicated in different historical contexts by different minds without some consequence for their meaning. A romantic return to the past is not possible for those like us who are mired in time and language.

Mindful of the historicity of understanding and the other that remains other, hermeneutical reflection seeks to understand that which is different. More to the point, it seeks to understand what is covered up, even what we think is most evident and obvious. Therefore, when I say that the second task of this book is the critical reconstruction of mimesis, I clearly do not mean a return to lost origins or a repristination of past ideas. Of course, to be mired in time and language does mean that the past has effects on the present. There will be continuity as well as discontinuity in the reading of mimesis I am proposing. Yet given that, what I am undertaking is an alternative interpretation of mimesis enriched by contemporary critiques seeking to inform the task of reflection. I think that the current criticism of mimesis and the manifold forms of anti-mimetic thought have diverted us from what is covered up, even though it is close to us — as close as our own understanding, action, and the struggle to be selves with others.

The pressing question for this second level of my argument is then: Why mimesis? I contend that it is a valuable interpretive key to current hermeneutics, theology, and ethics because it crosses through the array of problems now facing us. These are questions about meaning and power relative to language and understanding, text, and personal existence. The fragmentation that marks the postmodern *ethos*, a dissemination regarding language, self, and world, is understandable in part as the breakdown of classical and modernist mimeticism. Thus I am simultaneously employing mimesis as a clue both for reading postmodern thinkers and for critically reconsidering its hermeneutical import for current thought.

As a work in hermeneutics there is a bit of irony in the book's title. Mimesis has often been used to speak about thinking or art as an activity of copying or mirroring what is under question, and "reflection" also has been taken to imply that mental acts "reflect" and "refract" the world they represent through ideas and images, themselves "mirrors" of reality. Thus the title of the book seems to suggest a form of realistic thinking currently under attack by theologians and philosophers as well as literary theorists and cultural critics. The irony is that the reconstruction of mimesis I undertake provides the means for the deconstruction of imitative thought about language, understanding, and the human condition. At least this is my argument.

But there is more. To title this text *Mimetic Reflections* is to suggest that current thinkers continue to wrestle with the problem of understanding a meaningful world, the relation of time and action, and the task of being a self. And it is to claim that these are questions we should continue to explore. The book carries on an inquiry into these problems by attempting to think with and yet beyond previous ways of considering them. The reason for this approach is simply that our thinking cannot escape the past even as it seeks to address the specific questions that confront us now. The concern of this study is to explore the ways we think and speak about the human condition in all its complexity and ambiguity. Such thinking arises out of and returns to the welter of life or it becomes vacuous and pointless. Our interpretations, in other words, must wrestle with the claims of others and the world.

This leads to the third level of my argument. The final concern of this book is not simply to reconstruct mimesis and provide a reading of current thinkers. It is to make a modest proposal for ways of thinking theologically and ethically about the questions we face. Of course, in this book I do not attempt to put forward a comprehensive construal of the being and activity of "God," the status, import, and possibility of such thinking and speaking, or the relation of the divine to world and human being and doing. In short, this is not a theology. Nor is it an ethic. I have not attempted a comprehensive account of the meaning and value of human being and doing, modes of practical reasoning, or the examination of ways of life relative to an articulable measure of the well-lived life. Nevertheless, though this work is not a theology or an ethic, it is oriented by them and seeks to provide a mode of reflection to help carry them out.

At present there is considerable suspicion about the relation of hermeneutics to theology and ethics. On the one hand, there are theologians who argue that reflection on the status of theological and ethical discourse removed from the particularities of a community's narratives begins in error. These critics hold that hermeneutical reflection necessarily takes human being-in-the-world as *the* subject matter of any text, including religious ones. Given this, a hermeneutically informed theology becomes an interpretation of existential questions, reducing without remainder religious beliefs and symbols to present concerns. On the other hand, there are thinkers who claim that all hermeneutical reflection will, by the nature of the case, undo itself, given the playful character of language. To claim that reflection on the way we think and speak about human being and doing will advance any constructive understanding of the human project or of the divine is naïve. The task, these critics claim, is to deconstruct our pretenses to such projects.

It is important to note that mimesis is central to each of these criticisms of hermeneutics. And my own substantive argument will draw on insights from each. However, I contest their conclusions about the kind of inquiry this work must represent. Hermeneutical reflection, as I use the term, is indeed concerned with human being and doing, but it also seeks to understand what confronts us as different and other, whether that other is the Word of God, the face of the poor, or the strange claims of the past. It is concerned with the *Sache*, the subject matter, in question, but always in relation to some interpreter. And because this kind of reflection is a form of practical thinking, it is not reducible to the structure and play of sign systems. Hermeneutical thinking is irreducibly tied to the problems of life. Such reflection does not necessarily attempt to escape or control our finitude; nor must it attempt to reduce all texts and traditions to existentialist questions about the meaning of authentic human life as an act of freedom. It is a way of carrying on the task of theological and ethical reflection. However, regarding the third level of the argument, the constructive one, the question returns: Why mimesis? Beyond the presence of mimetic strategies in current forms of theological and ethical reflection, why consider it in the constructive task of thought?

As has often been noted, theologians currently face a twofold "crisis" regarding the status and import of their reflection: a crisis of cognitive claims about the truth and meaningfulness of religious discourse, and a crisis of praxis relative to religious symbols, beliefs, and claims about human moral and political existence. If nothing else, this dual problematic means that for any theology to be persuasive it must surmount the separation of theology and ethics and struggle to be truly theological and truly ethical. As one step in this direction, I have attempted in this book to unfold a set of questions and to develop a mode of reflection that can address these issues on their own grounds and in their own way.

Thus mimesis is important for the task of theological and ethical reflection because it signals a constellation of problems inherent in Western discourse about the divine and human life. This tradition has become gravely problematic and even oppressive for most, if not all, of us. I contend that its problematic and heteronomous character is related in great part to classical and modern mimeticisms. Yet even the notion of a "tradition" poses difficulties. Given this, the task of thinking with and beyond received problems and modes of discourse is both a challenge and a necessity: a challenge because what has been bequeathed us is not sufficient to meet our questions; and a necessity because thought is irreducibly finite and mired in time and language. Taking up this challenge and that necessity is the task of any hermeneutically informed mode of reflection, whether in theology and ethics or not. It is the form of thinking I am attempting to practice in this work.

Obviously, any critical and reflective work is undertaken from some perspective or point of view. This is certainly the case with the present work. My standpoint is mentioned and employed throughout even as the argument seeks to unfold some of its import. It entails the contention that knowledge of the human condition cannot simply be derived from theological claims or religious narratives, and that discourse about the divine is not easily reduced to claims about authentic human being and doing or the natural world. Given this, the argument seeks to unfold those practices crucial for understanding the human condition, even as these imply the question of our relation to the divine as that in which we live, move, and have our being. This stance, which entails substantive and interpretive claims, is hardly unproblematic. However, it is crucial if we are to make any sense of the symbol "God," the human experience of the divine, religious and moral discourse, and the complex character of the human condition. At least this is what part of my argument tries to show.

The specific stance and mode of reflection that I seek to practice in this work helps to explain why I have chosen to explore the thinkers I have. After all, it might appear odd to read hermeneutical thinkers on the way to theology and ethics. Of those I explore in depth only Kierkegaard is customarily called a theologian. Yet since I am trying to explore questions that permeate the ways we think and speak about human being and doing with others and in relation to the divine, it is necessary to explore those thinkers who directly address these issues. This is all the more the case regarding mimesis. Thus the task of reconstructing mimesis and contributing to theology and ethics has shaped my selection of thinkers to consider. Any constructive work in theology and ethics along these lines must finally think beyond those whom I have explored here. It must also, I believe, think with them.

This book seeks, then, to carry on an argument at three interrelated levels. It is a contribution to understanding central postmodern thinkers, the reconstruction of an important notion in our intellectual and cultural traditions, and a step toward the tasks of theology and ethics. In the end it remains inconclusive while indicating a direction of thought and a set of problems that I think must be explored by theologians, philosophers, literary theorists, and cultural critics. If my argument is found persuasive, my hope is to follow this direction of inquiry further and to explore the problems that still call for some response.

Chicago, December 1989   WILLIAM SCHWEIKER

Mimetic Reflections

1

A Shattered Universe

OUR AGE IS ONE of suspicion and critique. It is one also turned against itself. There is a deep and pervasive challenge to the way we understand our lives and our world in all their wonder and ambiguity. *Homo faber, Homo dialogicus*, the "thinking reed," and the "image of God"—these images of the human, and many others as well, are all under critical examination. And so they should be. Part of the task of life for us is reflection on our being and doing. After all, the human is, as Iris Murdoch has put it, "a creature who makes a picture of [itself] and then comes to resemble the picture. This is the process which moral philosophy must attempt to describe and analyze."[1]

The problem we face is the breakdown both of what is meant by "image" and of the specific images we have used in understanding ourselves. Still we confront the ancient demand to "know thyself," even as we seek to orient the exercise and burden of our freedom. We confront this demand with the knowledge that the forms of discourse, images, symbols, and "pictures" used to interpret life concretely inform what it is we become. Given this, there are criticisms and suspicions of all attempts to find *the* image of the human and to inscribe our self-understanding within its analogical logic. In this, our age turns against itself; we seem condemned to the criticism of images of life while we remain strangers to ourselves.

Under the current challenge to traditional notions of the human, the import and logic of the image, and the continual search for understanding, it is necessary to take stock of the way we think about our world and ourselves and of the images and ideas we use in doing so. This taking stock is not simply at the service of conceptual clarity and reflective precision. More fundamentally, an inquiry into the way we think and speak about human life and our world seeks to understand basic questions and problems about the human dilemma. This book is a taking stock in both these senses: it is an examination of ways of thinking that have informed our images of the human, and it is an inquiry into human life and its world.

My contention is that for much of Western thought a cluster of issues surrounding the way we understand human being and doing, the meaningfulness of our world, and our relation to that world has been encapsulated in the notion "imitation." Traditional imitation theory, as we shall see, held that thought is a "reflection" of transcendent ideas, the divine mind, nature, or the transcendental act of mind itself. And it also held that works of art, language, and ideas are imitations, representations, or copies of some external reality or mental acts. Thus the meaning and veracity of thought and language consisted in a relation between them and their referent. For us this neat parceling out of reality is problematic, to say the least.

But naturalistic and idealistic ideas and criticisms of mimesis as "imitation" tend to camouflage important insights and problems. The terminology of mimesis actually arose from mime drama and cultic action. Through the action of the mime a play is presented, just as in cultic action a sacred myth is enacted. This performative character of mimetic praxis is missed when "imitation" is dominated by the logic of representation. The historical questions of why and to what end the Greeks first used cultic and dramatic language in philosophical discourse are not the concern of this study. Perhaps it is simply an example of the priority of symbolic and everyday discourse over critical reflection. Be that as it may, these historical questions are ones for classical scholars and historians of philosophy. What is of interest for the thinkers I shall explore is the import of mimesis for thinking and speaking about fundamental philosophical and theological topics. My contention is that the postmodern hermeneutical use of mimesis rests precisely on reclaiming its performative roots in a variety of domains of thought about the human condition.

Most basically my claim is that mimesis helps us talk about the way human beings participate in the generative power of their world to render it and human existence meaningful. The full import of this claim can be unfolded only through the course of this work, but two things should be noted at the outset. (a) Mimesis in classical thought attempted to articulate the manifestation of being as meaningful, either in art and language or in the physical world itself. This concern continues in the postmodern thinkers we shall study. Yet they reclaim a performative understanding of mimesis in order to overturn classical metaphysics, theories of thought and language, and reflection on the human.

(b) Mimesis, true to its performative roots, implies a question about how Being is rendered meaningful and how the meaning of being human is disclosed. This concern is found in classical thinkers, whether in Plato's use of mimesis for moral theory or in Aristotle's theory of plot and moral edification, and continues in the current discussion as well. But can mimesis serve to help us think and speak about the ways humans render the world meaningful and realize their own existence? The authors I shall study think so. Mimesis is, then, a notion for moral philosophy; it is a way to speak about human being and doing relative to the world in which we live, move, and have our being.

Mimesis is a notion that bridges reflection on the meaning of Being and on human being and doing through the act of figuration in action and language. It helps us consider the problem of the image and its logic while providing ways to think with and yet beyond it. My suspicion is that this is the reason mimesis has again captured the attention of postmodern hermeneutical thinkers. The task of this chapter is to show the plausibility of this claim, and in order to do so, I must isolate the dimensions of the problem inherent in discourse about mimesis.

DOMAINS OF THE PROBLEM

Human life, whatever else we wish to say about it, is a quest for meaning carried out through language and action. We are symbol-using and -interpreting agents. At present there is a reconsideration of the truth of symbols and language through the exploration of the figural character of all linguistic expressions. The assumption that literary works, for instance, are "pictures" of a prior non-linguistic reality is problematic for anyone who is aware of the symbolic character of human culture and consciousness, and who has questioned a vision of reality parceled out between the ideal and the actual, the transcendental and the categorical.[2] These distinctions were the hallmark of classical and modernist theories of texts and symbols. Symbols and works of art, so these theories went, participate in some antecedent reality that they "represent." Through representation the human mind has the power to capture within its system of signs and analogies that which is represented. Thus "representation" denoted not only the dependency of thought and language on reality but also their power to inscribe it, and hence any conceivable other, in a total system. The contemporary challenge to "representation," as a mainstay of Western thinking about human knowing and communicating, demands attention.

But human life is not only the search for meaning within its world; it is also a response to a world of power and the quest for truthful existence. We are moral beings, agents who interpret our world and our lives. The problem of what counts for a good life is perplexing and troubling. Once the radical historicity of human life is granted, the incommensurability of cultural values, standards, and mores seems inevitable. How do we speak across cultural lines to evaluate human desires, aspirations, and actions in the quest to speak about authentic human life? Perhaps we must admit that universalizable moral claims are impossible. Yet given that conclusion, can we avoid the reduction of moral claims to personal preference or communal ideology, thereby abandoning all critical perspective on the human project? Likewise, the claim that the self is infinitely plastic and hence formed simply by its cultural context curtails all talk about human "nature." But given this assumption, can we speak of the value and status, not to mention moral failure, of the self? Is moral reflection limited simply to evaluating and justifying public acts, mores, and ideologies? Put differently: Is the domination of the political so thorough that we cannot explore the dispositions, desires, and passions that drive individual and communal existence with some idea of the genuinely human?[3]

Within the Western religious traditions these questions about symbols, human agency, and reflection become all the more complex. Modernity has relegated religious beliefs and convictions to the private sphere and hence deprived them of any status in the assessment of our condition. The power of religious texts and symbols to inform thinking, being, and doing does seem problematic simply because of the cultural and historical distance between their origin and the present conditions of life. More important, the experience of massive suffering that scars the face of this century, coupled with the rise of critical reflection, challenges the plausibility that religious traditions have much to offer our self-understanding. Appeals to the wisdom of religious traditions seem facile and glib, perhaps self-deceptive. Clearly, the import of these traditions for our self-examination is not ambiguous or intuitively obvious. In this situation, how can personal or communal existence be informed in any small way by the classic texts and beliefs of a religious tradition?

The complexity of these questions about language, experience, agency, and reflection is doubled by the fact that they are interdependent. They mark out the problems I shall consider in the following chapters, and they implicate the mode of reflection I hope to practice. The task here is to articulate a way of reflecting on the shape, texture, and fragility of human experience and its world. The winds sweeping our culture challenge this type of reflection. The wild plurality and fragmentation of our situation rightly oppose all oppressive structures and monisms, but they also threaten us with conceptual, moral, and religious chaos.[4] Any attempt to reflect on the coherence of our experience seems undone or beside the point.

Of course, a host of methods and theories has been developed to explore the moral, religious, and linguistic dimensions of experience. What is unique about our situation is not the pluralism of approaches and interpretations of the human condition—that has always been the case—but the seeming fragmentation of our discourse about the myriad dimensions of human experience. This fragmentation is often taken as the mark of the postmodern situation. No doubt it is. Yet there are wider problems germane to this inquiry that mark out the postmodern mindset.

The pressing problems of our day have to do with our relation to the natural world, the shape and texture of human existence and action, and the crisis of meaning seen in the despair and anxiety that mark Western culture in the face of technology, the erosion of confidence in transcendental accounts of subjectivity, and the failure of any progressivist view of history and culture, even given the startling developments in Eastern Europe. Along with the sense of fragmentation just noted, I take these problems and the breakdown of the modern answers to the human dilemma to mark out the postmodern *ethos*. Indeed, this chapter can be seen as an inquiry into the domains of that *ethos* as they bear on theological and ethical reflection and cohere with the problem of how we "picture" human life, as Murdoch puts it. Of course, it is too much to claim that rethinking mimesis will help us address these global problems. The task here is more modest: to reflect on how we speak and think about human being and doing in relation to our world and the universe of meaning.

The task before us is to develop a construal of human life that will allow us to see the relation of understanding, language, and human agency, while facing squarely the current criticism of traditional visions of human life. The problem we face is the full implication of our escape from an "imitative" image of the human, its world, language, and even the cosmos. But what does that mean? In the remainder of this chapter I want to try to answer that question.

I make no pretense of providing in a single chapter anything like an exhaustive interpretation of our situation. Moreover, I am not providing a detailed interpretation of the thinkers I shall use in illustrating the problem of imitation. My aim throughout this chapter is simply to isolate the various dimensions of the problem of imitation and to determine what it means to escape a vision of human world marked by an imitative mindset. The postmodern *ethos*, I suggest, is marked by several traits I have already noted that signal it as an escape from an imitative world. There are, first, criticism of and concern for the image or figure beyond imitative logic which touch not only aesthetics but also our understanding of the human project. Next, there is the sense of fragmentation and gaming in our conceptual as well as our cultural and political lives. And, finally, there is a radical questioning of modern thought itself, specifically its concern for self-reflective critical rationality grounded in freedom.[5] My contention is that imitation provides both a way to understand the relation of these aspects of our situation and a clue to the perduring questions we face. In this chapter we shall see in brief fashion that aesthetic and ontological uses of imitation have formed the backdrop for religious and moral imitation. Correspondingly, religious and moral imitation take up and express differently these ontological, aesthetic, and hermeneutical issues. I hope this chapter will shed some light on why imitation is again an issue for us and not simply a topic for the history of ideas.

THE ESCAPE FROM IMITATION

Throughout much of the Western intellectual tradition imitation was used to render conceptual and perceptual chaos into an harmonious universe of thought and value. Texts were seen as the imitation of nature or of an author's intentions and genius. The moral life was to be the imitation of the "good man," the gods, or the One God. And the world was a theater of God's glory, the shadows or images of divine things, so that, armed with a sacred text, one could read the world in order to speak analogically about the divine purposes. The human stood amid an imitative and symbolic universe and interpreted itself in its matrix of meaning. What is more, every aspect of reality derived its purpose and value from its cosmic station. The power of imitation was that it allowed one to see the connections of meanings, world, value, and God and hence to articulate an ordered existence. That order was strict but elusive because the various levels of reality more or less mirrored each other. The ancient theory of imitation meant, then, that human discourse and symbols take their meaning not from their immanent subject matter or the presentation of human being and doing in the world, but from their representation of external or natural reality.[6] Truth was the correspondence between a representation and its "referent."

Ancient mimeticism has fallen under suspicion, and with good reason. Human life is indeed a search for understanding, which we undertake by interpreting a symbolic, linguistic world. No doubt this is why ancient interpretive practices, ranging from allegory to narrative, hold perduring hermeneutical import.[7] And yet, we know the meaning of a text, an event, or our world only through the text itself or the conceptual framework within which we place events. It is difficult, perhaps impossible, to know how that meaning matches or represents the world outside the text, let alone how the "world" might reflect deeper reaches of Being. In fact, the most powerful texts, events, experiences, and actions do not so much copy the world as refigure it.[8] The travail of interpretation is to explore the clash of meanings that texts and events generate, not their simple correspondence to "reality." Yet "imitation," as an aesthetic concept, implied that interpretation, and hence understanding, is primarily about checking references to "reality." We simply cannot perform these checks in any definitive sense. The dream of an imitative totality, a system of coherent signs referable to "reality," remains just that, a dream.

With the Enlightenment and the rise of critical philosophy in the West, the vision of the human enmeshed in a pre-given symbolic universe completely broke down. The soul and the cosmos no longer enjoyed a simple imitative relation. Critical thought turned to the active powers of the mind to understand our world. Texts were seen as expressions of human genius, and the problem of meaning became one of interpreting these expressive figurations against the backdrop of the transcendental character of human freedom and feeling. Ironically, in our context this critical turn itself has fallen to criticism. The current concern for language shows that transcendental interpretations of the human and its symbolic world are not sufficient. We are too aware of the way interpretive action shapes meaning and what is meant by "text" to assume that we can easily interpret a text by isolating the author's intention, even if that were possible. The turn to language as crucial to human world explains the retrieval of ancient interpretive practices just noted, because a concentration on language and figural interpretation demonstrates the abiding relation of being and linguistic praxis.

The criticisms of premodern and modernist thought demonstrate that the problem with imitation is manifestly not only aesthetic and epistemological but ontological. That is, "imitation" implied some understanding of the meaning and structure of Being. Not surprisingly, the classical ontology of imitation is under suspicion since it meant that ideas and relations had reality devoid of any relation to human thought and language. The human mind was depicted as a mirror with little part in the construction of its world of meaning and value. This suggested that what is real is going on, as it were, behind our backs and that the phenomenal world of language and action had to be transcended to grasp the real. Ancient mimeticism often devalued the phenomenal and along with it all the bearers of reality, like the body, nature, and words or signs. Ironically, while striving for realism, traditional imitation rested on an intuition of the real, beyond the mediation of thought and language, in order to test the truth of our thought and actions.

Modernist expressivism and constructivism, in which the human mind fashions a meaningful world from the givens of intuition, also seem problematic. Such constructivism fails to acknowledge the dependency of thought on language, on the givenness of our linguistic world and practices. Modern idealism isolated the transcendentally free self, the "I," from a world of causal and affective relations. The "I" designated the power and unity of the self that must be thought but cannot be grasped since the "I" in the reflexive act is still the power and unity of the self in its own self-reflection. In this way the "I" was taken to transcend and even constitute its world even as it retreats within reflection. Such an "I" announces one dimension of alienation suffered by our culture. Imitation has again become a topic of inquiry, it would appear, because through this notion we are asking about the human relation to its world through figuration. Better yet, it prompts consideration on the ways in which an environment becomes a meaningful world.

The problem of imitation challenges fundamental assumptions about the way things are and our relation to the world. Because we have only an interpreted access to reality, any claim to the "way things are" is an evaluative stance. What much of our intellectual and cultural traditions assumed, and we reject, is that a criterion of value is simply written into the fabric of existence and free from our participation in its construal. We seek to escape a hierarchical and imitative universe in thought and in action, and yet our traditions are wedded to imitative ways of speaking about human and natural existence. At least since Nietzsche, it has been clear that the human participates in the creation of values. The rise of modernity was a celebration of human capacities for creativity. Yet it sought to free the human from the givenness of participation in the patterns of the natural and social world. The question now is how best to understand the ways in which we participate in our world both to disclose and to enhance relations that sustain, order, limit, and make possible all life.

Our escape from an imitative image of life touches, then, on the basic ontological, epistemological, and axiological assumptions that undergird our cultural tradition. Understanding what our escape from an imitative universe means demands a more detailed look at the metaphysical and ontological uses of imitation. This, in turn, will provide an entrance into moral and religious questions.

IMITATION AND METAPHYSICS

Jacques Derrida has argued that classical mimesis was ruled by the "system of truth," by which he means a correspondence theory of truth.[9] One level of the problem of imitation, in classical thought, centers on the relation or mediation of the ideal and the real (Plato), or the particular and the universal (Aristotle), that inscribes the problem of truth. In a word, mimesis has to do with the "embodiment" of ideas and values in concrete reality, action, language, and art. For example, Plato argued in the *Timaeus* that the cosmos is an imitation of its artificer's idea and that time is a moving imitation of the eternal. In the *Republic* he argued that the work of art also is an imitation of the idea of the artist and then derivatively of the archetypal idea that the artist's idea copies. The work of art is, therefore, thrice removed from the "truth." One judges the real (the work of art) as an imitation (a copy or representation) of the idea. Since an imitation derives its significance from what transcends it, to judge the relation of copy and idea, one needs an intuition of the idea outside its mediation in the concrete. Judging requires, in Plato's terms, "philosophy" because the philosopher is the one who has seen the Idea unmediated by language and symbols. Mimesis, as a concept, allows the thinker to describe the mediation of ideal and real while remaining free of the ambiguity of the actual as the basis of knowledge. It provides a logic for the image. And imitation also explains the painful disparity between our ideas and actual reality, a disparity that sparks moral and cognitive dissonance.

Aristotle argued in his *Poetics* that in (tragic) poetry there is an expression of a universal insight into the human condition. The disclosive power of drama makes it closer to philosophy, which deals in necessary universals, than to history, the domain of the particular and contingent. According to Aristotle, what mimetic art does is disclose the universal through the particular. Specifically, tragedy reveals the travail and fragility of human life through the actions, characters, and events in the play. In reasoning out a plot and the fate of its characters we learn something about the human condition. We derive insights about how to live from the portrayal of the actions and suffering of others. Specifically, we learn how certain people act in particular, concrete situations.[10]

Mimesis answered the problem of the mediation, even incarnation, of the ideal in the real, or the disclosure of the general in the particular, even as it was used to express different ideas of human knowledge. In a word, imitation was a conceptual framework for classical Greek metaphysics; it expressed the intelligibility of any particular act of being as the precondition for speaking analogically about the whole of what is. Hence, the task of Greek metaphysical thinking, as thought about first principles, involved the attempt to think and articulate the systematic and logical unity of all reality in relation to those principles.[11] Being, God, and the Good, True, and Beautiful have all been used to denote that first principle. What imitation allowed was a way to think and articulate the unity of reality since it explained the relation, proper or distorted, of concrete entities to the first principle, however conceived.

Metaphysical reflection not only is about the unity of what is; it also can take the form of fundamental ontology as the attempt to think the relation of Being and beings. According to Heidegger, the history of Western thought is the forgetfulness of the difference between Being and beings. And here too "imitation" was crucial to the metaphysical enterprise. In classical ontology it denoted that difference of beings and Being by accenting the duality of idea and reality. Yet the classical thinkers failed, according to Heidegger, to explore adequately the appearance of Being in beings by concentrating on the idea. Hence imitation signaled the devaluation of the phenomenal as an appearance of Being. To understand the world one had to look elsewhere, to the archetypal idea that the world dimly imitated or to first principles of thought.

Heidegger saw clearly that the demise of the question of Being was implicit in the rise of imitative thought since it devalues the phenomenal realm. More specifically, he saw the decay of Western thought as a movement from *physis* (nature or emergent power) to the domination of the Idea. This transition from "nature" to idea is signaled by imitation. Heidegger wrote: "What appears —the phenomenon—is no longer *physis*, the emerging power, nor is it the self-manifestation of the appearance; no, appearing is now the emergence of the copy. Since the copy never equals its prototype, what appears is 'mere' appearance, an actual illusion, a deficiency."[12] For Heidegger, the phenomenal appearance and concealment of being are denied by an imitative vision of things as mere copies of Ideas inscribed in a certain logic. The problem of imitation reaches into how we understand the structure and meaning of Being itself. What Heidegger attempted to think was the emergent power of phenomena through its appearance and concealment in beings.

Greek metaphysical imitation reached into all domains of reflection. Plato saw how imitation provided a conceptuality and logic for relating aesthetics, education, politics, morals, and cosmology. And Aristotle, with modifications, agreed. That is, they saw not only that imitation signaled the mediation of the ideal and the real, the particular and the universal, but also that it allowed one to conceive of the unity of the transcendentals (the True, the Good, and the Beautiful) in relation to particular domains of being. If all reality is the imitation of the Ideas, as Plato suggests, then it finds its unity at the transcendental level. Art, politics, and education are to be imitations of the ideal forms. The plurality of the world is explained through the diversity of imitative actualizations. That diversity, while apparent, is not ultimately the way things are. For Aristotle, the artistic presentation of the human condition in tragedy means that art serves moral knowledge even as it pushes toward theoretical insight. Poetry, after all, is closer to philosophy than to history. In a word, mimesis allowed the ancients a way to articulate the unity of human claims, experiences, and aspirations. Given this, it was as crucial to pedagogical reform and political theory as to metaphysical reflection.

At this point Derrida's claim that classical imitation-theory is ruled by the system of the true is germane. That is, imitation articulated the transcendental unity of the good and the beautiful under the claim of the true as the correspondence of the real to the ideal (Plato) or the particular classified under the universal (Aristotle). Acts and dispositions are seen as "good" when they correspond to or embody the "Good." The same logic held for aesthetics and hence the beautiful. Thus for much of ancient Greek thought, imitation provided a conceptual way to mediate ideals and actuality *and* a way to articulate the synthetic unity of the transcendentals (Good, True, Beautiful). Imitation answered the human anxiety about the unity of life and its purpose while providing criteria for judging the veracity of beliefs, ideas, and action. Mimesis thus served fundamental ontological and epistemological purposes; it embodied the project of classical metaphysics. At least this is true for Plato, the first philosopher of mimesis.[13]

The final breakdown of the classical world came with the Enlightenment and its awareness of the human participation in the construction of social, political, moral, and religious realities. Kant gave this new self-awareness its most systematic expression. His project was to isolate the foundation for knowledge-claims in the transcendental dynamic of the knowing subject—it is interesting, of course, that the three *Critiques* are still structured around the problem of the true, the good, and the beautiful—and the problem of the relation of the categorical to the transcendental remained central to his thought. Through the synthetic act of the productive imagination, precepts are wedded to concepts affording knowledge of the world. In a word, figuration remained a crucial epistemological and ontological problem for Kant.

What Kant did was to ground knowledge-claims reflexively while elucidating how synthetic judgment reveals a transcendental unity. The problems of mediation, or realization, and unity were thereby rearticulated through a reflexive philosophy of the subject. Because of this, the vocabulary of imitation, which had served this function, virtually dropped out of eighteenth-century discussions of human knowing. In many respects, however, Kant, through his understanding of the synthetic power of mind, opened anew the problem of mimesis, only now in relation to the transcendental activity of the human. That is, while imitation was dropped as an aesthetic and metaphysical concept, the problem of mimesis remained. It reappears in Kant's discussion of the imagination.[14] But it was really the Romantics and other idealists who made explicit this turn to imagination and linguistic expression in speaking of our figural world of meaning.

The height of the Romantic vision is aptly illustrated by Coleridge. For him the imagination of the artist is the repetition of the eternal I AM: "The primary imagination I hold to be a living power and prime agent of all human perception, and as a repetition in the finite mind of the eternal act of creation in the infinite I AM."[15] Coleridge announces a critical, reflexive metaphysics of the self, with imitative action at its core. The "I" is the unity, power, and prime agent of the self and its knowing of a world. The "I" is a repetition of the divine creator, and just as elusive. Moreover, Coleridge's exalted vision of the imagination means, correspondingly, that language must be understood around its power. "The best part of human language, properly so called, is derived from reflections on the acts of the mind itself. It is formed by a voluntary appropriation of fixed symbols to internal acts, to processes and results of imagination."[16] Though Coleridge's romanticism is problematic, a crucial theme is announced here that will concern us throughout this study: the relation of language and action. For him, linguistic action is the self-expression of internal acts of the mind that are in turn the imitation of the infinite I AM. Through this activity the eternal is related to and expressed through the temporal and the finite while the unity of the self as an "I" is enacted. Hence, the work of the artist is the expression of the reflexive relation through the "I" of the self to the eternal. The "I," the author, becomes, in effect, the artist-god voicing the words of the infinite I AM.

The current suspicion of critical foundationalism and Romantic expressivism arises from a deeper attention to the problems and power of language. Thus although the thinkers I shall be reading in the following chapters acknowledge the reflexive character of all thought, they claim that such reflexivity has a linguistic character. That is, current thinkers argue that one cannot capture an absolute foundation, a unity and power of "Being" or "thought" in the "I" or the "Absolute," because the depths of our linguisticality disallow a total mediation of thought and being. This does not mean, however, that discourse about Being and understanding is fanciful or meaningless. It means, rather, that one must speak of them in and through their linguistic figuration and performance. This opens the possibility of ontological claims through language while signaling the death of traditional imitation and its metaphysics. The question of the meaning of Being can be explored without reducing it to one about the unity of what is in relation to first principles or the "I." The first move of postmodern thought is, then, away from the primacy of the *cogito* as the foundation for all knowledge-claims or as the primary referent of language.

Another criticism of Romantic and critical thought concerns the assumption that expression is primarily self-expression, a claim made by Coleridge and others. The escape from the imitative universe of the ancients, in which the human was immersed in a larger universe of meaning and levels of reality, meant in the eighteenth and nineteenth centuries a concentration on the autonomous self as a center of desire, freedom, and will. In the name of freedom, this concentration removes the human from its deep participation in the world and potentially neglects language as a crucial medium for that involvement. As Charles Taylor puts it: "What comes about through the development of language in the broadest sense is the coming to be of expressive power, the power to make things manifest. It is not unambiguously clear that this ought to be considered a self-expression/realization. What is made manifest is not exclusively, not even mainly, the self, but a world."[17] The issue, then, for contemporary hermeneutics becomes the presentation or expression of *a world*. Crucial to the failure of Romantic expressionism is the realization that language helps to shape consciousness and the human condition even while through it a world comes to expression or presentation. Beyond the ancient imitative cosmos we seek again to grasp our being in the play of the world.

I have traced ever so briefly the problem of mimesis in classical, critical, and Romantic thought. What we have seen is that ontological/metaphysical and hermeneutical uses of imitation rested on and announced basic antinomies: ideal *vs*. real, authorial intention *vs*. textual representation, transcendental self *vs*. action in the natural world. In each case the interpretive and reflective task was to move by analogy or intuition through the imitative image (the real, the representation, the natural) to the idea or consciousness behind it that is the unity, power, and prime agent of the image. Thus imitation, while attempting to articulate the expression and participation of being in beings, consciousness in language, and self in world, actually broke them apart. The failure of ontological and representational imitation comes with the suspicion that beings are not copies of transcendent Ideas and that texts, though perhaps presentations of a world, are not icons of private consciousness.

My contention is that postmodern thought rejects classical mimeticism for its failure to acknowledge the human participation through language and action in the figuration of its world. This challenges the imitative image and its logic. Current thought also represents a criticism of Romantic and critical obsessions with the self as an autonomous center of desire and will mimetically presenting itself in language. The human is a responder to a world in which we find ourselves and which we help construct. As Taylor suggests, expressionism for postmodern thought becomes radically anti-subjectivistic just as it is radically anti-imitative. The question then becomes: What vocabulary can we use to help us interpret ourselves and our world?

Ironically enough, it is precisely at this juncture that we must turn anew to mimesis. It is crucial to realize that Plato and Aristotle, the usual place to begin discussions of mimesis, are actually a second step of reflection on more basic human practices. As noted before, mimetic action and the terminology of mimesis arose in cultic action and Sicilian mime, in worship and theater. Although classics scholars have long understood the dynamic and dramatic origins of mimesis, the hermeneutical import of these roots is just now being explored. The perplexing question then is: What import does mimesis have for us once we see that it is not iconic copying but the praxis of figuration?

Mimesis, true to its roots in cult, may open to us the presentation of world and the play of linguistic meaning as well as provide insight into the human condition. Indeed, my contention is that mimesis so understood provides postmodern thinkers with a way to speak about how we live, move, and have our being. What the thinkers explored in the following chapters achieve is a fundamental shift from "imitation" as copying or the expressive power of the imagination to mimesis as performative praxis in understanding, human self-hood, and narrative texts. Given this, mimesis is a way for them to think and speak about the fundamental acts of understanding and its world, human action and time, and the self.

This turn to mimetic praxis is not without its difficulties, however. Jacques Derrida has also explored the performative shape of mimesis as crucial to the deconstruction of traditional and hermeneutical reflection, and his work provides a critique on all attempts to return to imitation. It does so through mimesis.

THE DECONSTRUCTION OF MIMESIS

Derrida continues Heidegger's destruction of Western metaphysics. Heidegger, as we saw, read the decay of Western thought as beginning with a movement from the truth of *physis* (nature as emerging power) to the domination of the "idea." Derrida notes, however, that the original impulse of Greek thought saw no separation between *logos* and the mimetic action of *physis*. He writes:

> Mimesis thus determined belongs to logos, and is not animalistic aping, or gesticular mimicry; it is tied to the possibility of meaning and truth in discourse. At the beginning of [Aristotle's] *Poetics* mimesis in a way is posited as a possibility proper to physis. Physis is revealed in mimesis, or in the poetry which is a species of mimesis, by virtue of the hardly apparent structure which constrains mimesis from carrying to the exterior the fold of its redoubling. It belongs to physis, or if you will, physis includes its own exteriority and its double. In this sense mimesis is therefore a "natural" movement.[18]

Physis is disclosed in phenomena precisely through its "redoubled exterior." Mimesis denotes the intelligibility of reality, its *logos*, inherent in the dynamics of nature. Put differently: mimesis is a way to speak of Being itself becoming meaningful in phenomena without an appeal to some antecedent realm of "ideas" to explain the value and meaning of the world. Derrida capitalizes on this dynamic of redoubling, on mimesis, in connection with Being or *physis*. But he shifts his concern to language. This turn to language, and specifically to text, is taken in order to trace out the implications of redoubling for undoing all claims to final truth or presence while speaking as well about the production of meaning.

Derrida's way of putting the relation of Being and language is to say that "there is nothing outside of the text." Of course, he is not suggesting that all we have are books. The point is that we live in a web of symbols and signs that refer in complex ways to yet other symbols and signs. We dwell in a free play of figuration where signs point to other signs, symbols to symbols, and so on. Little wonder then that premodern interpretive practices, like allegory or narrative, have captured the postmodern deconstructionist mind. We live in a free play of signs. As Rodolphe Gasché puts it:

> Derrida has made it clear that the word text can be substituted for the word Being. Text is a translation of Being. It is a word, the use of which is indispensable to him in a very specific historical situation. For this very reason its importance is only strategic, and there is no intrinsic value to it. Thus while naming Being, the text is also something very different, if not without relation to Being. . . . The word text, the denotation of the text, for re-making the word being, is precisely what is no longer answerable to the meaning of Being. With the word text, Derrida names an instance which, crossing out all the modalities of presence, at once *intersects* with that from whence the presencing of the presence comes to be, Being as the phenomenon par excellence.[19]

Language is Being's Other in and through which Being always withdraws. Being is a free play of figuration and not something antecedent that is poorly embodied in things, words, or ideas. Given this, it is best understood as "textual."

Derrida's move to textuality is a trenchant criticism of any and all ontologies that seek to reduce difference to the same or assume that talk about Being does not entail problems of figuration. His deconstruction of texts also stands as a critique of linguistic idolatry in the identification of any sign, thing, or system with the fullness of truth. Derrida's strategy is, in my judgment, to show how mimesis undoes Western "mimeticism" from the inside.

Derrida's argument about mimesis moves on two levels. (*a*) He shows that mimesis is the differential, redoubling movement in *physis* itself. That is, mimesis signals the production of doubles or traces for what is not present and hence always defers direct reference to that which is represented. But this also means that this non-present reality is known in and through that which is different, a sign, which itself is known only in its specific difference from other signs. Derrida's term for this is *différance*, meaning to defer in and through difference. My contention is that mimesis is best understood within the scope of Derrida's texts as the dynamic of *différance* so crucial for his reading of the textuality of being. Indeed, as he says in "Economimesis," mimesis is the "free unfolding–refolding of the *physis*."[20] *Physis* is productive of meaning; it is the emerging power of any reality. This breaks the logic of imitative representation and concentrates reflection on the production, or economy, of meaning. In a word, *physis* is disclosed and deferred through its exteriority.

Being may be understood, then, as productive redoubling in which the movement is concealed by its generation of doubles. This dynamic constitutes the economy of meaning. In realizing this, Derrida's retrieval of mimesis turns against itself. If *physis* is mimetic, then (*b*) truth as presence and correspondence is suspect. At the heart of *physis* we find only the productive movement of redoubling. Derrida's interpretation of mimesis concentrates on this mimetic movement. Once we see this relation of mimesis and *physis* moved to the level of language and text, the importance of mimesis to deconstruction is clear. I shall explore the economy of Derrida's use of mimesis by tracing his reading of specific thinkers, since through them he deconstructs the topics of concern to us: text, self, and even God.

In the texts of Plato, Derrida locates a network and logic of mimesis. Plato's concern for *logos* means that mimesis is ironically condemned in human acts of figuration (poetics) but not in Being. That is, it is crucial to Plato's form of idealism that thought be able to move from given reality to the ideas that reality imitates. The problem with human acts of imitation is that they are yet another step removed from the idea and thus open the possibility that the mind may falter and mistake the imitation for the reality. Derrida calls this the "double inscription of mimesis" in Plato's thought since the logical necessity of affirming likenesses (*eikastic*) between idea and reality nevertheless entails a denial of semblances (*fantastic*) in art and writing. The internal duplicity of mimesis forced Plato to attempt to separate good from bad mimesis.

In Plato's texts, as Derrida reads them, mimesis is the production of a thing's double. This double, this supplement, has a curious status. On the one hand, it has value only as it is related to its referent. In this sense the double does not have complete reality, and its veracity counts on pointing beyond itself. Yet the supplement does have some independent status, since it can be condemned by the philosopher as deceptive and as blocking true knowledge of its referent.[21] The problem is that Plato at once affirms the value and reality of mimesis and denies the truth of the double. Most important for Derrida is the fact that the question of mimesis marks the crossing in Plato's texts of ontology and language. The same ambiguity is accordingly found in each.[22] Given this, Being can be understood as "text" and thereby seen as troubled by the same mimetic dynamic. Plato's theory of truth curiously condemns and needs mimesis. His thought allows Derrida to see mimesis as deconstructing traditional ontology by reading it as textual.

Aristotle's position is more difficult. Mimesis, as we have seen, is related to *physis*. In the *Poetics* it is also related to the human. This marks the humanization of *physis* into the truth of human nature. Derrida notes about the *Poetics* that "Mimesis is proper to man. Only man imitates properly. Man alone takes pleasure in imitating, man alone learns to imitate, man alone learns by imitation. The power of truth, as the unveiling of nature (*physis*) by mimesis, congenitally belongs to the physics of man, to anthropophysics."[23] This transformation of *physis* to human *physis* follows a trajectory that runs all the way to Kant and beyond. It signals the anthropocentrism of much of Western thought and logic. Yet if *physis* is mimetic, then the human itself is a play of *différance* and is known only in its productive exteriority. The human being is known in those acts that mimetically figure its being. Given this, mimetic tragedy becomes the means for understanding something about the being of the human;

in Aristotle's terms, the mimesis of action discloses something about the way various human characters live and act in their moral world.

Derrida's point is that if there is a mimetic relation between the act and being of the human, then the "self" is deconstructed through its very acts since they always defer reference to the self. The emplotment of human action in narrative texts likewise undoes itself in both the texture of action and the action of the mimetic (narrative) text. This further confounds Aristotle's mimeticism since for him mimesis forms the bridge between being and knowing because it is related to human *physis* and to the pleasure of knowing through figures. For Aristotle, mimesis yields pleasure only on the condition that it shows in narrative action that which is not to be seen in particular acts: the essence of the human. Nature reveals itself precisely by figuring itself in the mimetic double, the plot, through the act of the artist. The path to knowledge is through plot as the unreal, the untrue, and the non-present.

In Aristotle's thought, mimesis is controlled by a theory of truth. But mimesis seems to undo that notion of truth even as it is a basic element in it. Derrida's tactic has been to locate the mimetic play in these texts as the deconstruction of the ideas of truth as well as the understanding of text and language found in Plato's and Aristotle's own texts. He turns then from classical mimeticism to its transcendental retrieval in critical philosophy.

In "Economimesis" Derrida makes many of the same arguments against Kant. The target is again the complex relation of the human, world, and text, but now as they are found in Kant's critical transformation of philosophy. Derrida's critique centers on the relation of imagination and nature in Kant's texts.

> Pure and free productivity must resemble that of nature. And it does so precisely because as free and pure, it does not depend on natural laws. The less it depends on nature, the more it resembles nature. Mimesis here is not the representation of one thing by another. . . . It is not the relation of two products but of two productions. And of two freedoms. The artist does not imitate things in nature, or, if you will, in *natura naturata*, but the acts of *natura naturans*, the operation of *physis*. But since an analogy has already made *natura naturans* the art of an author-subject, and, one could even say, of an artist-god, mimesis displays the identification of human action with divine action—of one freedom with another. . . . "True" mimesis is between two producing subjects and not between two produced things.[24]

The analogy between art and nature in Kant is fantastic. Genius imitates nothing. This is the final apotheosis of the human and the expansion of a specific economy of meaning to a general economy of truth. Through the mimetic act of imagination the human is identified with the divine. Much as God's act is the condition for the creation of all that is, so here, for Kant, the imaginative act of the human is the condition for the intelligibility of its world. And yet if ontological mimeticism undoes itself, so will transcendental, imaginative mimesis.

Through imaginative mimesis the human totalizes all being and gives closure to truth. Art circumvents nature. "One must not imitate nature; but nature, assigning rules to genius, folds itself, returns to itself, reflects itself through art."[25] At the end of this path blazed by Kant stands the triumph of the idea, the ultimate mastery of meaning. Derrida's point is that the project of metaphysics, of grasping the unity of all and thinking the being of beings, is bound to the notion of mimesis. This is true of Kant as it is of Plato. And yet, precisely because they are mimetic, each system of thought undoes itself.

Thus Plato began a tradition of reflection by subjugating the mimetic redoubling of *physis* to a theory of truth, to the idea and *logos*. Aristotle raised the stakes by identifying *physis* with human nature and thus relating both nature and mimesis to the human. Kant, for his part, drew the conclusion that the artist does not "make" (*poiesis*) the work of art but is analogous to the divine creator. The effect of Derrida's argument is to deconstruct self and Being with the mimeticism of classical and transcendental thought.

Derrida traces out the final implications of his argument about mimesis by reading Mallarmé's text *Mimique* and its concern with the mime. He notes that the "Mime ought only to write himself on the white page he is; he must inscribe himself through gestures and the play of facial expressions."[26] The mime re-presents nothing and conforms to no-thing that exists prior to the silent act of the mime. The mimetic act is outside the system of truth that is built on correspondences between ideas and things. By reclaiming the theatrical roots of mimesis, Derrida deconstructs imitation while exploring the production of meaning as mimetic in character.

At this juncture Derrida anticipates a possible response to his argument and disallows it.

> The mime produces, that is to say makes appear "*in praesentia*," manifests the very meaning of what he is presently writing: of what he *performs*. If one followed the thread of this objection, one would go back, beyond imitation, toward a more "originary" sense of "aletheia" and of "mimeisthai." . . . One could indeed push Mallarmé back into the most "originary" metaphysics of truth if all mimicry had indeed disappeared, if it had effaced itself in the scriptural production of truth. But such is not the case. *There is* mimicry. [B]ut it is difference without reference, or rather a reference without a referent. . . . Mallarmé thus preserves the differential structure of mimicry or mimesis, but without its Platonic or metaphysical interpretation, which implies that somewhere the being of something that "is," is being imitated. . . . The operation, which no longer belongs to the system of truth, does not manifest, produce, or unveil any presence; nor does it constitute any conformity, resemblance, or adequation between a presence and a representation. . . . This "materialism of the idea" is nothing other than the staging, the theatre, the visibility of nothing or of the self. It is a dramatization which illustrates nothing.[27]

Heidegger wanted to understand beings, and particularly *Dasein*, as the unveiling, the *aletheia*, of Being. Derrida's point is that such a project may seem possible through mimesis itself. And yet, once mimesis is understood theatrically, as the pure free play of miming, then such a project is not possible. What is left is pure dramatization, pure theater or spectacle, with the complete displacement of all presence or reference.

Mimesis, as Derrida reads it, is the continual dramatic productivity unfolding and refolding itself. He has bracketed all consideration of the content of that movement and centered on the movement itself. It is pure reflexivity in the differential structure of language. Thus talk of reference is compressed into a theory of indeterminate meaning, with mimesis as its capstone. For Derrida this is not a disparaging conclusion. It means that we must forgo claims to foundations and mastery. We are implicated in an endless dance of meaning that always deconstructs our pretenses to a final representative system of truth.

The importance of Derrida's texts is that they deconstruct imitative notions of the self, being, and text through mimesis itself. Yet he also places the human once again in a web of signs and symbols, a figural universe. This is the curiously premodern aspect of his talk about mimesis. That symbolic world is not one that reflects or imitates a non-symbolic higher world. There is, as he says, "nothing outside of the text." The movement of that text is the unending mimetic play of differences; it is a free play of figuration in which we must attempt to understand our lot and life.

Derrida presents a challenge for our reflections: to explore language and human being without a totalizing theory of truth. He has shown that mimesis challenges simple identity and that discordance is written into the fabric of mimetic works and actions. So understood, mimesis provides any hermeneutic with a critical principle at the level of language. And it forces us to reconsider what we mean by talk about text, self, and world. Before doing so it is important to grasp the full scope of the problem of imitation. And this entails moving from its ontological and hermeneutical dimensions to its moral and religious import.

Our Most Anti-Imitative Self-Image

Ours is an age of photocopying and mass culture. Yet we pride ourselves on being anti-imitative; we celebrate our capacities for action, originality, and insight. Ours is also an age in which the human domination over natural processes has reached into biological engineering and nuclear physics. And yet as the ecological movement attests, we are also struggling to overcome the technological alienation from our natural home. The tension we live with is the desire to assert at one and the same time our capacities for creative and constructive transformation of our world while acknowledging our interdependence with the wider environment. Sadly, all too often that interdependence is denied. Transformation, rather than being creative, can be the destructive manipulation of our shared natural world.

The escape from an imitative picture of the human and its world has meant simultaneously a celebration of our capacities for change and the potential valuation of the natural world simply in terms of human desires and needs.[28] This anthropocentric valuation of the world has reaped tragic consequences.[29] The question is: Why is it that we react so forcefully against any suggestion that human freedom is always dependent freedom and human value always interdependent value? As a culture we have rejected "imitation" as an element in the interpretation of what it means to be human. Yet our current framework of self-interpretation, a technological and economic one, itself is destructive.

The failure of traditional mimetic claims about the human reveals a central moral and religious problem: namely, what it means to be a self, an agent in the world. Mark C. Taylor argues that the "relation between God and the self is thoroughly specular; each mirrors the other. In different terms, man is made in the image of God. This *imago* is an imitation, copy, likeness, representation, similitude, appearance, or shadow of divinity. . . . The recognition that man is believed to be the *imago Dei* suggests that the self is a 'theological conception.'"[30] We are living in the age of the eclipse of former ideas of the self. The notion that the self is an icon of God, a substance that can be variously formed and informed, or that we can easily locate the transcendental ego as the grounds for our claims and ideas, is suspect in a culture deeply aware of the drives of the unconsciousness. However, the idea of an "iconic self" and talk about human nature, found in ancient and medieval faculty psychology, sustained much Western reflection on what it means to be human. When this discourse becomes problematic, how then are we to think and speak of the human condition? As Taylor suggests, the best place to begin exploring this question is with the *imago Dei* itself.

Given the biblical injunction against images, it may seem foolish to speak of imitation in the Bible. Actually it is only St. Paul who uses the specific terminology of "mimesis." Nevertheless, the problem of existential imitation is found throughout the biblical texts. Though the making of images is condemned, there is one image, a living one, that holds pride of place: the *imago Dei*.

It is within the context of interpreting the human as the image of God that the biblical understanding of imitation is worked out. Martin Buber wrote: "For in the image of God did he make man. It is on this that the imitation of God is founded. We are destined to perfect from out of ourselves, in actual life, the image in which we were created and which we carry in us that we may—not any longer in this life—experience its consummation."[31] Buber's language signals one reason for the failure of moral and religious imitation: it is "man" that is the full image of God and hence the *imitatio Dei* too often bolsters a sexist ethic. Traditional Christianity and Judaism have often seen women as derivative males and dim reflections of the divine.

The sexism of much Christian and Jewish thought exposes another problem with imitation for postmodern thought. The intelligibility and plausibility of the *imitatio Dei* depend on an idea of God and human nature. Yet once the conceptual stability of "God" and of "image" is lost or seriously questioned, then what and who the human is again calls for reflection. That is, the *imago Dei* ironically locates reflection on the human within discourse about *imago* and *Dei*, both of which are now under suspicion and criticism. We have already traced the critique of imitation vis-à-vis "image," and shortly we shall turn to the problem of imitative construals of the divine. At this point we must explore the way imitation co-implicated the human within the conceptual framework of image and God.

However, we must first acknowledge that Buber's point is elsewhere. It is that although humans are not divine our actions can be godlike and that this perfects the being of the human. The imitation of God rests on normative claims about the nature of the human. Biblical imitation describes those actions that will realize, present, and perfect this image. It is a way of perfecting who and what the human is in relation to the divine and thus is a crucial element in the religious and moral interpretation of the human. The question then becomes: What are the particular ways of God that the human is to follow?

The details of what the Jewish and Christian Scriptures mean by the "ways of God" are too complex to survey here, but some general observations are possible. There are three ways of "following" the divine outlined in the Hebrew Scriptures, and these are attributed to Jesus in the New Testament Gospels. As E. J. Tinsley noted years ago, the three ways include the way of Torah (moral and religious edification through following the commands of God), the way of "Sonship" (concrete discipleship modeled on the Israelite kings), and the way of Wisdom (discerning God's purposes through nature, history, and society).[32] These three strands of biblical thought, representing different periods in Israel's history, are exceedingly complex.

The New Testament Gospels weave these themes into the pattern of Jesus' relation to his disciples. The follower of Jesus was called to participate in his destiny by walking in the way of Christ as teacher of the Law and the Son of God. The most significant transformation of the Jewish *imitatio Dei* comes with Paul. He understood the image of God not as any given human being, but as Christ, who is the true "icon" of God (Col. 1:15–16). The realization of the image of God in the human can be achieved only through the mimesis of Christ, in his death and resurrection, and by being, in Paul's terms, *in Christ*. Paul uses the language of mimesis to speak of the believer's salvific relation to Christ and to Paul's own ministry of the Gospel.

The biblical tradition takes "following" and "walking" as descriptive of human existence shaped by a relation to the divine. Human practical existence, how we "walk," is formed by the God or gods we follow. The imitation of the One God was seen as a way to actualize the human within the horizon of time. Given this, the ways of God and the *imitatio Dei* and *imitatio Christi* are simultaneously a disclosure of the good of the human in relation to the divine and guides for action appropriate to that good. The conceptual matrix of *imago/imitatio* touches, then, on the being of the moral agent, the good, and guides for action and thought.

The conceptual pair *imago Dei/imitatio Dei* has failed as a viable interpretive key for our self-understanding. Why? Most obviously, this vision of life seems to lead to appraisals of human action that cannot account for our freedom or the complexities of judgment in specific situations. Furthermore, the cultural distance between us and the life of Jesus or the experience of the Israelites counts against a simple "imitatio" ethic. Finally, as I noted above, the imitation of God entails an understanding of God and idea of human good that is problematic.

Despite these obvious problems, a vision of the human as the image of God and of the religious life as the imitation of God has been retrieved of late. Yet in the process the imitative meaning and logic of the image have been reconstructed, and so too discourse about the divine. Arthur Cohen, attempting to think theologically after the "Tremendum" of the Holocaust, speaks of the Jews as enacting the divine purposes in the world. He states:

> The world is the divine *scenum*, the mime theater where only the passivity of God's essence is displayed. . . . The world (which is the passivity of God) is complemented by man whose essential character is freedom. . . . The life of man through God, both as imitation and as real presentation, is not surety enough unless enacted within community, where . . . collective language makes audible the silent speech of creation.[33]

This claim about the world as "mime theater" and the human as the "presentation" of the divine is striking. Cohen retrieves the language of mimesis in the service of a post-Holocaust theology, and in doing so radically transforms classic religious and moral imitation. The human is not simply given as the *imago Dei*, and the world must be understood as the silence of God. The *imitatio Dei* is both a way of life through God, as Cohen puts it, and the struggle in freedom to let creation speak. In this sense, the *imitatio Dei* is taken into the being and activity of God. Here the human is "pictured" as the voice of creation.

Christian theologians have also reclaimed imitation to speak of human being and doing. Johann Baptist Metz understands the *Nachfolge Christi*, the following of Christ, in relation to the apocalyptic interruption of the Kingdom of God. The *Nachfolge* provides a point from which to denounce oppressive political and economic systems and announce liberation. Metz writes that the "Christian idea of *Nachfolge* and the apocalyptic idea of imminent expectation belong together. It is not possible to 'follow' Jesus radically, that is, at the roots of life, if 'the time is not shortened.' Jesus' call: 'Follow me!,' and the call of Christians 'Come, Lord Jesus!,' are inseparable."[34] The shape of "following" is given in the apocalyptic praxis of Jesus whose liberating work is the Kingdom of God interrupting history. The following of Jesus entails, for Metz, a prophetic, liberating vision of human life. The Christian is one who stands in a solidarity of memory with the victims of history and with the dangerous memory of Jesus. Given this dual solidarity, the task of discipleship is to break the logic of developmental history in the struggle for liberation.

A different position is voiced by John Howard Yoder. In his *The Politics of Jesus* he treats *Nachfolge* and *imitatio* as a conceptual pair. And he argues that to "follow after Christ is not simply to learn from him, but also to share his destiny."[35] Yoder takes this sharing to entail a "revolutionary subordination" or "the readiness to obey amidst suffering; trusting God for not yet discernible vindication."[36] The mark of following Jesus is the cross as the social meaning of Christian faith and action.

Yoder's position is the near-opposite of Metz's. There is no call by Yoder to change the world. The Christian is to witness to the world through voluntary subordination and obedience despite the consequences. But this is not a form of quietism; it is genuinely revolutionary in countering the usual logic of power. And at bottom, like Metz's, Yoder's position entails a theological vision. Hence Christian imitation, as either liberative or revolutionary praxis, pushes toward theological issues. As Taylor noted, the self and God are hermeneutically related.

In the face of the cultural eclipse of the "self," we must reflect anew on human existence. What is interesting about Cohen's, Metz's, and Yoder's retrievals of "imitation" is that each suggests a vision of human agency. Human life can be seen as a performance through which convictions, beliefs, and loves come to presentation on the *scenum* of the world. Praxis, like language, is the figurative presentation of our being in a situation, a world, and entails a hermeneutic of human acts as the being-at-work of human nature. As Robert Sokolowski has put it, human nature "is both achieved and shown for what it is" in moral action.[37] My contention is that mimesis is used by postmodern hermeneutics to understand the being of human action and the acts of being human beyond the inscription of the human within the logic of the image. Yet in claiming this, I meet another criticism of the hermeneutical reconstruction of mimesis that must inform these reflections.

THE SACRED AND MIMETIC DESIRE

In much the same way as Derrida's work isolated discord in the fabric of mimetic texts, René Girard's exposes the discordance in our social life. While Derrida retrieves theatrical mimesis to deconstruct "imitation," Girard turns to the cultic roots of mimesis to explore the mechanism of violence in society. Like Derrida's, the importance of Girard's thought for this study is that he isolates critical aspects of mimesis. He does so not at the level of language, but in human action and desire.

Mimesis plays a double role in Girard's thought: to explain both the genesis and trajectory of desire into social violence and the victimage mechanism in religious traditions. Mimesis is central to the "triple audacity" of his project: developing a fundamental anthropology, a critique of modernity, and an explanation of religion and Christianity.[38]

Girard's thesis is that violence is the core of cultural life. Desire, he claims, is the generating force of violence that arises out of the attempt of two or more persons to appropriate the same "object," thereby engendering rivalry. "When any gesture of appropriation is imitated," he notes, "it simply means that two hands will reach for the same object simultaneously: conflict cannot fail to result."[39] Desire is neither self-generating nor simply evoked by what is desired. Indeed, "the subject desires the object because the rival desires it."[40] Thus not only is the rival an obstacle to what is desired, but he or she also mediates desire for the object.

The triangle of desire of subject, object, and mediator/rival is what Girard takes to be the true meaning of mimesis. The curious origin and shape of desire mean that the subject and mediator of desire are unaware of their triangular situation. Mimetic, triangular desire transfigures its ostensive object and conceals the origin of the subject's own desiring. Given this, as desire accelerates between rivals, two things happen. First, through the act of appropriation and identification there is an obliteration of difference between subject and mediator by their common desire. The denial of difference is the condition for violence simply because the "participants become each other's conflictual doubles or 'twins.'"[41] This leads Girard to the startling conclusion that the "ultimate meaning of desire is death."[42]

Mimetic desire threatens to accelerate to the point of social violence and breakdown, to a "mimetic crisis" as Girard calls it. When violence does erupt in human community, how is it to be abated? According to Girard, this is the primal social question that myths and rituals address. Religion, as the second consequence of the acceleration of desire, is the social answer to the problem of violence. It answers this problem through an act of violence that ends the disruption by imputing the cause of the social breakdown to a suitable victim, a scapegoat, who is then sacrificed. As he notes, sacrifice "is the resolution and conclusion of ritual because a collective murder of expulsion resolves the mimetic crisis that ritual mimics."[43] Girard, like Emile Durkheim, sees religion as the generative force of culture. More important, he holds that sacrifice and the sacralization of the victim are the heart of religion and thus the primal fact of the social order. Freud was right about collective murders, the repressive power of civilization, and the drives of desire. He failed, in Girard's eyes, to see their mimetic structure.

The sacrificial rite controls the spread of violence by providing punitive action against its ostensive cause represented in a victim. The criteria for determining the victim can be religious, cultural, or even physical, but the implicit concern is to reintroduce difference, through the sacrifice of the despised victim, into a situation where mimetic desire has obliterated it and evoked violence. Sacrificial violence is mimetic in that the desire for violence is directed at the being of the representative mediator, the victim. Hence the scapegoat must be a mimetic substitution for the true cause of the violence. This leads to the curious fact that the scapegoat is simultaneously despised as a "monstrous double" of the cause of social conflict and venerated as the means to social stability and redifferentiation.

The sacrificial act is mimetic on Girard's reading in that it enacts the foundations of the social order through the sacralization and destruction of the victim. And just as desire trades on illusion and ignorance about its origins, so does religion. Religious "misapprehension figures largely in the very real protection offered by society, by ritual sacrifice, and indeed by religion in general."[44] There are three levels of difference crucial to explaining the social function of religion: the loss of difference that works through mimetic desire and leads to violence; the illusion of sacred difference in the mechanism of victimage that is crucial for the resolution of violence; and the real difference between violence and love that transcends religion itself.[45] Religion reintroduces difference into a situation of undifferentiated desire, but it does so through the illusion of the mimetic victim. The real task is to escape mimetic religion.

Girard's work is helpful for noting the import of mimesis for exploring the generation of a social world and the primal place of religion in relations of power. Religions are, if nothing else, responses to a world of power, even if we do not want to reduce them to that. The objects of religious interpretation on his reading are those texts and events that hide and disclose the primal event of culture. While concentrating on the generative act of culture, Girard is also concerned with the representative mechanism crucial to concealing it. Given this, his seemingly cultic- and ritualistic-based method opens onto the textual, psychological, and cultural dimensions of religion as well. For Girard, mimesis serves to explain the character of desire, religion, and violence, and thus becomes the key to analyzing texts, events, actions, and cultures.

Girard argues that through the complex of desire, sacrifice, and the scapegoat he has isolated the unity of all rituals and the actual foundations of society. "All rites," he claims, "amount to a theatrical reenactment of mimetic crisis in which the differences that constitute society are dissolved."[46] This unity of rites is of course highly debatable. But the pressing issue is how is it possible for us, locked in our triangular desires, to recognize that religion and violence trade on illusion and ignorance? In *Deceit, Desire, and the Novel*, Girard offers answers to these questions which he has developed further in more recent studies.

First, Girard argues that the trajectory from desire to death is diverted in the novel when the hero repudiates desire and pride through a conversion generating a new non-triangular relation to self and others. This resolution is the mark of the great novelists: they provide answers to mimetic desire in the person of the hero who finds reconciliation with others. Second, because the novel finds this resolution, it provides a way to criticize the illusions of desire that taint our culture. The novel unmasks false transcendence and the mechanism of desire. In fact, Girard claims that the repudiation "of a human mediator and renunciation of deviated transcendency inevitably call for symbols of vertical transcendency whether the author is Christian or not."[47] Thus for the modern West, the novel introduces a critique of desire dependent on a more primal revelatory insight. Girard holds, surprisingly enough, that Christianity is that revelation.

Girard explores Christianity for its introduction of the critique of religion and violence. What interests him about the Scriptures is that in them Christ as "the victim is declared innocent of the evil of which [he] is accused."[48] Because of this, the sacrificial process is exposed for what it is, and with it the structure of violence and religion. In the light of the Christian revelation we see that choice "always involves choosing a model, and true freedom lies in the basic choice between a human and a divine model."[49] Christianity is a way beyond religion, a path that has shaped our culture and allowed us to see what was hidden in illusion and sacrality: victimage and violence.

Girard's explanation of Christianity is problematic, however. Paul Valadier notes that on Girard's reading "revelation is therefore *the* true knowledge of social processes," and this implies a Christian gnosticism toward violence and desire.[50] It must be remembered that Christianity claims to be primarily about the revelation of God and not about violence. In a similar way, Robert North questions Girard's interpretation of biblical texts. He argues that the key to Girard's reading is Jesus' refusal to enter the spiral of violence. "His redemptive life-work consisted rather in 'turning the other cheek' (Matt. 5:39) and showing only love where a scenario of violence was proposed to him."[51] Love breaks the spiral of mimetic violence by introducing difference and transcendence. But there are texts, specifically Pauline ones, that use sacrificial language about Jesus' death, and the Christian tradition is replete with sacrificial soteriologies from the Church Fathers to Anselm's *Cur Deus Homo*. More important, Girard's concentration on the problem of violence seems to collapse Jesus' concern for the Kingdom of God into its social utility as ideology critique. The same can be said for Girard's penchant for understanding God as non-violent love. The divine is conceived of in relation to its utility for political and cultural thought and action.

Girard offers, then, a novel, if problematic, reading of Christianity. He isolates its particularity not in terms of New Testament modes of discourse, but in relation to what he sees as the non-violent and non-sacrificial act of Christ. "The Christ of the Gospels," he claims, "dies against sacrifice, and through his death he reveals its nature and origin by making sacrifice unworkable, at least in the long run, and bringing sacrificial culture to an end."[52]

Christianity is anti-mimetic; it overturns the generative act of culture by introducing a critical, non-violent, differentiating principle. And this principle, Girard claims, is the Paraclete who "is the universal advocate, the chief defender of all innocent victims, the destroyer of every representation of persecution. He is truly the spirit of truth that dissipates the fog of mythology."[53] Given this, the task now is to expose the dynamic of culture and religion and thereby to undo mimetic violence.

Girard's reading of mimesis is curious. He seems to recognize and perpetuate Plato's suspicions about it since both thinkers claim that imitative representations hide their referents. Of course, for Girard mimesis is not simply reducible to a cognitive or aesthetic representation. "That conception of imitation—which goes back to Plato and marks the whole Occidental tradition—masks the fact that imitation is more originally the desire for the appropriation of that which the other possesses."[54] The emphasis on desire, rather than representation or textual production, also separates Girard from poststructuralist thinkers like Derrida. Girard writes:

> The classical structuralists repress conflictual mimesis as much as anyone ever did. That is why the poststructuralists, beginning with Derrida, could turn mimesis into a weapon against the structuralist theory of sign. . . . Lacoue-Labarthe and poststructuralism see mimesis as a factor of undecidability, and this is not radical enough. As a result they never reach the other side of mimesis already perceived by religion in a purely religious and fantastic light. They do not understand that mimesis can also play a crucial role in the genesis and practical stabilization of cultural difference.[55]

Girard seeks to explain the genesis of violence and cultural systems through mimetic desire. His reading of mimesis frees it from structural semiotics, deconstructionism, and realistic "imitation" while allowing him to explore relations of power.

It may seem that Girard's reading of mimesis is an attempt to escape figural understanding, an escape Derrida would hold as impossible. Girard's point is that mimesis is not only about presentation and figuration; it is also about power. More specifically, mimesis has to do with the generation of a social world. Girard's critical, even negative, reading of mimesis must be retained in its reconstruction. But mimesis must also be situated within a hermeneutic of the problem of figuration and thus of meaning. But that is not all. What has become apparent in this brief summary of imitative thought is that the problems of moral and social mimesis are also religious ones. To complete my problematizing of imitation I want to turn now to the theological questions we face.

GOD'S EMPTY THEATER

John Calvin voiced an ancient sentiment about God's relation to the world by speaking of the world as the theater of God's glory. He also claimed that God is the fountain of goodness refracted in the world. For the eyes of faith, and interpreted in the light of revelation, the world is the image or shadow of divine things from which one can speak about God's governance and goodness. At least one can argue *that* God is, even if "revelation" is required to make more specific claims about the divine.[56] Likewise, Augustine found in memory, will, and reason traces of the divine Trinity. The human, as the *imago Dei*, provides yet another analogue for our talk about God.[57] Both these claims —that the world is a reflection of divine purposes and goodness and that the human is the image of God—are forms of religious mimeticism. But for us God's theater is empty. It is empty not because human experience is devoid of a religious sense, but because the divine no longer seems to appear in our world. What is more, the value and integrity of our worldliness do not seem dependent on a relation to some transcendental actor.

Attempts in this century to respond to the crisis of theism seem spent, whether in existentialist interpretations of Christian faith, the rehabilitation of *Heilsgeschichte* by Neo-Orthodox theology, or, more recently, appeals to Christian community by narrative theologians. For many in our culture, believers and nonbelievers alike, the contention that God is an agent in the drama of the world is not compelling. The horrors of two world wars, the Holocaust, and the religious legitimation of inequality contest such claims. Seen theologically, the crisis of imitation is nothing less than the crisis of theism. The world theater stands empty; the actors are dead, and the script about salvation is forgotten.

The religious criticism of imitation touches on how we interpret and understand our world and ourselves and on claims about the "object" of religious experience. In a nutshell, the imitative vision of the world led to forms of theism that reified "God" into an independent existing being, and valued the human as the image of the deity while limiting our capacities for change. Some attention to these levels of the religious problem of imitation should expose why it is a theological problem. More specifically, I am drawing together the ontological, hermeneutical, and existential levels of the problem of imitation described above to show their confluence in the problem of God.

Religious traditions that take texts, world, or self as disclosive of some ultimate reality develop methods or strategies of interpretation to discern the meaning of that reality for human existence and action. In the West these strategies have been legion. For example, Origen, in *De principiis*, argued that there is a relation between the soul and the levels of meaning in Scriptural texts. The struggle of interpretation was to move from the literal to the spiritual plane of meaning. Interpretation was a way of knowledge, a process of edifying the soul in relation to God.[58] Typological interpretation was used by St. Paul to show that Adam was a type of Christ, the true Adam. His interpretive strategy was a way of seeing all reality and history from a religious perspective. The Kabbalistic masters developed intricate methods of interpreting

Torah. Earlier this century Rudolf Bultmann, drawing on Heidegger's work, developed an existential hermeneutic. And feminist and liberation theologians have espoused new hermeneutic approaches linked to praxis.[59] The list could go on endlessly. The point is that religious traditions develop methods of interpretation that aid in understanding human existence and the divine.

These interpretive strategies, despite their differences, generally have two aspects. First, texts, symbols, and ritual actions are taken to have a disclosive power. They provide ways to understand and explain life and the divine purposes; they are schemes for interpreting reality and for understanding the human within the activity of the divine. On this level, religious texts and their interpretations are making strict truth-claims. More correctly stated, they demarcate the field, or plausibility structure, in which we understand claims to truth. The problem is, of course, that traditional interpretations have been challenged by modern science and historical study. The contention that there is an analogy between text and soul, or that the book of Scripture interprets the book of the world, is problematic indeed. Imitation was crucial to these ancient interpretive methods, both at the level of the text's reference to "reality" and in the process of interpreting itself. Hence the criticism of imitation challenges a religious hermeneutic of the world.

Beyond the disclosive character of religious texts and their interpretation there is also, second, an edifying dimension. Religious texts, symbols, and actions are *used* to form the character and conduct of persons and communities.[60] A religious tradition not only gives food for thought and insight into the meaning of human life; it also shapes the heart and affections of its members. An agent comes to be through the edifying process of learning and appropriating a community's memory, story, and symbolic action. The problem is that this edifying process can be deeply ideological and oppressive, as the experience of women and the poor within Christianity aptly shows. The Scriptures, and their interpretations, have supported voluntary powerlessness in the name of religious virtue. Insofar as "imitation," from Plato onward, has been a pedagogical category, then this critique also impinges on imitation. The problem is how to speak of the formation of the self, the agent, in community and action.

Implicit in the criticism of the disclosive and edifying power of religious texts and interpretation is the challenge to understanding religious belief systems as explanations of reality. The rise of natural science, various forms of ideology critique, and the universality of the hermeneutical condition challenge all claims intent on explaining the way things are. Within Judaism and Christianity this threatens the basic claims of theism. That is, the imitative view of the world as the theater of God's glory and goodness and the biblical hermeneutic of the human as *imago Dei* have supported a theism with God depicted as cause or creator of the world, as the highest good, and as in some sense an agent. The problem of "theism" relative to imitation arises, then, in metaphysical, hermeneutical, and ethical levels. I want to show this now even though we shall not return to it until the last chapter of this study.

Ever since Kant the end of classical metaphysics has been announced. I have already touched on imitation as a metaphysical concept, so at this point I am concerned with the theological use of metaphysical imitation. It is important to recall what the task of metaphysics included: the attempt to think about and articulate the systematic and logical unity of all reality from first principles, and to understand the relation of Being to beings. The theological purchase of the metaphysical project has meant conceiving of "God" as the first principle or the horizon of unity of all reality and as Being itself. This twofold purchase has shaped the way we speak of God's relation to world and to human being and doing. Again, though I am not attempting an exhaustive interpretation of particular thinkers, a few examples will illuminate the problem of imitation in this kind of theological discourse.

Thomas Aquinas speaks of God as the cause and end of all being. This allows him, through the analogy of being, to articulate the nature of God since all else is sustained by its creator and hence in some way manifests that creative power. He notes: "Being, however, is not the nature or essence of any created thing, but God alone. Therefore no thing can remain in being when the divine operation has ceased."[61] The biblical metaphor of "creator" is interpreted metaphysically, while reality is given a theistic grounding and orientation. The difficulty is to think the difference between Being, even divine being, and beings, and to understand, without religious bias, the phenomenological character of reality. Joseph O'Leary has noted that the onto-theological pattern of metaphysical thinking "seeks to locate being in a 'logical' way, as the ground or cause of beings, either in the sense of that which beings as such have in common (ontology) or that source of being which grounds the unity of beings as a whole (theology)."[62] Most simply stated, "metaphysical" theism seems to reify God into *a* being or to classify the divine under the genus of Being and thus deny the transcendence of God. And in the same way such onto-theology tends to neglect attending to the phenomenological appearance to the world in its own integrity. The meaning and purpose of the world lie outside of it in God.

Seeing "God" as the ground and source of unity need not be articulated metaphysically; the same impulse can arise in transcendental interpretations of God. For example, Gordon Kaufman speaks of "God" as that image/concept that serves as a center or focus of devotion and orientation. Given this, he contends that we "must not be misled here into repeating the common error of searching for some particular being or reality to which the name 'God' can be applied. . . . 'God' is the focal term of an overarching conceptual framework (in terms of which all experience is grasped, understood, and interpreted), and is not the name of an agent perceived or experienced apart from that frame."[63] Despite Kaufman's transcendental turn, which does avoid confusing God and Being, this is still a metaphysical God. God is the unity of all else constructed analogically from the transcendental structure of the human self. The project of understanding God as the unity and source of all else continues in Kaufman's position and with it the risk of failing to attend to the phenomenal world in its own appearance. A theological answer seems applied to the world, and more specifically to the evolution of the cosmos. The attraction of his position is that without seeing God as a being Kaufman articulates the relation of God and world. God is the frame for understanding human world. And yet, like Thomas' onto-theological vision, Kaufman's constructivist theology rests on unexplored mimetic assumptions that are under fire.

If Being is the nature of God and not the essence of any created thing, then categorical realities are dim reflections or imitations of Being (God) that present in their appearance the power of Being. Imitation provided a way to think of the appearance of Being in beings, "God" in "world." The practical import of this insight was developed in the natural law tradition in Roman Catholic moral theology, and in the idea of the "orders of creation" in Protestant thought. Given the ontological relation of God and world, it was possible to discern the moral implication of the ordering of reality. What is evident is that the breakdown of metaphysical imitation spells the loss of the mediation of God and world and with it classical theistic moral theories. We are at a loss for any cogent way to relate God and world, and hence to conceive of reality as the presentation of the divine ways. The theater stands empty.

Likewise, if God is the interpretive framework for the orientation of our being, doing, and knowing, how can we speak of God? Aesthetic imitation provided a way, either realistically or expressively, to explain the referential power of religious symbols. With the breakdown of this form of imitation, our religious images and concepts seem vacuous; they point nowhere. This being the case, the concept of God, despite Kaufman's rejoinder, provides little concrete orientation for life. The crisis of metaphysical and aesthetic imitation, noted before, redounds upon traditional and contemporary claims about God.

The criticism of imitation, as we have seen, touches on human being and doing. "God" has also been understood relative to the human as a moral agent. For instance, Kant claims that human reason has "need of an idea of highest perfection to serve as a standard according to which it can make [moral] determinations."[64] God as the idea of a highest perfection serves the moral self-understanding in two ways: as a standard for interpreting and judging our moral situation, and as a motive for action in the "kingdom of ends." Thus the idea of God functions as a standard for judging moral obligations and claims. God also provides motivation for action since under divine sovereignty we can be assured, Kant claims, that our actions and intentions will be justly judged.

Interestingly, the crisis of imitation infests this form of theism too. It does so simply because the idea of God is dependent for its cogency and motive power on being an imitative, imaginative figuration of forms of the categorical imperative. To treat all persons not simply as means but as ends as well finds its theological representation in God as the ruler of the kingdom of ends. And the imperative to will only what one could will as a universal law of nature is expressed theologically by the idea of God as lawgiver. In each case the idea of God has an imitative relation to its foundation in a form of the categorical imperative. Yet once expressive imitation becomes problematic, either through the demise of the iconic "I" or the introduction of the ambiguity of language, then a transcendental moral theism becomes problematic. We cannot articulate the relation and mediation of moral obligation (transcendentally grounded) and its representation in the idea of God. Given this, we are forced to consider again the hermeneutical and expressive dimensions of mimesis in our God-talk.

Another form of moral theism that is instructive for our problematizing of imitation sees God as the highest good (*summum bonum*). Augustine and Aquinas were one in claiming that God is that toward which all beings ultimately strive in seeking their specific good. This idea of God correlates with the human as *imago Dei* driven by loves and desires for its own end. Moreover, God as highest good articulated an ontological and axiological claim. As St. Augustine put it, all that is, is good. This formula infuses existence with value derived from its (created) status before God. Being is good, and the highest being is logically the highest good. The human moral quest is, in reality, a search and longing for God. Human existence participates, in its very being, in that goodness. So understood, God is the source and unity both of being and of moral motive and evaluation.

The most obvious difficulty with this form of theism in a postmodern world is to make sense of "highest" good without reifying God into *a* good. That is, the problem is to avoid forgetting the ontological difference, a forgetfulness of which classical imitation was too often guilty. Yet for our purposes what is important is how the crisis of ontological imitation signals the death of this form of theism. If we can no longer speak of the presentation of the good through specific goods, how can we understand the human search for God through its quest for specific goods? The main actors of the drama are dead, it would seem, and the script of the grand narrative of the human quest is lost.

The problem of imitation entails, then, the presentation of the "good" and so undercuts important forms of classical theism. Given this, we are forced to rethink the appearance of the good. Robert Sokolowski has signaled this task: "The good is essentially attractive, always promissory. A thing's being good for us signifies that we can act with it in such a way that the acting is good. The primary sense, the prime analogue of the human good, is not a feature of something but an exercise and an involvement, an activity of something."[65] Sokolowski's point here is that we must drop a speculative idea of the good, the good as the "seen" inhering *in* something, and recognize our involvement in the good. This requires a new account of act, one task of the following chapters.

The crisis of imitation helps undermine moral, metaphysical, and transcendental forms of theism. Conversely, traditional theistic claims gather up the uses and problems of imitation as I have charted them. With the demise of "theism" theologians have responded differently. I want to note these responses and then return to them in the conclusion of this study. First, some now see the task of theology to be its own deconstruction. To avoid idolatries of all sorts it is crucial to undo the reifying tendency of our God-talk. Mark C. Taylor claims that the dissolution of the Western philosophical and theological tradition, with imitation as a conceptual linchpin, means "that deconstruction is the 'hermeneutic' of the death of God. As such, it provides a possible point of departure for a postmodern a/theology."[66] My contention is that a postmodern theology, to be cogent and complete, must rethink mimesis. This rethinking will entail a deconstruction of imitative understandings of "God's" relation to the world, language, and human existence. Yet because I am rethinking mimesis in relation to language and action I hope to avoid the fragmentation of theological discourse that threatens deconstructionist theology with moral and political paralysis.

Another response to the demise of classical theism rests on a hermeneutic of the "classic" religious texts, events, or persons. Such a hermeneutic, as David Tracy argues, attempts to think anew the disclosures of the horizon of human existence. Eberhard Jüngel, also taking a hermeneutical route, attempts to think the unthinkable God through the divine revelation in its other, in humanity, through Christ.[67] Again, my claim is that discussions of "disclosure" or "revelation" at least implicitly draw on some theory of presentation. They depend on some notion of mimesis. With the failure of classical and expressivist theories of imitation, we are forced to rethink mimesis within the task of religious reflection. This is crucial not only for the status of theological discourse, but also for an understanding of the kinds of texts on which we reflect.

Finally, thinkers like Kaufman, Arthur Cohen, and James M. Gustafson have in different ways tried to think about God in relation to human being and doing.[68] Kaufman, as noted earlier, understands God as the framework within which we orient our existence. More specifically, he speaks of the image/concept "God" as having a humanizing and relativizing function for human life that aids in guiding our lives. Cohen, it will be remembered, sees the calling of the Jews as that of enacting on the *scenum* of the world the divine presence. To be human and, specifically, to be Jewish is to take on that activity. Gustafson attempts to discern what God is enabling and requiring us to be and to do through the patterns and processes of our natural and social world. Theology is a way of construing the world evoked by piety and serving to guide human existence. All these positions entail claims about human agency and the way moral agents attempt to enact beliefs and convictions. Yet because all these positions attempt to relate the human and divine, the criticism of imitation and the "iconic" self must be reconsidered.

We no longer see the universe as a house of mirrors where levels of reality reflect each other and each has its proper place and station. We are skeptical about our ability to jump outside our culture and our language to see if they match a naked uninterpreted reality. Human symbolic expressions are seen, not as imitations or representations of their "referents," but as presentations of human being in the world and the construction of a world of meaning. Accordingly, we interpret ourselves not as icons of a transcendent deity but as actors who struggle for goods and values we deem important even while acknowledging the interests and desires that drive our thought and action. And because we help construct our world it is difficult, if not impossible, to see it as the images and shadows of divine things. The imitative universe, as the expression of God's sovereignty of the world, is taken as oppressive, static, and untenable. With that conclusion, all talk about God seems outdated or trivial before the real questions and problems facing us. Carrying on God-talk in a postmodern context requires attending to hermeneutical and moral concerns that come to a head in the problem of the theological use of imitation.

BEYOND IMITATION

In cursory fashion I have isolated the problems of imitation that form the context for this study. Aside from the history of reflection on mimesis and related concepts, the context of the present discussion is the *ethos* of postmodernism. That *ethos*, I have argued, is marked by the fragmentation of discourse about God, self, world, and text, a critique of image and yet a reconsideration of figuration, and a challenge to the adequacy of modern reflective and critical reason. The relation of these developments can be understood through the current critique of ancient and modern mimeticisms. The crisis of these forms of thought, I have argued, strike at the roots of our lives since we are creatures who understand ourselves in and through those images, forms of discourse, and pictures we form and accept of what we are to be and to do.

The postmodern condition is marked by a problem and a possibility. The problem is the confluence of various global crises: the technological mastery and destruction of our natural home, the pervasive reality of sexual, racial, political, and economic oppression, challenges to received accounts of subjectivity, and the sense of despair that follows the breakdown of modern cultural progressivism. In the face of these problems, the postmodern *ethos* seems to be one of simple resistance. (Witness, for example, the flurry of events in Eastern Europe and China.) This resistance rests, in part, on a possibility seen in that *ethos* itself: the possibility of rethinking human being and doing in its world beyond imitative paradigms of thought.

The escape from imitation has meant many things for us as a culture. It has meant the celebration of human freedom and capacities for change. At the same time it has introduced questions about the value of given reality and the veracity of our beliefs and actions; we seem cast on a sea of uncertainty. The escape has also meant the awareness of human action in the construal of its world and the expression of itself in art and literature. But this has also meant the loss of a naïve apprehension of "sacred" texts and symbols. We no longer see reality as a graded system with each part of the universe assigned a place. This has raised questions about our own identity and value in the larger scheme of things. Our freedom from the imitative cosmos is an escape from traditional theism and all attempts to reassert it. And yet religious questions continue to arise, and the idea of God still calls for attention. Ironically, we have escaped an imitative universe, but not its lure.

This study is a taking stock of how we think and speak about, how we picture, our world and our lives in their many dimensions. The hermeneutical path beyond imitation rests, I shall argue, on a shift from the imitative logic of the image to performative praxis. The constructive claim of this study is that such a shift will help in describing and understanding the elusive dynamic of human life. To that end, I shall trace this shift in areas that traditional imitation addressed: understanding and its world, text, and self. Through the interpretation of central postmodern thinkers, we are attempting to think about the texture of the acts of understanding, narrative, and being a self. Doing so takes us into reflection on language, time, and action as the media of human being and doing. And we shall see how mimesis, beyond classical and modern paradigms of thought, may still help us think about the coherence of life vis-à-vis these media of our being in the world. Yet because of this, it is not possible to define mimesis since it is the shape of the basic acts of understanding, narrative configuration, and self. The full import can be shown but not neatly stated. The structure of the argument attempts to do this.

What has been learned from Derrida's and Girard's criticisms of mimesis is that this notion marks the meeting place of power and meaning. They have shown us that mimesis disallows any easy conceptual totality, given the figural dynamics of language, or an understanding of the human that avoids the question of power. Girard and Derrida have also reconsidered mimesis in relation to its ancient performative roots in theater (Derrida) and cult (Girard). They explore those forms of mimetic praxis that are crucial for the thinkers we shall read. Despite the fact that my argument moves in directions different from theirs, Girard and Derrida help signal a turn to a performative notion of mimesis in speaking about the world and human life. I shall return to them later in this study.

In a word, the task of this book is the hermeneutical reconstruction of mimesis and its problems through the interpretation of central postmodern hermeneutical thinkers. "Reconstruction" does not mean the return to the lost origins, as if it were possible to reclaim without remainder premodern mimeticism. By reconstruction I mean an alternative interpretation of mimesis enriched by modern and contemporary critiques of imitation seeking to inform understanding and action. And my thesis is that the reconstruction of mimesis can serve us in understanding world, our experience of time, and the ambiguity of selfhood. I hope my interpretation of thought about mimesis will preserve the best insights of our tradition in a genuinely self-critical and postmodern way. Once we see mimesis as a form of structured praxis, as our participation in and enactment of our world, then perhaps it can help us think and speak of our being and doing.

NOTES

1. "Metaphysics and Ethics," in *The Nature of Metaphysics*, ed. D. F. Pears (London: Macmillian; New York: St. Martin's, 1957), p. 122. H. Richard Niebuhr has noted that the West has used several images to understand and orient human life. He isolates three as particularly crucial: *Homo faber, Homo politicus*, and, the one he considers most adequate, *Homo dialogicus*. These images entail different patterns of thought about the human project. See his *The Responsible Self: An Essay in Christian Moral Philosophy* (New York: Harper & Row, 1963). As will become clear throughout this study, part of the problem we face is the breakdown of what is meant by "image," to say nothing of those images, symbols, and metaphors we use to understand ourselves. Given this, my turn to mimesis is not an attempt to find *the* image of the human; it is to explore the dynamics within which human life, action, and being are enacted. For another helpful study on the hermeneutical shape of our moral self-understanding, see Martha C. Nussbaum, *The Fragility of Goodness: Luck and Ethics in Greek Tragedy and Philosophy* (Cambridge: Cambridge University Press, 1986).

2. See Richard Rorty, *The Consequences of Pragmatism: Essays, 1972–1980* (Minneapolis: University of Minnesota Press, 1982).

3. On the chaos of our moral world, see Alasdair MacIntyre, *After Virtue: A Study in Moral Theory* (Notre Dame: University of Notre Dame Press, 1981). For a feminist thinker who emphasizes the importance of the political and yet insists on the need to escape its hegemony, see Julia Kristeva in *The Kristeva Reader*, ed. Toril Moi (New York: Columbia University Press, 1986).

4. For a discussion of theology and pluralism, see David Tracy, *The Analogical Imagination: Christian Theology and the Culture of Pluralism* (New York: Crossroad, 1981).

5. There are numerous recent discussions of postmodernism. See James L. Marsh, "The Post-Modern Interpretation of History: A Phenomenological and Hermeneutical Critique," *Journal of the British Society of Phenomenology*, 19 (1988), 112–27, and Jean-François Lyotard, *The Postmodern Condition: A Report on Knowledge*, trans. Geoff Bennington and Brian Massumi, Theory and History of Literature 10 (Minneapolis: University of Minnesota Press, 1984). See also Andreas Huyssen, "Mapping the Postmodern," *New German Critique*, 33 (1984), 5–52.

6. Classical art, so the common history goes, was realistic even when its "mimeticism" was never exact. Given this, studies of "imitation" as an aesthetic concept generally end with the nineteenth century and the rise of Romanticism. On this see John D. Boyd, s.J., *The Function of Mimesis and Its Decline* (Cambridge: Harvard University Press, 1968; repr. New York: Fordham University Press, 1980). Perhaps

more than any other book on imitation, Eric Auerbach's monumental *Mimesis* has served to reinforce the assumption that "mimesis" denotes the representation of reality. See his *Mimesis: The Representation of Reality in Western Literature*, trans. Willard R. Trask (Princeton: Princeton University Press, 1959). Though my argument is a sustained attack on the adequacy of understanding "mimesis" solely as representation, it is nonetheless true that theories of art as the imitation of nature are no longer tenable. We simply cannot escape the awareness of the intentionality of the artist in the production of art. The paradox of our situation is that pure Romantic expressionism is also not a plausible account of art. Forces beneath the surface, like the unconscious, shape intentional artistic expression. It is in this context, I contend, that mimesis and representation are being reconsidered by postmodern thinkers. For a trenchant criticism of a mirror image of thought and mind, see Richard Rorty, *Philosophy and the Mirror of Nature* (Princeton: Princeton University Press, 1979).

7. See Harold Bloom, *Kabbalah and Criticism* (New York: Seabury, 1975). For a discussion of post-critical understandings of science, see Richard Bernstein's *Beyond Objectivism and Relativism: Science, Hermeneutics, and Praxis* (Philadelphia: University of Pennsylvania Press, 1983).

8. This is Paul Ricoeur's understanding of the metaphoric power of texts, a position I shall explore later. See his *Essays on Biblical Interpretation*, ed. Lewis S. Mudge (Philadelphia: Fortress, 1980).

9. See his *Dissemination*, trans. Barbara Johnson (Chicago: The University of Chicago Press, 1981).

10. See Karl F. Morrison, *The Mimetic Tradition of Reform in the West* (Princeton: Princeton University Press, 1982) and James M. Redfield, *Nature and Culture in the* ILIAD: *The Tragedy of Hector* (Chicago: The University of Chicago Press, 1975).

11. Joseph S. O'Leary has outlined the metaphysical elements in traditional theism. See his *Questioning Back: The Overcoming of Metaphysics in the Christian Tradition* (Minneapolis: Winston, 1985).

12. *An Introduction to Metaphysics*, trans. Ralph Manheim (Garden City: Doubleday Anchor, 1961), p. 154.

13. For a helpful study of mimesis in pre-Socratic Greek culture, Plato, and Aristotle, see Herman Köller, *Die Mimesis in der Antike: Nachahmung, Darstellung, Ausdruck* (Berne: Francke, 1954).

14. For a discussion of Kant's aesthetics, see *Essays on Kant's Aesthetics*, edd. Ted Cohen and Paul Guyer (Chicago: The University of Chicago Press, 1982).

15. *Biographia Literaria*, ed. George Watson (New York: Dutton, 1965), p. 167. For a discussion of the current debate over the problems of reflexivity, see Hilary Lawson, *Reflexivity: The Post-Modern Predicament* (La Salle, Ill.: Open Court, 1985). On Romantic strands in hermeneutics, see F. D. E. Schleiermacher, *Hermeneutics: The Handwritten Manuscripts*, ed. Heinz Kimmerle, trans. James Duke and Jack Fortsman, American Academy of Religion Texts and Translations 1 (Missoula, Mont.: Scholars Press, 1977).

16. Coleridge, *Biographia Literaria*, p. 194.

17. *Philosophical Papers*. 1. *Human Agency and Language* (Cambridge: Cambridge University Press, 1985), p. 238.

18. *Margins of Philosophy*, trans. Alan Bass (Chicago: The University of Chicago Press, 1982), p. 237.

19. "Joining the Text: From Heidegger to Derrida," in *The Yale Critics: Deconstruction in America*, edd. Jonathon Arac, Wald Godzich, and Wallace Martine, Theory and History of Literature 6 (Minneapolis: The University of Minnesota Press, 1983), pp. 172–73. See also Susan A. Handelmann, *The Slayers of Moses: The Emergence of Rabbinic Interpretation in Modern Literary Theory* (Albany: State University of New York Press, 1982), and Christopher Norris, *Deconstruction: Theory and Practice* (New York: Methuen, 1981).

20. "Economimesis," trans. R. Klein, *Diacritics*, 11 (1981), 6. For convenience, reference will be made to the English translation. I have made corrections as needed from the French version. See "Economimesis," *Mimesis des articulations* (Paris: Aubier–Flammarion, 1975), pp. 57–93.

21. *Dissemination*, pp. 186–87.

22. Derrida notes the relation of mimesis and truth in Plato's thought. He writes that Plato "is obliged sometimes to condemn mimesis in itself as a process of duplication, whatever the model might be, and sometimes to disqualify mimesis only in function of the model that is 'imitated,' the mimetic operation in itself remaining neutral, or even advisable. But in both cases, mimesis is lined up alongside truth: either it hinders the unveiling of the thing itself by substituting a copy or double for what is; or else it works in the service of truth through the double's resemblance (*homoiosis*)." See ibid., p. 187.

23. *Margins of Philosophy*, p. 237.

24. P. 9.

25. Ibid., 4.

26. *Disseminations*, p. 198.

27. Ibid., pp. 206–208.

28. The relation of mimesis to naturalism and cosmology are important for my argument. For a recent rethinking of the moral status of nature see Erazim Kohák, *The Embers and the Stars: A Philosophical Inquiry into the Moral Sense of Nature* (Chicago: The University of Chicago Press, 1984). See also Hans Jonas, *The Imperative of Responsibility: In Search of an Ethic for the Technological Age*, trans. Hans Jonas and D. Herr (Chicago: The University of Chicago Press, 1984).

29. Feminist criticisms of hierarchy are bountiful, of course. For a recent systematic and theological treatment of this, see Rosemary Radford Ruether, *Sexism and God-Talk: Toward a Feminist Theology* (Boston: Beacon, 1983).

30. *Erring: A Postmodern A-Theology* (Chicago: The University of Chicago Press, 1984), p. 35.

31. *Mamre: Essays in Religion*, trans. Greta Hort (London: Melbourne University Press, 1946), p. 39.

32. *The Imitation of God in Christ: An Essay on the Biblical Basis of Christian Spirituality*, The Library of History and Doctrine (London: SCM Press, 1960). See also Hans Dieter Betz, *Nachfolge und Nachahmung Jesu Christi im Neuen Testament*, ed. Gerhard Ebeling, Beiträge zur historischen Theologie 37 (Tübingen: Mohr, 1967).

33. *The Tremendum: A Theological Interpretation of the Holocaust* (New York: Crossroad, 1981), pp. 92, 94.

34. *Faith in History and Society: Toward a Practical Fundamental Theology*, trans. David Smith (New York: Crossroad/Seabury Press, 1980). I have corrected Smith's translation, which renders *Nachfolge* as imitation! The distinction between "following" and "imitating" is crucial to Metz's argument.

35. *The Politics of Jesus: Vicit Agnus Noster* (Grand Rapids: Eerdmans, 1972), p. 128.

36. Ibid., p. 129.

37. *Moral Action: A Phenomenological Study* (Bloomington: Indiana University Press, 1985), p. 27.

38. This point is made by Paul Valadier, "Bouc émissaire et Révélation chrétienne selon René Girard," *Etudes*, 357 (1982), 253. I have presented this reading of Girard elsewhere; see my "Sacrifice, Interpretation, and the Sacred: The Import of Gadamer and Girard for Religious Studies," *The Journal of the American Academy of Religion*, 55 (1987), 791–810.

39. *To Double Business Bound: Essays on Literature, Mimesis, and Anthropology* (Baltimore: The Johns Hopkins University Press, 1978), p. 201.

40. *Violence and the Sacred*, trans. Patrick Gregory (Baltimore: The Johns Hopkins University Press, 1977), p. 145.

41. René Girard, "Mimesis and Violence: Perspectives in Cultural Criticism," *Berkshire Review*, 14 (1979), 10.

42. *Deceit, Desire, and the Novel: Self and Other in Literary Structure*, trans. Yvonne Freccero (Baltimore: The Johns Hopkins University Press, 1965), p. 290.

43. "Mimesis and Violence," 11.

44. Girard, *To Double Business Bound*, p. 206. See also Benoît Garceau, "La violence et le vrai savior de l'homme," *Sciences Religieuses/Studies in Religion*, 10 (1981), 5–14, and René Girard, *The Scapegoat*, trans. Yvonne Freccero (Baltimore: The Johns Hopkins University Press, 1986).

45. Paul Dumochel, "Différences et paradoxes: Réflexions sur l'amour et la violence dans l'oeuvre de Girard," in *René Girard et le problème du mal*, edd. M. Deguy and J.-P. Dupuy (Paris: Grasset, 1982), pp. 216–18.

46. "Mimesis and Violence," 10.

47. *Deceit, Desire, and the Novel*, p. 312.

48. Valadier, "Bouc émissaire," 255. The argument that the Christian faith is not a religion was proposed by key Neo-Orthodox theologians. Perhaps the most powerful statement of this is made by Karl Barth, who argues that religion, as the human attempt to reconcile itself with God, is sin. True faith, contrariwise, holds fast to God's act in Christ. What seems clear is that while Girard wants to argue that Christianity is in some sense not a "religion," he differs significantly on this with Barth. For Barth the problem centers on the human relation to God; for Girard the concern is with the structure and shape of social reality. Girard's non-theological reading of Christianity seems clear on this point. See Karl Barth, *Church Dogmatics*, edd. G. W. Bromiley and T. F. Torrance, 12 vols. (Edinburgh: Clark, 1956–1969), I/2, pp. 280–361.

49. *Deceit, Desire, and the Novel*, p. 58.

50. Valadier, "Bouc émissaire," 257.

51. "Violence and the Bible: The Girard Connection," *Catholic Biblical Quarterly*, 47 (1980), 18.

52. "Mimesis and Violence," 18.

53. *Scapegoat*, p. 207.

54. Claude Troisfontaines, "L'identité du social et du religieux selon René Girard," *Revue Philosophique de Louvain*, 78 (1980), 73.

55. *To Double Business Bound*, p. 203.

56. *Institutes of the Christian Religion*, trans. Ford Lewis Battles, ed. John T. McNeill, 2 vols., Library of Christian Classics 20–21 (Philadelphia: Westminister, 1960). See I.v.8, I.vi.2, I.xiv.20, II.vi.1, III.ix.2.

57. *On the Holy Trinity*, ed. Philip Schaff, Nicene and Post-Nicene Fathers 3 (Grand Rapids: Eerdmans, 1980), pp. 1–228.

58. *On First Principles*, trans. G. W. Butterworth (Gloucester, Mass.: Smith, 1973).

59. The literature on feminist hermeneutics is extensive. See *Feminist Interpretations of the Bible*, ed. Letty M. Russell (Philadelphia: Westminster, 1985) and Elisabeth Schüssler Fiorenza, *Bread Not Stone: The Challenge of Feminist Biblical Interpretation* (Boston: Beacon, 1984).

60. For a narrativist account of the moral use of Scripture, see Stanley Hauerwas, *A Community of Character: Toward a Constructive Christian Social Ethic* (Notre Dame: University of Notre Dame Press, 1981). See also Paul Nelson, *Narrative and Morality: A Theological Inquiry* (University Park: The Pennsylvania State University Press, 1987).

61. *Summa contra Gentiles* III, ch. 65 (Rome: Marietti, 1925), p. 290. I have not entered here into the debate on the importance of Trinitarian thought for current theology, although my argument has implications for it. At this point I am interested in general claims made for God's relation to the world and to human moral existence.

62. *Questioning Back*, p. 11.

63. "Constructing the Concept of God," *Neue Zeitschrift für systematische Theologie und Religionsphilosophie*, 23 (1981), 48–49. See also his *The Theological Imagination: Constructing the Concept of God* (Philadelphia: Westminster, 1981).

64. *Lectures on Philosophical Theology*, trans. Allen W. Wood and Gertrude M. Clark (Ithaca: Cornell University Press, 1978), p. 21.

65. *Moral Action*, p. 30. On the importance of *actus* as a fundamental philosophical and theological category, see David B. Burrell, *Aquinas: God and Action* (Notre Dame: University of Notre Dame Press, 1979).

66. Taylor, *Erring*, p. 6.

67. See Tracy's *Analogical Imagination*, and Jüngel's *God as the Mystery of the World*, trans. Darrell L. Gruder (Grand Rapids: Eerdmans, 1983).

68. In addition to the Cohen and the Kaufman works already cited, see Gustafson's *Ethics from a Theocentric Perspective*, 2 vols. (Chicago: The University of Chicago Press, 1981, 1984).

2

Understanding as Mimesis of World

IN THE PREVIOUS CHAPTER I tried to outline some of the problems found in classical and modernist notions of imitation, especially when it articulated the logic of the "image" or "idea." These problems ranged from basic issues in aesthetics to metaphysics, epistemology, moral philosophy, and even theology. In each case, the relation of ideal and real, universal and particular, intention and expression were thought and spoken about in imitative ways. The lure of imitation theory was to show the relation and distinction of each of these even as it actually broke them apart, taking one side of the relation as a dependent representation of the other. More important for our purposes, the human was placed in the logical framework of the image and imitation, either as one who knows through images or, in the case of biblical thought, as the one who realizes its being by imitating the divine. The criticisms of image/imitation, and of "God" as well, challenge not only aesthetic and metaphysical rationality, but also discourse about human being and what it means to be human.

While we were uncovering the layers of the problem of imitation, we discerned a contrary mode of reflection on mimesis, one that was hinted at in dialogue, plot, and imagination, and in moral and religious existence. To be sure, these strands of reflection remain tied to the "image," but it is not interpreted within a conceptual framework dominated by mirroring or imitation. For this mode of thought, mimesis is a way to speak of an activity, a praxis, of figuration through which the being of something is presented and deferred. How might we understand mimesis in this way? Is it possible at all, given the long history of discourse about "imitation"? What might this kind of mimetic thinking contribute to our reflection on the human condition, world, texts, and even the divine? Our inquiry is oriented by these questions, ones that can only be addressed throughout the course of this entire study. The first step in addressing them is to explore mimetic figuration itself in the areas of reflection that imitation previously articulated. In this chapter I do so by turning to the problem of understanding in exploring the work of Hans-Georg Gadamer.

Although my purpose is not to explore Gadamer's place in the history of hermeneutics, a few words about his project will set the context for examining his mimetic strategy of thought and for the conclusion I draw from his work.

Gadamer stands within the development of hermeneutics initiated by Schleiermacher and decisively redirected by Heidegger. That is, Schleiermacher began the turn in hermeneutics away from the exegesis of texts, particularly sacred ones, toward the problem of understanding. Yet, as Gadamer sees it, Schleiermacher took the problem that hermeneutics seeks to solve to be that of misunderstanding an author or texts, and his hermeneutics was developed as a way to overcome misunderstanding. With Wilhelm Dilthey, who followed Schleiermacher, hermeneutics meant a turn to the question of the origin of the work and the use of methods employed in the human sciences in the search for understanding. Heidegger redirected hermeneutics away from the problem of misunderstanding toward the task of exploring understanding itself as *Dasein*'s way of being-in-the-world. Gadamer continues this concern for the ontological import of understanding. *Truth and Method*, his major work, is an attempt to provide a comprehensive hermeneutic relative to art, history, and language.

Gadamer takes philosophical hermeneutics to be inquiry into understanding in general. "Understanding [*Verstehen*] for Gadamer is primarily coming to an understanding [*Verständigung*] with others."[1] Understanding is dialogical and communicative in character. But more to the point, Gadamer is concerned not only with the dynamics of understanding, but with its *truth*. In exploring the question of truth, he marshals a critique of the rise of epistemology as the search for the foundations of knowledge and for the methodological control of inquiry. Within the constellation of questions about method and truth we can understand both Gadamer's own work and his reading of mimesis.

What does Gadamer mean by "truth" and "method"? The rest of this chapter will explore what he means by the event of truth; by method he means something specific, even if he does not carefully define it. As Joel Weinsheimer notes, "Method, and epistemology in general, Gadamer contends, is primarily a response to *Fremdheit*, the condition of being no longer at home in the world. To be at home means to belong, to live in surroundings that are familiar, self-evident, and unobtrusive; its contrary, *Fremdheit*, consists in the schism between past and present, I and others, self and world."[2] Method is an attempt to overcome alienation. Yet it is one that heightens the schism because it seeks to dominate and explain the objective world by controlled processes of thought and action. In the process even the one undertaking the inquiry becomes an object for methodological explanation. Hence method, in its cognitive and technological forms, is destructive of the very conditions for belonging.

The pretense and task of method is knowledge through control. Logically this task has two sides since a "total knowledge and control of the world requires a total knowledge and control of ourselves."[3] Gadamer holds that such total knowledge is not possible, and still less so through control. Furthermore, method does not reap the self-knowledge, the moral wisdom, that is a mark of the life well lived. Understanding, for him, is overcoming the alienation that all life instanciates, since life itself is a process of differentiation and assimilation; yet genuine understanding reaches this overcoming without domination and in such a way as to form the one who is understanding. In a word, Gadamer believes that genuine understanding is a participation in the event of truth, and he seeks to explore this event and participation beyond mastery or total knowledge.

Gadamer's hermeneutics attempts to give an account of the truth of understanding. For our purposes, it is important that there are parallels between Gadamer's treatment of mimesis and his criticisms of previous hermeneutics. Isolating these will move us one step closer to reading his works. Here we should recall that imitation, under the logic of the image, articulated specific relations (ideal/real, etc.) demarcating their separation, a separation that is overcome by understanding one side of the relation (real) by the other (ideal). In modern hermeneutics this imitative strategy manifested itself in two ways that Gadamer seeks to challenge, and he does so through mimesis.

First, classical imitation theories in prioritizing *eidos* over *physis*, as Heidegger put it, provided the impetus for the working out of method in aesthetics, history, and philosophy of language. That is, imitation theory signaled the *Fremdheit* of Being and beings, the ideal and the real, such that this separation must be overcome by controlling one side of the relation by the other—either through pure intuition bypassing the "imitation," or by judging the imitation by its denotative or analogical relation to its (ostensive) referent. Method in modern thought is, then, one legacy of imitation theory. In this respect Gadamer's criticism of method in modern hermeneutics is part of the challenge to imitation. Imitation holds out the possibility of total control while instanciating alienation. Gadamer's first criticism of modern hermeneutics is that it became methodologically centered, concerned with developing strategies of explanation to control an object under inquiry, whether that object is a text or an historical period. This development I am suggesting is a working out of imitation theory. And yet Gadamer seeks to reclaim mimesis.

Most simply put, Gadamer contends that with Dilthey and others hermeneutical reflection shifted from understanding the truth-content of a text or event to explaining the conditions of its genesis. "The question of understanding thus becomes the genetic one: what were the conditions under which agents acted, spoke, or wrote as they did?"[4] The rise in modern thought of historicist approaches to events, texts, and persons, the concern with the artist's intentions and genius in the production of texts, and the development of the myriad forms of textual and historical critical methods all mark, in Gadamer's opinion, a shift in the focus of hermeneutical attention. And it is this shift that gave rise to the dominance of method. Of course, his judgment on this point is debatable, but it is a debate we cannot enter here. What is important is the way his criticism of these developments coheres with his turn to mimesis.

Gadamer's retrieval of mimesis is a way to speak of our belonging to history and language beyond the *Fremdheit* instanciated in method. Reclaiming a performative notion of mimetics challenges the logic of imitation and its working out in method.[5] Understanding is not the control of what is other and objective; it is an enactment of commonality that is an event of truth. As performative, understanding is always practical; and giving an account of understanding, the task of hermeneutics, is concerned, not with the possible objectivity of such understanding, but with what that understanding *is*. For precisely this reason mimesis remains important. As Gadamer reclaims it, mimesis focuses attention not on the origin of a work in the artist's intention or on its historical locale, but on its content, its *Sache*. Mimetic works, as Georgia Warnke writes, "do not refer back to an original in the sense that they could be evaluated with regard to their faithfulness to it. Instead that which is depicted comes to light only through the depiction itself. In other words, it is through the artistic representation itself that we can comprehend the artistic subject matter."[6] Thus the retrieval of mimesis is an attempt to center hermeneutical reflection on the claim to truth of a work, its subject matter, and not the conditions of its genesis. However, in order to do so Gadamer must also undertake a critique of imitation theory and its legacy in method. His use of mimesis is central to his criticism of method and to his attempt to focus hermeneutical reflection on what is understood, the *Sache*, in the act of interpretation.

Gadamer's hermeneutic overturns classical imitation theory, even as it attends to the areas of thought and action that mimesis previously explained. In fact, his mimetic strategy is a way to speak and think about being and understanding. On the way to showing this, I want to offer an interpretation of his hermeneutic. His position provides us with a general understanding of mimesis that will be refined in the following chapters. Isolating Gadamer's position requires a detailed reading of his works on mimesis and a judgment of how they fit within his general hermeneutic.

Because of the complexity of Gadamer's thought on mimesis, I want to foreshadow issues and conclusions that will emerge from my reading. (*a*) Gadamer interprets mimesis around forms of social interaction, or play (*Spiel*), ranging from cultic dance to dialogue. In each case through the specific praxis something is brought to figurative presentation. It is important to recall that the terminology of mimesis arose around cultic action and mime theater. In the cultic art there was an "epiphany" of the god through the action and the actors. I contend that Gadamer is attempting to grasp this epiphanic element as crucial to understanding experiences of meaning, the *Sache*, of a text, event, or conversation. Mimesis is, then, a transformation into figuration of *Spiel*-activity that allows the being of the play and the players to present themselves as an event of truth. This "transformation," Gadamer argues, signals an increase of being by rendering possible our understanding of world and self.

(*b*) The dynamics of bringing human belongingness to world into presentation has a threefold structure: the activity of the presentation, its temporal character, and the presentation as a figured work. In each aspect of the "presentative action," there is reference both to human experience and to the "objective spirit" of the activity. At times Gadamer gives preference to the structured work, the text or work of art, in his reflections on mimesis to counter any reduction of the work to authorial intention or historical origin. Yet his position entails all three moments of the performative action with reference to the objectivity of the action and to the human participant. So understood, "mimetic action" helps us articulate the relation of Being and understanding beyond the pale of classical and modern mimeticism.

(c) Gadamer works out his hermeneutic in three areas: the experience of art, historical understanding, and language as the horizon of human world. Each of these areas of concern manifests a mimetic structure, as does the relation between them. Thus *Truth and Method*, as I shall interpret it, develops a comprehensive hermeneutic that articulates the mimetic character of understanding and Being while showing the relation of art, historical traditions, and language. A "mimetic hermeneutic," if I may call it such, exposes the relation between the domains of human existence that traditional imitation theory attempted to show.

(d) The ontology of human belonging means that Gadamer's hermeneutic opens the question of the shared commonality of the human. At this point he specifically links hermeneutics with practical philosophy and the question of the good. Here we reach the final concern of this chapter. That is, after isolating Gadamer's mimetic strategy and what it says about human belonging to world we can raise the question: What is the horizon of that belongingness? In commenting on Aristotle's practical philosophy Gadamer notes something that applies equally well to his own thought: "Not only art imitates nature. Human practice does so too insofar as it aims at nothing other than the highest fulfillment of human existence itself. The fact that it does, however, shows that at the same time human existence points beyond itself to the divine."[7] Thus we are led, within the discussion of mimesis, into basic issues of human being and doing and, hence, into religious and moral questions.

My thesis about *Truth and Method* is that it proposes a complex hermeneutic that itself is clarified when seen as mimetic. Indeed, I shall argue that Gadamer's understanding of mimesis, as temporal, dynamic action that comes to presentation, is a way to speak about understanding and Being becoming meaningful in a world. To show the plausibility of this claim I must first isolate Gadamer's retrieval of mimesis to see if it provides insight into that work. Accordingly, my interpretation of his thought will move in three broad steps that correspond to the parts of *Truth and Method*. First, I want to examine his understanding of mimesis in relation to the experience of the work of art as well as his specific essays on mimesis. Next, I shall explore the mimetic shape of understanding as it is represented in Part II of *Truth and Method*. Finally, I shall argue that for Gadamer language also has a mimetic structure while it dynamically relates understanding and the disclosure of Being in the work of art. Thus *Truth and*

Method presents a complex mimetic strategy crucial to the rest of my argument.

My substantive claim is that Gadamer interprets mimesis in art and understanding around forms of social praxis through which Being comes to presentation. This overturns classical ontology and the hermeneutic of imitation while providing a way for us to retrieve and use mimesis in our reflections on world and understanding. "World" is the social performance of our commonality, a belongingness, that is the good of the human. In art and in historical understanding that solidarity comes to figurative presentation. Because of this, that commonality is always deferred, elusively escaping our grasp, and always calling for further acts of understanding. The medium of that presentation and deferral is the mimetic play of language in which we are the actors. Yet given this, we are pushed beyond Gadamer into considering more specifically both our act of understanding within time and what it means to be a self, topics I shall consider in the remainder of the book. Thus reading Gadamer advances my own reflections on postmodern hermeneutics by retrieving mimesis as a basic notion open to ontological, ethical, and even religious issues.

ART AND EXPERIENCE AS MIMETIC

The complexity of Gadamer's retrieval of mimesis rests on the fact that he interprets it in relation to another notion, that of *Spiel* or "play." This suggests that the dynamics of figuration must be interpreted in relation to social praxis and power. Moreover, he isolates both experiential and ontological aspects of mimesis and *Spiel*. Given this, I want to begin by investigating the dimensions of play as these open onto Gadamer's rethinking of mimesis. What is immediately clear is that the turn to *Spiel* as a basic ontological concept breaks the imitative universe of mirrors, and it does so by accenting, not the static correspondence of artifact or world to "idea," but the self-disclosure of the world. "What Gadamer is describing is the process by which worlds come to be, an event of being and truth. The event of truth is the *unabgeschlossenes Geschehen*, the unconcluded event, in which we are always caught up, even and especially when we are playing. The player in truth is being played."[8] My concern is to show the place and importance of mimesis within this ontology of presentation in which being and understanding are two sides of the same event of truth.

In his short work *Die Aktualität des Schönen: Kunst als Spiel, Symbol, und Fest*, Gadamer asks: What is the basis of our experience of art?[9] His answer emerges from studying art in relation to "*Spiel*," "festival," and "symbol," and he begins the essay by considering the fundamental character of play in human culture. Pointing out that "*Spiel* is an elementary function of human life so that human culture is generally not thinkable without a play [*Spiel*] element" (AS 29),[10] Gadamer pauses to consider the mode of being of play.

Gadamer highlights the cultic roots of *Spiel* and the metaphorical use of the term as in the play of light and the play of wills, and he links *Spiel* to the free movement of self-presentation.

> [This] movement must have the form of self-movement [*Selbstbewegung*]. Self-movement is the basic character [*Grundcharakter*] of living being, which, after all, Aristotle . . . had already described. What is living has the force of movement in itself; it is "self"-movement. *Spiel* appears only as self-movement, which through its movement strives for neither purpose [*Zweck*] nor aim [*Zeile*], but rather movement as movement . . . , which means the self-presentation [*Selbstdarstellung*] of the being of life [AS 30].[11]

Gadamer draws the surprising connection between cultic *Spiel*-action and the self-movement of nature, or *physis*, implying that an ontology is possible through an analysis of social performance (*Spiel*). Understanding this, Gadamer seeks to isolate the character of *Spiel* on his way to a social ontology.

Gadamer notes, in *Truth and Method*, that the to-and-fro (*hin und her*) movement of play reveals the original meaning of *Spiel* as dance (*Tanz*). Cultic dance is the context within which to understand the mode of being of *Spiel*. Dance has no goal outside of itself and has a repetitive character. It may be repeated as often as liked, and it "is" only in its performance. That is, dance has a self-presentative nature and a unique temporal character. Therefore, three characteristics are evident in the relation of *Spiel*, dance, and life: movement, a presentational character, and temporality.

Gadamer's idea of *Spiel* is multi-layered, one level of which is manifest in his comment on a child's ballplaying:

> The goal that is pursued here is indeed a purposeless activity, but this activity itself is meant. It is that which the play intends. . . . This is the first step on the way to human communication because here something was presented—if only the movement of play itself—so it was there also for the spectator [*Zuschauer*], who intends [*meint*] it. . . . In the end, play is the self-presentation of its own movement [AS 30–31].

Spiel, as purposeless activity, is communicative; it is a way of insight into the human condition through the participatory communion that it establishes. This kind of knowledge is participatory; "it is nothing other than *participatio*, the inner taking part [*Teilnahme*] in this repetitive movement" (AS 31). As Jean Grondin has correctly noted, it "means that the subject participates in the verbal contents in which an action [*Handlung*] for itself or in itself takes place."[12] The first mark of *Spiel* is that it is participatory action that is purposeless beyond self-presentation.

Gadamer also isolates the rule-governed character of human *Spiel*. In the essay "Das Spiel der Kunst" he notes that what "constitutes the play-character of human play [is] that rules and forms become set up which are valuable only in the continuity of the world of play."[13] Participation always entails involvement of some structural relations that guide and limit viable courses of action.[14]

Through this participation there is an apprehension of self-consciousness as players come to know themselves in the context of relations and rules. The rule-governed character of play enhances commonality and self-consciousness as viable social goals.

Gadamer insists, however, that *Spiel* cannot be grasped simply by attending to the attitude or the subjectivity of the creator, the audience, or even the players. As he sees it, this was the error of modern hermeneutics and its domination by method. Gadamer wants to focus on the movement itself. In fact, he claims that the "players are not the subject of play; rather the play comes to a particular presentation [*Darstellung*] through the players" (WM 98/TM 93). In *Spiel* "the to-and-fro movement [*Bewegung*] is meant which has no goal [*Zeil*] outside of itself in which it ends" (WM 99/TM 93). The to-and-fro movement is constituted by the interaction of the players, though it cannot be reduced to their subjectivity, and gives rise both to the players *as* players and to the rules of the play. The being of *Spiel* is not analogous to the being-for-itself of subjectivity; it is interactive movement that has its own proper character of spirit.[15]

The basic ontological character of *Spiel* is central to Gadamer's entire hermeneutic: *Spiel* is dynamic participatory interaction. "The movement [*Bewegung*] back and forth is so central for the essential determination of *Spiel* that it is not important who or what performs [*ausführt*] this movement. The movement of *Spiel* as such has no substrate [*Substrat*]. It is the *Spiel* that is played regardless of whether or not there is a subject who plays. The play is the execution [*Vollzug*] of the movement as such" (WM 99/TM 93). By *Spiel* Gadamer means, then, performative movement, a *kinesis*, having no substrate. The search for some foundation outside of the movement or for a genesis in the subjectivity of the players is misguided. In this sense, Gadamer's ontology signals both the presentation and concealment or deferral of Being through the very *Spiel* of self-presentation. And yet his retrieval of mimesis, unlike Derrida's, does not rest with pure figuration.

Gadamer's reading of *Spiel* is an elaboration of certain Heideggerian insights. As I noted in the first chapter, Heidegger understood *physis* as the emerging power of Being such that any particular phenomenon is the self-manifestation of its being. All phenomenal reality, as "nature," is its own self-presentation and is to be understood as such even while it is an appearance of *physis*. The ideality of reality, its meaningfulness, is not antecedent to phenomenal presentation, as in classical imitation theory, but is won through that figuration even as this figuration does not exhaust its meaning. It must always be understood anew and hence differently. For Gadamer, the mimetic transformation of reality is precisely what signals the ideality or meaningfulness of being. Life becomes meaningful when it is transformed into a figure that can be understood. Mimesis denotes, in this sense, the meaningfulness of Being in phenomena; that is, Being becomes meaningful in its concrete presentations. Given this, Gadamer's hermeneutic must begin with and aim toward understanding the concrete expressions of Being. He understands *Spiel* as a way to explore this self-movement of Being into meaningfulness.

Heidegger speaks of *Spiel* in his Heraclitus lectures: "It plays because it plays. 'Because' sinks into play. The play is without 'why.' It plays while it plays. There remains only play: the highest and deepest. . . . Nothing is without ground. Being and ground: the same. Being and ground has no ground; it plays as abyss that playing which, as mission, plays up to as Being and ground."[16] Heidegger's language is unduly obscure even if he is trying to escape onto-theological modes of thinking. His point is that the play of Being is ontologically basic. It is the "way" of Being. Being is not a static some-thing antecedent to physical reality; nor is it an ideal realm crudely actualized in bits of reality or in reality as a whole. Rather, Being is the interactive movement and power of reality manifesting itself in various phenomenal dimensions.[17] Following Heidegger, Gadamer uses *Spiel*, as a social praxis, to speak about the dynamic character of Being, confounding any static or foundationalist view of Being and world and signaling that his ontological reflection is deeply social. Being is understood as social performance, as the world of play.

Beyond *Spiel* as the dynamic of being, Gadamer discerns another layer of *Spiel*, which suggests a correlation between the phenomenal structure of Being and consciousness, through the dynamics of *Spiel* itself. In fact, according to Hegel, *Spiel*, festival, is the way of consciousness.

> Appearance is the arising and passing away that does not itself arise and pass away, but is "in itself" [i.e., subsists intrinsically], and constitutes the actuality and the movement of the life of truth. The True is thus the Bacchanalian revel in which no member is not drunk; yet because each member collapses as soon as he drops out, the revel is just as much transparent and simple repose. . . . In the whole of the movement, seen as a state of repose, what distinguishes itself therein, and gives itself particular existence, is preserved as something which recollects itself, whose existence is self-knowledge, and whose self-knowledge is just immediately existence.[18]

Spiel is ontologically basic; it is interactive self-governed movement, the dynamic of *physis* and consciousness. And the goal of *Spiel*-action is self-presentation. Beyond the alienation of understanding and world, Gadamer is attempting to show their primal relation. Accordingly, we should expect to find an analogous character to the *Spiel* of Being and of understanding. However, the full import of this turn to *Spiel* is clarified only when we deepen our interpretation to include its temporal and presentative character.

For Gadamer the "movement of *Spiel* has no goal in which it ends; rather it renews itself in constant repetition [*Wiederholung*]" (WM 99/TM 93). This comment on the repetitive character of *Spiel* is reminiscent of Kant, for whom aesthetic pleasure is the free play of the faculties without a theoretical or practical goal. Gadamer's analysis is formally similar to this, as he himself notes (AS 57), yet for Kant the purposelessness of the free play of the faculties betrayed a lack of moral and theoretical *content* in aesthetic experience—even if art is a symbol of morality. Gadamer explores the temporal structure of *Spiel's* mode of being beyond the relation of faculties concerned about the content of this activity, interpreting this temporal structure through "festival." Again, my claim here is that Gadamer is retrieving the cultic and theatrical framework in which mimesis is to be understood and reconstructed. Hence from dramatic action (*Spiel*), we turn to the temporal shape of that action, to festival.

"While one celebrates the festival," Gadamer writes, "the festival is always and the whole time 'there' [*Da*]. That is, the time character of festival is that it 'happened' and is not disintegrated into the duration of detached moments" (AS 54). The temporal character of festival is that it is *event-full*. Festival time is not ordinary time. Gadamer derives three characteristics of the repetitive event-structure of festival: its unique temporality, the social character of festival, and its experiential quality.

Festival time is "fulfilled time." Our normal experience of time is "*Zeit für etwas*" and even empty time (*leere Zeit*). Festive time breaks up this time-for-something. It is a holiday from the humdrum and predictable path of ordinary time. The experience of festival time is not one of emptiness or discrete moments of "now." The festival "brings one to stay and linger." It provides us with continuity through time. This "lingering" is the truth of festival, and it is generated from its interactive dynamics. Thus the temporality of festival opens up an interactive mode of being contrary to the isolated pellets of "nows" in ordinary time.

The paradox is that festivals exist only in their celebration. In this sense the being of festival is always present (its celebration) and not present (between celebrations). Festival has its being in becoming, and this "does not mean mere possibility but rather imperfect present or, better, movement into presence."[19] Hence the enactment itself is a deferral of complete presence even as it is a move into some presence. The ontological and temporal structure of festival is always a repetitive movement in and out of presence. Gadamer argues that this unique character enables continuity through becoming. I shall return to this shortly. First I must isolate the sociality of festival.

Festivals are social events. "The festival is mutuality [*Gemeinsamkeit*], and it is the presentation [*Darstellung*] of the community in its completed form. Festival is always for all" (AS 52). This public character of festival counters the private aesthetic consciousness. It also signals an event within which the *Fremdheit* of self and other is overcome without reducing the other to the same through manipulation and control. Indeed, the festival "properly exists only when it is played—that is, when object and subject coalesce so that object is no longer object and subject no longer subject."[20] There are no private festivals precisely because a festival is the interactive celebration of a community. Festival sends its roots down into the *ethos* of the community and presents it anew. Through festival the community comes to presentation for all. The community ex-ists, or stands out, in the festive performative presentation.

The being of festival is a self-presentation—for example, a religious community presents itself as a particular community in its celebration of worship —and yet precisely because it is self-presentative a festival is also public. "And yet the cultic act," Gadamer notes, "is actually a presentation for the community, and equally so a theatrical drama [Schauspiel] is a playful act [Spielvorgang] that essentially calls for an audience [Zuschauer]. . . . The audience completes what the Spiel as such is" (WM 104/TM 98). The festive presentation is for someone; all presentation is, at least potentially, for an audience. In the spectator, Gadamer contends, the festival is raised to its completion. This is a clue to the cognitive dimension of the festival.

The experience that properly takes place in "festival," with its repetitive nature, is contemporaneity. In isolating the experiential element in festival we turn from the analysis of the movement of festival to the experience of the spectator. Jean Grondin has suggested that the "movement between the work and the spectator presents a self-display which does not go out from us. It makes itself indeed an open event of truth, in which we simply participate, a ground experience [Grunderfahrung] which Gadamer wants to define as the event of truth in general."[21]

Festival is structured Spiel, and as such its truth is participatory. But festival is also repetitive. Through it the identity of the participants and the festival is engendered. There is a dialectical relation between the temporality of festival and the contemporaneity that its repetitive character elicits. The experiential level must be understood between these poles of participatory repetition and continuity through time.

There is a dimension of continuity through the experience of festival because presentation is its mode of being and hence each repetition is equally original to the work itself. The temporal structure confounds any search for origins to the festival outside of its enactment. Repetition is not the repeating of a beginning in a literal sense. Rather, our temporal experience of festival is through its celebration and includes memory and expectation (Erinnerung und Erwartung). The performative character of the celebration is the structure of its temporality: its mode of being is always to become something different. Festival is marked by this radical temporality.

Festival calls for an audience to participate (Teilhabe) or to take part in the event, and this participation is for Gadamer the meaning of theoria. The theoros, he notes, was someone who took part in the mission to the Greek religious festivals. Greek metaphysics conceived of theory in relation to what is ulti mately and unchangeably true and real, and shifted "theory" from participation at the festival to the intentionality of the knower in attending to something. This shift gave rise to a metaphysics of vision, which culminated in the drive of method to overcome alienation through control and total knowledge.

For Western epistemology, as Gadamer reads it, theory is an attitude of intending pure presence.[22]

The festive character of *theoria* subverts the subjectivity, atemporality, and drive for pure presence seen in much metaphysical thinking. *"Theoria,"* Gadamer writes, "is actually participation [*Teilnahme-methexis*], not doing, but a passivity [*Pathos*]: namely, being totally involved and carried away by what one sees" (WM 118/TM 111). However, we should not interpret the spectator in terms of her or his subjectivity. Being present, participating, is a being outside of the self; it is ecstatic being with someone or something else. The spectacle, the work, places a claim on the spectator. It is the claim of beauty. To withdraw into one's self here is to disassociate oneself from participation in that event. The claim of the spectacle means that there is a contemporaneity between spectator and the event.[23]

Festive experience is ecstatic participation in which the spectator ex-ists through time in relation to the celebration. The spectator is set in the world of the festival, which, as a circle of meaning, serves no immediate utilitarian ends. The distancing from self and everyday world is productive; one shares in what is presented and thus gains, so Gadamer claims, continuity with the self. The being of the spectator is like that of the festival: being in becoming through which identity is presented and preserved.

In this interpretation emerge the two elements of the experience of festival and art: participation and continuity. By exploring the human experience of art in and through festival, Gadamer radically challenges traditional aesthetics. The work of art does not reflect some temporally prior origin either by imitating nature or by expressing the author's genius. Through interpretive action, it is originative in its mode of being and brings something to a specific figuration. Because of this, the criterion of validity in interpretation cannot be the intention or purpose of the author. Rather, interpretation follows the trajectory of the work itself, the presentation of its *Sache*. "Interpretation is probably in a sense a re-creation [*Nachschaffen*] but this re-creation does not follow the process of the creative act; rather, one has to bring to presentation [*Darstellung*] the figure [*Figur*] of the created work in accordance with the meaning [*Sinn*] therein" (WM 114/TM 107). The experience of the work is not aesthetic differentiation between the interpreter and the text or work, an alienation of subject from the artistic object, but the aesthetic non-differentiation (*Nichtunterscheidung*) of the work and its subject matter in interpretive presentation. It is an overcoming of differentiation relative to the *Sache* of the work, its truth-content.

For example, in interpreting a text we experience its meaning in becoming. We participate in the bringing to presentation of the subject matter of the text, realizing, implicitly at least, that each interpretation is a different celebration of it. Because of this, Gadamer argues that to understand at all is to understand differently. Each interpretation, on analogy to festival, is different and yet equally originary. Thus the presentation of the festival in performance, or of a text in interpretation, is part of their being. Festival and interpretation have the character of an event (*Ereignis*). This is also true of the interpreter. The participatory relation between the spectator and the spectacle, between text and interpreter, is such that one *becomes* through participation. We learn and understand the meaning of a text through interpretation and are changed by it. In a word, this is the way of edification and culture; it is the path of tradition. This is why, as we shall see in greater detail shortly, Gadamer gives an ontological formulation to *Bildung* (culture). "What the interpreter is—not just what he thinks and does—changes in interpreting; it is an event of being that occurs." In fact, "this event changes what he is in such a way that he becomes not something different but rather himself."[24]

Unlike Plato and Aristotle, then, Gadamer does not take art to be a productive science. Art is not a *techne* in which the product is to correspond to the idea of the artisan or an archetype and is methodologically explainable as such. Gadamer begins with *Spiel* and festival and therefore with performative action, that is, with dance, drama, and cult. This seemingly simple shift has drastic consequences. The truth of art is not its imitative relation to an archetypal idea or origin in the act of genius, but the presentation of a figured meaning. The kind of understanding made possible through the festival of interpretation is interactive and participatory. It is not the attempt to discern some idea behind the presentation. Knowledge is an appropriation of the truth-content of the work through participation that engenders an identity. These aspects of being and understanding are what Gadamer means by the event (*Ereignis*) of the experience of the work of art. The event is a double mimesis, a movement and an appropriation.[25]

Further, Gadamer observes that artistic presentation is always for someone. What is required for this perfection of human play in art is a *Verwandlung ins Gebilde* (transformation into structure or figuration). Through this transformation play achieves its ideality (*Idealität*). The artistic transformation is the figurative structuring (*Gebilde*) of human *Spiel* for an audience. So transformed, Gadamer claims, play is meant and understood. "Only now does it detach itself from the presenting act [*Tun*] of the players and consist in the pure appearance [*Erscheinung*] of what they were playing. . . . It has the character of a work, or an *ergon*, and not only of an *energia*. In this sense, I call it a *Gebilde*" (WM 105–106/TM 99). This is a complex statement. Gadamer is claiming that *Spiel* denotes the pure "energia" of Being (*physis*). In art as a work, an *ergon*, this energy is transformed into a figure that is the presentation of the play for someone else. Correspondingly, the *Gebilde* (image or figure) is structured energy through which the play achieves public meaning.

What precisely does Gadamer mean by transformation and figuration? In *Die Aktualität des Schönen* he writes that the "*Gebilde* is first of all not a thing one can think of as purposefully made (an idea still implied by the concept 'work'). Whoever has made a work of art 'stands,' in truth, before the *Gebilde* of his hands no different from anyone else. There is a leap [*Sprung*] through which the work of art distinguishes itself in its particularity and irreplaceability" (AS 44). This is strange language. Whereas the movement of *Spiel* was rhythmic dance to-and-fro, in speaking of *Gebilde* Gadamer resorts to the disjunctive Kierkegaardian language of a leap. The dynamic quality of the transformation *into Gebilde* is an entirely different movement from *Spiel*. The *Gebilde* is the leap of figuration through which art distinguishes itself as art and escapes its origin. To follow Gadamer's thought at this point we must inquire into each dimension of his claim.

Gadamer argues in *Truth and Method* that what he means by transformation (*Verwandlung*) in this context is the autonomy of presentative play relative to the players. In art the play escapes its bondage to the artist; its subject matter reigns. This suggests that the movement character of the work of art, as opposed to pure *Spiel*, is not a simple change; it is a radical trans-formation.[26]

> A change [*Veränderung*] always means that what is changed also remains the same and is held on to. . . . In terms of categories all change [*Alloiosis*] belongs to the sphere of quality, i.e, an accident of substance. Transformation [*Verwandlung*] means that something is suddenly and as a whole something else, that this transformed thing it has become is its true being [*wahres Sein*] in comparison with which its earlier being is nothing. . . . Thus the transformation into structure of what previously was here is no more. But also . . . what is now presents itself in the *Spiel* of art [*was sich in Spiel der Kunst darstellt*], is what is abidingly true [WM 106/TM 100].

The formation of the work of art is a trans-formation of *Spiel* into *Gebilde*, into figured energy. Mimesis, he claims, is this transformation into figure. It shows the truth of some reality.

Gadamer is making a claim which, if it can be sustained, virtually overturns the traditional framework in which mimesis was understood. His claim is this: the transformation into figure (*Gebilde*) means that the original or archetype (*Urbild*) is in and for itself through its presentation in a figurative way. The figure does not refer to some transcendent pre-existent archetype or to the imagination of the genius which it inadequately imitates or represents; the work is the presentation, even enactment, of the archetype. The relation of art, of an image, and its "meaning" must be reconceived on the basis of presentation or performance (*Darstellung*).[27] As Grondin correctly notes:

> Not only is the *Bild* [image] an *Abbild* [copy] that refers to something else; it is a presentation-event to which comes, due to its evidential power, one particular existence of the *Urbild* [archetype]. This in no way means the detachment of the image from its archetype; or vice versa. It is in the copy that the archetype comes to itself. Through the presentation the presented experiences a qualitative increase in Being (WM 133), in which it gains "more" in meaning [*Bedeutung*].

By coming to presentation, a new meaningfulness and presence are apportioned to the presented.[28]

Grondin's observation is understandable only when we realize that Gadamer reconceives the event of truth around social interaction (*Spiel*) marked by festival temporality. The usual categories for defining Being and understanding are destroyed and rethought in a social, temporal, and active manner. What we see now is that through the work of art something comes to presentation for someone, and it does so through a specific image or figure (*Bild*).

Gadamer claims that the "image is an ontological event [*Seinvorgang*], in which Being comes to a meaningful appearance [*Erscheinung*]." He continues:

> The quality of being archetype is an essential movement which is founded in the presentative character [*Darstellungcharakter*] of art. The "ideality" of the work of art is not through its relation to an idea which is to be an "imitated" and "reproduced" [*nachzuahmendes, wiederzugebendes*] being, but, as with Hegel, as the appearance [*Scheinen*] of the idea itself [WM 137/TM 127].

The ideality or meaning of art is its presentation. Gadamer's tactic is to destroy traditional ontology in order to reconceive Being as meaningful socio-temporal interaction. The work of art is a specific figuration and appearance of the essence of play. In the transformation of play into figuration, the performative action reaches its ideality in that it is phenomenally presented to an audience. Thus the audience enters the festival action itself. The dynamic and presentative character of the work of art is thereby achieved only in and through the action of the audience that completes or perfects the work.

I can now summarize what I have argued regarding the context in which Gadamer understands mimesis.

> (1) The mode of being of art is interactive participatory movement (*Spiel*). This movement is the *work* of art, and there is no prior substrate behind this movement. There is also no utilitarian goal beyond the *Spiel* and its self-presentation.

> (2) The unique temporality of art is that it is repetitive and self-renewing. This repetitive character is, moreover, the ground for continuity through time. Given this, festival is the ground of ordinary time. It is the performance of human sociality. The truth of festival is the basis for other modes of human temporal experience.

> (3) Art is presentative. That is, it is symbolic in its performance. This presentative character is always potentially for someone. In art human *Spiel* as symbolic is completed by the presence of the audience for whom the festival presents a meaningful whole. Thus it is a disclosure of human sociality under a structured figure of presentation.

These three levels of the mode of being of art (play, festival, and symbol) are separable only for the sake of argument. The mode of being of the work of art entails them all.[29] What this demonstrates is that art is related to the being of human sociality and temporality. In connecting *Spiel*, festival, and symbol we can say that in the experience of the work of art a truth about Being and human being-in-the-world is rendered available. To participate in this presentation is to be edified, formed through participation, and hence to overcome the *Fremdheit* of self and world. For Gadamer, the dynamic of mimesis is a way to speak of the relation of *Bild* (image) and *Spiel*/festival as basic to a meaningful world.

Before exploring in detail Gadamer's notion of mimesis itself, we can also draw together the experiential side of his argument. There are three levels of experience correlate to the dynamic of the work of art just noted. Together these make up the other aspect of the double mimesis found in Gadamer's work.

(1) Understanding is participatory; one takes part in the event of truth. Such taking part is a constitutive element of the nature of truth made available in the experience of art. The participatory character of understanding is Gadamer's retrieval of the Greek idea of participation (*methexis*). It relates to the interactive character of *Spiel*. There is no realm of ideas prior to or beyond this participatory level. The interactive character of *Spiel* gives rise to thought and ideas.

(2) The modality of experience made possible through art is contemporaneity with the work and self. Through participation we recognize what was previously missed. We learn something about ourselves not available in other ways. This marks the cognitive dimension of the experience of art.

(3) Both participation and identification are deeply social and are ways of understanding and recognition. They are ways of understanding self through another encountered as symbolic, as calling for interpretation. Such self-understanding is interpretive knowledge won through encountering what is alien and strange, the work of art. Through participation, contemporaneity, and recognition, consciousness is formed into self-consciousness.

All these dimensions of hermeneutical experience are conceptually distinct but actually related. Understanding is participatory, entails a recognition of what presents itself, and marks a contemporaneity between the work and the "reader" through which self-consciousness is formed relative to what is disclosed in the experience. Thus the strategy emerging in Gadamer's discourse is the interrelation of disclosure and understanding on a number of levels. This interrelation, I am arguing, is the double mimesis at the heart of his hermeneutic.

What should be clear by now is that Gadamer is rejecting a simple correspondence idea of truth and being in favor of one that centers on disclosure and deferral as well as participation. More particularly, he understands disclosure to take place through a performative act (*Spiel*) when it is transformed into a work, a specific figuration. Understanding is not intuiting the ideas behind the appearance, checking an image to its referent, or the methodological control of "objects" by a knowing subject. Understanding is marked, therefore, by the same character as the work of art since it is part of the being of the work.

These seemingly modest claims, ones now standard in hermeneutics, provide the context for us to reconsider mimesis in Gadamer's thought and our own. I have already anticipated this since his discussion of mimesis is located between the lines of the argument discerned thus far. These include the dynamic, living movement of *Spiel*, the transformation into figure, and the interactive and temporal character of festival along with the experiential correlate to each of these. The levels of his argument dictate the texture of my reading of mimesis and will lead, finally, to the ontological import of Gadamer's project.

Gadamer is actually developing philosophical insights gleaned from classics scholars. Herman Köller, whom he cites, notes that the central meaning of mimesis "is dance; [*mimeisthai*] means primarily: 'to bring to representation through dance.' Greek dance was always bound together with rhythm, musical accompaniment, and narrated word. . . . [M]*imos*, and all derived from that concept, originally resides in the sphere of cult. . . ."[30] Köller goes on to show how this dramatic presentation of *mythos* in cultic action includes the audience. Moreover, the mimetic action seeks to bring the myth, the human, and the god to an epiphanic presentation. The trajectory of Greek philosophy, as I noted in the previous chapter, in its epistemology, metaphysics, and aesthetics was to move away from this dramatic sense of mimesis and toward imitation as "copying." Ironically, the dynamic elements of mimesis remain in Plato's dialogical strategy and Aristotle's idea of narrative emplotment. Not surprisingly, these are precisely the domains of language in which Gadamer (dialogue) and Ricoeur (narrative) retrieve a dynamic understanding of mimesis.[31] What we see here is that Gadamer attempts to reclaim and reinterpret mimesis as dramatic presentation in art, understanding, and dialogue.

In *Die Aktualität des Schönen* Gadamer writes about mimesis in a way reminiscent of Köller:

> Mimesis here does not mean making something after [*nachahmend*] something already known, but, rather, bringing something to presentation [*etwas zur Darstellung bringen*] so that it is present in this way in sensual fullness. The ancient use of these words was derived from the dance of the stars. The stars are the presentation of pure mathematical laws and proportions that mark the order of the heavens. In this sense the tradition, I believe, is right when it says "art is always a mimesis," i.e., it brings something to presentation [AS 47].

Gadamer is not concerned with the Pythagorean claims about the relation of stars to mathematical laws. He is interested in mimesis as *bringing something to presentation*. The presentation, we saw, is a transformation into a sensual fullness that manifests the energy of life. Moreover, in art what was previously a self-presentation is now presented for an audience. In the work of art reality is presented as trans-formed. The figuration *(Gebilde)*, Gadamer claims, is the transformation into the true. What "is" is brought to light. "The work of art, in which *Spiel* expresses itself fully in the unity of its course, is in fact a wholly transformed world. By means of it everyone recognizes that that is how things are" (WM 108/TM 101–102). Much like Aristotle, Gadamer is claiming that something true about the way things are is revealed in the abstractive quality of the work of art. A rush to explore this dimension of recognition and its implications for understanding must be avoided at this point in the argument. Gadamer is actually making three claims that must be isolated first.

Gadamer's leading notion is *Darstellung* (presentation). The mode of being of *Spiel*, we saw, is self-realizing movement. In mimetic *Darstellung* that energy is presented as an autonomous being, as a work. Because of this, the mimetic presentation marks, as he says, an increase in being of what is presented. "By coming to presentation a new meaningfulness and presence are given to the presented."[32] This increase in being is the transformation into the true that is the mark of mimesis. Hence mimesis stands as the link between artistic presentation (the work) and the character of human being in the world as one of understanding. This is why, as we shall see later, language is uniquely mimetic, and why a mimetic act marks a correlate increase of being and meaning. Mimesis is the process of rendering Being meaningful and thereby of making an increase in Being.

However, care must be taken here because terms like "Being" and "meaning" can be the emptiest of words. Is Gadamer, when all is said and done, merely playing a metaphysical game where Being somehow escapes all avenues of thought? Does noumenal being-in-itself finally rule, and if so, how can mimetic presentation possibly signal an increase in being? What, if anything, does Gadamer mean by these sentences?

In response to these queries Gadamer replies: "The way in which a thing presents itself is . . . part of its particular being" (WM 450/TM 432). We can make a distinction between Being and the way it presents itself, but it is not a rigid one. All presentation is ultimately presentation for someone, is dramatic and symbolic in character. For one who can understand, being and meaning are related. This arises from our participation in what is understood as disclosing the sociality of Being. Hence the best way to speak of "Being" is as "world." Being as such is an abstraction; it is not some metaphysical reality but the dynamics of concrete reality. Being becomes meaningful through a transformation into concrete reality. Gadamer is trying to explore how worlds come to be.

Categorical phenomena are, when understood, the figurations of "Being." Through this transformation something new is manifested metaphorically: being is understood *as* presented, and any given reality is Being itself *as* figured. Joel Weinsheimer is correct when he writes about any reality that "this *as* belongs to its being means that (rather than being self-identical) it differs from itself: it is / not itself, and this is the case of everything that exists historically."[33] Later we shall see that Being and meaning are related through the mimetic and metaphoric character of language. At this point it is clear that this increase in meaning is the experiential side of Gadamer's hermeneutics. Not only is mimetic *Darstellung* a presentation of human action such that it enjoys an increase in meaning, but mimesis also suggests a primal relation of Being and meaning relative to the non–self-identical character of historical beings.[34]

In his essay "Dichtung und Mimesis" Gadamer writes about this primal relationship constitutive of mimesis:

> Mimesis is and remains an original relationship [*Urverhältnis*] in which there appears not so much an imitation [*Nachahmung*] as perhaps a transformation [*Verwandlung*]. It is, as I have called it in another connection with art, aesthetic non-differentiation [*die ästhetische Nichtunderscheidung*] that marks the experience of art (WM 111ff.). When we revive this original meaning of mimesis, we are liberated from the aesthetic construction that the classical theory of imitation [*Nachahmungstheorie*] meant for thought. Mimesis is not so much that something refers to another thing, that is, its archetype [*Urbild*], as that something is indeed in itself as *Sinnhaftes* [full-of-meaning].[35]

Mimesis suggests a fullness of meaning through the figuration of fundamental relationships between reader and text, self and other, and, finally, an entity and its own meaning. Contrary to Kant, with his aesthetic differentiation, in which aesthetic consciousness is abstracted from the work, Gadamer claims that presentation and experience are related. Mimetic action allows the audience, the communicants, to participate in the presentation. This is what Gadamer means by "aesthetic non-differentiation."

In genuine understanding the alienation of reader and text, for instance, is transcended. Gadamer takes this moment of unitive appropriation to be the mark of understanding beyond the methodological attempt to overcome alienation. But he does not explore the possible dark side of this. That is, he does not inquire as Girard did into the conflict that can originate when two subjects are seeking to appropriate the same thing. Nor does he explore the ways in which the other resists appropriation by standing over against the one seeking to understand, to appropriate what is other. These questions of power and otherness are of considerable import for religious and moral reflection. They will concern us later. At this point it is enough to note that Gadamer's purpose is to show how genuine understanding can occur between a subject and a text, or work of art, that is radically alien, culturally, linguistically, or historically.

Mimesis is a presentation of some subject matter through figuration, a work of art or image. What is finally disclosed in any particular act of understanding, if we reflect on that act itself, is a basic relation of Being and meaning. As Gadamer puts it, "mimetic presentation is not *Spiel* that simulates; rather, it is a *Spiel* that communicates itself, so that it is known for nothing else than its possibility to be: pure presentation."[36] The *Gebilde* of art, he goes on to say, is a true shining (*wahrer Schein*) that communicates itself. There is being-in-itself only in the most conceptually abstract sense. In fact, the being of any reality is always for another rooted in the *Ur-relation* of Being and meaning. What this exposes for Gadamer is actually the relatedness of human and its world. The human, as the one who can raise the question of the meaning of being, discloses, in that questioning, a belongingness to world. Art is one place in which this relation is presented, but so too is the very act of understanding in response to the work of art, a text, another person, or tradition. The point here is that this fundamental relation of human and its world is articulated by mimesis, and by interpreting mimetic works we recognize our interdependence with world.

What we see, then, is that art is a mimetic phenomenon in the deepest sense of the term: it has a temporal, or festive, character even as it is figuratively or symbolically presented *Spiel*. This is its claim to truth and the reason one must attend to the subject matter of any particular work. Aesthetic non-differentiation means that experience overcomes the historical distance of work and audience even as that experience provides continuity for the audience itself. In viewing Shakespeare's *King Lear*, for example, we enter anew that festive and tragic tale only to find how we have changed and yet endured since the last encounter. And we learn something there not found elsewhere about the troubled yet gallant human condition.

Mimesis is a way to speak about the figurative presentation of *Spiel* with its festive temporality. Yet we should ask: What is the import of mimesis for Gadamer's hermeneutics? After all, why use the terminology of mimesis, with all its attending difficulties, if the notion adds nothing to the argument? Gadamer turns to mimesis on analogy to cultic action, I think, to demonstrate the abiding relation of the experience of the work of art to what is disclosed through the act of understanding. This counters the subjectivism of the modernist turn to the reflexive "I," or *cogito*, as well as the rise of method in the human sciences without negating the fact that it is I or we who understand and in so doing understand our world and ourselves. As Georgia Warnke puts it, the "truth of works of art is a contingent one; what they reveal is dependent on the lives, circumstances, and views of the audience to whom they reveal it."[37] Thus Gadamer's ontological reading of mimesis opens up the dimension of understanding. Shortly I shall explore understanding as a mimetic phenomenon. On the way to that discussion, it is important to isolate specifically the relation of understanding and mimesis.

In "Dichtung und Mimesis" Gadamer spells out what he means by recognition as crucial to understanding. This returns us to the question of understanding that I set aside earlier to explore mimetic action more specifically. Gadamer writes:

Something known as something means: to know again [*Wieder-erkennen*], but recognition is not merely a second re-knowing after a first acquaintance

[*Kennenlernen*]. It is something qualitatively different. When something is recognized it has already been liberated from the uniqueness and accidental elements of the circumstances in which it is met. It begins therein to raise itself to its perduring essence and to become unraveled from the accidental character of its occurrence [DM 231].

Recognition is not a simple recollection of what was known. It is, rather, the insight into the meaning of what is presented in the work of art. Insight into existence is gained through a concrete expression of life in figuration. Through the transformation into *Gebilde*, meaning is raised from its particularity and achieves a cognitive ideality that can be recognized *as* figured.

Gadamer echoes Plato, in that for him recognition is the apprehension of some perduring essence. But, contrary to Plato, essence is never separated from the character of the mimetic *Darstellung*. As Aristotle argued, art is the avenue of recognition and understanding. Poetry is closer to philosophy than to history because the poem and the idea are concerned with universals.[38] And like Aristotle, Gadamer is claiming that the universal is recognized and presented only in the particular.[39] Recognition is won through interpretive enactment; it is insight into the meaning disclosed only in the concrete.[40] The moment of recognition is the transformation of presented figured meaning into significance for us. What something "is" is recognized in its presentation.

What is at stake in all this is an understanding of truth. We might even say that it is the contest between imitative (correspondence) amd mimetic (performative and figurative) ideas of truth. The truth of recognition is that through the presentation something more becomes known than was previously understood. "In recognition what we know emerges as if through an illumination [*eine Enleüchtung*], from all chance and variable circumstances that condition it, and is grasped in its essence [*Wesen*]. It is known as something" (WM 109/TM 102). What is "is" insofar as it is recognized *as something*. This signals the basic metaphorical and analogical character of all human knowing, as noted before.[41] The metaphoric character of understanding is, moreover, rooted in the phenomenal presentation of Being. Thus what Gadamer has done, following Heidegger, is to make truth-as-disclosure (*Aletheia*) the condition for any other specific forms of truth-claims and understanding. In various situations we can make statements that correspond to some reality, but that notion of truth itself is dependent for its condition of possibility on the presentation and understanding of the world.

Recognition marks an increase of being in what is known through the participation of knower and known. That is, it signals the participation of one who can understand in what presents itself for interpretation. The act of interpretation, through which understanding is reached, enacts an increase in being and meaning because a common world between interpreter and what is understood is realized. This relation made evident by interpreting works of art is the primal relation of mimesis. "Imitation [*Nachahmung*] and presentation [*Darstellung*] are not merely a copied repetition [*abbildende Wiederholung*], but a recognition of the essence. Because they are not merely repetition, but a bringing-forth [*Hervorholung*], the spectator is involved in them. They contain in themselves the essential relation [*Wesensbezug*] for everyone for whom the presentation exists" (WM 109/TM 103). Mimesis as presentation has, then, a cognitive function. Indeed, it is a way to speak of understanding as dependent upon a revelatory and epiphanic presentation of something in which the audience, the one understanding, participates in the bringing forth. The form of knowing found here is an insight into the being of something, its essence, *as* something. To understand is to be related to the being and meaning of what is understood. And this participatory character of recognition returns us once again to the ontology of play isolated above. Thus mimesis is interpreted by Gadamer relative to *Spiel*-action even as it opens that action to its cognitive and ontological depths through figuration.

Gadamer escapes a crass version of mimesis because he correctly sees it as a form of social praxis, as *Spiel*. More specifically, what he has done is to interpret art and the experience of art through the social, interactive, temporal, and presentative dynamics of *Spiel*, festival, and symbol. Given this, we can discern the shape of his mimetic strategy. In art (human) *physis*, with its dynamic character, is presented as figured. The work of art is the mimesis of that being that enjoys an increase in meaning when grasped by an audience. The audience, when it understands that presentation as meaningful, has a corresponding increase in being: consciousness is formed and raised to a more comprehensive perspective. The entire event is festive. In the performance of interpretation, the work and audience ex-ist and yet become different. *King Lear*, to draw on an earlier example, comes to be in its presentation and is meaningful only when grasped by an audience. When we understand that tragedy in all its power, are we not changed? Is there not insight into the travail of our tumultuous existence? For a moment Lear stands out of the text, and we reach to meet him. In that meeting we, and even Lear, are changed. We become more of what we most profoundly are.

Gadamer places the question of mimesis in a new context: the intimate relation between the disclosure of Being in figurative presentations and the event of appropriation. This double process Gadamer calls a transformation. Truth for Gadamer is precisely this dialectical double mimesis of disclosure and appropriation in which meaning and Being are actualized. Mimesis as a whole, it seems, is this path of actualization disclosive of what is dramatically realized through its presentation. The dynamics of mimesis finally express in the medium of language the *Ur-relation* of meaning and Being, human and the world, subject and object. Again, expression here is not Romantic self-expression; it is the power to make things manifest. And what is manifested, finally, is not only a self but also a social world. Thus I am suggesting that for

Gadamer mimesis is the coming-to-meaningfulness of Being through a trans-formation into figurative structure, into world and understanding.

With these main features of Gadamer's mimetic strategy in mind, I want to turn in greater detail to his discussion of understanding in *Truth and Method*. My thesis is that it too has a mimetic shape and correlates to his analysis of the work of art. The plausibility of my claim for the importance of mimesis in Gadamer's hermeneutic can be sustained only if it opens up the other dimensions of his project. So first I shall explore his discussion of understanding and then turn to the problem of language itself.

UNDERSTANDING AS MIMETIC

Gadamer begins his hermeneutic of understanding in *Truth and Method* with Heidegger's discussion of the "fore-structure of understanding." The circle of understanding is one in which we project a meaning of a whole from some initial hints about it. Each time we read a novel, for example, we engage in working out an interpretation by projecting a meaning of the whole and cor-recting these guesses based on further reading. "The constant process of new projections," Gadamer suggests, "is the mode of being of understanding and interpretation [*Auslegung*]" (WM 252/TM 236). Inappropriate fore-meanings simply come to nothing in this process of working out (*die Ausarbeitung*) an understanding. Our hunches about a character in a novel are proved wrong, or right, as we continue to read. Our projections can, indeed must, be open to revisions. The very act of reading demands an awareness and critique of one's bias to allow for revision. This openness to revision does not detract from the importance of our prejudices, our prejudgments (*Vorurteile*), about the mean-ing of the whole. They remain basic to understanding simply because we make revisions of bad projections by forming new ones, themselves prejudg-ments about the meaning of something. Prejudgments are the mark of our preapprehension of a meaningful whole, whether that be of a novel or a tradition.

Interestingly, if we reflect on the importance of prejudgments in all acts of understanding, we see that they signal the finitude of human existence. The movement of understanding shows that we are rooted in history simply because we have inherited a language and view of the world that shapes our initial response to any phenomenon. "In truth, history does not belong to us; rather, we belong to history. Prejudgments more so than judgments constitute the historical reality of [our] being" (WM 261/TM 245). Without detracting from the projective structure of understanding and thus the transcendence of the human over brute facticity, Gadamer has turned to focus on the thrownness of our existence as the condition for understanding: "The futurity of *Dasein* —the basic projection that befits its temporality—is limited by its other basic determination, namely its "thrownness," which not only specifies the limits of sovereign self-possession but also opens up and determines the positive possibilities that we are."[42] Understanding occurs within our historicity. Indeed, it is the human form of historicity. We are limited by and dependent upon our world. And yet this interdependence is precisely the condition of possibility of all understanding and all novelty. Understanding bears the signs of our thrownness into tradition and culture.

The radical historicity of understanding requires, contrary to the ambitions of the Enlightenment, a frank admission of our indebtedness to tradition. Tradition has its being in becoming. "In truth, tradition itself is constantly a moment of freedom and of history. . . . It is, essentially, preservation [*Bewahrung*] such as is active in all historical change. Preservation is a deed of reason [*Vernuft*], freely as such, though an inconspicuous one" (WM 265–66/TM 250). The dialectic of change and preservation is, we can say, the festive structure of tradition since it exists only in the interactive process of handing on (*traditio*) what was received.

The festive structure of tradition suggests that its meaning is not located solely in some primal origin, even a foundational event. Meaning is located, not in a discernible origin or *telos* of tradition or genius, but in the process of tradition itself. Like a festival, traditions exist in their performance. Meaning is generated through the performance of handing on something anew, which, in each case, is the act of understanding. And every new understanding will correspondingly be a different figuration of tradition just as each celebration of the festival is equally originative. Thus in the quote cited above, Gadamer can justly claim that preservation is an act of reason. But that act is bound to the tradition even as in its performance it extends that tradition. This festive structure of tradition marks its unique temporality, a being in becoming that is a passing in and out of presence.

The temporal structure of tradition is also characteristic of understanding; tradition is the presentation of past acts of understanding in cultural artifacts. The festive character of tradition means, correlatively, that understanding achieves continuity through interaction with a tradition. The interaction we have with our past is called interpretation. "Tradition is not," Gadamer writes, "simply a precondition under which we always already stand; we produce it ourselves, inasmuch as we understand, we participate in, the happening of tradition [*Überlieferungsgeschehen*] and hence further determine it ourselves. The circle of understanding is thus not a 'methodological circle,' but describes an ontological structural moment of understanding" (WM 277/TM 261). *Traditio* is the condition of possibility for understanding, even as a tradition comes to be in new ways in each different articulation of it. Thus although human understanding is always historically dependent, it is also paradoxically creative, contributing to its own future conditions.

The temporality of understanding and tradition is a curious dialectic of continuity in becoming. Gadamer's analysis expands to include the participatory and presentative elements of tradition and understanding that we have isolated in any mimetic practice. The rubrics under which these appear in his analysis are "effective historical consciousness" (*wirkungsgeschichtliches Bewusstsein*) and the "fusion of horizons" (*Horizontverschmelzung*).

Gadamer contests the subjectivism of aesthetic consciousness, found in critical and Romantic thought, by concentrating, as we have seen, on the power of the work of art to confront us. And against historicist notions of understanding that depict the mind as able methodologically to escape historicity, he argues, in Part II of *Truth and Method*, for the historical rootedness of consciousness. This means that the task of historical knowledge is not, as thinkers like Ranke and others have claimed, a matter of the way reason constructs an historical totality to discern the meaning of particular events *in* history. The problem is rather that of the application (*Anwendung*) of tradition to our situation.[43] Gadamer insists that we "have come to see in the course of our reflections that an understanding always involves something like an application [*Anwendung*] of the text to be understood to the present situation of the interpreter. . . . [We] consider application to be as integral a part of the hermeneutical process [*Vorgang*] as understanding and interpretation [*Verstehen und Auslegen*]" (WM 291/TM 274–75).[44] The task of understanding and interpreting our past occurs through the application of that tradition to our current needs. This application is not a highly speculative construction; it is rooted in the effects of history that form understanding. Gadamer takes this dimension of application and effective-history to be basic to hermeneutical experience.

Application, as Gadamer understands the term, has a twofold dynamic. First, it is the application of a text or tradition to the interpreter. This is the event of understanding. The heart of the hermeneutical problem is that a tradition and text confront us as alien, as strange, and thus are always understood differently. There is, in understanding, a relation of a general meaning and the particular situation of the interpreter. "Understanding is, then, a particular case of the application of something general to a concrete and particular situation" (WM 295/TM 278). Understanding is fundamentally practical both in being directed to particular situations and in being formed through the action of understanding anew. It is, as Gadamer says, practical wisdom or *phronesis*.

The second dynamic of application is the use of a tradition in a situation and its needs. On the analogy of legal and theological hermeneutics, the work of interpretation is to make the law or a text concrete in specific cases. Application here has a performative character because through it a general meaning, e.g., legal precedent, is disclosed in the concrete action. It is revealed in its transformation into figure: a particular case becomes the presentation of the meaning of the law now enacted. This dynamic of application is the mechanism of tradition; it is the productive movement of understanding. It bears the marks of mimetic action.[45] The twofold character of application constitutes the shape of effective-historical consciousness. It also shows Gadamer's retrieval of insights, noted in the previous chapter, about the relation of the ideal to the actual, the particular to the universal, found in classical thought. And yet although Gadamer returns to these basic questions, he approaches them with a different mimetic hermeneutic.

Understanding–interpretation–application is a complex process in which a given tradition or text is appropriated by an interpreter through the concretization of meaning in a specific situation. This actualization marks an increase of Being and meaning in tradition and understanding. Effective-history is, therefore, both the work or production (*Wirken*) of history and history's effects on consciousness.[46] The mimetic and productive character of hermeneutical consciousness is that meaning is presented and recognized through the application of tradition to self that forms (*bildet*) an *ethos*. Thus Gadamer links, in an important way, the formation (*Bildung*) of culture, and we can say individuals, with the appropriation of the figures (*Bilder*) of a tradition. We come to be as agents through the appropriation of a tradition that helps shape dispositions, skills, and virtues as well as a view of the human good. Later we shall see how Kierkegaard's analysis of the self and Ricoeur's notion of narrative identity further articulate this process of formation.

Significantly, Gadamer ties the process of culture to "nature," or *physis*. "*Bildung* resembles Greek *physis*; like nature it has no goals outside of itself. . . . In *Bildung* that by which and that through which one is formed becomes completely one's own. To some extent everything that is received is absorbed, but what is absorbed is not like a means that has lost function. Rather, in acquired *Bildung* nothing disappears; everything is preserved" (WM 8/TM 12). *Bildung* is analogous to the emerging power, the *physis*, of nature. It is the power of the being of the human, its nature, and its community figured in particular lives. Given this, we might expect that for Gadamer culture will have a *Spiel*-character that overcomes through appropriation the *Fremdheit* of life. This is no doubt true, but the unique thing about human culture is that it is formed by figurations (*Bilder*) through which we come to understand ourselves. The character of culture is figured activity; it is a mimesis of human being.

Understanding and tradition, as the dynamics of *Bildung*, have their being in becoming. The process of their being is a fusion or melting of the horizon of the past and our own situation through interpretation. "In the process of understanding," Gadamer notes, "an actual fusion of horizons [*Horizontverschmelzung*] takes place, which means that as the historical horizon is projected, it is simultaneously taken up and preserved [*Aufhebung*]. We describe the conscious act of this fusion as the task of effective-historical consciousness. . . . It is the problem of application that exists in all understanding" (WM 290/TM 273–74). Understanding and tradition involve a mimetic transformation into figuration of the present and past historical horizons. How does this take place?

Hermeneutical consciousness involves an openness to what is alien; it is a response to what presents itself to us. To be open is to question and so to open the self to what is unknown. Questioning is a mark of human finitude and transcendence; we do not know and yet we question, we seek. So the act of questioning opens the stage for an answer. Gadamer takes the logic of question and answer as the structure of knowledge. Knowing is a constant, open search. "The art [*Kunst*] of questioning is the art of being able to go on questioning, i.e., the art of thinking [*Denken*]. It is called dialectic because it is the art of conducting an actual conversation [*Gespräch*]" (WM 349/TM 330). Dialectic, thought itself, is dialogical; conversation is the *Spiel* of thinking.

The dialogical character of thinking means that thought has a *Spiel*-like movement. Gadamer isolates this in the to-and-fro of question and answer between interlocutors. Thinking, as dialogic, has the same characteristics as *Spiel*; it has active, temporal, and self-presentative dimensions. A conversation, he contends, is the process of verbal movement whose aim, understanding, is internal to itself. Dialogue is verbal dance. Moreover, conducting a conversation "means allowing yourself to be conducted by the object to which the partners in the conversation are directed" (WM 449/TM 330). To suppress the question about the subject matter or *Sache* under inquiry is to withdraw from the dance of thought into the solitude of opinion. Through dialogic action the actors come to be and are formed by participation in the movement. Finally, what is presented is the *logos* of the conversation.[47]

Commenting on Socratic dialogue, Gadamer writes:

> What emerges in its truth is the logos which is neither mine nor yours, and thus so transcends the subjective opinion of the conversation partners that the conversation leader is always also ignorant. Dialectic as the act of conducting a conversation is also the art of seeing the connection of things [*zusammenzuschauen*] in a unity of an aspect (*sanoran eis en eidos*), i.e., it is the art of the formation of concepts as the working out [*Herausarbeitung*] of a common meaning [WM 350/TM 331].

Through dialogic action there is participatory knowledge, true *theoria*, about a common meaning. But the dance of conversation also presents itself in the formation of concepts (*Begriffsbildung*) that are the transformation into figuration of this common meaning. The formation of ideas (*eidos*) is not separated from dialogical *kinesis* but occurs through the movement itself. Dialogue, we can say, is the mimesis of a common meaning because through it what is common, the subject matter, is transformed into meaningful concepts and presented as such. Gadamer uses the analogy of conversation to describe the shape of historical understanding since our relation to the past is an interpretive one. What we are seeing, then, is that historical understanding has a mimetic character.

The telos of a conversation is understanding. This is certainly our goal in historical inquiry. Understanding formed through a conversation with a tradition is what Gadamer means by the effects of history on consciousness. "I have pointed out," he writes, "that effective-historical consciousness is something other than the inquiry into the effective-history that a work has, the trace [*Spur*] that a work leaves behind. It is rather a consciousness of the work itself, and hence has an effect" (WM 324/TM 305). Effective-historical consciousness is understanding formed by the influence of the tradition. It is our consciousness of effective history. "We stand in history as, according to Heidegger, we stand in the 'world.' That being-in-the-world, in which the way of understanding and effective-history are correlative concepts, is characterized in the nature of the self."[48] Understanding is always in the world; it is always in tradition.

If understanding is always in history, then, correspondingly, through formed consciousness, tradition is again enacted in each act of interpretation. Tradition is transformed through that act into the living present of human action and intercourse. Significantly this means that understanding is a concretization of a universal (tradition) in a particular. It bears the marks of the movement of Being I traced earlier, and no doubt this is why Gadamer draws a parallel between *Bildung* and *physis*, thereby opening ontological reflection on tradition itself. Moreover, in that understanding is the concretization through application of tradition in a specific situation, Gadamer's discussion also returns us to themes isolated in the previous chapter. Aristotle, Plato, Kant, and Hegel too, it will be remembered, explored differently the relation of the universal and the particular and ideality and reality. Gadamer takes up these problems in a thoroughly post-critical hermeneutical way, but he is doing so through mimetic action. And his point is that by understanding the alien voice of the past we are formed even while supplementing the formation of history. We join the liturgy of history as part of what it means to be human.

The character of historical experience correlates with Gadamer's discussion of art. The ludic nature of art reached its culmination in the disclosure of meaning through the interaction of work and audience. In discussing the inverse side of this process — namely, understanding — Gadamer has shown how consciousness comes to self-awareness through encountering what is alien, the past or present configured in a culture's artifacts. Understanding comes to be by interpreting human ideas, beliefs, and dreams set down in writing or handed on and yet alienated from us. By understanding those expressions of human world the tradition is figured anew and hence passed on even as we overcome our estrangement from the past.

This relation of understanding to its past expressions suggests a formal dialectic of alienation/reconciliation that spans Parts I and II of *Truth and Method*. It is a mimesis of life since it too "embodies the circular structure of forage and assimilation, excursion and reunion, alienation and appropriation, self-differentiation and self-integration."[49] The past confronts us like the work of art; it presents something to us. Ultimately, the past through distanciation shows us our belongingness to a shared world even while through interpretation we help to enact that commonality. The same structural components are present in each part: *Spiel*, festival, and symbol; that is, in Part II we have isolated the dynamic of understanding as interactive (dialogue), temporal continuity or fusion, and figuration in the work or in understanding and tradition *(Bildung)*. Thus each of the Parts of *Truth and Method* we have explored has accented one dimension of this mimetic process, without excluding the others. Part I concentrates on "symbol" or the disclosive character of mimetic figuration in art; Part II emphasizes the festive, temporal structure of understanding and tradition; Part III, we shall see, finds its center in linguistic *Spiel* as the ontological horizon for disclosure and appropriation. To complete this reading of Gadamer's mimetic strategy we turn to language.

LANGUAGE AS MEDIUM OF WORLD

Gadamer claims that the basic hermeneutical phenomenon is the relation of thinking and speaking. Language, in fact, is "the universal medium in which understanding itself is realized. The mode of understanding is interpretation" (WM 366/TM 350). Elsewhere he notes that the "world presents itself" in language. And he even claims that "Being that can be understood is language." To grasp the import of these broad statements we must begin on a more modest level.

In Part III of *Truth and Method*, Gadamer attempts to isolate the horizon in which hermeneutical experience takes place. An horizon "is the range of vision that includes everything that can be seen from a particular vantage point" (WM 286/TM 269). One's horizon is not solely a limiting factor of existence, however. It is not a frozen frontier but "something that moves with one and invites one to advance further" (WM 232/TM 217).[50] As horizon it is that in which we live, move, and have our being. Gadamer claims that language and world are the horizon of human life.

> Not only is language [*die Sprache*] one of the human's possessions in the world; but it depends on the fact that the human has a world. For humans the world exists as world in a way that no other living being has its existence in the experience of the world. But the existence of the world is linguistic. . . . [Language] has no independent life apart from the world that comes to language within it. Not only is the world only world insofar as it comes to language [*zur Sprache kommt*]; language too has its particular existence only in that the world is presented [*darstellt*] in it [WM 419/TM 401].[51]

Clearly, Gadamer must explore the relation of language and world as the horizon of experience. This relation is actually the primal relation that is the condition of possibility for understanding. Understanding is, finally, the concretization or realization of that basic belongingness of human understanding to its world. This has considerable import for religious and moral reflection, as we shall see later.

In his discussion of language, Gadamer repeats the criticism he makes about former philosophies of understanding: any attempt to isolate the human from the ambiguity of ordinary language simply removes us from the condition necessary for understanding. "The essential relation between linguisticality [*Sprachlichkeit*] and understanding is itself seen primarily in the way that it is the nature of tradition [*Überlieferung*] to exist in the medium of language, so that the preferred object [*Gegenstand*] of interpretation [*Auslegung*] is of a linguistic nature" (WM 367/TM 351). This passage clarifies two points. First, language allows the objects of understanding to come to expression, specifically in the words of the interpreter. Language is the medium for the fusion of horizons that marks understanding, and "tradition" is best seen as a process of handing on (*Überlieferung*) rather than simply a deposit of concepts and beliefs. Within this process, as we have seen, understanding and its coming-to-presentation in tradition are mimetic activities. Language as medium means that it is the condition of possibility for the festive and presentative dimensions of tradition and its correlate experiential dimensions.

Second, if language is a medium, then it helps determine the object of hermeneutical reflection: the transformation into structure of some subject matter in text and tradition. "So written texts present," Gadamer notes, "the unique hermeneutical task. Writing is self-alienation [*Selbstentfremdung*]. Its overcoming [*Überwindung*], the reading of texts, is the highest task of understanding" (WM 368/TM 352). A relationship to what is meant is established through the transformative act of understanding.[52] This is not to grant a special status to writing. Gadamer readily admits that writing and speaking share the same plight: a tension between appearance and true thought (cf. WM 371/TM 354). The hermeneutical task is to transform alienated meaning back into understanding. Thus not only is language a determination of the object of hermeneutical experience and the medium of that act, but it also specifies the hermeneutical act itself.[53]

Gadamer does not explore this process of appropriation in a particular community; rather he sets out the broad lines of the process as a feature of understanding. His point is a general and philosophical one: language and thought form a unity. The objects of human thought admit no distinction between word and object, just as understanding relies on, while also forming, linguistic concepts through its commerce with the world. Gadamer notes that we "are always already biased in our thinking and knowing by our linguistic interpretation of the world. To grow into this linguistic interpretation means to grow up in the world. To this extent, language is the real mark of our finitude. It is always out beyond us."[54] This returns us to the announced issue: the relation of language and world.

To explore this relation Gadamer takes a complex historical approach. He traces the emergence of the "concept" of language in Western thought through three stages: *logos*, *verbum*, and concept formation. He then sets out to explore language as the horizon of hermeneutical experience under the rubrics of experience of the world, the speculative structure of language, and its universal aspect. Embedded in this analysis is the strategy of reflection I have already isolated. Not surprisingly, his historical and constructive presentation is guided by language as *Spiel*-like (*logos*), festive (*verbum*), and symbolic (concept).

The heart of Gadamer's project is the relation of meaning and truth. "In the earliest times the intimate relation of word [*Wort*] and object [*Sache*] was so self-evident that the proper name was considered part of the bearer of this name, if not, indeed to substitute for it. . . . Thus it seems to be part of its being" (WM 383/TM 366). Word is the productive figurative presentation of a subject matter. And yet Greek philosophy began with the supposition that word is only a name, or sign, for a thing. Hence, the philosophical consideration of word and object centered on the correctness and rightness of names to objects. This constricted the referential power of language to the level of the word rather than to the sentence.[55] Plato, in the *Cratylus*, described the different relations of word and object, thereby introducing the troubled relation of *Bild* and *Urbild*, and hence "imitation," to thought about language. He isolated two theories about the relation of word to object: conventionalist theory, which bases the relation on the agreement and practice of language users; and "imitation" theory, which sees a natural relation between word and object. These two theories dominated the consideration of language from then on.

Gadamer weaves his way between the poles of these two theories. A "common language use" (*allgemeinen Sprachgebrauch*) approach, like Gadamer's, claims that we do not and cannot arbitrarily change the meaning of words. "A common world, even if it is an invented one, is always a presupposition of language" (WM 384/TM 367). The worldhood of language contests the conventionalist theory: the relation of word and object is not through any consensus; it is within the horizon of world. Language is not simply a tool constituted for whatever use we give it. Likewise, the failings of the "imitation" theory are evident. We have no vantage point outside of language to test whether it corresponds to reality or not. We stand on the inside of language; unlike tools, language is the medium of all of our understanding, a horizon of our world.

Plato also despaired of both theories. He argued that being must be understood by transcending words altogether. Language is banished from his ideal City just as its poets are. Gadamer cannot follow this path. His approach is to explore the commonality of language and "things." "But in all of this," he writes, "the point is missed that the truth of 'things' [*Sachen*] is in the speech [*Reden*], which means, ultimately, in the content of a unified meaning concerning things and not in the individual words—not even in the word-stock of an entire language" (WM 389/TM 374). A unified meaning in speech means understanding language by a turn to the use of words, to speech or *logos*. Language and experience are intimately bound. We cannot leap outside of language to construct a system of truths. We are mired in linguistic experience. The process of understanding and edification is, in no small measure, to acquire a language that dialectically expands and draws on experience.[56] This intimate relation of language and experience extends to *Dasein*'s horizon: world.

Gadamer's reading of Greek thought on language isolates the priority of *logos* (speech) over word. In speech there is a primordial relation of thought and thing; through *logos* experience comes to presentation. *Logos* is, we can say, the ludic or *Spiel* dimension of language: interactive, participatory, and self-presentative. Gadamer retrieves this character of *logos* under the rubric of "language as the experience of the world" (*Welterfahrung*). Commenting on Wilhelm von Humbolt, he emphasizes that a view of language is a view of the world, and that living speech as "linguistic *energia*" is the essence of language. We have seen this talk about *energia* before in Gadamer's description of *Spiel*. Here language is seen as the play of human world. "Not only is the world only the world insofar as it comes to language; language, too, has its unique existence only in that the world is presented to it. The original humanity of language means thus the original linguisticality of human being-in-the-world [*In-der-Welt-Sein*]" (WM 419/TM 403). But his contention that the horizon of *Dasein* is linguistic can be sustained only if it can be argued that humans ex-ist through language. And if that argument can be made, then the relation between *Spiel* and language will also have been shown. My contention is that this is precisely Gadamer's tactic.

Taking the relation of language and world as his focal point Gadamer asks: What is it to have a world? For us to have a world means to have an attitude toward it, and so to have some freedom from what we encounter. Drawing on Heidegger, Gadamer distinguishes between world and the habitat or surrounding world (*Umwelt*) of all living things. To have a world is freely to stand out (ex-ist) from *Umwelt*. It is, as we now know, to have *Bildung* or culture through language. And though Gadamer does not explore the tragic underpinnings of culture, he does claim that this standing-out is a linguistic event. *Logos* is the presentation of *Dasein*'s relation to the world as the basic relation of what is uniquely human. To recall the earlier discussion of *Spiel*, the ludic is the dynamic presentation of its *eidos*, its ideality. Gadamer is making the same argument here: a language is the play of a particular world. By entering the play of *logos* we enter a world. What does this mean?

First, language, on analogy to *Spiel*, is a dynamic process when it is living in conversation. It is a participatory action that displays its own world as common ground. "For language," Gadamer notes, "is the language of conversation [*Gesprächs*]. It forms through the process of understanding [*Verständigung*] its first actuality" (WM 422/TM 404). Like *Spiel*, language, as *logos*, only "is" in its performance, in conversation. Conversation creates a common playground (*Spielraum*) or world in which we find ourselves. *Dasein* dwells, as Heidegger said, in the house of language. Second, the linguistic world is not a barrier to knowing; it is the condition for understanding, the primal relation of *Dasein* and its "world." And so the horizon of hermeneutical experience stretches to the limits of language and world. This means that the world has a basic intelligibility, a "logos" to it. "Obviously language is able to do all this," Gadamer avers, "because it is not a creation of reflective thought, but helps to fashion the world-relation in which we live" (WM 426/ TM 408). Language, with the power to manifest a world, is the horizon of experience.

"Whoever has language 'has' a world" (WM 429/TM 411). This phrase neatly summarizes Gadamer's point. We ex-ist, stand out, of the *Umwelt* into *Welt* through linguistic communication. The dance of language in conversation presents the primal relation of understanding and world as the condition for understanding. Moreover, insofar as the acquisition of language is a growing into a world, it also characterizes the being in becoming of *Dasein*. This is true of both the formation of the individual and the formation of a common shared social world. The *logos*-dimension of *Dasein* is its particular ludic mode of being. The mimetic power of language is the condition for the formation and ex-istence of world.

The second strand Gadamer isolates in his history of the concept of language is that of *verbum*. He retrieves this dimension of language from reflection on the Incarnation and the Trinity in Christian thought.

> The interpretation of the mystery of the Trinity, the most important task confronting the thinking of the Middle Ages, was based . . . on the relationship between human speech and thought. . . . The uniqueness of the redemptive event introduces the historical object into Western thought, bringing the phenomenon of language out of its immersion in the ideality of meaning [*Sinn*], and offers it to philosophical reflection. In contrast to the Greek logos, the word is the pure event [*Geschehen*] (*verbum proprie dicitur personaliter tantum*) [WM 396/TM 379].

The fine details of Trinitarian reflection, the limitations of analogical thought about the Trinity, and the adequacy of Gadamer's reading of the theological tradition need not concern us.[57] What interests him in Trinitarian and Incarnational reflection are three characteristics of the event-character of *verbum*. These are its revelatory, dialogical, and productive or creative aspects.

Following Augustine's *De Trinitate*, on the "inner word" as the analogue for the Trinity, Gadamer notes: "The mystery of the Trinity is mirrored in the miracle of language insofar as the word that is true, because it says what the object is, is nothing by itself and does not seek to be anything. . . . It has its being in its revealing. Exactly the same thing is true of the mystery of the Trinity" (WM 396/TM 381). Language as *verbum* has its being in presentation for others, in revelation (*Offenbarung*). It is, as Grondin says, the "*Aletheia*-function" of language.[58] Contrary to the *Spiel* of self-presentation in *logos*, *verbum* is a public presentation. This is, we recall, one aspect of the being of festival. Language is not a closed game. Its being is in becoming an incarnate event of meaning. What comes to speech is potentially presented for all, all who have ears to hear![59]

From *verbum*'s presentative character Gadamer considers more explicitly the inner word. *Verbum*, he notes, cannot be reduced to the Greek *logos* as "the dialogue of the soul with itself" precisely because the *verbum* is presentative or incarnational. "The inner word," he writes, "remains related to its possible manifestation" (WM 399/TM 382). When thought conceives of an object, it is ordered, on analogy to the Trinity, toward being known. This orientation of *verbum* to an object means that language is primarily reflective, not of the "I," but of the subject matter. Moreover, the orientation is not a strict temporal sequence, and yet it does connote the modal character of *verbum*. It suggests the discursive character of understanding. This is not, again, a strict temporal sequence. It is rather a mental process in which thought celebrates a subject matter. Like a festival, thought is not a line of "nows." It has a peculiar modality that interphases the *ek-stases* of past, present, and future. Augustine recognized this himself in his reflections on memory and the "distention" of the soul in his *Confessions*.[60] Understanding is marked by festive temporality, which fuses past with present through the originary act of interpretation and therefore passes in and out of presence while projecting a future.

Beyond its modality, the Trinity, for much of the Christian tradition, was understood as a processive emanation. This understanding allows Gadamer to turn from the movement of thought to its productive dimension. On analogy to the *verbum* Gadamer writes that the "process and production of thought is not a process of change (*motus*) or a transition from potentiality into action, but an emergence [*Hervorgehen*] *ut actus ex actu*. The word not only is formed after the act of knowledge has been completed . . . but is the act of knowledge itself" (WM 400–401/TM 383). The divine Trinity in its procession obviously does not move from potentiality to actuality. It is always in *actus*. The unique modality of the Trinity is from actuality to actuality. By analogy, the *verbum* means that word and thought are not separable; they are one. Thus if language as *logos* was the presentation of the basic relation of understanding and world, here we see that language is also the relation of word and thought. Thought comes to be in its presentation in word. The unique modality of *verbum* is "out of nature into nature."This suggests that thought is directed to public presentation; it is not grounded simply in the reflexive act of the *cogito*.

The analogy between the Trinity and thought is, of course, strained. The human word is potential before actual even though word and thought are always one. Likewise, human words are imperfect in conveying unambiguously human thoughts and in the orientation to the object or subject matter. Gadamer, following St. Thomas, grants these failures in the analogy. But what interests him is that the unity of speaking and thinking means that a word is not formed by a reflexive act. The word or expression expresses not simply the mind but the intended object. This confounds Kantian transcendentalism and Romantic expressivism and heralds the productive character of language.

Gadamer's analysis of *verbum* reappears, I think, in his discussion of the center of language and its speculative structure. We should not be alarmed by this talk of speculation since, as shown earlier, he interprets theory as *theoros*: the spectator at the sacred festival. Contrary to the Greek impulse to flee into epistemological foundationalism, Gadamer's concern is with language as the mediation of finite, historical experience.

The mediating function of language is sustained in its *verbum* character, specifically in its orientation to productivity and its intended object. As he notes, every word "breaks forth as if from a center and is related to the whole, through which it alone is a word" (WM 434/TM 415). Each and every word or sentence potentially makes an entire language resonate and hence lets a world appear. This is why Gadamer speaks of the speculative center of language. Human speaking is finite, but there is in it an infinity of meaning that may be interpreted.[61] This discloses the "belongingness" (*Zugehörigkeit*) of the human and its world. Gadamer, we know, previously explored this belongingness as effective-historical consciousness. His concern here is to isolate the linguistic horizon of that consciousness. The productivity of language reveals and constitutes this belongingness.

Gadamer contests any *a priori* rigid division of subject/object. Drawing on his discussion of tradition, he claims that the belongingness of *Dasein* to the world has an event-character. This event is made possible "only because the word that has come down to us as tradition and to which we are to listen really encounters us and does so in such a way that it addresses us and is concerned with us" (WM 437/TM 419). We are in the festival of tradition as *theoroi* called to participate in that event. Our participation is primarily linguistic since it begins in "uninterrupted listening" and being formed by the tradition. In the event of understanding, as the mode of being of *Dasein*, tradition itself is being in its becoming. The dialectic is not one of progressive emergence from language (the Greeks) or its culmination in consciousness (Hegel); the dialectic is the relation of an infinite meaning presented in a finite way.

The speculative character of language, more specifically stated, is in "the realization of meaning [*Sinn*], as the event [*Geschehen*] of speech, of communication, of understanding. Such a realization is 'speculative' in that the finite possibilities of the word are oriented toward the meaning intended, as toward the infinite" (WM 444/TM 426). The speculative element of language is the relation of the said and unsaid in the concrete unity of meaning. Such speaking, Gadamer contends, may express a relation to the whole of Being. But the speculative power of language is not the ability by speakers to copy some external reality. It is speculative in presenting a "new sight of a new world." This new world, whether in a present word or a traditional parable, meets us as alien. But it also reveals our belongingness in a world. The sayings of Jesus, for example, place before us a new world and a new insight into that world. In those sayings a radical vision of life is presented even as our loyalties to this world are exposed and questioned. Such sayings express the speculative power of language.

Understanding begins as a response to the speculative power of language. Interpretation, as moving toward the fusion of horizons, joins this speculative dance. It is a coming to language, as Gadamer says, of a totality of meaning. "What this means is that all interpretation is speculative as it is actually practiced, quite apart from its methodological self-consciousness. . . . For the interpreting word is the word of the interpreter; it is not the language and lexicon of the interpreted text. This means that appropriation [*Aneignung*] is no mere repetition of the text that has been handed down, but a new creation of understanding" (WM 448/TM 430). Meaning is wrought in the concretization of understanding not in reference to an "I" or an "author" behind the text but in what Gadamer calls the "understanding I." This means, surprisingly, that language is the point at which the self and the world appear, a point, as we shall see, that Kierkegaard seeks to understand. Through interpretation we come to be in relation to the presented world. Gadamer's hermeneutic takes the modern *cogito* from its throne and places it again in the world.

The third strand in Gadamer's history of language is "concept formation" (*Begriffsbildung*). Anyone who speaks uses the general meanings of words to articulate particular meanings about specific persons, things, and events.[62] Involved in this process is the curiosity that what is said shares in the particularities of the circumstance. Our words rely for meaning on their concretization in particular sentences about ideas, words, events, or persons. But this means "that the universal concept that was meant through the meaning of the word is itself enriched by the particular thing in view [*Sachanschauung*], so that in the end a new, more specific word formation [*Wortbildung*] emerges that does more justice to the specific thing" (WM 405/TM 388). The process of concept formation, and therefore the development of language, is through this concretization of general meaning. The process is fundamentally metaphoric and corresponds to the practical character of understanding noted above. On the basis of perceived likeness, linguistic consciousness gives expression to that similarity. The metaphoric transfer is the basic thrust of language formation and the widening of the realm of experience. If we recall the unity of thought and language, this metaphoric process means that the "order of things" becomes apparent in speaking about them. Stated differently: the metaphoric process of concept formation presents the relationality of things. "Universals" are metaphorical expressions born of the concretization of meaning.[63] I shall explore metaphor in greater detail in the next chapter.

One consequence of forgetting the relation of thought and language is the degrading of language into mere signs, which allows the application of modernist scientific techniques to the human sciences. Our forgetfulness is understandable in that language recedes in our use of it. In the very process of bringing to expression our experience of the world, language conceals itself, and we attend from it to what is presented. Ironically, the recessive nature of language is integral to its being communicative and the condition for its devaluation into mere signs. We can communicate only when we turn our attention from the medium of understanding to the subject matter (*Sache*) of the statement. This diversion, though necessary, allows one to treat words as signs of their "what," and gave rise to the classical imitation theory regarding language. Yet it is clear that the subject matter is in fact intimately bound up with the mode and medium of its presentation.

The other consequence of forgetting the relation of thought and language is a simple nominalistic conventionalism in which meaning is dependent solely on the needs and wishes of the community of speakers. The irony of this position, from Gadamer's perspective, is that a common language is a condition for a community of speakers. Our language plays a role in the formation of the understanding of our needs and wishes, and it is integral to the communities in which we seek to satisfy and express them. In a word, language is central to our social world. It is not simply conventional since it always bears ontological depth in relation to a "world."

Between these forms of forgetfulness Gadamer recalls the fact that all language is oriented toward some meaning. The metaphoric process of concept formation means that language discloses its universality only in a transformation into figuration in specific uses or concepts. The metaphoric process of transformation is the presentation of a general meaning in specific ways, words, or concepts for others. Through concept formation, relations in the world are figured into concepts that, mimetically we might say, present those relations. Language reveals our being in the world and is productive of the meaningfulness of those relations. As such, language has ontological import. And this import is Gadamer's real concern.

"Being that can be understood is language" (WM 450/TM 432).[64] This is Gadamer's greatest claim. What it means is that in language being comes to presentation, becomes world. In this sense the self-presentation of any being that can be interpreted and understood is finally "linguistic." Insofar as nature can be understood it is linguistic; it speaks to us. "This means that it is of such a nature that of itself it presents [*darstellt*] itself to be understood. . . . To come to language [*zur-Sprache-kommen*] does not mean to acquire a second existence. The way something presents itself belongs, rather, to its particular being [*Sein*]" (WM 450/TM 432). The primordial relation of understanding and world heralds the fact that all "phenomena" are linguistic. This is why I noted earlier that for Gadamer the self-presentation of any reality is in a sense linguistic. That is, a reality presents something to be understood, to be responded to and appropriated. Hence in all our commerce with the world we are continually responding through interpretation; we read the book of the world. Gadamer calls this the universality of hermeneutical experience. Hermeneutical reflection rests on the contention that reality presents itself for interpretation, that all Being is meaningful if nonetheless ambiguous.

Self-presentation and being-understood belong together. Put differently: the world is self-presentative (linguistic) and the mode of being of *Dasein* is understanding. Whereas Part I of *Truth and Method* explores the presentative dimension of the world on analogy to the work of art and Part II the mode of being of understanding, here we grasp the horizon of both in language. Language is, finally, the presentative and temporal mimesis of meaning and Being; it is the medium of human world relating understanding and Being.

Gadamer forwards this remarkable argument by considering the relation of the Good and the Beautiful. The nature of the beautiful is that it makes itself manifest. "The beautiful reveals itself in the search for the good. That is the distinguishing mark of the human soul" (WM 456/TM 437). What manifests itself evokes love and so disposes people toward itself. The beautiful then is the "mediation of idea and appearance" (WM 456/TM 438) since it is an appearance, or shining (*Schein*), in which a "what" appears.[65] "Beauty," he writes, "has the mode of being of light" (WM 457/TM 439), and is "the mode of appearance of the good in general, of Being as it ought to be" (WM 457/TM 439). This signals that understanding has a basic moral dimension.

The point here is not to repristinate a metaphysics of the beautiful or of light. Nevertheless, thought about the beautiful does help us to explore two further points about the relation of appearance and comprehensibility. First, the beautiful justifies, for Gadamer, the priority of the "activity of the object" in hermeneutical experience. This is the grounds for contesting the subjectivism of the Enlightenment. It is also the reason, in my judgment, that *Truth and Method* begins with the experience of the work of art. A proposal, idea, or text asserts itself first, and we respond to it. Thought does not generate itself *ex nihilo*; it is born in response to a world. That which asserts itself disturbs our horizons. It encounters us and demands understanding. Gadamer goes so far as to speak of it as a "Thou." In the event of understanding we encounter something that asserts itself and makes a claim on us. This confrontation, and hence the activity of the object, are the condition for understanding.

The event-character of the beautiful, as the way of being and of understanding, is thus an insight into the nature of truth. The beautiful closes the gap between idea and appearance through *Bild*. By extension, the truth of human being is the identification of idea (values, beliefs, and loyalties) with appearance (existence) in a particular culture or character. This leads us to the edge of Ricoeur's and Kierkegaard's thought. Ricoeur will claim that human identity comes to be through understanding itself vis-à-vis narrative portrayals of life. Kierkegaard's entire authorship seeks to examine the concrete act of being a self, and in doing so, helps us explore further the problem of the human orientation in and comportment before the world and itself. Gadamer's point, nevertheless, is that understanding is an encounter in which something asserts itself as true, whether that be the world of a text or Jesus Christ. This encounter takes place through the linguistic performance of interpretation.

Appearance and participatory *Spiel* take place in the dance of language. "Language games [*sprachliche Spiele*] are where we as learners—and when do we cease to be that—rise to the understanding of the world" (WM 464/TM 446). Understanding is participation in an event through which meaning asserts itself. The truth of understanding is the truth of *Spiel*. Language is, finally, the *Spiel* of human world. It entails a mode of knowing and a truth that involves our being. And our being is formed through the ludic, festive, and symbolic engagement with a world of meaning mimetically presented to us.

GADAMER AND THE RECONSTRUCTION OF MIMESIS

Truth and Method as a whole presents Gadamer's mimetic strategy. I have traced its steps and turns. It encompasses the presentation of meaning in the work of art in which we gain insight into our being and world (Part I). Understanding is the festive dialogue between us and tradition that enables a fusion of horizons that forms us as it extends the tradition (Part II). The medium of insight and identity, presentation and contemporaneity, Being and understanding is the dance of language (Part III). That dance presents a world even as we participate in it. Human understanding is the mimesis of world as ludic, temporal, and symbolic.

This is obviously not imitation as crass copying. It is the presentation by a transformation into figuration of the belongingness of the human and world that creates a common world of meaning. We might say, using Kantian terms, that mimesis is a schematizing action. Through the mimetic performance the "belonging" of human and world is schematized and presented figuratively.[66] What is presented is not the transcendental structure of the human, but our belongingness in the world. Gadamer's reading of mimesis subverts the critical turn to the subject and places the human on the stage of the world.

Gadamer's mimetic strategy involves rethinking the relation of understanding and Being through language. That relation is interpreted on three levels: a *Spiel*-dimension of interaction/participation; festive temporality marked by contemporaneity/identification; and the symbolic power of presentation/recognition. The direction of my argument actually has been to show that these are Gadamer's recastings of the meanings of Being. Tracing the etymology of Being Heidegger wrote:

1) The oldest, the actual radical word is "es" . . . life, the living, that which from out of itself stands and which moves and rests in itself: the self-standing. . . . 2) The other Indo-European radical is "*bhu*, *bheu*." To it belongs the Greek "*phuo*," to emerge, to be powerful, of itself to come to stand and to remain standing. . . . 3) The third stem occurs only in the inflection of the Germanic "*sein*": "*wes*"; Sanskrit: *vasami*; Germanic: *wesan*, to dwell, to sojourn. . . . From the three stems we derive three initial concrete meanings: to live, to emerge, to linger or endure. These are established by linguistics, which also establishes that these initial meanings are extinct today, that only "abstract" meaning "to be" has been preserved.[67]

We have seen these various levels of being in Gadamer's mimetic strategy. *Spiel* connotes living motion, which, as festive, causes one, and itself, to linger, and has symbolic power to emerge in presentation. What is significant, it seems to me, is that Gadamer rethinks Being along these lines, but also as performative social action. This opens up the reconstruction of mimesis in several areas of thought, including religion and morals. That is, Gadamer's social ontology has implications for our understanding of "texts" and what we mean by human understanding and life. I want to trace some of these implications here, although the rest of this book is devoted to developing them in full.

First, Gadamer's mimetic strategy explores the relation of Being and meaning in language. Being is self-presentative. Etched into the way things exist is a mimetic character: to bring to presentation. That presentation involves a transformation into structure that manifests through our participation the meaningfulness of human world. Gadamer's general ontological claim provokes reflection on the import of our social and natural world. We might ask: Where is the image or picture of the human presented? Answers abound, as we saw in the first chapter. For the *imago hominis* Plato looked to the soul; the Hebrews, to the living "image of God"; and St. Paul, to Christ. The task is to think through the mimetic structure of human being. This requires further investigation of how we make sense of the temporal structure of life and how the self comes to be.

Gadamer's hermeneutic also suggests an approach to texts, and this provides a way to explore human temporality. First and foremost, texts are understood through performative action. Though most commentators take Gadamer's primary analogue for texts as dialogue, I have shown that a cluster of ideas structure his thought. Texts and dialogues are understood through *Spiel*, festival, and symbol. Texts are mimetic insofar as they present or perform a world through a particular transformation into structure. That figuration means that the text escapes its original social or artistic point of origin and achieves a level of ideality. Scriptural texts, for example, that present the message of Jesus do not slavishly represent it. Through that presentation the message enjoys an increase in meaning—it is potentially open to all. The message ex-ists through its mimetic figuration bringing a world (e.g., the reign of God) to presentation. At this point the mimetic process of texts *necessarily* dovetails with the mimetic action of understanding. It makes little or no sense to speak of texts presenting a world *by themselves*. That presentation happens only in relation to the dance and festival of understanding. Ricoeur's work on mimetic narrative, I shall argue shortly, expands these insights.

Along with providing a way to think about texts as mimetic, Gadamer's exploring of human appropriation or understanding raises the question of how the self comes to be a self. Understanding is the transformation into structure of a presentation so that one is formed (*Bildung*) in specific ways. The process of formation is participatory and identity-engendering, and moves toward self-presentation. This provides us with a way to think and speak about the formation of moral character (edification) as born out of and oriented to practical action. At this point we are pushed into Kierkegaard's analytic of the self. That is, his analysis of existence will help us to deepen Gadamer's insight into the mimetic character of understanding.

Gadamer understands hermeneutics to stand within the tradition of classical practical philosophy. Accordingly hermeneutics is interested in practical wisdom (*phronesis*), and, more generally, the human good. Given this, Gadamer's mimetic strategy, as the process of human community itself, opens up fundamental ethical inquiry. He does so through the notion of practice, demonstrating once again the priority of practical understanding over "method" in his hermeneutics.

"Practice," writes Gadamer, "is conducting oneself and acting in solidarity. Solidarity, however, is the decisive condition and basis of all social reason."[68] Society is organized for the sake of a common order of living. This means that human sociality is something which is choiceworthy beyond utility. That which transcends the useful or the necessary, Gadamer notes, is what the Greeks called the *kalon*, meaning both good and beautiful. And it is accessible to all; it is not diminished by being shared but actually gains through participation. "In the end, this is the birth of the concept of reason: the more what is desirable is displayed for all in a way that is convincing to all, the more those involved discover themselves in this common reality; and to that extent human beings possess freedom in a positive sense, they have their true identity in that common reality."[69] The step into human nature is the realization of a shared reality through the interpretive discovery of ourselves in solidarity. The task of social reason and practical philosophy is to lead to this recognition and to direct action in rendering that common reality actual.

The chief task, as Richard Bernstein puts it, "is to justify this way of reason and defend practical and political reason against the domination of technology based on science."[70] The way of reason, personally and socially, is dialogical. It is, to recall our earlier discussion, the way of conversation. Dialogical understanding is *phronetic* in that it mediates a universal, a shared *ethos* and concern, and a particular situation. This mediation is not merely placing particulars under universal principles. Universal and particular, as noted above, are co-determined. The shared *ethos* of the community is only as it is mediated and embodied in particular ways. This means that the mode of knowing involved here is one that includes our being and our doing relative to what is discerned as good in a particular situation. Because of the polysemy of *kalon*, good/beautiful, social reason must be responsive, and it works aesthetically. That is, it seeks to discern what is fitting or appropriate in a particular situation, an insight I shall explore in concluding this study.[71]

Social reason demands and moves by reasoned discourse about the common good even as the moral and political task is to enact, to present, that good. In this dialogic process of application, our common reality is presented even as it is transformed and passed on. "Achieving this concretization is the vital concern of one who possesses the virtue of *phronesis*."[72] This does not assume a static normativity of tradition. On the contrary, tradition is always in revision. Gadamer's main point is that understanding, as dialogical, is phronetic: a realization of a universal in a particular situation. Through this concretization a shared *ethos* is presented. In the act of understanding, something radically other is taken as sharing our common world; alienation is overcome in the solidarity of understanding. If the good manifests itself in the beautiful, as Gadamer contends, then one moral and political task is to enact our world as beautiful, as rightly ordered life. We might say that the moral and political task is to enact a just and peaceful world as the mimesis, the presentation, of what it means to be human. Gadamer's argument here raises the question of the power of solidarity that enables and transforms understanding and a common world. This too will concern us later.

Gadamer rethinks mimesis as the transformative figuration of Being and understanding. His insight, as I have interpreted it, is to have reconsidered these notions around the elements of performative action, and hence to have reconceived the framework for interpreting mimesis *and* human understanding as our coming-to-be in a social world. I have shown that on analogy to performative action mimesis involves a mode of participation in a world, edification through participation and festive repetition, knowledge through recognition of what is demanded and fitting in a situation, and, finally, a presentation of self and world to others. To alter a phrase of Theodore Jennings, we can say that to "participate in [mimetic action] is to know how the world acts, how it 'comes to be,' and to be formed by it ourselves."[73]

Gadamer's mimetic strategy virtually destroys traditional imitation theory and yet his hermeneutic speaks to many of the areas of concern that classical thought addressed. He provides a reconception of mimesis as the figuration of performative enactment in works of art, or texts, and understanding, and he shows the abiding and yet dynamic relation of meaning and Being, human and world, through mimetic interpretation and the dynamics of language. Even more specifically, he has provided the beginnings of a vocabulary to speak about mimesis. Mimetic action, we have seen, has interactive, temporal, and figurative dimensions whether one is considering understanding, language, or the work of art. The moments of the mimetic act also have a correlate dimension in understanding: interpretation, the fusions of horizon, and effective-historical consciousness. And all this, Gadamer contends, takes place in language. Thus the deepest trajectory of his mimetic strategy is into the being of human world.

NOTES

1. Georgia Warnke, *Gadamer: Hermeneutics, Tradition, and Reason* (Stanford: Stanford University Press, 1987), p. 4. For other helpful studies of Gadamer's work, see Jean Grondin, *Hermeneutische Wahrheit? Zum Wahrheitsbegriff Hans-Georg Gadamers*, Monographien zur philosophischen Forschung 215 (Tübingen: Athenäum, 1982) and Joel C. Weinsheimer, *Gadamer's Hermeneutics: A Reading of TRUTH AND METHOD* (New Haven: Yale University Press, 1985). Gadamer's relation to nineteenth- and twentieth-century hermeneutics is detailed by Richard E. Palmer in *Hermeneutics*, Northwestern University Studies in Phenomenology and Existential Philosophy (Evanston: Northwestern University Press, 1969). David Couzens Hoy explores Gadamer's thought in relation to more recent hermeneutical thought. See his *The Critical Circle: Literature, History, and Philosophy* (Berkeley: University of California Press, 1978). For a collection of essays on Gadamer's work, see *Hermeneutik und Dialektik: Hans-Georg Gadamer z. 70. Geburtstag*, edd. Rüdiger Bubner, Konrad Cramer, and Reiner Wahl, 2 vols. (Tübingen: Mohr, 1970). For an important recent reading of Gadamer, see Bernstein's *Beyond Objectivism and Relativism*. These scholars provide the historical and textual study of Gadamer's corpus assumed in my reading.

2. *Gadamer's Hermeneutics*, p. 4.

3. Ibid., p. 12.

4. Warnke, *Gadamer*, pp. 9–10. For a contrasting position and a criticism of Gadamer on this point, see E. D. Hirsch, Jr., *Validity in Interpretation* (New Haven: Yale University Press, 1967).

5. Gadamer relies at this point on Köller's *Die Mimesis in der Antike*. Gadamer's use of this work as well as his claims about *Spiel* are the reasons for my translating *Darstellung* as "presentation." By doing so I hope to signal its relation to dramatic enactment rather than visual representation. I also seek by this rendering to capture the originary character of each enactment missed by translating it as "re-presentation."

6. *Gadamer*, p. 59.

7. *The Idea of the Good in Platonic–Aristotelian Philosophy*, trans. P. Christopher Smith (New Haven: Yale University Press, 1986), p. 172.

8. *Gadamer's Hermeneutics*, p. 113.

9. (Stuttgart: Reclam, 1977). All references will be cited in the text as AS and page number. Translations are mine, although I have checked them with *The Relevance of the Beautiful and Other Essays*, trans. Nicholas Walker, ed. Robert Bernasconi (Cambridge: Cambridge University Press, 1986). See also Gadamer's *Wahrheit und Methode: Grundzüge einer philosophischen Hermeneutik*, 2nd ed. (Tübingen: Mohr, 1965). Henceforth all references will be cited in the text. I include references to the

English translation (TM) as well, although my translation differs at key points with it. See *Truth and Method*, trans. Garrett Barden and John Cumming (New York: Seabury/Continuum, 1975).

10. Elsewhere he notes that "human play and the ability to play is a specifically human distinction. One speaks, as you know, of the play element that is present in all human culture. One discovers forms of play in the first human working, in cult, in the administration of justice, and in social relations . . ." ("Das Spiel der Kunst," *Kleine Schriften*. IV. *Variationen* [Tübingen: Mohr, 1977], p. 235).

11. For a helpful article on Heidegger's reading of being and motion that shows affinities with Gadamer's, see Thomas Sheehan, "On Movement and the Deconstruction of Ontology," *Monist*, 64 (1981), 534–42. I shall use the Latinate "ludic" (sport, game, cultic action) as synonymous with Gadamer's German *Spiel* and the English "play."

12. *Hermeneutische Wahrheit?* p. 104. The Hegelian impulse behind Gadamer's reading of the movement of *Spiel* is clear throughout. Likewise, as Grondin points out, Gadamer's notion of participatory knowledge shows Platonic overtones. My reading acknowledges these connections but argues that his retrieval of performative mimesis signals a new direction for reflection.

13. P. 235. Because Gadamer makes a connection between *Spiel* and culture, it is clear that, by extension, he is speaking here of the nature of human law. The ethical implication of this assertion will be explored later.

14. The rule-governed character of *Spiel* shows the deep difference in the thought of Gadamer and Jürgen Habermas. Habermas seeks what he calls a "universal pragmatics" in which an "ideal speech situation" can be used to judge all distortions in human communication. Gadamer does not cast rules to the wind. He is noting that although they are internal to "games," they are also contextually bound to those games. Though all human play and culture is rule-governed, the content and force of the rules are relative to that game. For a good introduction into Habermas' thought, see his *Communication and the Evolution of Society*, trans. Thomas McCarthy (Boston: Beacon, 1979).

15. We should recall that Kant speaks of the work of genius, the truly great work of art, as having its own spirit. What Gadamer has done, in response to Kant, is to understand the spirit or logos of *Spiel* as interactive. Thus it is social and not subjective as Kant's understanding of the beautiful is. See Immanuel Kant, *Critique of Judgment*, trans. J. H. Bernhard (New York: Hafner, 1951).

16. John D. Caputo, "Being, Ground, and Play in Heidegger," *Man and World*, 3 (1970), 38, 40. These are his translations of Heidegger's *Der Satz vom Grund* (Pfullingen: Neske, 1977). Sheehan's "On Movement and the Deconstruction of Ontology" is also helpful on this issue.

17. Grondin, as I noted before, contends that Gadamer's notion of *Spiel* and participatory knowledge is Platonic. I think that through the notion of *Spiel* Gadamer is actually overcoming Plato through a pre-Socratic reading of being, one drawn from Heidegger. What is important for us is that Gadamer's argument against Heidegger is made on social and cultic grounds.

18. *The Phenomenology of Spirit*, trans. A. V. Miller (Oxford: Clarendon, 1977), para. 47. It is interesting that Hegel would associate the movement of truth with cult! I think this is one more connection Gadamer is making between mimesis and later thought.

19. Sheehan, "Movement and the Deconstruction of Ontology," 537.

20. Weinsheimer, *Gadamer's Hermeneutics*, p. 103.

21. *Hermeneutische Wahrheit?* p. 104.

22. Elsewhere Gadamer has written that mimetic *"Darstellung* is a part of the cultic event, perhaps the procession, as we know of the carnival or festival. It is an act of identification and not of difference in which something is recognized" ("Dichtung und Mimesis," *Kleine Schriften* IV, p. 231).

23. See Jerald Wallulis, "Philosophical Hermeneutics and the Conflicts of Ontologies," *International Philosophical Quarterly*, 24 (1984), 283–302.

24. Weinsheimer, *Gadamer's Hermeneutics*, p. 71.

25. Weinsheimer, in ibid., uses the terminology of "double mimesis." He means by it the artist's presentation of something through the work and then the performers' presentation of the play. Accordingly, he writes that "Gadamer's notion of double mimesis leaves art especially vulnerable to the charge of being a double removed from the truth" (p. 118). I contest this reading even as I am speaking of a double mimesis. What I mean by the term is that there is a performative transformation into figuration of both the being of the work and the being of the one understanding. This renders more complex the Platonic reading of Gadamer that Weinsheimer seems to suggest.

26. Gadamer's German raises problems of translation. *Verwandlung* can be rendered as "transformation," "transfiguration," "metamorphosis," and even "transubstantiation." In all cases the work of art is a *Spiel* transformed into structure or figuration *(Gebilde)*. The work of art is *Spiel* that has its own structure and figure. The closest analogues to Gadamer's position, I think, are discussions of the Eucharist that hold that through the festive action of the community Christ's presence is presented anew through that figuration. The analogy is important since for Gadamer interpretation is the re-activation of the dance or festival itself. Though I shall not explore this analogy to the Eucharist further, the polysemy of *Verwandlung* must be kept in mind.

27. Edward S. Casey has noted that "in the symbolizing act the actual or imagined referent of the work is brought into symbolic relation; it becomes internal to the act as something that is symbolized or meant, not merely indicated or denoted" ("Truth in Art," *Man and World*, 3 [1970], 362).

28. *Hermeneutische Wahrheit?* p. 115. Gadamer is making a claim similar to that of Elisabeth Schüssler Fiorenza. She argues for a shift from defining Scripture as archetype to that of prototype, opening Scripture to critical revision. Her hermeneutics is guided by a pragmatic impulse. That is, Scripture functions to guide modes of liberating action. Although Gadamer's notion of text is not pragmatic, it is clear that he is seeking to overcome understanding the text as pointing to some archetypal meaning that does not change. See Fiorenza's *In Memory of Her: A Feminist Theological Reconstruction of Christian Origins* (New York: Crossroad, 1983). See also my "Iconoclasts, Builders, and Dramatists: The Use of Scripture in Theological Ethics" in *The Annual of the Society of Christian Ethics* (Washington: D.C.: Georgetown University Press, 1986), pp. 129–62.

29. Paul Ricoeur, as we shall see later, has offered a similar analysis of mimesis which demonstrates that there are levels of action, temporality, and symbolic figuration in mimesis. Ricoeur's mimetic strategy moves from prefiguration to configuration through refiguration. His position is heavily dependent on Aristotle, as we shall see.

30. *Die Mimesis in der Antike*, p. 119.

31. My point here is that Gadamer and Ricoeur rethink mimesis relative to its first

classic philosophical articulations in Plato and Aristotle. Their insight is to have done this relative to festival or play (Gadamer) and human action (Ricoeur).

32. Grondin, *Hermeneutische Wahrheit?* p. 115.

33. *Gadamer's Hermeneutics*, p. 255.

34. This is, I think, Gadamer's way of addressing the forgetfulness of being that Heidegger hailed as the legacy of the West. Heidegger saw the question of meaning as related to that of being. He entered the problem of Being through the one *(Dasein)* who can ask the question of the meaning of Being. Gadamer, in offering his hermeneutics of understanding, must avoid the error Heidegger isolated. He does so by showing the primal relation of being and meaning. This is why the discussion of *Bildung* is central: human coming-to-be, formation, is in relation to the meaning of world.

35. Pp. 232–33. Henceforth all references will be cited in the text as DM and page number. Translations are mine.

36. "Das Spiel der Kunst," p. 239.

37. *Gadamer*, p. 66.

38. Aristotle, *On Poetry and Style*, trans. G. M. A. Grube, Library of Liberal Arts (Indianapolis: Bobbs-Merrill, 1958).

39. See *Idea of the Good in Platonic–Aristotelian Philosophy*, pp. 159–78.

40. Gadamer's affinities with Hegel are again evident. The work of art is for Gadamer, in conjunction with the experience of art, a "concrete universal." I have tried to show throughout the discussion that Gadamer's own position, as Grondin argues as well, is constructed through conversation with the Greeks, Hegel, and Heidegger.

41. On this see Sallie McFague, *Metaphorical Theology: Models of God in Religious Language* (Philadelphia: Fortress, 1982).

42. "On the Problem of Self-Understanding," *Philosophical Hermeneutics*, trans. and ed. David E. Linge (Berkeley: University of California Press, 1976), p. 49.

43. *Anwendung* can be translated as "use," "application," or "employment." I use application throughout since I am arguing that *Anwendung* is two-sided: application to our situation and application to our selves in forming *Bildung*. *Anwendung* is, nonetheless, the pragmatic element in Gadamer's hermeneutical theory. It is significant that in his discussion of application he looks to the Preacher and the Judge as the paradigmatic figures for this aspect of interpretation.

44. Gadamer acknowledges the distinction between *subtilitas intelligendi* (understanding), *subtilitas explicandi* (interpretation), and *subtilitas applicandi* (application) that Hirsch demands (cf. WM 290/TM 274). His point is that these are interrelated moments in understanding. They are not separate "methods" of interpretation.

45. Georgia Warnke makes the same point. See her *Gadamer*, pp. 91–100.

46. See Grondin, *Hermeneutische Wahrheit?* pp. 143ff. See also Weinsheimer, *Gadamer's Hermeneutics*, pp. 181ff.

47. In this regard Gadamer relies on Collingwood's hermeneutical prioritizing of the question. See R. G. Collingwood, *An Autobiography* (Oxford: Oxford University Press, 1970). For Gadamer's discussion of Collingwood see WM 351–52/TM 333–34. Warnke *(Gadamer*, pp. 100–106) argues for the Socratic understanding of dialogue in Gadamer.

48. Grondin, *Hermeneutische Wahrheit?* p. 147.

49. Weinsheimer, *Gadamer's Hermeneutics*, p. 159.

50. Bernstein puts the matter well. "A horizon, then, is limited and finite, but it is *essentially* open. For to have a horizon is not to be limited to what is nearest but to be

able to move beyond it. Indeed the very idea of a closed horizon is a false abstraction"
(*Beyond Objectivism and Relativism*, p. 143).

51. There is difficulty with Gadamer's German here. His term is *Sprache*, which
may be translated as "language," "speech," or even a particular tongue. The polysemy
of his term must be kept in mind. Likewise, to say that the world is linguistic is merely
to assert that all human culture and social reality are constructed through modes of
communication. The mode of communication, or particular tongue, is always specific
to cultural contexts. Thus although Gadamer is making general claims about human
language-users, he is also asserting the particularities of specific languages.

52. In this light Ricoeur is surely correct when he notes that the distanciation involved
in writing is productive of meaning. See his "The Hermeneutical Function of
Distanciation," in *Hermeneutics and the Human Sciences: Essays on Language, Action,
and Interpretation*, ed. and trans. John B. Thompson (Cambridge: Cambridge University Press, 1981), pp. 131–44.

53. This clarifies what Gadamer means by hermeneutics. "The best definition of
hermeneutics is this: to let what is alienated by the character of the written word or by
the character of being distanciated by cultural or historical distances speak again. This
is hermeneutics: to let what seems to be far and alienated speak again" ("Practical
Philosophy as a Model of the Human Sciences," *Research in Phenomenology*, 9 [1979],
83).

54. *Philosophical Hermeneutics*, p. 64.

55. For a discussion of this shift see Paul Ricoeur, *The Rule of Metaphor: Multi-Disciplinary Studies in the Creation of Meaning in Language*, trans. Robert Czerny,
Kathleen McLaughlin, and John Costello (Toronto: University of Toronto Press, 1977).

56. George A. Lindbeck, in *The Nature of Doctrine: Religion and Theology in a
Postliberal Age* (Philadelphia: Westminster, 1984), makes the argument that becoming
religious is a matter of learning a language. Gadamer is in agreement with some of this
argument, yet it is clear that he holds to a dialectical relation of language and experience. Without that relation it is difficult to understand change in language or experience. Surely Lindbeck's position is one-sided in this regard. Moreover, as we have
seen, what Gadamer means by *Sprache* is not simply a language system, as Lindbeck
seems to think, but living discourse itself.

57. Two central treatises on the Trinity with hermeneutical import are Augustine's
De Trinitate and Karl Barth's *Church Dogmatics*. Referring to the inner word, Augustine explores the Trinity and its analogy in the internal processes of the soul. Barth
turns to the revelational history of the Word of God and thus counters the *analogia entis*
implicit in Augustine's position. What may be demanded, but cannot be done here, is
to rethink Trinitarian language as interactive, uniquely modal, and presentative. This
task is beyond the scope of the present study although my argument suggests directions
for such work.

58. *Hermeneutische Wahrheit?* p. 189.

59. Gadamer notes (WM 438/TM 420) that this is the reason hermeneutical reflection
begins with audition and not with vision. To use broad generalizations, his position has
more affinities with biblical thought than with the Greek emphasis on knowledge as
visual. This is not to claim that Gadamer's argument is biblical. It is not. Rather, he
retrieves the priority of listening over seeing through his retrieval of the cultic dimensions of play.

60. Trans. R. S. Pine-Coffin (New York: Penguin Books, 1961). See particularly Books Xff.

61. On the infinity of meaning and interpretation see Frank Kermode, *The Genesis of Secrecy: On the Interpretation of Narrative* (Cambridge: Harvard University Press, 1979).

62. We should note that this is the reason Schleiermacher felt it necessary to add psychological interpretation to grammatical exegesis. Authors use language differently to communicate unique thoughts and in different styles. Schleiermacher's claim was that the text was the expression of the author's intention, and not, as for Gadamer, oriented to the presentation of a subject matter. Thus Schleiermacher moves beyond grammatical exegesis to empathy with the author. Gadamer holds that interpretation must address the subject matter (*Sache*) presented and not the mind of the author. See Schleiermacher's *Hermeneutics*.

63. This is Gadamer's Hegelian point: finally nature imitates art and language in that its being comes to speech. This is why it was possible to say earlier that *Bildung* is the mimesis of nature, because, in fact, both are processes of presentation, of language.

64. "Sein, das verstanden werden kann, ist Sprache."

65. Gadamer is continuing Heidegger's argument that truth is a "lightening." See Martin Heidegger's "Letter on Humanism," *Basic Writings from* BEING AND TIME *(1927) to* THE TASK OF THINKING *(1964)*, ed. David Farrell Krell (New York: Harper & Row, 1977), pp. 189–242. For Gadamer's discussion of this, see WM 457/TM 439.

66. By drawing on Ricoeur's thought I shall isolate the schematizing power of mimesis in narrative imagination.

67. *Introduction to Metaphysics*, pp. 58–59.

68. "Practical Philosophy as a Model of the Human Sciences," 87.

69. Ibid., 77.

70. *Beyond Objectivism and Relativism*, pp. 145–46.

71. Bernstein has noted this element of "fittingness" as has Jerald Wallulis in "Philosophical Hermeneutics and the Conflict of Ontologies." This is the cathekontic aspect of Gadamer's thought. The ethical import of his position will concern us in the conclusion of this study.

72. Hans-Georg Gadamer, *Reason in the Age of Science*, trans. Frederick G. Lawrence (Cambridge: MIT Press, 1981), p. 134.

73. "On Ritual Knowledge," *The Journal of Religion*, 62 (1982), 121. His statement is actually "to participate in *ritual* etc." What Jennings shows is that ritual action is a way to know, is pedagogical, and is a knowledge of what is fitting. We have found all these elements, as well as temporality and presentation, in mimetic action. The reason is simple: mimetic action, as Gadamer has seen, is rooted in ritual and drama.

3

Narrative as Mimesis of Time

THROUGH MY READING of Gadamer I have isolated the complex character of mimesis that destroys classical and modernist notions of imitation but speaks to some of the domains of experience they articulated. Gadamer undoes classical imitation by interpreting mimesis in relation to social dramatic performance, interweaving its roots in cult and theater. For him mimetic action includes active, temporal, and presentational dimensions, and his mimetic strategy is an interpretation of the meaning of Being and the human participation in the event of truth.

Gadamer elucidates the dimensions of his hermeneutic in language (*logos, verbum*, concept), art (*Spiel*, festival, symbol or *Gebilde*), and understanding (dialogue, fusion of horizons, effective-historical consciousness). In each case, the mimetic character of these includes a transformation into figuration through which human belonging to world and tradition is mediated and presented. This belongingness is the condition of the possibility for human good. Practical wisdom (*phronesis*) struggles to enact this commonality into concrete social and personal existence. Hermeneutical reflection and the moral life are, then, acts of practical reason.

Gadamer provides us with an understanding of mimesis freed from Greek metaphysics, critical foundationalism, and Romantic expressionism. Against classic metaphysics, he understands being as the dynamic of self-presentation of world in which we are the participants; it is not a substance but the dynamic of reality. Being becomes meaningful in its transformation into figuration as "world," whether in art, understanding, or most generally in language. This means that Gadamer, as I read him, has developed a social, mimetic ontology.[1] The escape from Romantic expressionism is no less complete. Understanding is the creative refiguration of our belonging to tradition. What is presented is not the genius of the author but the transformation of our shared world. Understanding is fundamentally social. The travail of our existence is to enact a shared world as the condition of the possibility for all other dimensions of the human quest. Understanding, as mimetic, is a practical and deeply moral task. Genuine thinking is critical reflection on human praxis and shared world.

At this point we are pushed to think with and yet beyond Gadamer. That is, though he has helped us retrieve mimesis from the ashes of metaphysics, what of the problem of imitation at the level of text and self? Of course, Gadamer's hermeneutic does explore text and human practical existence. Yet his discussion of mimesis, as we saw, concentrates on ontological reflection. Given this, first, we must consider more specifically linguistic presentations, or texts, since these form the entrance point for interpreting the human dilemma and thus to self-understanding. Such understanding is the crown of an examined life, carried out in and through language by way of interpretation. Second, we must explore further the human orientation to the horizon of existence in order to isolate specifically religious and moral questions. Therefore, the systematic reason for moving beyond Gadamer is to address more explicitly textual mimesis and what can be discovered from it about the orientation of human existence calling for religious and moral reflection.

In this chapter my concern is to examine more closely the mediation of "world" and the human agent through language. I shall do so by exploring narrative as the most obvious example of the mimetic use of language, as thinkers from Aristotle to Paul Ricoeur attest. My concern is not simply with narrative as story, but more fundamentally with the mimetic character of language relative to agency. Any narrative conveys a story, of course. And different communities, whether religious or not, employ stories to shape their identity, express their fundamental beliefs about the world and human life, and structure their experience. Yet given that obvious fact, my concern in this chapter is not with the content of a specific community's story and its import for moral and religious existence, but with the more basic problem of the mimetic shape of narrative in relation to understanding and agency.[2] This is why Ricoeur's work is crucial to my argument. He argues that through mimetic narrative the human orientation to death and eternity, as the horizon of our temporality and hence a meaningful world, becomes exposed. Thus by turning to Ricoeur's work we can explore further the mimetic shape of language relative to our temporal condition.

This reading of Ricoeur coheres with his own understanding of the philosophic task. He has noted that "hermeneutical philosophy is a philosophy that has accepted all the demands of this long detour [of interpretation] and resists the dream of total mediation . . . of the self to itself as an absolute subject."[3] This means, moreover, that "there is no understanding of the self that is not mediated through signs, symbols, and texts; the understanding of the self coincides in the last instance with the interpretation that employs these mediating concepts."[4] Ricoeur understands hermeneutics in continuity and discontinuity with reflexive philosophy and phenomenology. These relations are important for grasping his interest in mimetic narrative.

First, contrary to the tradition of reflexive philosophy, which owes its modern expression to Descartes, there is for Ricoeur no simple primacy of the *cogito* or the possibility of a transparent, immediate relation of the "I" to itself. As he puts it, there is no total mediation of self to self. Given this, critical self-understanding cannot take the journey of direct introspection; it must make the detour of interpretation through texts, signs, and symbols. In a similar way, hermeneutics draws on and yet surpasses Husserlian phenomenology. Although phenomenological reflection has always insisted that consciousness is always *of* something and not simply of itself, for Ricoeur such reflection remains concerned with the intentionality of the subject. Yet there is, for him, no simple route to the meaning of this dynamic of consciousness. As we shall see, this is particularly the case with the problem of time. It becomes evident in the perplexing fact that there are two possible perspectives on time, the cosmological and the phenomenological, which, though always distinct, continually imply each other. Given this, a phenomenological account of time concerned solely with consciousness is not sufficient in itself to understand the experience of time. Some detour of interpretation is needed.

What hermeneutics does continue from phenomenology is the concern for the *Lebenswelt*, that life always takes place in some world of meaning. Hermeneutics does so, specifically, by exploring *Dasein*'s way of being-in-the-world as understanding, as Heidegger puts it. Here too, understanding is always mediated through interpretation, specifically of *Dasein*'s relation to the world in care. However, though Heidegger understands care (*Sorge*) as *Dasein*'s basic mood of being-in-the-world, he understands authentic care as a resoluteness in being toward death. Ricoeur, as we shall see, follows this turn to care, and does so from the paradigm of consciousness and intentionality, but he challenges the claim that being toward death is the sole authentic posture in life. Thus with phenomenology and Heideggerian hermeneutics Ricoeur turns to explore our being-in-the-world. Against these options he is concerned with the dynamic of the texts, not the intentional structure of consciousness, and he widens the scope of possible forms of authentic moods as ways to live in a world disclosed by these texts. Thus, as he puts it, "the task of hermeneutics, as I have said, is a double one: the reconstruction of the inner dynamic of texts and the restoration of the ability of the text itself to point from itself to the idea of a world in which I can dwell."[5]

Thus Ricoeur, following Heidegger and Gadamer, begins with human being-in-the-world. This perspective has several important implications. First, it entails a turn to the human, to *Dasein*, as the entrance point from which to explore "world" and Being. Yet because *Dasein* is always already in a world, the methodological turn to understanding does not lead to subjectivism or to only a philosophical anthropology. The concern is with fundamental ontology, specifically the problem of time. Nevertheless, Ricoeur's approach is in and through narrative configurations of human doing and suffering. Second, Ricoeur would agree with Richard Rorty that language "goes all the way down" and thus is the condition for all understanding.[6] But "all the way down" for Ricoeur means that our language reaches our being-in-the-world. Because of this, language can make referential claims; it is not a system closed in on itself. Language breaks beyond itself in practical existence, as we shall see.

Because language is the medium of world, it is possible to discern some general characteristics of our worldliness. Ricoeur does so through the interrelation of temporality, language, imagination, and feeling. What is crucial for my argument is the way the pre-understanding of our being in the world is itself understood. By reading *Time and Narrative*, we shall see that Ricoeur, following Aristotle, takes the pre-understanding of narrative to be the order of purposive human action. The basic problematic is the relation of the poetic configuration (plot) to the given world of human commerce and interaction.[7] This means that although Ricoeur begins with action, he ends with insight into the human experience of time through the interpretation of narratives.

Given Ricoeur's place in the development of thought from reflexive philosophy to post-Heideggerian hermeneutics, his mimetic strategy takes on particular significance for my argument. First, it suggests that the examination of life, as a task of ethics, is carried out in part through the interpretation of signs, symbols, and texts that open the possibility of understanding human being-in-the-world. In this regard, his work on mimesis mediates my interpretation of understanding in world in the previous chapter and the problem of the self in the next. Second, Ricoeur's challenge to the primacy of being toward death as the fundamental mood of authentic life is important for my argument. As we have seen, the question of human solidarity as the good of the human is the pressing question for Gadamer. And for Kierkegaard, it is the passion for existence, not being toward death, that marks the authentic life as one of faithful discipleship. In word, Ricoeur's mimetic strategy not only provides a way to understand the interpretive detour on the way to understanding; it also opens up inquiry into the basic affective and passional shape of the human condition. And, finally, Ricoeur's reflection of narrated time itself raises questions for religious thinking that turn us back to Gadamer and move us forward toward Kierkegaard and beyond.

To aid in reading Ricoeur I want to foreshadow some of my argument, as I did with Gadamer. First, through metaphor Ricoeur works out his claim for the referential power of language with its implications for religious reflection. Moreover, he sees *Time and Narrative*, which contains the main discussion of mimesis, as a companion to *The Rule of Metaphor*. The discussion of metaphor and imagination sets the context for the claims to truth Ricoeur wants to make for mimetic narrative.[8] It also returns us to the problem of language I bracketed in the last chapter.

Second, Ricoeur's concern, in his discussion of mimesis, is the way narrative relates to cosmological and phenomenological accounts of time. He develops a complex mimetic strategy, which he calls the "threefold mimesis." Within each of the aspects of mimesis there are three elements: action, temporality, and "symbol." His reading of mimesis, I contend, is best seen in the framework of Gadamer's mimetic strategy outlined earlier. What Ricoeur does is to concentrate more specifically on the act of figuration in plot and reading.

He speaks of narrative as the "con-figuration" ("with-figuration" or with-*Gebilde*) of the prefigured order of lived experience. By interpreting narratives, the reader, in an act of imagination, refigures lived temporal experience. One refigures human time within a dual orientation to death and eternity by interpreting and appropriating fictive and historical configurations that help generate identity. This allows narrative to be seen as the mimesis of human action and thus opens up the question of the act of being human. Ricoeur pushes us in this direction when he notes that "to speak of the identity of an individual or of a community is to answer the question: *Who* has done such action? *Who* is the agent, the author? . . . Without recourse to narrative, the problem of individual identity is in effect given up to an antinomy without solution . . . " (III 355/246).[9] He goes on to speak of narrative identity (*l'identité narrative*) as the solution to the antinomy of self-identity in a diversity of acts.

Third, Ricoeur turns to mimesis at the level of lived experience, plot, and the act of reading. In doing so he destroys classical imitation theory at the epistemological and aesthetic levels. As he notes, the act of reading brings forth the refiguration of human world. In fact, "without the reader who accompanies it, there is no configuring act at work in the text; and without a reader to appropriate it, there is no world deployed in front of the text" (III 239/164). The moment of refiguration, where there is a crossed reference (*référence croisée*) between fictive and historical configurations of time, requires a reader. Ricoeur even states that the "effects of fiction, effects of revelation and transformation, are essentially effects of reading. It is by way of reading that literature returns to life, that is, to the practical and affective field of existence" (III 149/101; cf. I 116–17/76–77). In reading, text and life meet.

Narrative, then, is not an icon, an imitation, of its subject matter outside of human action. Narrative mimesis must be reconsidered around human action, and so too its revelatory power. Narratives are disclosive of our lot and life only because they are anchored in human temporality and action and, in historical narratives, in some relation to "cosmological" time over against consciousness. This makes the act of reading a refiguration of our prefigured lives inasmuch as there is a crossing of fictive and historical figurations of time. Two issues emerge from this. First, how do we understand narrative identity, how does the self come to be? Kierkegaard will help us address this question. Second, Ricoeur speaks of the mediation of historical time into a unified whole as a practical task guided by the idea of one humanity and one history (III 370–71/258–59).[10] This leads us back to Gadamer's concern for the shared world of human solidarity.

Thus Ricoeur's thought draws us forward to Kierkegaard through the idea of narrative identity and back to Gadamer in the discussion of mimesis and the practical idea of one humanity and history. My reading seeks to show how narrative configuration mediates world and agency even as it depends on them for its meaning and truthfulness. Narrative mediates self and world because in it language (the medium of world) and human action meet in a temporal horizon. Given this, narrative provides the paradigmatic example of the mimetic power of language.

Finally, my central claim is that mimesis articulates the relation of understanding, in its ontological depth, and action, in its temporal ambiguity and orientation. In a word, Being and time are understood through metaphor and narrative, and the relation between them is expressed in mimesis. If this interpretation is plausible, then we have a way to grasp the metaphoric and narrative shape of reflection as itself mimetic and related to human being and doing. Thus though all discourse and texts involve metaphor and narrative, they are best understood as mimetic: figurative presentations of the intersection of human temporality and being that call for interpretation.[11]

My reading of Ricoeur will concentrate on his principal discussions of mimesis found in *The Rule of Metaphor*[12] and *Time and Narrative*. Even the most superficial comparison of these works shows his concern: to explore the disclosive power of language through metaphor and narrative in order to address aporias of thought and temporality vis-à-vis human action. But Ricoeur's project is more complex than a simple theory of reference. Basically he is interested in developing a hermeneutic that follows an arch from a pre-understanding of our being-in-the-world, a first naïveté, through critique and explanation, to a new post-critical understanding of our relation and interaction with the world, namely, to a second naïveté.[13] In a word, his hermeneutic articulates and interrelates the classical threefold task of literary hermeneutics—understanding (*subtilitas intelligendi*), explanation (*subtilitas explicandi*), and application (*subtilitas applicandi*)—and it does so in the search for critical understanding. His reading of mimesis instanciates these three concerns.[14]

The logic of this chapter is to discern Ricoeur's mimetic strategy in relation to our shared world and the self. My argument will contextualize the discussion of mimesis in claims about metaphor, and then explore his specific claims about narrative and its limits.

MIMESIS, METAPHOR, AND LANGUAGE

In reading Gadamer, I isolated the metaphoric character of knowing as rooted in the *Spiel* of Being. That is, Being comes to be understood *as* something through a mimetic transformation into figuration. Understanding involves, therefore, seeing something *as* something, as a figurative presentation of reality. We know this "thing" *as* a tree, a double figuration of Being in the actual tree and in our language. What ultimately is understood in Gadamer's hermeneutic philosophy is the common world of the human through its presentation in art, tradition, and language. Ricoeur, in *The Rule of Metaphor*, also explores the relation of mimesis, metaphor, and Being. That is, metaphor as a specific kind of linguistic action forms one context for Ricoeur's reading of mimesis just as *Spiel* did for Gadamer. In both metaphor and narrative, as Stephan Strasser has noted, "something new arises thanks to a synthesis of heterogeneous elements. The productive imagination [*die produktive Einbildungskraft*] plays the roll of a matrix here: it originates a new 'schema' that makes a higher form of intelligibility possible."[15] Given this, we must isolate the dynamics of metaphor and imagination on the way to understanding Ricoeur's mimetic strategy.

Ricoeur's first concern is the relation between poetics and rhetoric precisely because metaphor belongs to both spheres of discourse. Behind this relation lies a difference. Rhetoric is the "art of inventing proofs," of persuasive argument. The poet, however, is to "compose an essential representation of human action." Given this difference, Ricoeur sets out to discuss the structure of metaphor against the background of persuasion and the poetic arts. This allows the interpretation of metaphoric reference to shift from the level of the word or noun to that of the sentence or discourse. He notes that while Aristotle's *Poetics* relates metaphor to parts of diction, in the *Rhetoric* metaphor is understood relative to the modes of speech. The history of criticism has related metaphor to the noun. Ricoeur's basic task is to attempt a theory of metaphor at the level of discourse. As he notes:

> The bearer of the metaphorical meaning is no longer the word but the sentence as a whole. The interaction process does not merely consist of the substitution of a word for a word, of a name for a name—which, strictly speaking, defines only metonymy—but an interaction between the logical subject and a predicate. If metaphor consists in some deviance, . . . this deviance concerns the predicative structure itself.[16]

Ricoeur seeks to develop an interaction theory of metaphor, as he calls it, as opposed to a substitutionary one. Metaphor is not the substitution of one word for another but the clash of semantic fields between literal and nonliteral statements. Metaphor involves, therefore, deviant predication rather than deviant denomination, and shifts the discussion of metaphor to the level of the sentence and the interaction of the logical subject and predicate.

Ricoeur's emphasis on the function of rhetoric and poetics allows both a move from the noun to the sentence as the locus of metaphoric reference, and a concentration on audience or reader reception as itself related to the basic constitution of metaphor. He contends that metaphor, "or better to metaphorize, that is, the dynamic of metaphor . . . [rests], therefore, on the perception of resemblance" (RM 24). This perception of resemblance by a reader is basic to metaphor, and permits Ricoeur to follow a twofold trajectory in his analysis.

On the one hand, our ability to see resemblances opens up the possibility of exploring the productive imagination of the poet and the audience as the grounds for the possibility of that perception. Imagination is the transcendental correlate to the semantic clash inscribed in metaphor at the level of the sentence.

Our insight into similarity-in-difference is a synthetic operation of the productive imagination relative to metaphor. As he says, imagination "is this 'ability' to produce new kinds by assimilation and to produce them not 'above' the differences as in the concept, but in spite of and through the differences."[17] On the other hand, the notion of resemblance provides the ground for Ricoeur's discussion of sense and reference in the metaphoric process. "This brings us very close to our most extreme hypothesis: that the 'metaphoric' that transgresses the categorical order also begets it" (RM 24). Such an understanding of reference is crucial to Ricoeur's formulation of "split reference" or, as he puts it in *Time and Narrative*, intersection or crossed reference in narrative refiguration. Although he readily admits to having abandoned in this later work the terminology of sense and reference in favor of configuration and refiguration, it is important to understand his claims for narrative in the context of metaphoric truth.[18] Poetic discourse is about the world, but is so by an indirect strategy that suspends regular description.

By isolating the functions of rhetoric and poetics, Ricoeur opens up a new interpretation of metaphor and metaphoric reference. However, in terms of my argument it is interesting to note what he has passed over. Ricoeur claims that although rhetoric arose out of oratory, before that "there was undisciplined common speech [*l'usage sauvage de la parole*]," and notes that the "properly dramatic character of rhetorical activity is explained by the 'savage' roots of rhetoric" (RM 10). His discussion of rhetoric and mimesis touches on Plato only as a step to Aristotle. That is, he never examines the domain of cultic action isolated by Gadamer. Thus his inquiry into the tradition of reflection on mimesis stops with Aristotle. What he does not consider is the possibility that mimesis and metaphor may have been re-interpreted and applied to poetics or rhetoric from dramatic and cultic activity. That is what I have attempted to do with Gadamer's help, and why a narratology must rest on a notion of mimesis developed vis-à-vis understanding and language. Yet given this, we can still draw insights from Ricoeur on the mimetic power of language.

Given the location of his argument, it is not surprising that Ricoeur isolates features of the Aristotelian understanding of metaphor important for his treatment of mimesis. For Aristotle, metaphor is something that happens to the noun. It is defined in terms of movement. Metaphor is a kind of displacement or transposition; it is, specifically, the transposition of a name. Aristotle's understanding of metaphor is one of substitution at the level of the noun. What interests Ricoeur in all this is the notion of transposition. From this he advances an hypothesis. By centering on the *relationship* between the pairs in metaphoric activity it is possible to understand metaphor as a phenomenon productive of meaning through categorical transgression. Ricoeur claims that "metaphor destroys an order only to invent a new one; and that the category-mistake is nothing but the complement of a logic of discovery. . . . [M]etaphor bears information because it 'redescribes' reality. Thus the category-mistake is the de-constructive intermediary phase between description and redescription" (RM 22). The semantic impertinence of the metaphoric predication is a means to redescribe the world. From this Ricoeur goes on to claim that there is a "metaphoric" at work at the origin of all logical thought. Metaphoric reference exceeds the bounds of the linguistic system; it is a path of insight. But insight into what?

In his earlier work, Ricoeur follows Frege in making a distinction between sense (*Sinn*) and reference (*Bedeutung*). "The sense is 'what' the proposition states; the reference or denotation is 'that about which' the sense is stated" (RM 217). This basic division marks out different disciplines of study: semiotics explores sense while semantics is concerned with reference. This has important implications for the relating of signs to discourse and the releasing of mimesis from its domination by a theory of signs. Ricoeur makes the distinction this way:

> [The] implication of the distinction between semiotics and semantics that concerns us here is the following: grounded on the predicative act, what is intended by discourse points to an extra-linguistic reality which is its referent. Whereas the sign points back only to other signs immanent within a system, discourse is about things. Signs differ from signs; discourse refers to the world. Difference is semiotic; reference is semantic . . . [RM 216].

Ricoeur's concern is to break the closed wall of language created by concentrating, as forms of structuralism have, on the logic of signs. He does so through metaphor and narrative. What is important for my argument is the way he understands the referential act.

Most particularly, semantic impertinence is "the violation of the code of pertinence or relevance which rules the ascription of predicates in ordinary use. The metaphoric statement works as the reduction of this syntagmatic deviance by the establishment of a new semantic pertinence."[19] All this takes place at the level of predication where something is predicated of something else or judged as another. Such predicative acts demand an insight into similarities between subject and predicate in order to produce and/or understand metaphoric predication. At this point the semantic question once again implicates the imagination. I shall return to this in a moment.

Through the semantic impertinence of the metaphor, meaning is generated. This impertinence, stated most pointedly, is the clash between literal description or predication and nonliteral predication. A person's disposition, for instance, is and is not "sunny." The clash between the literal and the nonliteral generates a new way of seeing the world. It is a world portrayed and redescribed by the text that suspends literal description, and this "world" is what Ricoeur means by the semantic import of the text. The structure of the work is its sense, but the *world* of the work is its reference. "Or to put it another way, discourse in the literary work sets out its denotation as a second-level denotation, by means of the suspension of the first-level denotation of discourse" (RM 221). Ricoeur calls this a theory of "split reference." This means that poetic discourse refers to the world, but does so through an indirect strategy of suspending normal predication. The poetic reference establishes another world having analogical relation to our lived experience.[20] Metaphoric reference allows us to see the world "as" it is depicted poetically. Metaphor, as a transformation into figuration, spells an increase in meaning: something is understood *as* or *like* something else. The Reign of God, for instance, is seen *as* a mustard seed in one of the parables of Jesus.[21]

Metaphoric reference implies and establishes an analogy or resemblance between the metaphorized world and the world of common predication. Insight is precisely the grasping of that relation through the structure of the world; it is a synthetic act in and through the metaphor itself.[22] This analogy and its attendant synthetic act are the backing for the claim to truth by metaphoric statements. They are made possible by several layers of tension in metaphor: between a principal subject (literal) and a secondary subject (nonliteral); between a literal and a nonliteral interpretation; and in the relational function of the copula (to be) between "identity and difference in the interplay of resemblance." I have already explored the first tension, that is, between literal and nonliteral claims. The third tension, the ontological dimension of poetic discourse, will concern us only at the end of our reading of Ricoeur. The second tension regarding forms of interpretation moves us beyond metaphoric structure to interpretation and hence to the imagination.

Ricoeur has noted that his theory of the imagination is an attempt to understand it in relation to a theory of semantic innovation. He is aware of the problems in speaking of the imagination, the principal one being the relation of imagination and image with its logic. That relation sets up two different axes along which Western philosophy has historically understood the imagination, both of which are infested with traditional assumptions about imitation.

One axis concerns the status of the image and ranges from presence to absence. That is, the "image" both is present in the mind and yet represents something not present. On this reading the imagination forms an image of what, strictly speaking, is absent and transcendent. At one end of this axis, image is related to perception as a trace and a matter of the reproductive imagination. At the other, "the image is thought of essentially in relation to absence, of other-than-present, the various key figures of the productive imagination all refer[ring] in different ways to this fundamental otherness."[23] The other axis on which imagination has been understood concerns consciousness as fanciful or critical. Coleridge, as noted in the first chapter, distinguishes between two powers of the imagination. The range here is from the confusion of image and reality in pure fancy to the point at which "the critical distance is fully aware of itself, [and] imagination serves as the instrument in the critique of reality."[24] Imagination understood in this way clearly draws on Romantic mimesis and its theory of image.

Now, these two axes arose because imagination has traditionally been defined by its relation to perception. Ricoeur, for his part, proposes to understand it around a type of language use: the semantic innovation of metaphoric discourse. This shift undoes a spectator or representational theory of knowledge and its reliance on imitation theory. The imagination is discursive in character.

Metaphor, as we saw, produces a shock between semantic fields. Imagination is operative precisely in mediating this shock.

> Imagination is apperception, the sudden view, of a new predicative pertinence. This could be called "predicative assimilation" in order to stress the point that resemblance itself is a process of the same nature as the predicative itself. None of this is taken from the old association of ideas as it relates to the mechanical attraction of mental atoms. Imagining is first and foremost restructuring semantic fields. It is, to use Wittgenstein's expression in the *Philosophical Investigations*, "seeing as. . . ." In this we find what is essential to the Kantian theory of the schematism. Schematism, Kant said, is a method for giving an image to a concept. And again, schematism is a rule for producing images.[25]

Imagining, then, is not having mental pictures but "display[ing] relations in a depicting mode." The imagination is a mimetic activity of transforming basic relations into figuration. It is a synthetic operation. Through this operation new configurations of meaning are produced. The imagination is the transcendental correlate of semantic innovation. Indeed, Ricoeur has consistently argued that the imagination is, in the Kantian sense, a schematizing of this synthetic operation through metaphor and narrative. As he notes, the "imagination is this competence, this ability, to produce new logical spaces through predicative assimilation, and it produces them in spite of—and thanks to—the initial differences between times that oppose assimilation."[26] The imagination is productive through a schematizing act.

Ricoeur argues that the imagination is operative at the personal level through the projection of courses of action in accordance with some anticipatory schema. It is also at work on the social level through ideology and utopia as critical projections for action. Thus imagination is a way of insight and critique. Its imaginal products may function as regulative ideas for moral and political action.[27] In fact, we shall see that in *Time and Narrative* III he claims that one aporia of temporality (the plural *ek-stases* of time within the unity of history) requires a practical idea of one humanity and one history to render it productive for human action. Thus the imagination renders the paradox of our temporal experience morally and politically productive. Likewise, the aporia of personal temporal experience, as we shall also see, requires the practical idea of narrative identity. The imagination mediates individual and communal identity and courses of action. What is striking is that Ricoeur retrieves the Kantian productive imagination on a linguistic level. When we turn to mimesis, we shall see how imagination is related to time. This will mark Ricoeur's complete recasting of Kant's theory of the imagination in order to bridge the semantic innovation of metaphor and plot as the production of mediating synthesis in the midst of semantic impertinence, and as the grasping together of the manifold of events into a fictive, narrative whole.

Thus far I have been tracing the productive aspect of the imagination or the poetic act of making metaphors and fictive narratives. The productive imagination is also operative in interpretation. This is particularly the case when the metaphoric reference is to a world "in front of the text."

> [T]he meaning of a text lies not behind the text but in front of it. The meaning is not something hidden but something disclosed. What gives rise to understanding is that which points towards a possible world, by means of the non-ostensive references of the text. Texts speak of possible worlds and of possible ways of orienting oneself in these worlds. . . . Interpretation thus becomes the apprehension of the proposed worlds which are opened up by the non-ostensive references of the text.[28]

Interpretation follows an arch from pre-understanding through the configuration of the world in the poetic text to appropriation of the world displayed by it.[29] This appropriation is between the reader's world and the world of the text. I shall explore this process further when we turn to *Time and Narrative*. At this point in our reading we can say that the act of appropriation is an imaginative one.

Ricoeur's notion of metaphor rests, then, on a shift from the priority of the word to the priority of the sentence. Metaphoric reference arises from the clash of literal and nonliteral claims, and through this clash insight into our world is won. We see the world *as* metaphorically depicted. Metaphorizing and interpreting require an act of imagination that renders productive the semantic clash of metaphor. Metaphor "redescribes" the world through figuration. Given this, metaphor interlocks epistemological and ontological elements at the level of both language and imagination.

Ricoeur has made this point forcefully. "I dare to say," he writes, "that to see something as . . . means to make manifest the *being as* of the object. I place the 'as' in the position of a clarification of the verb 'to be,' and I make out with the *being as* the last reference of the metaphorical expression."[30] Thus Ricoeur claims that metaphor opens up ontological reflection: being has an "as" structure, a synthetic power known figuratively as presented. Given this, we can say, along with Gadamer, that metaphor and imagination are transformations into figuration through which there is an increase in meaning and Being.

Metaphor seems to be the mimetic power of language at the level of the sentence, the smallest unit of meaning. The question now becomes: How do we understand larger units of discourse, say texts, also as mimetic? With that question we turn to *Time and Narrative* where we shall see the same strategy worked out through mimetic narrative. Indeed, as Ricoeur puts it, "the mimesis of narrative works and the distinction of the threefold mimesis—prefiguration, configuration, refiguration of the world of action through the poem—expresses that endeavor to unite the precision of analysis with ontological determination."[31]

MIMESIS IN NARRATIVE AND ACTION

The Rule of Metaphor and *Time and Narrative* form a pair because both are concerned with semantic innovation.

> With metaphor the innovation consists in the production of a new semantic pertinence by means of an impertinent attribution. . . . With narrative [*le récit*] the semantic innovation consists in the invention of a plot [*intrigue*] which, also, is a work of synthesis. In both cases the semantic innovation is carried back to the productive imagination and, more precisely, to the schematism which is its signifying matrix [I 11/ix].

Understanding a metaphor is grasping the new semantic pertinence from the ruin of the clash of literal and nonliteral predication. Understanding a plot is grasping the "operation which unifies it into a whole and complete action." The parallel between metaphor and plot exceeds epistemological claims. Ricoeur notes that mimetic narrative is a particular application of metaphoric reference to the sphere of human action.

For Ricoeur, mimesis, it would seem, is controlled by a general metaphorics even though, with Gadamer, we can understand metaphor as itself mimetic. Nevertheless, Ricoeur sees mimesis controlled by a notion of metaphoric truth grounding logic while being located within the field of narrative and human action. As he notes, it "is in the capacity of fiction to refigure this temporal experience, prey to the aporias of philosophical speculation, that the referential function of plot resides" (I 13/xi). Thus Ricoeur's entire discussion of mimesis falls within the compass of a metaphorics of truth and theory of narrative. And the problems of language, time, and action form the horizon of his discussion. In this he has broken from the logic of classical imitation while still exploring problems it sought to address, problems like that of knowing through figures.

The general problem that *Time and Narrative* addresses is, most simply put, the relation of narrative and time. More specifically, Ricoeur hopes through narrative to explore the relation of phenomenological approaches to time, centering on human internal consciousness, and cosmological theories that isolate time in natural motion. Here again we see how mimesis is employed to think and speak of the mediation of the human and its world, now relative to the problems of time. The "mimetic activity of narrative," Ricoeur notes, "is perhaps schematically characterized as the invention of a third-time [*tiers-*

temps| . . . " (III 354/245). This third-time is a mediation of phenomenological and cosmological time through the making of a plot. We shall grasp the importance of this "third-time" later in relation to the aporias of temporality. Indeed, Ricoeur wagers that narrativity helps render productive the constant aporias of temporality even as these aporias mark out the limits of narrative.

Ricoeur begins by turning to St. Augustine in order to isolate the discordance that infests our desire for concordance in lived experience. That is, he finds in Augustine a "phenomenological" approach to time that concentrates on the "soul" and its experience of time, an approach that, in Ricoeur's eyes, is enriched by Husserl. He finds in Aristotle, and then in a more subtle form in Kant, an objective account of time relative to the soul. These two approaches form the arena for Ricoeur's reflection on time and narrative. Although my concern is not to explore these various thinkers, it is important to place Ricoeur's discussion of narrative within this dual history of reflection on time. He hopes to show the levels of discordance and concordance in our experience of time and in fictive and historical narratives as they cross and inform each other. The aporias of temporality are rendered productive by the reader in the cross-referencing of experience and objective time so that they inform each other through narrative configuration. In this sense, narrative renders practically productive the *Fremdheit* of objective and subjective accounts and experiences of time.

To isolate the details of Ricoeur's mimetic strategy, it is helpful to grasp in cursory fashion what he means by mimesis. Most succintly put, his concern is to ask "what happens to the *mimesis praxeos*, to the mimetic activity applied to human action (and suffering), when we make the question of time the touchstone of the meaning of this mimesis?"[32] Thus although Ricoeur continues to understand mimesis relative to action and *mythos*, as Aristotle did, he reclaims the notion by understanding it vis-à-vis time.

In *Time and Narrative* I Ricoeur describes aspects of mimesis that are found throughout the hermeneutical trajectory. His task is to illumine the arch between everyday lived time, its configuration in fictive or historical narratives, and its reception and appropriation in reading as a return to lived practical existence. The reader is crucial to this movement since she or he brings together life and narrative, thereby refiguring experience and rendering productive narrative emplotment. The act of reading constitutes the relation of time and narrative and, specifically, the crossing of fictive and historical figurations of time. And as we shall see, this intersection of narrative and time happens at the level of the agent, history, and temporality itself.[33]

Ricoeur isolates three aspects of mimesis: lived experience, narrative, and reading. In each aspect there are three elements: action, symbolic expression of the significance of experience, and the temporality of lived experience. Thus his notion of mimesis is actually threefold, and in each aspect of mimesis there are three component elements. It should be clear that Ricoeur's threefold mimesis, with its internal complexity, articulates, in more specific terms, the character of mimesis that I isolated by reading Gadamer. Mimesis includes action and self-movement, a temporal structure, and symbolic or figurative dimensions. Gadamer used mimesis to explore understanding and the presentation of human world, the coming to meaningfulness of Being. Ricoeur is concerned more with the narrative configuration of human temporal experience as this helps us understand and render intelligible the paradoxes of our temporal existence. He moves us more explicitly into considering the place of narrative in theological and ethical reflection even as he opens up the question of the self, the agent, for further inquiry. I take this reading of mimesis as a helpful refinement vis-à-vis human action and time of the mimetic strategy discerned in Gadamer's hermeneutic.

Ricoeur calls the prefigured order of human action Mimesis I (M1). The practical order of acting and suffering, including interaction with others, is marked off from mere motion by the fact that actions have goals, motives, and, most important, agents. Action is also deeply temporal. After all, we act through and in time; our being and doing are a temporalizing of Being. Finally, experience is given its significance through the cultural symbols we employ to articulate the meaning of experience and ourselves as agents. M1 is the backing for the intelligibility of narrative in these three areas. That is, narrative is understandable relative to human actions and agents the temporal structure of experience as past/present/future, and the fact that human action is always already shaped by cultural signs, rules, and norms. In this way, M1 provides the condition of the possibility for narrative while emplotment, or Mimesis II (M2), configures the order of action. As Ricoeur puts it "time becomes human time in the measure that it is articulated in the narrative mode, and narrative attains its full significance when it becomes a condition of temporal existence" (I 85/52).

M1 marks out the domain of lived experience prior to narrative configuration. M2 is the emplotment of M1 through the composition of a plot, or what Aristotle meant by *mythos*. Plot has a threefold mediating function that corresponds to the levels of each element of mimesis. First, it mediates individual events into a story as a whole. As Aristotle put it, the poet is the maker of a plot that brings episodes together. Next, plot mediates discordant elements, like reversals of fate, with agents, intentions, goals, and the like. In this way plot has within itself discordant elements even as it creates a concordant whole. Finally, plot mediates the temporal characteristics of action, in two ways: it relates action chronologically in the sequence of episodes that are narrated; and it mediates time in "the configurational dimension properly speaking, thanks to which the plot transforms the events into a story" (I 103/66). Ricoeur explicitly relates this configuration to the Kantian notion of a synthetic judgment. In fact, each mediation of plot relies on some synthesis of a manifold into a whole. We have already seen with Gadamer that mimesis is a way to think about synthetic power, but here it is expressed at the level of plot. M2 mediates, then, the prefigured order of action (M1) and understanding through interpretation. Understanding is always won through interpreting life transformed into a figurative presentation.

Finally, Ricoeur argues that "a new quality of time emerges" when the reader can view the whole story and understand the episodes that make it up. Mimesis III (M3) is precisely this act of reading and understanding that refigures practical existence. "By refiguration," he notes, "I mean, therefore, the power of revelation and transformation achieved by narrative configurations when they are 'applied' to actual acting and suffering."[34] What is important about M3 is that it constitutes the arch between the real world of action and its configured emplotment. In reading, life is refigured even as the referential power of narrative is released; a world is disclosed in front of the text and life (potentially) transformed.

Like M1 and M2, M3 manifests each of the elements of mimesis. Reading is an act through which experience is refigured and identity is engendered. M3 entails a "symbolic" refiguration of the world of experience that marks out the possibilities and limitations of narrative reference by crossing history and fiction. Finally, M3 suggests a poetic solution to the aporias of time by rendering them practically productive. I shall return to this later since the aporias of time will lead us beyond Ricoeur to Kierkegaard. The point now is that M3, the act of reading, is understood through the elements common to each aspect of mimesis even as it designates the refiguration of the world of the reader through interpretation.

With this sketch of Ricoeur's mimetic strategy in hand I now want to explore it in greater depth. By doing so I shall develop a mimetic vocabulary for reflection and open areas for further substantive inquiry. My plan of reading is to begin with plot (M2) and move back and forth in its relation to prefigured experience (M1) and reading (M3). My purpose here is not to recount Ricoeur's analysis of the various theories of time he explores. I shall not examine the contrasts between history and fiction, as he does, or the intricate dual history of thought about time in "phenomenological" and "cosmological" positions. My concern throughout is Ricoeur's understanding of mimesis and narrative.

Ricoeur sets out to explore plot (*intrique*) as the poetic triumph of concordance over discordance, and mimetic activity (mimesis) as the creative figuration in plot of lived temporal action. Ricoeur seeks to separate these two aspects of plot, related in Aristotle's *Poetics*, while citing "all the notations in the text of Aristotle which suggest a relation of reference between the 'poetic' text and the real 'ethical' world" (I 55/27). He is clear on two points about Aristotle. First, poetic activity for Aristotle is not marked by a temporal character. Only if one explores mimesis vis-à-vis human action, and not simply plot, will the narrative figuration of temporality enter the discussion. Plot can then be seen as the artistic schematization or figuration of temporal experience into a concordant whole, whether in fiction or historical narrative. Second, Ricoeur is aware of the ambiguous relation in Aristotle between ethics and poetics. Ricoeur's distinction without separation of *mythos* and *mimesis* is the attempt to relate ethics and poetics: through plot something of the human condition is disclosed, while mimesis is grounded in the world and order of human action.

Ricoeur's specific concern is to develop a notion of what he calls interweaving reference (*référence croisée*) between fictive and historical narratives. His reading of plot, despite its revisions, follows Aristotle's *Poetics* at key points. "The mimesis of Aristotle," Ricoeur notes, "has one space in which it is unfolded: human making [*faire*], the art of composition" (I 60/34). This warrants the separation, for the sake of analysis, of plot (the organization of events) from the imitation or presentation of action (mimesis). Actually the action or the mimesis is the poetic construction of the plot itself as a figuration of action. This gives priority, as Aristotle said, to action over character in narrative. Plot is human action in a depicted mode. This is true of fictive narratives and of historical ones as well, although they are also grounded in historical "traces" and a sense of a debt to the past, as Ricoeur puts it. We might say that historical narratives draw on the reproductive imagination. In any case, the actual making of plots is an action of the productive imagination. And although action takes precedence over character in Aristotle's poetics, character is still important since noble or bad characters are the ethical criterion for the distinctiveness of tragedy. That said, the emphasis and abiding concern of Aristotle and Ricoeur are with plot.

Ricoeur interprets Aristotle's *Poetics* along two lines that intersect in plot. Each line correlates the structure of plot with a particular form of audience reception. Poetic configuration is the meeting of these lines or vectors. The first line correlates the making of plots as a whole and the pleasure of learning through recognition. This is the level of concordance and disconcordant episodes found in *mythos*. Accordingly, Ricoeur speaks of a "literary hermeneutic" that centers on "the primitive relation of knowledge and enjoyment that ensures the aesthetic quality of literary hermeneutics" (III 255–56/174). This relation reaches back to Aristotle, who explained that humans are the most mimetic of animals because we take pleasure in learning. This pleasure, Ricoeur argues, is related to bringing concordance to disconcordant elements.

The second line relates reversal in plot (*peripeteia*) and *catharsis* as it is found in plot and in the reader's response. These concern moments of discordance in the midst of concordant *mythos*. At this juncture Ricoeur speaks of the difference between types of readings. The first, "*la lecture innocente*," is a reading that enjoys the immediacy of pleasure. Rereading, as "*lecture distancée*," critically clarifies and questions the text and naïve readings. "A dialectic of expectation and of questions rules the relation between reading and rereading. Expectations are open but also more indeterminate, and questions are determinate but also more exclusive" (III 257/175). Here a third reading emerges, corresponding to the third-time noted above, which, we might say, holds pleasure and learning together, rendering productive the aporias of time in interpretation. Roughly, this is, if James Redfield is correct, what Aristotle means by *catharsis*. That is, *catharsis* is both a resolution in the plot of its manifold elements and the insight into the human condition gained by audience/reader reasoning out the plot.[35] By interpreting narrative we reason out our temporal experience and hence gain insight into the way specific kinds of characters act in particular situations. Narratives make the possible actual through figuration. Learning is achieved through reasoning out the plot relative to its own internal resolution.

These lines of pleasure/learning cross in plot. Two separate imaginative acts are found on each line and in their crossing: synthetic production and synthetic judgment. Thus Ricoeur has set up a complex strategy within the general rubrics of Aristotle's *Poetics*, one coherent with this notion of metaphor and imagination. Each line correlates production and *reception*, while the whole is inscribed in the poetic configuration. I want to explore this strategy further on the way to the aporias of temporality.

Plot is a "*modele de concordance*" through the arrangement of events. Plots are to be complete, whole, and of proper magnitude, as Aristotle said. For Ricoeur the notion of the whole (*horos*) is central. The whole does not have a temporal character but rather a logical one since wholeness is defined only in relation to a logical sequence of beginning, middle, and end. Plot is a "singular collective" of a manifold, an insight crucial to the aporias of temporality to be explored later. The same applies to magnitude as well. The plot is to be suitable in length. Artistic plot delimits, circumscribes, time. The "logic" of the plot is the internal connection that is not controlled by chronology but affords insight into temporal experience by ordering events into a whole.

Through the reductive and abstractive act of making plots, something is accomplished and shown. The ordering of the events is an act of "mythic intelligence." And it affords learning with pleasure as the telos of poetics.

Apprehending, concluding, and recognizing the form: here we have the skeleton of meaning for the pleasure found in imitation (or of representation). But if it is not a question of philosophical universals, what are these "poetic universals"? That they are universals, that is not doubted, because they can be characterized by the double opposition of the possible to the actual and of the general to the particular [I 68/40].

The sort of universality which plot comports derives from its order, which makes its completeness and its wholeness. . . . they are universals related to practical wisdom, and hence to ethics and politics [I 70/41].

What is displayed is the internal order of action as a unified manifold of experience. The act of making plots lets the universal, as Ricoeur says, "spring forth" because it is the making of a logical coherent order. As the narrative is viewed or read, the audience/reader has the experience of reasoning out the plot and thereby learns something about experience. This is the pleasure of recognition or insight into order in the flux of discordant lived experience. Ricoeur concludes that this pleasure of recognition presupposes "a prospective concept of truth, according to which to invent is to discover [*retrouver*]" (I 70/42). This prospective notion of truth coheres with the intentional nature of metaphoric reference. Therefore mimesis inscribes for Ricoeur a theory of metaphoric truth at the level of plot. The imaginative act of making a plot, when coupled with the act of reading, is to discover something about human time.

The making and reasoning out of plots is a pathway of insight into human action. As Redfield notes, "fiction is the outcome of a law of inquiry."[36] This making is not sheer creativity since it is the mimesis of the order or logic of action. Still, it is genuine making because it is the synthetic ordering of a manifold of episodes allowing the intelligible to spring forth. *Mythos* is controlled by a logic and intelligibility rendered through the poetic act and the reasoning out of the narrative. Put differently: the making of plot renders meaningful the already intelligible order of action.

The tragic plot is not pure concordance, however. It is, as Ricoeur calls it, "discordant concordance." In the midst of the plot are changes of fortune. Heroes fall, dreams are won or lost in the reversal of a narrative. These changes test the concordance of the plot. And it is the structure of the plot that engenders *catharis*, the purgation of pity and fear. The second line of Ricoeur's presentation is tied to the relation of plot reversals and emotion. As with the first line of his reading, these remain bound to the poetic structure and the activity of the reader.

According to Aristotle, the changes of complex plots include reversals (*peripeteia*), recognition (*anagnorisis*), and suffering (*pathos*) (*Poetics* 1452a–1452b). A complex plot provides paradox in its causal network. The change in fortune relates closely to the emotionalism of pity and fear. What a complex plot does is to render discordant incidences necessary and/or probable within its concordant structure. In doing so, the *plot* purifies and purges these incidences within its wholeness. Given this, plot conjoins the intelligible and the affective. "Aristotle thus comes to say that *pathos* is one ingredient of the imitating or representing of praxis. So poetry conjoins these terms which ethics opposes" (I 74/44). Ricoeur cites Redfield: "'*Pathe* and learning together constitute the characteristic values to us of a well-made narrative. I suspect that Aristotle meant by *catharis* exactly this combination of emotion and learning.'"[37] This reference to emotion is an important addition to the previous discussion of metaphor and imagination; it is also crucial to my own argument.

Elsewhere Ricoeur has shown the relation of imagination and feeling relative to the poetic reference. To grasp his argument about understanding and plot, we must clarify the import of feeling. In an essay on the metaphoric process, Ricoeur claims

> [A] feeling is a second-order intentional structure. It is a process of interiorization succeeding a movement of intentional transcendence directed toward some objective state of affairs. To *feel*, in the emotional sense of the word, is to make *ours* what has been put at a distance by thought in its objectifying phase. Feelings, therefore, have a very complex kind of intentionality. [T]hey accompany and complete the work of the imagination as schematizing a synthetic operation: they make the schematized thoughts our own. . . . Feelings, furthermore, accompany and complete imagination as *picturing* relationships. . . . Finally, the most important feature of feelings can be construed according to the third feature of imagination, that is, its contribution to the split reference of poetic discourse. . . . My contention is that feelings, too, display a split structure which completes the split structure pertaining to the cognitive component of metaphor.[38]

Feeling inserts us into the imaginatively figured world. It is a way *Dasein* is *in* the world, something that we shall explore further in Kierkegaard. And for Aristotle, feelings are aroused in tragedy through identification with the protagonist, particularly through discerning her or his fault (*hamartia*). Thus it is through feeling that we enter the world of the text as crucial for the refiguration of actual, practical existence. While the reader completes the signification of the text, she or he is also affected by it.

The importance of feeling in Ricoeur's mimetic strategy cannot be overstated. Indeed, he follows Heidegger's turn to the ontological import of basic moods, but contests the concentration of resoluteness in being toward death as the sole way to authentic existence. He does so by showing the various feelings that insert the reader into the historical or fictive texts, feelings such as a sense of debt to the past and the demand to initiate action in the present. What is at stake here is the possibility of "being-a-whole," of *Dasein*'s integrity. Heidegger's answer was that *Dasein* finds this integrity in being toward an end. And he argued that it is only in being-toward-death that provides such an authentic end (III 90–146/60–98). For Ricoeur, the integrity of our being-in-the-world is not linked singularly to this orientation toward death. Nevertheless, the problem of the integrity, the wholeness, of life remains. Ricoeur's answer is that though reading fictive and historical narratives the reader refigures life as a whole. Basic feelings insert one into the world of the text in order to achieve that wholeness.

Feeling and the act of reading are crucial, then, to the power of narrative to refigure life. In fact, Ricoeur goes so far as to say that the "recourse to the mediation of reading marks the most obvious difference between *Time and Narrative* and *The Rule of Metaphor*" (III 230/159). He claims that in the study of metaphor he believed it possible "to conserve the vocabulary of reference, characterized as redescription of the poetic work by everyday experience. I attributed to the poem itself the power to transform life by means of a short circuit operating between the 'seeing as,' characteristic of metaphorical utterance, and 'being as,' as its ontological correlate" (III 230/159). However, it is reading that is active in the refiguration of life. *Time and Narrative* signals a turn to the importance of the interpreter and accordingly to pleasure and learning as ways we insert ourselves into the world of the text. By doing this Ricoeur links Aristotle's idea of *catharsis* with a Kantian aesthetics of enjoyment. And it is precisely the interrelation of reading and narrative that marks, for Ricoeur, the escape from pure textuality. But this break, as we shall see shortly, is a practical one.

The relation of reading, plot, and emotion is not simply one in which the work of art evokes an aesthetic response. Given Gadamer's critique of aesthetic differentiation, such an interpretation is not possible. For Ricoeur, the relation of plot and emotion in reading is circular. "It is the composition of the plot which purges the emotions, in bringing the pitiable and the fearful incidents to representation, and it is these purged emotions which regulate our discerning of the tragic" (I 75/45). The discordant elements interlock with emotional receptions much as the concordance of the plot draws on the productive imagination. These two elements are linked precisely through poetic configuration and are the compass of *catharsis*. Reading narratives gives us insight into the way human characters act in specific situations; they are mimetic realizations of potential experience and possible ways of life. Thus plot moves along a line from the production of order to imaginal insight, and from reversal to emotional identification and purgation. Learning and pleasure are related even as these elements remain in tension precisely because they relate and express lived experience. Plots let us see the world "as" realized poetically. That is the contribution of dramatic poetry to our moral understanding. Interpreting them gives insight into life, practice in moral reflection, and the possibility of refiguring our actual lives.

The question now becomes the relation of plot and *mimesis*. Ricoeur notes that "praxis belongs at the same time to the real domain, covered by ethics, and the imaginary one, covered by poetics, one which establishes precisely the status of the 'metaphorical' transposition of the practical field by the mythos" (I 76/46). This claim begins to demarcate levels of mimesis that will correspond to the trajectory of the hermeneutical arch. That is, mimesis as noted above, marks the pre-understanding of the order of action, its configuration in plot, and its reception by an audience. Again Ricoeur follows Aristotle: mimetic works of art teach and please through presenting human action in the world. The point in calling the order of action and reception "mimetic" is to establish the ontological import of narrative, as we shall see. But the move from action to plot is a "mimetic displacement," a metaphorical transposition (I 78/47).

For Aristotle, the ethical dimension of plot is the portrayal of the complex, active relations of character, situation, and specific acts. This is what he means when he claims that a poem is a mimesis of action. Ethics and poetics each deal with happiness. Ethics deals with it in potential form and the conditions and virtues needed for its realization. What plot shows is the relation between those virtues and contingent or possible situations as real, as actual. Thus mimetic plot mediates the possible and the real, disclosing something universal about the human condition, and rendering a certain intelligibility to the contingent through artistic actuality. "For tragedy is not about imitation of men but of action and life. It is in action that happiness and unhappiness are found" (*Poetics* 50A17–18). This means that tragedy borrows from the foreknowledge of action. It does so through character, as good or bad, and through the order of action. This constitutes what Ricoeur called M1.

Poetic configuration (M2) is the mimetic displacement or transposition of the order of action to the level of plot. As we have seen, the two lines of plot each move toward reception, pleasure and learning, as the telos of poetics. In spite of the fact that Aristotle's *Poetics*, unlike his *Rhetoric*, is not explicitly concerned with audience but with composition, reception does enter the discussion. Ricoeur, as noted before, calls this reception M3. Interestingly, in *Time and Narrative* III he returns to an aesthetics and rhetoric of the reader (cf. III 232–43/160–66). And he notes that Aristotle's concern for structure does not lock "itself up within the closure of the text." Ricoeur is again seeking to explore the semantic movement of the plot. Plot makes this movement through the text and the reader's action. "The line which I am following is this: The *Poetics* does not speak of structure but of structuration; or, the structuration is oriented activity achieved only in the spectator or the reader" (I 80/48). The reader is the one who, through a productive act, structures, or figures, human action and temporality. Mimesis is a structuring activity, a synthesis (*suntasis*), which is the operation of organizing the events into a system. This corresponds to the "reasoning out" the audience carries on relative to plot.

Mimesis coheres with the pleasure of learning. Given this, it is, as Aristotle noted, natural to the human; we are mimetic beings. In tragedy, this mimetic dynamic is related to the text.

> The pleasure of apprehending is in effect the first component to the pleasure of the text. . . . [T]he pleasure of recognition is therefore at the same time constructed in the work and experienced by the spectators. The pleasure of recognition, in turn, is the fruit of the pleasure which the spectator takes in the composition as necessary or probable. These "logical" criteria are themselves at the same time constructed in the piece and exercised by the spectator [I 81/49].

What Ricoeur isolates in the *Poetics* is that pleasurable recognition is the criterion of the *persuasive*. There is a rhetorical dimension in all narratives, and this is what Aristotle meant by *catharsis*. In fact, *catharsis* is the crossing point of learning and emotion even as plot includes concordance and discordance. Ricoeur is clearly augmenting Aristotle in that the work takes on its full scope only when it displays a world the reader may appropriate. In a word, the reader constitutes the crossed reference of the text.[39]

The importance of reading for establishing a text's reference raises the question of the relation of self and language that will concern us in the aporias of temporality and lead to our reading of Kierkegaard. But initially, we see how Ricoeur retraces the hermeneutical arch on the level of plot. By starting with plot, as with metaphor, he has shown the way poetic texts are open at both ends: pre-understanding and reception. I want now to trace in still greater detail what he means by *la triple mimesis*. This will allow me to refine the discourse of mimesis and further the inquiry into the mimetic power of language seen in narrative.

Ricoeur is well aware of the ambiguity of mimesis linked, as it so often has been, to representation. Indeed, he notes that "representation is the great accused of contemporary philosophy. One speaks, here and there, of the representational illusion as Kant did of the transcendental illusion."[40] Mimesis has been tied to correspondence and representational theories of truth, to "imitation." Ricoeur discerns in Aristotle a way beyond this identification so evident with Plato and others. For Aristotle, "one part of mimesis has a place only in the region of human 'making,' of production, of *poiesis*. [T]he other part operates in the field of action . . . " (MR 51–52). These two lines of making and action as well as their crossing point guide Ricoeur's argument. His concern is to show their interrelation.

I am not interested here in testing Ricoeur's reading of Aristotle on poetics or ethics. My concern is to explore in greater detail his idea of mimesis as this helps forward my argument. In brief, Ricoeur's thesis

> is that this rational operation [of reading] is in a parasitic relation to an "intelligibility of the first order" only susceptible in actual fact to the mediation between the two ends of the text. It is this intelligibility—the intelligence of configured narratives—that I want now to describe, as the blending of the prefiguration and the transfiguration of the world of action, said otherwise, as the blending of mimesis I and mimesis III [MR 57].

Ricoeur's complex reading of the triple mimesis not only follows the hermeneutical arch but is the linguistic and temporal inscription of the productive imagination and synthetic judgment.

We have seen that the imaginal synthetic configuration of action (M2) as image (plot) mediates M1 (pre-understanding) and M3 (understanding) precisely by demanding an act of judgment (reading) about the artistic work. The complexity of Ricoeur's argument is that in each level of mimesis he must discern active, symbolic, and temporal aspects as these are lifted to hermeneutical understanding from lived experience through poetic configuration. What is more, understanding always returns finally to temporal lived experience.[41]

By discerning these three elements in each level of mimesis, Ricoeur is making ontological claims for the power of poetic texts to refigure life through the act of reading. Mimetic texts break the closed wall of language. He states the problem succinctly: "To say it otherwise, in order to resolve the problems of the relation of time and narrative, I must establish the mediating role of the emplotment between a stage of practical experience that precedes it and a stage that succeeds it. . . . We are therefore following the destiny of a prefigured time to a refigured time by the mediation of a configured time" (I 87/54–55). This problem and the trajectory he follows demarcate the levels of mimesis. As noted before, the composition of a plot is grounded in our pre-understanding of the world of action on three levels: its intelligible structure, its symbolic resources, and its temporal character. All these I have already isolated in Gadamer. Yet even at this point we can see that Ricoeur's concern is with the way plot is a mimesis of action and not, as was Gadamer, with mimetic action itself. The world of action is considered on three levels by Ricoeur in order to provide backing for the interpretation of plot.

Intelligible action is dependent on a distinction between action and physical movement. Action implies goals and agents with motives who act and suffer. Action, moreover, is always with others. It is a form of interaction marked by promises, duties, debts, and the like. These signal the various forms of feeling that also insert the reader into the world of the text, as I noted above. Ricoeur holds that the relation between narrative and practical understanding is one of presupposition and transformation. Narrative presupposes familiarity with human action, with the shape of character and the norms for the judgment of behavior. Narrative also transforms this understanding. It does so through the synchronic structure of signification that inscribes action. This structure is the semiotic level of plot. Yet plot also transforms practical action into a narrative whole. To understand a story is "to comprehend at the same time the language of 'doing' [faire] and the cultural tradition which precedes the typology of plots" (I 91/57). Cultural traditions provide the symbolic framework for intelligible action. Plot presupposes some order to action that is transformed through the act of making the plot.

The intelligibility of plot moves us to the symbolic level of the order of action. Human action is always symbolically mediated insofar as we make sense of our experience; action is also shaped and guided by social norms. This mediation means that action itself is public and meaningful, an insight that Gadamer made through the idea of festival. To understand a ritual act, for example, is to place it within the symbol system of a culture as the context for intelligibility of that action.[42] This cultural context provides a "readability" to action analogous to that of a text. Moreover, the symbolic mediation of action provides internal norms or rules for action. Meaningful action is rule-governed behavior. The customs and manners immanent in a culture are the context for judging action. Ricoeur claims that this warrants a linking of the ethical presupposition of narrative with cultural symbols.[43] As such, art is a laboratory for the experimentation of values.

The intelligibility and purposiveness of moral action shape the discussion of the third element of the pre-understanding of action: temporality. By exploring Augustine, Aristotle, Kant, Husserl, and Heidegger, Ricoeur discerns a three-fold understanding of the present as correlate to a pure phenomenology of action.[44] "What is important is the way that ordinary praxis orders in relation to one another the present of the future, the present of the past, and the present of the present. It is the practical articulation that constitutes the most elementary inductor of narrative" (I 96/60). In this Ricoeur is following Heidegger's *Being and Time* and the basic thematic concept of "care" (*Sorge*) as disclosing the structure of being-in-the-world.[45] If this is the case, then narrative will have ontological import insofar as it configures lived experience and care. Moreover, understanding has ontological depth inasmuch as it entails an appropriation of a configured world relative to our own temporality. Only by demonstrating this interlocking structure, which moves from pre-understanding through plot to understanding, are poetic articulation and hermeneutical understanding related to the world. Mimesis, in its threefold form, allows poetic reference to disclose a refigured world of experience. The most pressing question is about the temporality of *Dasein* and what constitutes its unity.

Ricoeur's reading of the dual history of reflection on time is complex, to say the least. On the one side, he explores phenomenological accounts of time, in Augustine and Husserl, that want, despite their obvious differences, to explore time relative to consciousness or the "soul." On the other side, there are positions that center on the objectivity of time. This begins with Aristotle's discussion about the relation of time and motion, and it is deepened, according to Ricoeur, in Kant's transcendental account of time as a form of sensibility. Heidegger represents the genuine advance on both fronts even as he attempts to move beyond ordinary notions of time. As Ricoeur puts it:

> For one thing, the existential analytic has as its referent not the soul but *Dasein*, being-there; that is, the being that we are. But, at the same time, "*Dasein* is an entity which does not just occur among other entities. Rather it is ontically distinguished by the fact that in its very Being Being is an *issue* for it" (*Being and Time*, p. 32). . . . What is more, for an existential analysis, nature cannot constitute an opposite pole, or much less an alien theme, in the consideration of *Dasein*, inasmuch as "the 'world' is something constitutive for *Dasein*" (p. 77) [III 92/61].

Given this, it is with Heidegger's interpretation of *Dasein* and time that Ricoeur seeks to address the problems of temporality and narrative. My task here is not to enter into a discussion of Heidegger on this point—that would take us too far afield—but to grasp how Ricoeur develops his argument.

Given the previously mentioned problem of the integrity of *Dasein* and the analysis of being-toward-death, Heidegger's approach to time depends on desubstantializing it into the three *ek-stases* of temporality: past, present, and future. The dialectic of the *ek-stases* relative to Care establishes a priority of the end if *Dasein* is to be a whole. This primacy, as we know, is located in the future and being-toward-death. This is a curious argument in Ricoeur's eyes. Heidegger seems, in the midst of an existential analysis, to have prioritized one "existential" posture, resoluteness toward death, as fundamental to the analysis. In doing so, Heidegger forgoes the possibility of other authentic moods, as I noted before. Ricoeur's concern is to widen this analysis.

Ricoeur argues that the primacy of being-toward-death slights the importance of our being *in* time. Given this, he challenges Heidegger's analysis of time in *Being and Time* and seeks to take seriously ordinary time as crucial to a full account of temporality. This is not to say that Ricoeur does not follow Heidegger in exploring different levels of temporality. He does. The level closest to our ordinary representations of time is that things take place "in" time. But this "within-time-ness" (*l'intra-temporalité* or *Innerzeitigkeit*) is leveled off by the ordinary representation of time. Through exploring narrative, Ricoeur hopes to show how this "intra-temporality" differs from linear time. Yet at a deeper level one encounters "historicality" as such. The emphasis here is placed on the receiving of the past, with all of its weight, in the work of "repetition."[46] Ricoeur understands this weight of the past as a debt we owe to the tradition that formed us. Narrative becomes then a repetition, not in the act of *Dasein*, but in historical discourse. Finally, Ricoeur follows Heidegger beyond historicality to where temporality springs forth in the unity of past, present, and future. Of course, Heidegger rooted this analysis of time in Care, specifically in *Dasein*'s being-toward-death. As will become clear, Ricoeur too seeks to understand the "unity" of the time in its plurality. And he seeks to do so through narrative and its limits. This will mean that he offers a different reading of Care from that concentrated on death.

The deepest trajectory of Ricoeur's concern is with narrative as the configuration of lived temporality. The being-whole of life is understood through narrative configuration and refiguration and not that specific resoluteness. The act of making the plot and the synthetic act of following a plot interrelate with the fundamental character of temporality itself and *Dasein*'s comportment within it. This is also why Ricoeur is concerned to include feeling in the analysis of *catharsis*. That is, *catharsis*, as Ricoeur has rethought it, now incorporates the dynamics of the productive imagination and Care. It provides a way, a practical one as we shall see, to speak of identity and integrity in life relative to narrative configuration.

Ricoeur wants, then, to explore our temporal experience of "within-time-ness" defined by the thrown character of human being. This is a move not unlike Gadamer's concern for effective historical consciousness. The thrownness of our lives tends to make us describe time by means of the objects we care about. And this is why Heidegger saw it as inauthentic. But Ricoeur's interest is with the pre-understanding that marks this care. Given our being "within time," human initiative, our acts of choice in time, is a "making present" inseparable from awaiting and retaining. The "now" is the discursive articulation of *making present* won by human initiative. There is, to Ricoeur's mind, an element of *poiesis*, of making, at the level of lived temporality just as human temporality is marked by action. Hence plot, as a product of human making and a mimesis of action, provides the figurative entrance point for understanding our experience of time.

"Within-time-ness" is not simply a linear representation of successive moments. Even in ordinary experience, preoccupation, and language, we can discern an act of making present. "Narrative configuration," Ricoeur writes, "and the most elaborate forms of temporality corresponding to it share the same foundation of 'within-time-ness'" (I 100/64). Thus poetic configuration allows us to move to the level of temporality as a response to the aporias of time. The full implications of this reading of narrative and time will become clear only at M3. First we must understand, in a way not possible before, the mediating function of plot through its synthetic integration.

The mediation is between individual events and a narrative as a whole. How do we make sense of particular events except by construing a narrative whole within which to understand them? Plot provides an intelligibility to this part/whole relation through the act of making the plot. Hence the poetic act itself is understood as mimetic. The plot functions "symbolically" by depicting the "what" (human action) of the imitation. Narrative "makes appear" the order of action by configuring it. This is the objective correlate to the reasoning out of the plot (M3) that will complete the "springing forth" of the figuration. Yet here we can see again how plot relates to the deepest level of temporality since through it a unity of the plurality of time is displayed by a human act. Plot is, as Ricoeur calls it, "a synthesis of the heterogeneous." It is the poetic resolution to an aporia of time as a tension between two temporal dimensions: the chronologic and one which disrupts chronology. Through the configurational act episodes are portrayed while also being "grasped together" into a whole. It entails an act of judgment. "It will be remembered," Ricoeur writes, "that for Kant the transcendental meaning of judgment consisted less in joining a subject and a predicate than in placing an intuitive manifold under the rule of a concept" (I 104/60). *Poiesis* is the making of a figure that configures the manifold of successive events into a whole, the plot.

Poetic configuration is a work of judgment. Kant showed that the reflective judgment itself is a reflection on taste and teleological judgments. Ricoeur relates this to the way the act of making plots derives a whole. The configurational dimension brings an intelligibility to the whole and provides a sense of closure. The act of repeating the story, for example, breaks strict linear time. There is a retracing of temporal experiences but now in narrative. The acts of making a narrative and of following a story are *productive* of meaning out of existential paradox. I think we may go so far as to say that plot is the aesthetic idea for the unity of Care without appeal to an exclusive orientation toward death. That is, plot is a synthesis of the plural *ekstases* of time while evoking and cohering with Care, itself a comportment relative to *Dasein*'s temporal character. Hence the problematic of Care shifts from being toward an end (death) to its orientation toward various historical and fictive narratives of life as a whole. This evokes feelings as far ranging as debt and fidelity. As I see it, this is Ricoeur's attempt to widen the possible authentic, ethical comportments for human being-in-the-world.

Ricoeur draws out the implications of this formulation: grasping together (synthesis) is characteristic of judgment, and configuration is an act of the productive imagination. These acts are inscribed linguistically and temporally in narrative. Plot is a schematism that renders a manifold (episodes) intelligible. Unlike Kant, Ricoeur sees this act of imagination and judgment as deeply linguistic and temporal while remaining rule-governed. It is thereby correlated to the cultural norms and rules discerned in M1.

To say that M2 is a work of the imagination and judgment is already to make the step to M3. In Volume I of *Time and Narrative*, Ricoeur isolates M3 at the level of what Gadamer called application. Ricoeur continues this mode of analysis along the lines we have followed. M3 is simply the "interaction of the world configured by the poem and the world wherein real action occurs and unfolds its specific temporality" (I 109/71). This interaction is the world of the reader.

The act of M3 is, to put it most simply, reading. Much as the action of making the plot moves M1 to M2, so too action here completes the hermeneutical arch because in reading, in reasoning out a text, we fuse plot with action in the world. Reading informs moral being and doing through the act of reasoning about how characters act in ambiguous situations. The reasoning entailed in reading a plot helps form moral judgment even as the act of reading takes up and fulfills the configurational act of making the plot. It has kinship with "judgment that com-prehends, that 'grasps together,' the details of action into a unity of plot" (I 116/76). The following of a story, then, is actualizing it through an act like the production of plot. Ricoeur, however, goes further than saying that plot and reading are ways of insight. He wants to claim that the "act of reading is thus the operator which conjoins mimesis III and mimesis II. It is the ultimate indicator of the refiguration of the world of action under the sign of the plot" (I 117/77).

What I have called the symbolic or figurative dimension of each level of mimesis also displays itself in M3. It is found in the move from configuration (sense) to refiguration (reference), that is, to the world projected by the text as this refigures life. There is an intersection, as Ricoeur calls it, between the world of the text and that of the reader. We might say there is a semantic clash from which refiguration is born. I shall return shortly to the dynamics of split reference in narrative.

We should note first that Ricoeur places his argument within the ontological presuppositions entailed in our lives. That is, with M3 he begins to spell out the ontological significance of narrative.

> This is the ontological presupposition of reference, a presupposition reflected in the interior of language itself as a postulate lacking immanent justification. Language is for itself the order of the Same; the world is its Other. The attestation of this alterity [*alterité*] arises [*relève*] from the reflexivity of language itself with regard to itself, whereby it knows itself as being in being in order to bear on Being [*se sait "dans" l'être afin de porter "sur" l'être*] [I 118–19/78].[47]

Thus the hermeneutical arch returns to the precondition of human experience in the world as its condition of possibility. Poetic texts give us particular insight into our condition by configuring it.

Here we have a clue to the ever-deepening analysis carried on in each level of mimesis. That is, Ricoeur moves from action through configuration, which exteriorizes and schematizes that action, to the ontological horizon of temporality. As David Klemm has noted, Ricoeur's thought constantly moves through poetic, conceptual, and speculative levels of discourse.[48] In the journey of interpretation no total mediation is possible. Nevertheless, the quest for understanding does not banish ontological reflection. Plot configures our experience of temporality and the ordering of action. On each level of mimesis a relation of action and the ontological shape of our experience of time is shown. Ricoeur's task, accordingly, is to undertake "reflective, speculative thought as a whole in its search for a coherent answer to the question: What is time?" (III 143–44/96).

The analysis before us is all the more complicated in that the tripartite consideration is operative at each level of mimesis. The move from M1 to M3 follows the same pattern. Thus the same trajectory is inscribed at each level of mimesis and in the argument as a whole, a pattern similar to that discerned in Gadamer's hermeneutics. Is this a clue to a speculative account of time? Ricoeur writes:

> I have not ceased, for several years, to maintain that what is interpreted in a text is the proposing of a world which I might inhabit and in which I might project my most proper powers. In *The Rule of Metaphor* I held that poetry, by its mythos, redescribes the world. In the same manner, I will say in this work that the making of narrative [*le faire narratif*] re-signifies the world in its temporal dimension, in the measure that narrative, telling, is to remake action following the invitation of the poem [I 122/81].

Thus all reference is co-reference; it is split, and it is a way of "seeing" the world as interweaving with human temporality.[49] This is the step beyond *The Rule of Metaphor*, as noted above. The referential thrust of the text is completed by the imaginative act of reading. Narrative reference arises in the domain of moral action, and it thereby touches the ontological horizon of time. It is the problem of time, as this is properly raised by *Dasein*, that controls the reading of narrative and hence mimesis. Indeed, it is time that forms the ontological context for mimesis and Ricoeur's theory of metaphoric truth. Ricoeur's wager is that if mimetic narrative will not allow any simple answer to the question "What is time?" it will provide a way to understand the mediation of time into human time. As he argues in Volume I of *Time and Narrative*, time becomes human in the measure to which it becomes actualized in narrative, while narrative takes on its full significance insofar as it configures the experience of time. This becomes clear in his discussion of M3.

The temporal dimension of the world refigured by the act of reading is understandable given our previous discussion of the threefold mimesis. Most basically, a refigured world is a fictive augmentation of all three levels of M1. Here schematized temporality affords insight into daily experience grasped through a *cathartic* act. More than this, plot is the resymbolization of the order internal to action itself. To understand (M3) the configuration (M2) is to refigure our own mode of action (M1) around the schematism presented in the plot. What is refigured in the configurational act is the time of action that responds and corresponds to the aporias of temporality.

Exploring the relation of narrative and history in *Time and Narrative* is beyond the scope of our study, but two observations are in order. First, the fact that mimesis is situated between temporality and narrativity indicates its centrality to Ricoeur's theory of time and action. His notion of mimesis provides both a way to articulate the ontological character (in M1) and a reference (M3) to his understanding of metaphoric discourse. The discussion of plot and mimesis touches on experience and *référence* as its two ends breaking the pure reflexivity of language and imagination. Second, it is in M3 that the hermeneutic arch returns to lived experience. Ricoeur's mimetic strategy is not a vicious circle since what is appropriated and seen refigured is life under a new emplotment. Hence the reflexive character of narrative interpretation is not vicious; it issues in ever new refigurations of life. At each level, Ricoeur seems to be saying that mimetic action pushes beyond itself by figuring life and time. This thrust of mimetic action is repeated on the level of poetic imagination and judgment. The poetic configuration is an aesthetic idea, a symbol of morality (M1). As with Kant, the imaginal works of art disclose the horizon of morality and, in freedom, Being itself.

Ricoeur concludes *Time and Narrative* III in a way that parallels, as he says, the last chapter of *The Rule of Metaphor*. It explores "the limits of our narrative enterprise" by addressing the perplexing speculative question: What is time? His contention is that narrated time can help render productive the aporias of temporality. Insofar as it does, narrative is meaningful because it contributes to temporal experience. Since Ricoeur's mimetic strategy is grounded in the active, temporal, and symbolic elements of action, we can expect two things: that the aporias will arise at these points, and that narrative must render them productive.

Given my concern with his discussion of mimesis, these aporias and narrative responses are important insofar as they open up a direction of additional inquiry and extend insights already gained by studying Gadamer. What we shall see is that Ricoeur's narratology helps us understand the problem of human solidarity as a practical (moral and political) task even as we must probe further into the problem of the self as agent. Given this, after isolating the aporias of temporality, I can draw some systematic conclusions and turn to the problem of the self.

THE APORIAS OF TIME AND MIMETIC NARRATIVE

Ricoeur discerns three aporias of time which, though not resolved by narrated time, are rendered practically productive through the act of interpretation. Not surprisingly, they are found, as I noted above, in the various elements of M1 (action, symbol, temporality) since these provide the backing for narrativity itself. I want briefly to isolate each aporia and describe what it contributes to my overall argument.

First, Ricoeur isolates the aporia of time that centers on the unity of the self, the agent, through the diversity of experienced states and actions. This aporia arises in the incongruence between the two perspectives on time, the phenomenological and the cosmological. That is, the aporia arises between our lived experience of time and the accounts of our acts and states. Both perspectives are warranted, and yet they conflict. The problem centers on how we speak of a self, given its diversity through its own past, present, and future. This is so even if, as Augustine argued in the *Confessions*, past and future are modalities of the present self (memory and expectation). Ricoeur's claim is that narrated time helps render this aporia productive while not resolving or exhausting the question of the integrity of the agent.

Ricoeur argues that through reading a narrative we synthesize the self in the act of reading. However, by exploring the limits of narrative, he raises the question of the identity, personal or communal, of the agent or author of action. As I noted before, he contends that without recourse to narrative the problem of identity, subjectivity in the diversity of acts and states, is unsolvable, even in Heidegger's form of being-whole in being-toward-death. In order to achieve some cohesion in life without recourse to a substantial self while granting the diversity of possible moods, we must understand the self relative to narrative. The self is then "refigured by the reflexive application of narrative configurations" (III 355/246). Such reflexive application, what we could call cathartic understanding, helps to bring identity to the self through time. We gain an identity through narration.

Ricoeur claims that this reflexive application engenders "the self of the knowledge of oneself" (*Le soi de la connaissance de soi*). It is the fruit of the examined life. Of course, such self-knowledge is not an idealist concept of self-reflection. The detour of interpretation makes such total mediation impossible. The self gains identity and continuity through the critical application of what is narratively disclosed about the human and its world. This application constitutes what Ricoeur calls "narrative identity." Such identity is possible since narrative, as Aristotle saw, articulates the intersection of character and action as well as prenarrative features of human desire. Hence in the reflexive application of the narrative to one's self, our act (reading) and character (self) intersect relative to the plot with a *cathartic* relation to our desire for integrity. Ricoeur sees this phenomenon operative even at the communal level in the biblical accounts of Israel. As he puts it, "the historic community that names itself the Jewish people has drawn its identity from the reception of those texts they produced" (III 357/248). Thus the identity of the self and community through time is related to the mimetic act of reading.

Ricoeur's notion of "narrative identity," constituted through the mimetic act of reflexive reading, is crucial to my further argument. As I noted in the first chapter, the classic imitative and substantialist understandings of the self have vanished under the heat of criticism. And yet human agents still exist, still think and act. Once a substanialist notion of the self or an idealism of the "I" proves implausible, how do we speak of the self through time?[50] Ricoeur's suggestion is that we speak of narrative identity appropriated through the critical, reflexive act of reading and appropriating a narrative. This also signals the first limit of narrative regarding this aporia: narrative identity is not a stable or seamless identity; it is problem and task as well as a response to this aporia of temporality. As a problem it exceeds narrative in the concrete demands of life.

Ricoeur goes so far as to say that "narrative identity is the poetic resolution of the hermeneutical circle" (III 358/248). That is, M3 helps constitute identity and thereby refigures life through narrative emplotment without an appeal to the "I," even as it gives rise to self-understanding. M3 engenders the power of M2 to refigure life, yet what this means is that mimetic narrative is saved from being a vicious, infinitely reflexive, circle insofar as it informs practical existence through the act of reading. Hence the resolution of the hermeneutical circle is not a speculative one; nor is it one that rests in the character of language or the "I." It is a moral and political resolution. This is the second limit of narrative regarding identity; it is the limit of making a choice relative to what is disclosed by the text. As Ricoeur notes, "it belongs to the reader, now an agent, an initiator of action, to choose among the multiple proposals of ethical justice brought forth by reading." And this means that "narrative identity encounters its limits and has to link up with the nonnarrative components in the formation of an acting subject" (III 359/249). Yet in responding to what is presented to the text, the reader does refigure concrete, practical life.

Ricoeur is quick to point out that any identity won through interpretation is

hardly static or even stable; it is a continual task. Hence there is an inner
dialectic of agent/action established at the heart of narrative. The reader in the
act of reading comes to be even while through reading something is disclosed
about what it means to be a self. Being a self requires that we interpret our
world, our narrative traditions, even as we are called to act. This means that
the question of the meaning of time is bound by its narrative configuration to
identity and the continual refiguring, or transvaluing, of the practical life, a
life of freedom and desire.[51]

Ricoeur has isolated the first aporia at the level of action. Narrative is
meaningful to us in that it reaches into who we are as selves, as agents. This is
true of reading a novel, like *Catcher in the Rye*, or Scripture. These texts gain
their cogency and compelling power in that they present human life in a
configured, and hence transformed, way. In them we see ourselves, and yet we
do so differently. The aporia centers on the self in diverse times and acts. And
it is inscribed in the synthetic whole of the plot by the act of reading. The
aporia is rendered productive in that identity is won through confronting and
reading narratives. As we shall see with the other aporia, narrative presentation of human temporality becomes productive in practical, not speculative,
thinking. The trajectory of mimesis completes itself by informing life.

Ricoeur's reflections on narrative identity move us toward a post-imitative,
and yet mimetic, notion of the self. And yet questions remain. Which narrative ought we to appropriate? Which "proposals of justice" are we to initiate?
How do we judge good, right, and fitting narratives? Perhaps by their power to
sustain self and community, or are other criteria involved?[52] Ricoeur does
not answer these questions; they form the nonnarrative limits to his inquiry.
Still, his analysis of reading helps us consider the act of being a self beyond
a substantialist or imitative anthropology. He suggests that the self comes to
be by mimetically appropriating a narrative. But what exactly is this act of
being a self initiated in the present, as Ricoeur notes? Can we be more precise
in our analysis? At this point Kierkegaard's reflections become germane.
What I shall argue, to anticipate a bit, is that Kierkegaard develops an analysis
of the self coming to be through mimetic action, specifically in the *imitatio
Christi*. Accordingly, his position calls for some narrative theory to explain
the textual disclosure of Christ. At this point Ricoeur's narratology supports
Kierkegaard's hermeneutic of the self. Yet Kierkegaard goes on to explore
the problem of the self as the act of coming-to-be relative to the power (God)
that establishes it. In Ricoeur's terms, Kierkegaard explores the initiative of
the self relative to a fundamental passion for existence, a *Care* not controlled
exclusively by beings-toward-death. Hence he helps explicate what Ricoeur
means by the reflexive appropriation of narrative while moving the discussion
of the self to its religious and moral depths. This takes us to the second aporia
of temporality.

If the first aporia concerns identity, then the second "arises from the dissociation of the three *ek-stases* of time: future, past, present, in spite of the unavoidable notion of time imagined as a singular collective" (III 359/249-50). This aporia is located not only in a self or a community as agents, but in history as well. Again, Ricoeur's argument is that the process of totalization, in which we grasp history as a whole, is a practical act. It marks out the context of human life.

To isolate this aporia Ricoeur rehearses his discussion of Augustine, Husserl, Kant, and Heidegger, a discussion beyond the scope of this study. But he does ask whether "the poetics of narrative is able to respond to this aporia of multiple visages of the totality" (III 367/255). He proposes an "imperfect mediation" (*mediation imparfaite*) relative to the horizon of expectation, the transmission of traditions, and the force of the present. This requires a shift from a monological and speculative understanding of the totality of history to a practical and dialogical one. And each dimension of the imperfect mediation entails an act and a mood on the reader's part: expectation or hope for an open future against the closure of being-toward-death; a sense of debt to the traditions that have formed us; and a making present initiated in response to the force of the present. In order to mediate the modalities of experience, Ricoeur must show how these are expressed in narrative.

In each *ek-stasis* of time Ricoeur discerns a projective element and a practical one. For instance, in the horizon of expectation, as this corresponds to the Heideggerian "being-before-self" or projection, Ricoeur isolates not only our being-toward-death but also a practical dimension. This practical transposition of projection opens onto the future of communities and even the future of the whole of humanity. Thus there is a dialectic within our horizon of expectation between being-toward-death of self and the future of humanity. An analogous dialectic is found in tradition and "the force of the present": the personal experience of time undergoes a transposition through a practical idea.

What Ricoeur is suggesting is twofold: first, that the notion of a collective singular, of "history," is a practical idea that is a transposition of our experience of the *ek-stases* of time—the question is how narrative mediates, imperfectly to be sure, the threefold character of our experience of time and its unity; and, second, that the practical idea of one history is just that, a practical idea. It is an idea that has a certain prescriptive, motive, and binding force on us, not only because it arises from our experience of time but also because of the vision it presents. If we recall the projective power of imagination to present utopias that both motivate and critique present life, then we see that the practical idea of history also has this dual function. "History" and "humanity" are limit ideas and measures to guide and judge our being and doing.

We are exploring here the aporia of time that arises in the "symbolic" element of mimesis since the ideas of history and humanity are symbolic ones. The question is how narrative relates to this aporia of totality, either in the self or in the community. Ricoeur's suggestion about the practical resolution to this aporia takes us back to Gadamer's work since it includes the presentation of the commonality, or solidarity, that the human shares. This commonality, as the good of the human, entails the duty to help forge a viable common world. The question of this aporia is then: How is mimetic refiguration related to human world? Here we see that the practical idea of a common humanity and history is a mimetic one that not only presents our commonality but sets a course for action.[53] Narratives that present history as a collective singular draw their plausibility from their mimetic relation to lived time. If these narratives are truly understood, they refigure experience into a whole that may serve to guide our thought and action.

The question is how narrative relates to this aporia. Is Ricoeur proposing a "meta-narrative" to help unify and make sense of the pluralism of communities and individuals?[54] Certainly he is not suggesting the simple adoption of religious narratives or ideologies of history. His concern for the critical and utopian power of imagination, rooted in interpretation and effective history, would count against such final meta-narratives. Rather, he is saying that the *idea* of "one humanity and one history" serves to guide and critique our struggle to enact our world. As he puts it, there "does not exist the plot of all plots capable of equaling the idea of one humanity and one history" (III 372/259). This signals the first limitation on narrative relative to the second aporia of temporality. As a discursive genre, narrative is an inadequate medium for thinking of general history; total mediation is not possible. Yet given this limitation, how exactly does narrative respond to this second aporia? Is the literary category of narrative adequate to historical thought?

Ricoeur notes, and argues extensively in *Time and Narrative* II, that historical thinking does have an affinity to the discursive genre of narrative. It does so through the transmission of traditions, themselves essentially narrative in character. Historical reflection is involved in the subtle dialectic of anticipation and retrospection under the demands of the present. In this it coheres with phenomenological accounts of the experience of time marked by memory and expectation. Plot, whether fictive or historical, brings together events into a discordant concordance, into a whole. Through such configuration something about our temporal experience is illuminated. Historical thought entails an act of emplotment analogous to fiction even if time escapes complete narrative portrayal.

Ricoeur concludes, however, that narrative does not respond to the second aporia of temporality as well as to the first since the scope of history is universal. Yet two maxims can be reached to show the importance and limit of narrative to the various aporias of temporality.

First maxim: the answer of narrativity to the aporias of time consists less in resolving these aporias than in making them work, rendering them productive. That is how thinking about "history" contributes to the refiguration of time. Second maxim: any theory, whatever it be, reaches its highest expression only when the exploration of that domain to which its validity is verified is completed with a recognition of the limits which circumscribe this domain of validity [III 374/261].

Narratology, aware of its limits, is helpful when it renders the aporias of time productive. It does so through the practical idea of one history and one humanity that can guide our moral and political praxis. More generally, the question of time is understood relative to expectation, tradition, and the present as this evokes feelings of hope, debt, and actual initiative. Human life is *in* time. Given this, a total grasp of time forever eludes us even though we can explore ways of being in time. Narrative helps carry out this task.

If the first aporia exposed the question of the self as a mimetic phenomenon and prompts us to read Kierkegaard, then this second aporia draws on and yet deepens insights from Gadamer.[55] Narrative opens the question of the common world, common history and destiny, that we share. Ricoeur has enhanced this insight by arguing, in the face of the aporias of temporality, that the commonality of effective-history is a necessary, but not sufficient, condition for grasping the totality of history. Indeed, such a totality eludes a theoretical grasp and must therefore be seen as a moral/political task guided by the imaginatively construed idea of one humanity. This practical idea informs the way we understand our experience, and through interpretation it refigures life. The point is that the refiguration of life is not completed merely at the level of our self-understanding as part of human world. The practical idea must be enacted in personal and social existence if it is to trans-form or refigure life.

Once again we are pushed beyond Ricoeur into an inquiry into moral existence as the enactment, the mimesis, of human solidarity in the world. Yet what I have isolated, through Gadamer and Ricoeur, is that such solidarity accords with the depth of human existence, disclosed in narratives and in culture, and also an idea calling for practical action through which we seek to make sense out of existence. And if that solidarity between humans and their natural world is part of the good of the human, as Gadamer avers, then the idea of that solidarity provides a way to interpret and measure experience under the aspect or figure of the good. It also means that the human good appears in concrete enactments of solidarity. Ricoeur's practical reading of the idea of human solidarity augments Gadamer's claims about the human good. Significantly, mimesis, it would seem, is crucial to exploring that good and our practical task of enacting it.

The first two aporias of temporality arose at the level of action and "symbol" and found their productive import in narrative identity, or practical selfhood, and the idea of one humanity and one history. The final aporia of time is more elusive, more troubling, since it involves temporality itself. Ricoeur speaks of it as the "inscrutability" of time that undoes all our attempts to master meaning. The final aporia is that time resists mastery, and yet, in an act of *hubris*, we seek such domination. This discloses the depths of human fault and also, ironically, a power that exceeds human being and doing. As Ricoeur puts it: "To this aporia, diffuse in all our reflections on time, will respond, from the side of poetics, the confession of the limits that narrative encounters beyond itself and in itself. These limits attest that not even narrative exhausts the power of the speaking that refigures time" (III 375/261). What we see here is the second maxim isolated above: the limits of narrativity arise internal to narrative itself. Yet, interestingly enough, Ricoeur approaches again the problem of the power to refigure time. We should recall that the principal shift from *The Rule of Metaphor* to the work on narrativity centered on his abandoning the assumption that the text had the power to refigure life. Here we learn that the power to refigure time in speaking exceeds and limits narrativity itself, that is, the way in which we render our temporality meaningful. We shall return to this problem of power in theological and ethical discourse later; here it is important to grasp the internal limits of mimetic narrative that point to the power of speaking to refigure time.

Although the first two aporias of temporality were rendered productive through a turn to the practical dimensions of agency and history, this aporia marks out the limits of narrativity itself. It shows the impossibility of grasping time or exhausting the power of speaking that refigures time. Ricoeur's task will be to isolate a fundamentally poetic figuration of temporality that lies behind philosophical reflection. Theory, in other words, rides on poetic configuration just as logic did on metaphoric truth. Given this, reflection on time can never escape symbolic expression and hence is strictly limited by that domain of validity. Yet on seeing this, we realize that human temporality, as always already figurative, cannot be resolved speculatively. It must be understood hermeneutically through the interpretation of narrative figurations of experience and rendered productive in practical existence. Hence this last aporia, while marking out the conceptual limits of narrativity, also demonstrates its hermeneutical and practical character.

Concerning this aporia Ricoeur rehearses his argument as it spans the volumes of *Time and Narrative*. The details of his summary are beyond my immediate concern. What he points out is that there are two basic approaches to time itself, what he calls "archaism," or reference to first principles, and "hermeticism," an interpretive approach. Moreover, Western culture is founded on two different forms of archaism: the Greek and the Hebraic. Thus in turning to the possibility of thinking through this last aporia, Ricoeur turns to these various options seen in Western thought and life.

Aristotle speaks of being *in* time. This suggests a vision, or myth, of time as an envelope in which existence takes place. Given this, time forms the limits of thought. Yet how is that "envelope" depicted? Ricoeur notes that theogonies as well as the pre-Socratic thinkers expose the archaism in Greek thought on time. The pre-Socratics attempted to isolate the *arche*, the principle, of all reality while mythic formulations express cultural assumptions about time and the meaning of existence. Hence the condition of possibility of philosophical reflection is the search for origins internal to thought or expressed in myth. Philosophical reflection seeks to establish its own principles and thus represents a second archaism. For instance, the Greeks saw time as organized around the cyclical movement of the cosmos in death and birth. This cyclic vision becomes thematized in Plato's *Timaeus*, as a philosophical story, where time is depicted as "a certain mobile imitation of eternity." It is also found in Aristotle's discussion of the relation of time and motion. The mythic portrayal of time helped set the stage for the cosmological bent of Greek reflection.

Yet time as such remains inscrutable since we cannot escape our cultural figurations of it. The conception of time is imprinted with the polymorphism of its poetic figurations.[56] The importance of this for the analysis of time and narrative cannot be slighted. It means that although time *comes to* language in narrative figuration, time is not *in* language. The power of mimetic narrative is to bring time to language; narrative is a transformation into figuration of human time, rendering it meaningful. Nevertheless, time remains inscrutable, and the power to refigure it is not exhausted by narrative figuration.

The other archaism of Western culture is that of biblical thought which, in Augustine and his heirs, takes it bearing less from cosmology than from the self. Here the contrast of time and eternity, specifically the eternality of the divine Word, is the limit idea against which Augustine attempts to think about his experience of time. Significantly, Augustine, and many before and after him, gave an ontological reading of the holy name (YHWH) revealed at Sinai: "I am who I am" (Ex 3:14A). Hence God is the *arche* of being itself. From this flows the tradition of theism that modernity has attacked, as I noted in Chapter 1. Yet, according to Ricoeur, the biblical world thought of the eternality of the divine as the fidelity of God within the history of election. This fidelity, and with it the confession of God as creator (Gn 1:1ff.), can be continually reactualized in cultic action. The eternality of God is thus contrasted with the transitoriness of human life. The inscrutability of time rests on the mystery and transcendence of God.

Next, Ricoeur places Kant between archaism and hermeticism, given Kant's attempt to isolate the transcendental grounding of time. And yet Kant was also aware that the representation of time is relative to the human heart (*Gemüt*) and affections. Time here opens onto the domain of human affection and desire. Of course, Augustine already signaled this dimension of feeling by exploring time's relation to the soul. And Husserl continues and refines a phenomenology of time consciousness. Yet for Ricoeur the Husserlian project cannot escape the metaphorics of its own discourse, talk about time "flowing," falling-back, and so on. The phenomenological approach seems to return to some cosmological concerns. It was Kant's insight to have addressed this problem.

As noted before, Hiedegger represents for Ricoeur a crucial turn in the reflection on time. Yet *Being and Time* tends to assimilate the problem of time into that of authentic being as being-toward-death. Hence the horizon of human temporality is not the immutably eternal (Plato) or the eternal fidelity of God (Augustine); it is death. We must note here that Ricoeur announced in Volume I of *Time and Narrative* that "the most serious question that this work may be able to pose is to what degree a philosophical reflection on narrativity and time may aid us in thinking about death and eternity at the same time" (I 129/87). What we now see is that in this final aporia, narrative raises the question not only of the human temporality as including the problematics of coming into being and passing away (Greeks), being a whole in a being-toward-death (Heidegger), but also of fidelity. Hence the inscrutability of temporality opens onto the human orientation to the horizons of death and eternity (fidelity), that is, onto religious and moral questions.

What are we to make of this? Clearly Ricoeur's concern is to think the human orientation to death and eternity (fidelity) in narrative. Now we see that temporality is inscrutable; it will not allow our mastery or representation of it. In fact, there are internal and external limits on narrative. Internally, narrative exhausts itself in attempting to draw near to the inscrutable. Time is not simply *in* language, as I noted above. The external limits on narrative are that it must overflow into other genres in speaking of time. Bringing time *to* language is not the sole task of narrative. In a word, time is the inscrutable horizon of meaning that ever escapes complete figuration.

Does this mean that narrative is finally reduced to the endless free play of time? Against this seductive option, Ricoeur has carefully noted all along that his concern is with the way narrative renders our lived experience meaningful. If narrative contributes to our being temporal, then its contribution, though limited, is significant. He claims that "it is in the way in which narrative reaches toward its limits that there resides the secrecy of its reply to the inscrutability of time" (III 387/270). Thus this third aporia, we might say, is rendered productive because it is insoluble. Narrative opens us to the mystery that surrounds existence by its reach toward its limit while being unable to represent it. This suggests that a refiguration of experience in the light of narrative entails an opening of the human to what is always and already transcendent. Significantly, our orientation to that transcendence cannot be resolved speculatively (the third aporia) even as it prompts us to practical responses to selfhood and history (the first two aporias).

The aporias of temporality as Ricoeur has isolated them arise from the elements of lived experience as narratively configured. On isolating these aporias we see how the trajectory of Ricoeur's narratology pushes us beyond narrative "text" back into understanding and world (Gadamer) and forward to the problem of the human self (Kierkegaard). The aporias of temporality mark out the limits of narrative while exposing its contribution to human religious, moral, and political existence through the linguistic mediation of self and world within the inscrutable horizon of time. Thus the question "What is time?" is understood in and through narrative and its limits. It is related to the problematic of freedom and identity, the practical idea of one humanity and one history, and the inscrutable horizon of these. Narrative is a way of bringing time to language, of figuring it, and thus it has the power to refigure the human experience of time. And yet time escapes this figuration; the power of speaking that refigures time likewise exceeds the capacities of narrative.

RICOEUR AND THE RECONSTRUCTION OF MIMESIS

It is now possible to draw together Ricoeur's contribution to the reconstruction of mimesis. Fundamentally, Ricoeur understands mimesis as synthetic figuration in intelligible action, text, or practical ideas, where an experiential, episodic, or cognitive manifold is rendered into a whole. Clearly, his understanding of mimesis, in its threefold form and with its various elements in each form, expands Gadamer's analysis. Most importantly, Ricoeur has allowed us to specify the mimetic character of lived experience, its textual figuration, and understanding. Thus he has provided us with a more detailed vocabulary to speak about mimesis as well as showing its importance to the dimensions of human experience. And like Gadamer, Ricoeur has decisively reinterpreted mimesis beyond the pale of classic imitation theory. He has done so by exploring it in relation to the question "What is time?"

Ricoeur's contributes to this study by exploring textual mimesis. What his strategy demonstrates is the claim to truth of narrativity as the paradigmatic example of the mimetic power of language. Again, it is debatable exactly which texts are relevant for religious discourse, but at this point the important thing is developing a mimetic understanding of text. What Ricoeur's theory of narrativity allows us to see is how plot sends its roots down into human action and the cultural symbols through which we make sense of our experience. And the limits of narrative enable us to ask about that power of speaking that refigures time beyond the pale of narrative.

Most important, narrative exposes how we make sense of the horizon of existence, death or eternity, and hence calls for religious and moral reflection. Yet the reference goes both ways. Not only does narrative reach into the order of action and existence; it also opens up prospective modes of being and doing against the horizon of the human condition. The aporias of temporality find a practical resolution that is uniquely futural when we formulate practical ideas to guide our being and doing.

In the aporias of temporality Ricoeur's thought turns us back to Gadamer and forward to Kierkegaard. We turn back to Gadamer because we now understand human solidarity as the condition of the possibility of under-

standing, but also as a moral and political task. We must move forward to
Kierkegaard because we need to ask about the one, the self, that can come
to be in the present before death and eternity by reading narratives. Thus
Ricoeur's mimetic strategy not only helps us develop a more specific concept
of mimesis, it also mediates these other areas of reflection. Indeed, the insight
gained here is that the mimetic power of language, seen in narrative, mediates
world and human agency in the horizon of time even as it calls for further
reflection regarding our religious and moral condition and the power of speaking to refigure time.

NOTES

1. For a discussion of social ontologies see Michael Theunissen, *The Other: Studies in the Social Ontology of Husserl, Heidegger, Sartre, and Buber*, trans. Christopher
Macann (Cambridge: MIT Press, 1986). Theunissen's contention is that there are two
basic routes to a social ontology, one seen principally in Husserl, who began with
intentionality, and the other in Martin Buber, who was concerned with the I–Thou
relation. His study neglects Gadamer. My point is that Gadamer's notion of understanding and being as mimetic *Spiel* establishes a social ontology.

2. There is considerable literature on narrative in theology, religious and philosophical ethics, and literary criticism. For representative works, see Hauerwas' *Community
of Character* and Hans Frei's *The Eclipse of Biblical Narrative: A Study in Eighteenth-
and Nineteenth-Century Hermeneutics* (New Haven: Yale University Press, 1974).

3. "Erzählung, Metapher, und Interpretationstheorie," *Zeitschrift für Theologie und
Kirche*, 84 (1987), 251. See also Ricoeur's "From Existentialism to the Philosophy of
Language," in *The Philosophy of Paul Ricoeur*, edd. C. Regan and D. Steward (Boston:
Beacon, 1978), pp. 86–94.

4. "Erzählung, Metapher, und Interpretationstheorie," 248.

5. Ibid., 251.

6. See Rorty's *Consequences of Pragmatism*.

7. See Dominick LaCapra, *Rethinking Intellectual History: Texts, Contexts, and
Language* (Ithaca: Cornell University Press, 1983). LaCapra makes the same point.
His reading of Ricoeur is hampered by deconstructionist convictions. He sees Ricoeur
as logocentric.

8. See David Pellauer, *"Time and Narrative* and Theological Reflection," in *Philosophy Today*, 31 (1987), 262–86. For a helpful discussion of Ricoeur and religious
reflection, see David E. Klemm, *The Hermeneutical Theory of Paul Ricoeur: A Constructive Analysis* (Lewisburg: Bucknell University Press, 1983).

9. Paul Ricoeur, *Temps et récit*, 3 vols. (Paris: Editions du Seuil, 1983–1985).
Translations are mine, although I have checked them with the English translation. See
Time and Narrative, 3 vols; trans. Kathleen McLaughlin and David Pellauer (Chicago:
The University of Chicago Press, 1984, 1986, 1988). Citations will be given in the text
by volume and page number. I cite the French edition first followed by the English trans-
lation. All references to Aristotle's *Poetics* will be given in the text. See Aristotle, *On
Poetry and Style*.

10. At this point Ricoeur is developing an insight of Kant's that the idea of a universal history is a practical idea in the service of peace. See Kant's "Perpetual Peace," in *Immanuel Kant: On History*, trans. Lewis White Beck (Indianapolis: Bobbs-Merrill, 1963). See also Paul Ricoeur, "The Fragility of Political Language," in *Philosophy Today*, 31 (1987), 35–44 and also his *Political and Social Essays*, edd. David Stewart and Joseph Bein (Athens: Ohio University Press, 1974).

11. See McFague's *Metaphorical Theology*.

12. Citations to *The Rule of Metaphor* will henceforth appear in the text as RM followed by pagination.

13. The most succinct statement of Ricoeur's overall hermeneutic can be found in his *Interpretation Theory: Discourse and the Surplus of Meaning* (Fort Worth: Texas Christian University Press, 1976).

14. A basic study of Ricoeur's early thought in English is still Don Idhe, *Hermeneutic Phenomenology: The Philosophy of Paul Ricoeur* (Evanston: Northwestern University Press, 1971).

15. "Zeit und Erzählung bei Paul Ricoeur," *Philosophische Rundschau*, 34 (1987), 2.

16. "The Metaphorical Process of Cognition, Imagination, and Feeling," in *On Metaphor*, ed. Sheldon Sacks (Chicago: The University of Chicago Press, 1979), p. 143.

17. Ibid., p. 146.

18. Ricoeur makes this point about abandoning the Fregean terminology of sense and reference in a recent essay. See his "Narrated Time," *Philosophy Today*, 29 (1985), 259–71.

19. Ricoeur, "Metaphorical Process of Cognition, Imagination, and Feeling," p. 144.

20. See Ricoeur's "Can Fictional Narrative Be True?" *Analecta Husserliana*, 14 (1983), 3–19, for another statement of these issues.

21. For a discussion of parabolic discourse see Ricoeur's *Essays on Biblical Interpretation*.

22. My point here is that Ricoeur weds Aristotle's concern with the structure of the work of art, in metaphor and particularly in plot, with a Kantian understanding of the imagination. See Ricoeur's "Erzählung, Metapher, und Interpretationstheorie" and Strasser's "Zeit und Erzähling bei Paul Ricoeur."

23. "Imagination in Discourse and in Action," *Analecta Husserliana*, 7 (1978), 5.

24. Ibid.

25. Ibid., 7–8.

26. "Erzählung, Metapher, und Interpretationstheorie," 241.

27. "Metaphor and the Central Problem of Hermeneutics," in his *Hermeneutics and the Human Sciences: Essays on Language, Action, and Interpretation*, ed. and trans. John B. Thompson (Cambridge: Cambridge University Press, 1981), p. 177.

28. Ibid.

29. On this see Paul Ricoeur, "Appropriation," in *Hermeneutics and the Human Sciences*, pp. 182–96.

30. "Erzählung, Metapher, und Interpretationstheorie," p. 253. See also Klemm, *Hermeneutical Theory of Paul Ricoeur*, pp. 140–76.

31. Ibid.

32. "Narrated Time," p. 360.

33. In *Time and Narrative* Ricoeur has moved away from the language of "reference"

to that of the "intersection" or crossing (*inter croissement*) of the world of the text and the world of the reader. This terminology of intersection seeks to avoid an iconic view of the relation of text to world without thereby sacrificing claims to truth for narrative.

34. "Narrated Time," 360.

35. See his *Nature and Culture in the* ILIAD.

36. Ibid., p. 79.

37. Ibid., p. 67. The importance of "feeling" in Ricoeur's general hermeneutics is often overlooked. I argue that it is crucial to his argument. In terms of my concerns, it is also one point where Ricoeur's narratology opens onto Kierkegaard's analytic of existence.

38. "Metaphorical Process as Cognition, Imagination, and Feeling," pp. 154–55. Ricoeur's use of Husserl's notion of intentionality is evident here and in his theory of reference. Exploring this dimension of his thought or his relation to Husserl is beyond the scope of this study.

39. Ricoeur notes his reliance on Hans Robert Jauss's aesthetics of reception even as he is using the reader-theory of Wolfgang Iser. This is traced out in Volume III of *Temps et récit*; see pp. 228–63.

40. "Mimesis et Représentation," *Actes du Congrès des Sociétés de Langue Français*, 18 (1980), 51. The translation is my own. Henceforth citations on this text (MR) will be made in the text. This essay is a summation of Ricoeur's discussion of mimesis in *Temps et récit*. Because it does not situate mimesis relative to plot, it is not as helpful as the main text. I shall rely, therefore, mainly on *Temps et récit*.

41. Ricoeur's language of "figuration" (to represent, to act, to figure, to appear, to shape, or to form) draws from the same domain of experience (dramatic presentation and artistic representation) as Gadamer's terminology of *Bild, Gebilde*, and their derivations does.

42. Ricoeur follows Clifford Geertz and others in taking a cultural–linguistic interpretation of action. See Clifford Geertz, *The Interpretation of Cultures* (New York: Basic Books, 1973). For an excellent discussion of this approach in comparison to other strategies, see Bernstein's *Beyond Objectivism and Relativism*. These issues have also been explored by James M. Gustafson in *Treasure in Earthen Vessels: The Church as Human Community* (Chicago: The University of Chicago Press/Midway, 1976). For a recent application of this approach, see Lindbeck's *Nature of Doctrine*.

43. This is an interesting shift and is one move away from Aristotle. It seems to follow Hegel's reading of *Antigone* more than Aristotle's own position (cf. I 94/59). For Aristotle, the evaluation of action is relative to the virtues and ends of the agent and not, strictly speaking, to cultural norms. To be sure, as Ricoeur notes, the judgment of good and bad character presupposes norms, which may be cultural, but it is not clear that this was Aristotle's concern.

44. For a brief summation of Ricoeur's notion of the relation of time and narrative, see the substance of the discussion of *Temps and récit* published in "Narrative and Time," *Critical Inquiry*, 7 (1980), 169–90.

45. Derrida turns to the later Heidegger. Thus in part the clash between Ricoeur and Derrida is a difference in Heidegger. That is, Ricoeur continues the concern for an analytic of *Dasein* relative to the problem of time while Derrida radicalizes Heidegger's "destruction" of metaphysics and the turn to language. I am suggesting that the turn to care and feeling is important in this dispute.

46. We shall see later the importance of "repetition" for Kierkegaard as this interlocks with the analysis of existence. This is the first clue that Kierkegaard will interlace a retrieval of mimesis with the problem of time and truth (existence) which will advance our discussion while continuing the concerns we see here in Ricoeur.

47. The language of "alterité" has been championed by Emmanuel Levinas in his *Totality and Infinity*, trans. Alphonso Lingus (Pittsburgh: Duquesne University Press, 1969). Levinas uses this language to undo ontology relative to the ethical confrontation of the self with an Other. The Other always remains transcendent to my power to control him or her.

48. See his *Hermeneutical Theory of Paul Ricoeur*, pp. 157–59.

49. For a further discussion of the nature of poetic referentiality, see Philip Wheelwright's *Metaphor and Reality* (Bloomington: University of Indiana Press, 1962). He points out that "Poetic language . . . does so contribute; it partly creates and partly discloses certain hitherto unknown, unguessed aspects of What Is" (p. 51). This is the nature of the ontological reference of poetic texts.

50. On the rejection of the unity of the virtues, and the attendant problems for the way we conceive of the self, see MacIntyre's *After Virtue*. MacIntyre ends by appealing to narrative and community to answer this problem. My point is that the issue cannot be adequately addressed unless we rethink narrative itself and with it mimesis. I am doing so through Ricoeur's retrieval of mimesis within narrative action.

51. For the importance of freedom in the transvaluation of life as an ethical task, see Paul Ricoeur, "Ethics and Culture: Habermas and Gadamer in Dialogue," *Philosophy Today*, 17 (1973), 153–65. My contention here is that the problem of time and freedom are intimately related in Ricoeur's work.

52. For a Christian ethicist who has explored the question of narrative and Christian identity, see Stanley Hauerwas, *Truthfulness and Tragedy: Further Investigations into Christian Ethics* (Notre Dame: University of Notre Dame Press, 1977). See also H. Richard Niebuhr, *The Meaning of Revelation* (New York: Macmillan, 1941) and Steven Crites, "The Narrative Quality of Experience," *The Journal of the American Academy of Religion*, 39 (1971), 291–311.

53. Ricoeur is drawing again on Kantian insights. In addition to Kant's "Perpetual Peace" see his "Ideas for a Universal History from a Cosmopolitan Point of View" also in *Immanuel Kant: On History*, ed. Lewis White Beck (Indianapolis: Bobbs-Merrill, 1963).

54. The idea of a meta-narrative has come under increasing criticism. This is true on the level of ideology critique and the decay of idealist philosophies of history or the myth of progress. Ricoeur's point is that any idea of history as a unity is a practical and not a speculative one. Manifestly he is not suggesting the march of the Hegelian *Geist* through time. What he is advocating, in his oft-stated phrase, is a "post-Hegelian return to Kant." I take this to mean a hermeneutical philosophy, one engaged with history and language, that finds its resolution in practical reason and not speculative thought.

55. I believe that Ricoeur's post-Hegelian return to Kant is actually a return to the Kant of the *Critique of Practical Reason* via Gadamer and Heidegger. It also signals the impossibility of a total mediation freed from the realm of the figural. What I am arguing, then, is that this return to Kantian insights about the practical significance of the idea of "history" can be seen as correlate to Gadamer's concern for

human solidarity, itself presented in various cultural configurations.

56. Ricoeur is working within the Hegelian dialectic of the relation between concept (*Begriff*) and representation (*Vorstellung*). His point is that poetic figuration grounds and permeates reflection even as reflection seeks to test and clarify such figurations. On this see his "The Status of *Vorstellung* in Hegel's Philosophy of Religion," in *Meaning, Truth, and God*, ed. Leroy S. Rouner (Notre Dame: University of Notre Dame Press, 1982), pp. 70–90.

4

Self as Mimesis of Life

AT THE BEGINNING of this study I noted that our situation is marked by the criticism of fundamental suppositions backing much of Western thought. These criticisms challenge the way we think and speak about texts, moral agents, and our world. A brief rehearsal of these criticisms and the progress made in considering them will help in the study of Kierkegaard.

The first supposition under fire is that words, ideas, texts, and human imagination are more or less cogent representations of reality. The urgency of this criticism arises no doubt from a deep awareness of the power of ideology and of illusion. The proponents of this criticism contend that it runs to the depths of Western thought and life.[1] That is, the claim of postmodern thought from Heidegger to Derrida is that the task of the metaphysics of light rests on the venture of capturing all reality through the power of the idea; it seeks to reach total mediation. To challenge this claim, either by asking anew the question of the meaning of being or by showing how all texts undo themselves, is to critique the Western project. Thus recent criticism concerns the very notion of representation itself; not surprisingly mimesis is often isolated as the core of the problem.[2]

I have argued that mimesis is best understood as a dynamic activity that is a transformation into figuration. On this reading, texts are webs of signs activated in interpretation. They are performances in which we are the participants. Gadamer has allowed us to make this turn to performative action and thus embrace and go beyond the criticism of crass representationalism. Ricoeur, for his part, has allowed us to chart the mimetic shape of narrative and human action by understanding mimesis in relation to time and its aporias. We now understand "images" and imaginative or textual schematisms on the basis of mimetic, temporal action. Through our interpretive action, texts and images are performances of their meaning calling for a refiguration of the field of human being and doing in time. This turn to performative action and time undoes both the spectator-rationality of classical theory and the drive for presence and permanence in traditional metaphysics. Understanding is participatory, as Gadamer argued. And the inscrutability of time means that all figurations of the human condition can never achieve total mediation.

Most critics of representation work from the perspective of "textuality" or semiology. Their reading of human (symbolic) reality on analogy to texts lends itself to a simple reduction of those realities to mere signs and hence to the problem of reference.[3] When textuality as a heuristic metaphor expands to include all of life, the many-faced, pluriform, and varied character of reality is suppressed. The consequence of this procedure is to rob human symbolic interaction, whether linguistic or not, of any disclosive power. Here we should recall Ricoeur's maxim that although time and human action can be brought *to* language in mimetic texts, they are not *in* language. My tactic has been to show the mimetic dynamic of human action, specifically understanding and interpretation (reading), and the way human temporality and solidarity are bought to language through mimetic works. This entails understanding text and language from the perspective of mimetic praxis. Indeed, by reading Gadamer, Ricoeur, and in this chapter Kierkegaard, I am reconstructing mimesis as a way to speak of the fundamental acts of understanding, narrativity, and selfhood. Of course, this procedure embraces the recognition of the disclosive power of texts, symbols, ideas, action, and persons, and hence the centrality of language in reflection. But the turn to performative action takes us far beyond "imitation," and hence representation, without forsaking our experiences of insight gained through interacting with texts. In a word, the mode of hermeneutical reflection I am developing interrelates language and action as crucial to understanding human being and doing in the world.

What is at stake here are metaphors for the human and its world. I am employing dramatic performative action (mimesis) in order to reflect on text, understanding, and human agency.[4] More specifically, I am arguing that mimesis provides a means to explore the ways Being becomes meaningful through basic forms of praxis. I am also suggesting that the unity and power of these activities cannot be apprehended in an unmediated way; mimetic activities are reflexive in this sense. However, I have argued that appeals to the "I," absolute *Geist*, or a metaphysical one are also not plausible in that they seek total mediation. Thus the reconstruction of mimesis that I am proposing takes within itself the full force of the critique of imitation. World is not the imitation of transcendent ideas but a dynamic transformation into figuration through forms of mimetic action ranging from understanding to the act of being a self. Through these mimetic acts being becomes a meaningful, if ambiguous, world. Given this, works of art and narrative texts are not imitative in any simple sense. They are mimetic and thus call for participatory understanding and the refiguration of life. Likewise, "truth" is not simply the imitative correspondence of idea to reality. Rather, "truth" is the mimetic process of presentation and deferral or concealment of reality that requires our participation. We have seen how these ontological conclusions regarding mimesis entail certain claims about the practical field of thought and action. We are implicated in the task of disclosing a meaningful and truthful world. The dream of metaphysical idealism and strict representational realism has vanished. Nevertheless, we do contend with and respond to reality even as we struggle to enact a world.[5]

Another supposition under criticism in our postmodern situation is that thought is capable of developing total explanations of all reality. This claim is co-implicated in the problem of representation just noted. After all, thought cannot grasp a totality without configuring it—a possibility, as Ricoeur shows, that ever eludes us because of time. We are increasingly aware of the plurality of ways of seeing the world and of the diversity present in all monistic systems. Again mimesis seems the culprit. From Plato's mimetic cosmology to Hegel's mimetic theory of history, totalization and mimesis seem almost inseparable.[6] That is, there has been a search for the one, archaic act, whether cognitive or representational, that would allow a total philosophical system.

Against these totalizing tendencies critics of ideology have come forward.[7] These thinkers herald the practical character of thought. What are we to be and to do? What ends should we seek, and are they good and fitting ends? Practical thinkers seek to confront the reader with these questions. Their concern arises from the admission that all thought, discourse, and action are fueled by interests, guided by ends-in-view, and expressive of loyalties. Therefore, we must also ask about whose thought and interests are served by any cultural or political system. This requires uncovering the mechanisms of ideology that cover up interest and power relations.

The other advance we have made beyond imitation involves the dynamics of thought. Because it is mimetic, understanding is always participatory, social, and guided by practical concerns. Practical reasons, therefore, must ever confront false and distorted configurations of life in text, culture, and the systems of knowledge-production and political legitimation in a society. The "speculative" character of thought arises from its embeddedness in tradition even while it is constantly revising and presenting that tradition anew. Yet given the possible distortions in this inheritance, practical reason also always stands under the expectation of the new marked by hope. By reading Kierkegaard, I shall isolate the dimension of passion and desire that drives existence. But I am not seeking to determine the archaic act that will allow the construction of a total system of thought and being. Rather, I am attempting to discover analogies in the mimetic shape of understanding, narrativity, and selfhood as a way to think about and respond to the questions facing theology and ethics.

Kierkegaard's thought takes us into another arena of concern in our postmodern situation. I want to recall Mark C. Taylor's comment quoted earlier: "The relation between God and the self is thoroughly specular; each mirrors the other. In different terms, man is made in the image of God. This *imago* is an imitation, copy, likeness, representation, similitude, appearance, or shadow of divinity. . . . The recognition that man is believed to be the *imago Dei* suggests that the self is a 'theological conception.' "[8] The notions that the self is the icon of God, a substance that can be variously formed, and a transcendental "I" are suspect or untenable in an age deeply aware of the drives and plays of the unconscious. Yet these older pictures of the self have sustained much of Western thought. The human as the image of God certainly was the supposition behind the standard reading of the *imitatio Dei* and the deep relation between the *imago Dei* and *imitatio* in biblical thought. It was clear that "though the self is made in the image of God, the *imago* presents the task of *imitatio*. Through imitation of the image, the self seeks to achieve identity or to become what it is."[9] Plato argued that through imitation one seeks to become like the gods. Biblical texts claimed that through following the Lord one becomes what one most fundamentally is, one realizes the *imago Dei*. The criticism of imitation becomes a critique of the self. The self, inscribed in the logic and analogies of the "image," seems as archaic an idea as imitation or God.

A substantial notion of the self or the soul is untenable. Yet the attack on the self must be countered when it denies the human. In light of the modern devaluation of the person, in technology, state capitalism, and late socialism, can we charge ourselves and others with the task of countering repression if it is impossible to speak of moral agency? And if we cannot call for moral responsibility, what is to stop the wanton destruction of the weak, the world, and nature? At a more simple level, the very act of reading confronts us with the demand to choose between options presented by a text, as Ricoeur notes. And more profoundly, to understand at all is to take a stand relative to human solidarity.[10] Thus we cannot evade the question of the self, even as we must realize that this self is not a substance but an agent, not a solitary "I" but a social self interdependent with others, its world, and the earth. It is to the problem of the self, the self as agent, that Kierkegaard makes his contribution to our study. As Louis Pojman notes, Kierkegaard's "purpose in writing is not primarily theoretical but practical. He wants to help men and women *exist*, not learn to speculate on 'existence'—even though he speculates on the concept a good deal himself."[11]

What is interesting is that Kierkegaard finds it necessary to think the self and its act of existing in relation to Christ. This necessity arises not only from the centrality of Christ in Christian faith. To be sure, since St. Paul the *imitatio* has been defined as the imitation of Christ; Kierkegaard follows Paul in this Christological turn, as he does in so many things. Yet a close examination of Kierkegaard's texts with their Christological focus opens up another avenue for exploring the human self, one that insists that the self always comes to be relative to another, an other power. Kierkegaard's thought can also be seen as moving from the problematic of the self to Christ. Thus by exploring the self's response to Christ, Kierkegaard attempts to think about the human against its religious depth and horizon. In a thoroughly hermeneutical manner, Kierkegaard argues that critical self-understanding is the fruit of examined life. But that examination is one of interpretation and not simple introspection. My contention is that the "*imitatio*" becomes crucial in his analysis even as he enriches our understanding of mimesis. Kierkegaard develops what I call a mimetic interpretation of human selfhood.

The final problem occupying current thought is that the questions just mentioned are interrelated. As noted, human thought cannot grasp all reality into one scheme without the power to represent that totality. Imitation has given thought a tool for picturing the cosmos as a universe, as one. Moreover, fundamental representations of reality, by an almost inherent force, expand to capsulize the whole. Surely this is the case with our most basic metaphors: Being, time, goodness, truth, process, God, and, more recently, text! It is hardly surprising that mimesis should be found on all sides of our dilemma and, in fact, link the sides into a whole. But the supposition I have challenged is that the standard picture of mimesis can be sustained. Obviously, I think it cannot. I have argued that mimesis-as-copy arises only when linguistic action is understood on analogy to plastic arts.[12] And human action and the self are seen as imitative only when imitation is taken as a way to relate to a past or transcendent reality and not as a mode of temporal existence itself. The task is to develop a vocabulary for reflection beyond the imitative universe.

Postmodern reflection raises the question of the relation of language, action, and time as categories for understanding human existence. If language is temporal and active, which it is in use, then no linguistic formulation can claim to be permanent or to exhaust what is. All language is a process of reference; a static conceptual totality is a linguistic impossibility. But for the same reason, language can render the flux of existence meaningful; existence can be brought *to* language. The limitations on discourse do not discount its power to render the world meaningful through figuration. The dual impulse of postmodern thought moves away from representationalism because of the temporal and active character of language and toward a linguistic, and thus unified, vision of that temporal process.

In view of this problem of action–time–language, we have turned to narrative as *one* central hermeneutical category.[13] The value of narrative is that by its very nature it links the temporal, active, and linguistic dimension of human existence. And because of this, it is hardly surprising that those concerned with the unity of the agent through time should find narrative a boon for their thought. Thus it is customary for some narrative theorists to postulate that life has a narrative structure. Yet the fathers of narrative theology and philosophy knew differently. Augustine knew that narrative was the presentation of a more basic process: memory. And *memoria*, as temporal and linguistic, was a mimetic phenomenon. Aristotle, as we have seen, understood narrative as the mimesis of human action. Thus not only the postmodern problem, but the current popularity of "narrative," lead us back to mimesis.

What I have accomplished thus far in my reconstruction of mimesis is to rethink the problem in relation to texts, understanding, and language. And although mimesis as I have reconstructed it does not allow for a static speculative totality, it does provide a way to see some analogical connections within the domains of experience. In a word, we have undertaken a critical retrieval of important insights from the "Greek" side of our cultural and intellectual heritage that has pushed us to specific moral and religious questions: What does it mean to be a self? What is human solidarity and how do we enact it? What is the power of speaking that refigures time? With these questions in hand we turn to Kierkegaard. His work takes us into another side of our cultural tradition: biblical thought. What I hope to show is that for him the *imitatio* is a form of existential communication, a strategy for existence, edification, and salvation relative to the object of faith.

Of course, reading Kierkegaard is a notoriously difficult undertaking. And I make no pretense to providing a definitive interpretation of his texts! Indeed, a "definitive" reading of Kierkegaard is impossible since his works are designed to confront each reader anew. My reading of his pseudonymous texts, and specifically those inscribed under the names of Climacus and Anti-Climacus, will move in four broad steps. I want to foreshadow this reading briefly so that the flow of the argument will not be lost in its details.

First, I shall uncover some of the suppositions that back his authorship and strategy of communication, looking specifically at his understanding of language, thought, and paradox. This expands the analysis from a concentration solely on his dialectics or poetic strategy by tracing their interrelation around his central religious concerns.[14] These three foci correspond to the elements of mimesis discerned before: language, understanding, and being. What we shall see is that Kierkegaard attempts to break away from all forms of immanence, in which the human is simply rooted in truth, in favor of a form of inwardness in which the relation to the truth becomes the problem of existence. Hence like Gadamer and Ricoeur, although more radically, Kierkegaard starts with what confronts the human and not the isolated soul or *cogito*. There is no total mediation. Given this, the problem of existence and understanding is a practical question, not a speculative or theoretical one. At bottom, the denial of immanence is rooted in the paradoxical character of human being. Thus Kierkegaard continues ontological themes I have already charted relative to an understanding of the self. I hope to show that the *imitatio*, or existential mimesis, is crucial to understanding his interpretation of being human.

Next, I shall turn to Kierkegaard's analysis of the self. The standard reading of his texts isolates certain polar elements and relations within an analytic of existence. As Stephen Dunning shows, Kierkegaard's "paradoxical dialectics" of the stages of existence is controlled by the self/other relation and by the dialectics of inner/outer in the self.[15] Though I accept this interpretation, I am interested in exploring the dynamic of existing itself. Here the temporality of the self comes to the fore as do the various forms of passion that constitute or fail to constitute it. Therefore, my reading of Kierkegaard's famous "stages" of existence centers on the passion that drives each mode of life. Here too we shall see that the self is paradoxical in its being. Since Kierkegaard's authorship is mimetic, as Ricoeur understood this, we shall see how textual mimesis and existential *imitatio* interlock. The question becomes then: How does the self relate to a truth transcendent of it? This leads us to Kierkegaard's discussion of the *imitatio Christi*.

At this stage in my argument I shall suggest a reading of *Training in Christianity* by Anti-Climacus, a text too often neglected in Kierkegaard scholarship. In this work *imitatio* is the way the self comes to be relative to the power that establishes it, and the question becomes, then: How is the self related to this power?[16] The subtle dialectic of *Training* manifests a mimetic character while accenting the importance of passion in human existence. The *imitatio* becomes the way to realize existence while engendering inwardness, or selfhood. Thus through the *imitatio* there is a double mimesis: the truth, in this case Christ, is presented anew in the world in the figuration of the self as the self comes into existence. Thus through the *imitatio*, Kierkegaard denies any simple understanding of the self while not forgoing concern for the inwardness of human life.

Finally, by relating Kierkegaard's mimetic authorship with existential *imitatio*, we can return to Ricoeur's notion of narrative identity to speak of the continuity of the self through time without denying the constant task of life. What is more important, we can raise the question of the self's relation to the power that establishes it, a question that returns us to the dual orientation of the human, through narrative figuration, to death and eternity. At that point we shall be pushed beyond Kierkegaard into theological reflection. Thus in the next chapter of this study I shall chart the analogies between the forms of mimetic action and the way they raise religious and moral questions vis-à-vis the problem of power.

THE ADVANCE ON SOCRATES

"The birds on the branches, the lilies in the field, the deer in the forest, the fishes in the sea, countless hosts of happy men, exultantly proclaim: God is love. But beneath all these sopranos, supporting them as it were, as the bass part does, is audible the *de profundis* which issues from the sacrificed one: God is love."[17]

Kierkegaard the author retreats behind the pseudonymous works. The use of pseudonyms denies the readers fascination or identification with the author and hence forces us to confront the text as it is given. The authorship establishes a maieutic relationship between the reader and the text so that we may encounter the modes of existing portrayed in the text.[18]

The pseudonymous works provide the occasion for readers to stand before the ways of life presented in the text. The works, in Ricoeur's sense, open up a world in front of themselves.[19] Given this, we have a key to the form and function of the authorship. As a strategy for the edification of the self, the authorship must be commensurate with the structure and character of the self. It must also have a disclosive function to allow the readers to encounter themselves. The interweaving of the authorship and Kierkegaard's notion of the self means that we must expect some overlap in the reading of his work.

Kierkegaard knew well the tension between poetry and Christianity. According to him, Christianity is, most profoundly, not a doctrinal system; it is existential communication. As he wrote in his *Papirer*, "For Christianity the question is: does or does not my personal life express what is communicated?"[20] The distinction between poetic communication and Christianity is that poetry expresses a possibility for life while Christianity is a personal life expressive of what is communicated. The issue, therefore, is how existence is communicated and expressed. The various pseudonymous authors have no intention of speaking with authority, of imparting truth to the receptive reader.[21] "Direct communication" would assert that existence could be reduced to conceptual terms and easily communicated to the reader: that being in love, for example, could be communicated by talking about one's being in love. The possibility of direct communication would signal the primacy of theoretical reflection over the practical task of thought and life. It would mean that the problem of life is answerable by speculation and not a decisive mode of life. For this to be the case, thought must be in unity with Being, and the act of appropriating existence, of coming to be as an individual, a cognitive exercise. This is one dividing point, as Kierkegaard takes it, between himself and Hegel or Socrates, despite similarities in their projects. That is, though Kierkegaard's thought has manifest dialectical characteristics and he seeks to help women and men to *exist* through edifying discourse, he breaks with the presuppositions of Hegel and Socrates.

While truth, for Kierkegaard, is the adequation of idea and reality, he understands this as an existential task and not a cognitive problem. The real issue is how to render the ideal actual and actual ideal in existence. Thus he does not grant a thoroughgoing principle of identity between thought and Being. Kierkegaard's reason for this, as Mark C. Taylor notes, is theological: the principle of identity threatens to deny the qualitative difference between God and humanity.[22] There is also an existential reason: the self is not a simple given or a substance self-identical through time; it is a task. Thus for theological and existential reasons, religious communication must be carried on in an "indirect" manner. The negation of the identity of thought and Being is what undergirds the authorship and its mode of indirect communication, and the strategy of the authorship is dictated by considerations transcending linguistic and poetic structures. It is dictated by the character of God and of the human.

Though the authorship seeks by its mimetic shape to bring forms of life to language, thereby confronting the reader with a choice, existence itself, and certainly God, are not, in any strong sense, immanent *in* language. Insofar as the pseudonymous works are mimetic, they are rooted in the shape of existence itself even as they are figures of ways of life.

The pseudonymous works are mimetic in Ricoeur's sense because the reader encounters ways of existing as real possibilities for life. The aim of the authorship is concrete existence *on the reader's part*, but the texts themselves are poetic. What the works do is to map out an education on the way to existence, specifically Christian existence. A reader's response to the works places her or him on this "map." Kierkegaard's famous stages of life (the aesthetic, the ethical, and the religious) do not follow in a necessarily sequential course.[23] Rather, existence is presented from various perspectives, embodied in the authors' lives, in an attempt to outline modes of existing. But the self may exist in different spheres or stages at different times. Each work confronts the reader with embodiments of existence seeking to ignite a reflective moment on his or her part. In this sense, the texts seek to confront the reader with the force of the present demanding an act initiating a mode of life. In this act the *ek-stases* of time are given figurative unity in life. Thus we see here the importance of Ricoeur's claim about reading relative to the problem of reference in texts. We shall also see how Kierkegaard's claims about the act of existence deepens our understanding of what reading entails. Indeed, to refigure life means to come to be as a specific self living a particular kind of life.

The works are mimetic in a twofold sense: they stand as mimetic presentations of ways of living in the world, as different configurations of life; and as mimetic they disclose through interpretation ways of existing to the reader. The authorship is a strategy for edification. Karl Jaspers is correct when he notes that "Kierkegaard gave his own writings no other meaning than that they should read again the original text of the individual, human existential relations."[24] Kierkegaard can speak of the "poetic actuality" of the various authors in his pseudonymous corpus because the works present actuality (the authors' lives) and possibility (the options opened to the readers) for existence. What the authorship as a whole represents is an intricate edifying strategy in which poetic structures and the self interlock. His poetics is mimetic since it presents a reality in a heightened mode of existence and demands a response from the reader. The configuration of existence in the authorship allows for insight into life, a claim as old as Aristotle's *Poetics*.

Louis Mackey,[25] and others, have stressed just this poetic character of the authorship. The burden of my argument is to show that the structure of the self is also mimetic. Doing so demands uncovering further strata in the authorship before exploring the question of the self. Initially, then, we are concerned with the presentation of existential possibilities, or with how the authorship works. To understand Kierkegaard's poetics we must consider three subsidiary notions:

the use of paradox, the epistemological assumptions that back and are evident in the works, and the notion of language that serves as the linchpin for the authorship. We are attending to those areas of concern isolated through Gadamer and Ricoeur: language, understanding, and the character of Being. This will establish the dialectic of narrative identity, in Ricoeur's sense, understanding, and mimetic existence. I realize that such an approach may sound confusing. I am not implying that Kierkegaard set out a system of thought—a more foolish reading of these texts can hardly be imagined. My concern here is to lay open those notions that help back the authorship, while realizing that Kierkegaard never developed, and never wanted to develop, a system.

I want to begin with the place of language in the authorship. Three short citations will take us to the core of Kierkegaard's understanding of its power and limits.[26]

> (a) "That which annuls immediacy therefore is language [sporget]. If a man could not speak he would remain in immediacy."[27]
>
> (b) "Hegel in any case deserves the credit for showing that language had thought immanent in itself and that thought is developed in language."[28]
>
> (c) "Language has time as its element; all other media have space as their element."[29]

Through language the human escapes natural immediacy. We have a world because of and mediated by language, as Gadamer argued. Language ruptures immediacy because it has temporal and epistemic dimensions. First, language has thought *in it*. Although time, as Ricoeur argued, and existence, as Kierkegaard claims, are not immanent in language, insofar as they can be understood as meaningful, they must come *to* language. Thought is bound to language; as Gadamer claimed, language is Being that can be understood.

But thought concerns possibilities, not actualities. To think is to break with the immediacy of given reality. On this point Kierkegaard agrees with recent deconstructionist thinkers: pure immediacy and presence are not open to lingual beings.[30] Thought apprehends immediate reality by reducing it to a conceptual possibility. This is true whether one undertakes the philosophical task of isolating the conditions of the possibility for phenomenal experience, or considers a simple plan of action. Regarding Kierkegaard's overall project, this means that thought cannot know existence *qua* existence. The connection of thought and language merely heightens the dilemma of the authorship since its subject matter, existence, escapes linguistic communication.

The primary connection of thought and language is functional: to present possible modes of existing to the individual and in doing so to break the immediacy of self and world. Thought does this because it moves from actuality (*esse*) to possibility (*posse*). The movement is the inverse of existing, which is always from *posse* to *esse* initiated by an act of the self, an act rendering one an agent. Climacus writes in the *Concluding Unscientific Postscript* that the "aesthetic and the intellectual principle is that no reality is thought or understood until its *esse* has been resolved into its *posse*" (CUP 288). Using Kantian language, we can say that thought seeks the conditions of the possibility for actual experience and life. Thought moves in two directions: from concretion toward abstraction, and when coupled with language (which it always is), from immediacy (identity) to a diastasis between what is and what may be.[31]

As Kierkegaard sees it, there are significant differences between imaginative thought, which generates possibilities, and the appropriation of these for life.[32] And it is precisely here, as we saw, that Ricoeur too had to move from narrative interpretation to practical existence. Imagination grasps something as possible *for me*. To appropriate something is to apprehend something in reality, and this affects the one who understands. Understanding itself is a double mimesis: what is understood, the *Sache*, is realized anew in its appropriation, and the one *who* understands is transformed, as Gadamer argued.

Understanding is a "reduplication" of thought in life. The object in question may well be the same for imagination and existential appropriation. The difference is that when "I understand something in possibility I remain essentially unchanged, remain in the old, and use my imagination; when it becomes reality, then I am the one changed and the question is now whether I can preserve myself."[33] Kierkegaard's point is that understanding something is a more comprehensive task and problem than imaginative apprehension. And here his notion of "reduplication" augments Ricoeur's and Gadamer's discussions of understanding. To understand at all is to understand differently. This is true not only because of the historical, cultural, and linguistic distanciations that inform understanding, but also because the one understanding is changed in the act. This brings to the fore the problem of existential realization.

The issue for Kierkegaard stated most boldly is this: thought cannot be identified with the being of the self. Coming into existence involves more than thought. It demands decisions, passion, and will. Existence has its own character and structure. Nonetheless, thought is important in the distancing of the self from the world, a break essential for the human to stand out from its environment into a world and selfhood. We have already charted this distanciation in historical understanding and narrative configuration; it is what disallows total mediation and thereby evokes hermeneutical reflection. Kierkegaard's entire analysis of the self moves toward deepening levels of individuality, given this problem of distanciation. The self must stand out from its immediate world, law, and even the holy. Yet in standing out, in ex-isting, the self struggles to relate itself to the power that establishes it. This differentiation of the self-coming-to-be from the world, law, and the holy begins with the breaking of the immediacy of self and world through thought. A primordial relation of immediate participation is thus shattered by thought and language and even more so by the act of existence itself. But the basic problem of the self's relation to the power that establishes it remains. The primacy of this dialectic of productive distanciation and participation relative to fundamental postures in life is what makes Kierkegaard's work a hermeneutic of existence beyond modernist hermeneutics of consciousness. It is an insight elaborated in Heidegger's notion of Care, Gadamer's claims about historical consciousness and language, and Ricoeur's arguments for the mimetic figuration of time in narrative.

Thought has the power to break immediacy because it is always linguistic, and this establishes the hermeneutical problem for Kierkegaard. That is, language is the medium of existence; it relates thought and thinker. But this also means that it is primarily through linguistic constructs that the self will lay hold of possibilities for existence. Hence Ricoeur's talk of narrative identity helps us to understand Kierkegaard's point. What Kierkegaard does is to accept the functional power of language to generate diastasis between thought and existence and to present possibilities for life even as he places the problem of the relation of thought and reality in the context of existence. Existence is the troubled attempt to reduplicate in life what is passionately held to be true.

The claim is, then, that human life must move from primitive immediacy to a mediated relation to the world in order to come to be as a self. Not surprisingly, those stages of existence that seek pure immediacy—specifically, the hedonistic aesthetic and the mystical—attempt to transcend thought and language. They rest on an "immediate animal instinct or primitive trust" that is broken and overcome in the second immediacy of genuine faith.[34] The aesthete seeks the immediacy of pleasure; the mystic, that of wordless contemplation. The breaking of immediacy through thought and language is crucial, then, to the analysis of existence. But it also sets up the unique problem of the authorship regarding Christianity: if Christianity is not a thought system, which Kierkegaard clearly holds it is not, then how is Christianity communicated? I shall return to this question later.

Thought is immanent in language. That was Kierkegaard's first point. Yet language is also tensive; language has time as its element. This is the second important aspect of language in relation to the self. Robert Widerman has shown that time is a central category of Kierkegaard's notion of the self.[35] Rather than as a substance or an eternal soul, he sees the self as a process, a continual struggle or striving to actualize itself by moving from the actual (past) to the possible (future) through the decisive present.[36] Because language has time as its element, it is uniquely suited to relate to the self as deeply temporal. Thus Kierkegaard is exploring how the self comes to be at all in time.[37]

Language is the medium for the relation of thought and the self. Language is also the meeting place of thought and time, just as existence is the meeting place of possibility and temporality. The dual nature of language gives it a twofold function: it is disjunctive of thought and Being, and yet conjunctive of self and its thought. Language is fundamental to existence precisely because it opens possibilities for the self and is a medium for the relation of these (and hence the future) to the self in time. The authorship is built on this dual capacity of language even if the problem of existence is not answered by it. As we shall see, it is in the decision of the self to come to be relative to a possible mode of life that there is a fusion of past, present, and future that marks the modality of the existential act. In the act of decision one becomes, in Kierkegaard's terms, "contemporaneous" with the past (specifically the event of Christ) even as a hoped-for future (eternal salvation) is instanciated. The importance of language to this act, particularly the Scriptures, is that in and through it options for the self are presented that demand a decision under the force of the present. Yet it is the decision that is crucial for the being of the self in all its temporal richness and ambiguity and not simply the linguistic form that presents options to the self.

Given the power and limits of language, we can isolate the epistemological assumptions backing Kierkegaard's authorship as they impinge on his analysis of self. He clearly wants to discern the limits of thought in the movement of existence and its relation to truth. The self and truth are existential; pure thought is not. In a word, Kierkegaard is willing to accept Kant's limitations on reason as well as the antinomies of thought.[38] He does not mark off thought and faith as two modes of knowledge. That is, Kierkegaard does not hold to a dual truth-theory in which religious "truths," while not cohering with other modes of knowing and their claims to validity, do have truth-value relative to their own specifiable conditions or rationality. Rather, he wishes "to set faith, as an experience and a commitment, over against all forms of knowledge."[39] Thus Kierkegaard opts not for radical subjectivism, but for "understanding," in which the individual is changed through encountering and appropriating what is understood. What then is the relation of thought to the self?

Climacus states in the *Postscript* that "the only thing-in-itself which cannot be thought is existence, and this does not come within the province of thought to think" (CUP 292). Existence is beyond the arena of thought, even the thought of the genius, the Professor, and The System![40] Existence cannot be thought for various reasons. As Climacus never tires of saying, thought is in another domain; it is in the realm of the abstract and the timeless. Existence is concrete, actual, and deeply temporal. Though intellect is the sphere of immanence, existence is a dramatic risk of actualization, of freedom, lived out in the world. Existence cannot be captured in thought because, as we have seen, thought moves from actuality to possibility. Existing is a move from possibility to actuality.

For instance, when we think about becoming something, say an author, our very thinking about that way of life reduces it to its possibility. If it were otherwise, we could not entertain the idea as a live option for us. But being an author, actually becoming one, is a demand to actualize a mode of existence. And this, so Kierkegaard contends, is not a matter of generating possibilities. Indeed, the continual generation of possibilities can, and often does, hinder actualizing a way of life. The point is that when thought turns to a mode of existence, that way of life is reduced to its possibility for me, for you, and hence no longer is properly existence. Existence by definition is beyond the pale of thought to grasp. This is not a nihilistic heralding of the irrationality of life. On the contrary, our apprehension of possibilities for life is crucial so that we might come to be as this or that person. Nevertheless, actually coming to be as someone cannot be realized in thought alone.

Kierkegaard is not simply heaping scorn on reason in the name of irrationalism. He is setting limits around the power and scope of thought. His authorship demonstrates these limits because it depicts ideal, possible, and poetic presentations of ways of living. The works perform an intellective function by opening possibilities to the reader. Yet it is the reader, as Ricoeur says, who must understand these possibilities and realize them in life. As H. A. Nielsen has noted regarding *Philosophical Fragments*, the "reader, Climacus hopes, will help himself, caring not at all about the author's private opinion, quite willing, in fact, to allow the author a sphere of purely personal concern corresponding to his own."[41] In coming to be, thought and the possible mode of life poetically presented are brought into actuality by the "reader," the agent. Yet the cause of this coming to be must lie in something other than thought, in pathos, will, and freedom. Existential realization is, therefore, a double mimesis: by becoming a self the possibility for existence disclosed in the work is realized even as the self comes to be relative to that possibility. In this sense the self is a figuring of life even as its possibility is presented to it.

At this point we are pushed to the ontological assumptions of the authorship neatly encapsulated in Kierkegaard's notion of paradox. What he means by paradox is itself a matter of dispute, of course. The problem is found at two points: Kierkegaard's distinctive uses of paradox, and whether existence and Christianity are irrational. We can address the second issue by way of the first.[42]

In his *Journals*, Kierkegaard wrote that the "paradox is not a concession but a category, an ontological definition which expresses the relation between an existing cognitive spirit and eternal truth" (J 633). This entry falls in the midst of a discussion of understanding. Kierkegaard's point is that when the thinker her- or himself is considered, a paradox arises, an ontological paradox.[43]

The paradox is on two levels: that of presuppositions, and that of the relation of the self to the truth, of thought to existing. The presupposition of idealism, as Kierkegaard takes it, is that the truth is *in us* ontologically. Given this identity of thought and Being, the relation of the self to the truth is conceptual or introspective. The way to that relation is either the flight of Hegelian dialectic or the struggle of Socratic recollection. In either case, some total mediation is possible, a mediation aimed at becoming godlike or the realization of absolute Spirit in time. But what if this is not the case? What if the truth is *not in us*? This would be an absolute shift in presuppositions. And since we must at least admit the plausibility of these questions, we are moved, according to Kierkegaard, beyond Greek and German idealism.

Climacus, in the *Philosophical Fragments*, calls this new situation being in error, being in sin. Nielsen, summarizing Climacus, puts it nicely: "Being in the state of Error through one's own fault we call *Sin*. If we suppose the individual could will himself out of this state, we fall back into the Socratic view of things in which the individual is not destitute of the Truth but only separated from it by forgetting, or by not yet having thought his way through to it."[44] This error is revealed not by thought itself, but by the paradox of the Incarnation, the infinite entering the finite in time. This makes the Teacher and history central to the existence of the self rather than a Socratic midwife in the birth of the self from itself. We can easily compare the difference, as Pojman has done.[45]

SOCRATIC WAY	CHRISTIAN WAY
1. Truth is within man and man is open to that truth.	1. The truth is not within man; rather, man is in error, closed to the truth.
2. The teacher is incidental to the process of discovering the truth.	2. The Teacher is necessary to the process of discovering the truth; he must bring it from without and create the condition for receiving it within man.
3. The moment of discovery of the truth is accidental. The opportunity is always available; we must merely use our innate ability to recover it.	3. The moment is decisive for discovering the truth. The Eternal must break into time at a definite point (the fullness of time) and the believer must receive the condition in a moment of contemporaneity with the Teacher.

The Incarnation of the Teacher, so understood, is a paradox, given the suppositions of any form of immanence: it is a conflict of categories concerning the human relation to the truth, and it results from a conflict of presuppositions about the human. The Incarnation is a limit where thought breaks down. In this sense the paradox of the Incarnation has a deeply ironic power. It strips bare all presuppositions about ourselves and the truth and destroys the power of thought to comprehend existence while exposing the being of the self.

The heart of the categorical paradox is the relation of the self to the truth.[46] If the truth is in us, if truth is reached by recollection through strategies of introspection, then there is no internal paradox in relating the human to the truth. But if truth is not in us and yet cognition by definition is immanent, how do we relate to the truth? That is Kierkegaard's question. And it seems that any appearance of truth in time will be paradoxical, even absurd! So too will our relation to the truth be a paradox, a conflict of categories beyond the pale of thought. The problem of relating to the truth shifts from the task of recollection to another capacity of the self. And this demands an entirely different edifying strategy, an advance on Socrates. That strategy is the *imitatio*.

Paradox is a category for relating the self to a radically transcendent truth. Neither Hegelian mediation nor Socratic recollection but paradox is the mechanism of Kierkegaard's authorship and its edifying strategy. The Incarnation confronts the self with a paradox not resolvable into a higher synthesis or mediation. Thus against dialectic as simple contradiction or as reciprocity between positions Kierkegaard offers us a dialectic of paradox.[47] This means that one's relation to this truth is within the sphere of existence and what stands over against existence. "He who understands the paradox will forget that by understanding it (as a possibility) he has gone back to the old notions and lost touch with Christianity" (CUP 515). The reason that intellect must be crucified in the face of the paradox of the Incarnation is that thought moves from actuality to possibility and hence destroys the paradox of the Incarnation. The problem is how to exist in relation to this truth. The structure of existence becomes here the presentation of its possibility. Existing is the criteriology of thought: truth is subjectivity, as Climacus puts it.

It is clear that paradox informs the authorship, particularly the work of Climacus, and Kierkegaard's understanding of the Incarnation. In fact, paradox summarizes the problem of the authorship: how is one related to the truth? This notion of paradox depicts a clash of categories, a limit-situation, brought on by the affirmation of the Incarnation and the diastasis of thought and Being because of sin. It is a clash not at the level of metaphor (Ricoeur) but in the self. Yet paradox is a literary strategy essential to the authorship, given the understanding of the human relation to the truth. My contention is that there is a relation between paradox and the centrality of *imitatio* in Kierkegaard's texts.

I have argued that the poetics of the pseudonymous works rests on certain notions of language, epistemology, and paradox: on language, because in language, as in the self, thought and time meet (I have already charted this relation in mimetic narrative); on epistemology in setting its own limit and sphere of influence; and on paradox because of the self's relation to the truth. We see, then, the medium of the authorship (language), its task (the presentation of possibilities), and its strategy (paradox). The central concern of the authorship is the human relation to the truth. That relationship is a matter of communication and understanding. The advance on Socrates involves in part a theory of communication, an authorship, that does not accept immanentalism and the strategies of communication demanded by it. The works demand reflection; they confront the reader with poeticized existence transcendent to the self and demand a choice, a decision, about existence. To grasp the full import of Kierkegaard's mimetic strategy, we must now turn to his notion of the self.

SPIRIT–RELATION–SELF

For Kierkegaard, the self is spirit and relation relating itself to itself in a twofold dialectic of inner/outer and self/other. In *Sickness unto Death* Anti-Climacus writes:

> Man is spirit (*Aand*). But what is spirit? Spirit is the self. But what is the self (*Selv*)? The self is a relation (*Forhold*) which relates itself to its own self. . . . the self is not the relation but (consists in the fact) that the relation relates itself to its own self. Man is a synthesis (*Synthese*) of the infinite and the finite, of the temporal and the eternal, of freedom and necessity, in short it is a synthesis.[18]

This is a complex statement. Clearly, there are several aspects of the self in which, as John Elrod puts it, "different expressions of the self as synthesis (*Synthese*) refer to the formal structure of the self's being to which spirit is bound in its development."[49] The actual relation is the process whereby the self is actualized by moving from a given to an end. Yet this entire process involves formal elements of the self. There are, in fact, various synthetic expressions of the self, various relations to the relation of spirit (*Aand*) and relation (*Forhold*), that are the self.

Elrod has also suggested five relations crucial to understanding Kierkegaard's interpretation of the self: (*a*) finite–infinite: concrete; (*b*) body–soul: spirit; (*c*) reality–ideality: consciousness; (*d*) necessity–possibility: freedom; (*e*) time–eternity: temporality. The self is a reflexive process of relating to itself as an internal relation. And given this, the authentic self is, in Elrod's helpful scheme, concrete, temporal spirit that is free and conscious. The point is that when the self relates itself to itself what actually happens is that the self as spirit relates itself to itself as a synthesis of polar relations. What interests us is this process of relating in those relations since this *is* the self.

The self is the existential reflexive act of relating, but always, as Anti-Climacus insists, to a third. In *Sickness Unto Death* that third is cryptically called "the power which establishes the self." To become a self is to relate the self to itself relating to the power that establishes it. Against those who look to the polar relations in Kierkegaard's notion of the self, my concern is with the relation of the self to the power that establishes it and the shape of that relationship. This opens up the religious depth of the analysis of the self while helping to forward my own argument. Accordingly, I shall center my reading not on the various structures of the self, or on its synthetic expressions, although these will be assumed. Rather, I shall concentrate on the mode of the relation, on the movement itself. My contention is that Kierkegaard has a kinetic idea of the self because he centers on the motion of the coming-to-be. We shall see that he is concerned with the middle term that is the cause of the motion of the self. This term is the *pathos*, the passion, that relates the self to the power that establishes it. It is through passionate decision that the self "is." We can hardly imagine a less substantialist view of the self. In fact, I shall argue that it is necessary to borrow Ricoeur's notion of narrative identity to speak of the continuity of the agent through time even as Kierkegaard's analytic of the self is called for by the limits of narrative identity.

Kierkegaard's notion of the self is a kinetic one. It has marked similarities with Aristotle's thought about motion, which Kierkegaard studied through the works of Trendelenberg. We should recall that in the fourfold order of causation the efficient cause initiates change. Of course, Aristotle was primarily concerned with the motion of the cosmos and the problem of time, as we saw in the previous chapter; yet in considering living creatures, he claimed that they are moved efficiently by desire for some telos. The end desired is in fact the actualization of the nature of any entity. Existence is the coming-to-be of the entity relative to its end, its perfection. Kierkegaard is interested in the passion entailed in the movement, and hence temporality, of coming to be as a self.

The similarities between Kierkegaard and Aristotle are striking. There is a motion from potentiality to actuality initiated by a cause, a *pathos* for some end. Yet there are points of difference between them. For Kierkegaard there are a variety of possible modes of existing open to the individual. The coming to be of a self is never a simple actualization of a "nature," even human nature as a rational animal. An essential self or subject with normative force to determine the self is simply missing in his thought. Human nature does not have a specific given telos; nor is the reflexive "I," the unity and power of the self in itself, impervious to relations to others in time. The problem of the self is thus not merely its formation. It is the coming to be of the self and within that existential process the formation of particular ways of life.

The root of *kinesis* in the self is freedom manifest in a present existential act and not the act of consciousness. There is no necessity to actualize the self, and becoming a self is not simply a matter of consciousness. That is precisely the dilemma of human life. Thus George Stack is correct when he notes that for Kierkegaard "becoming is a change in actuality brought about by freedom. It is the 'category' of movement that enables Kierkegaard to describe the actuality of existence as a dialectical process of striving (*Straeben*) and becoming (*Vorden*)."[50] Climacus, in the *Fragments*, writes that this "coming-into-existence kind of change, therefore, is not a change in essence but in being and is a transition from not existing to existing" (PF 91). If this is the case, then we must explore the character of this motion and its cause.

Like Gadamer, Kierkegaard distinguishes between two kinds of motion: *alloiosis* and *kinesis*. *Alloiosis* presupposes the existence of what changes and is thus accidental change in the attributes of a being. This is true of natural processes. A picture, for instance, darkens and fades with age. We need not assume any doctrine of "substance" to grant that the picture remains even as it decays. In kinetic change the prior being is in fact a non-being, is possibility. Climacus continues the passage cited above: "But such a being, which is nonetheless a non-being, is precisely what possibility is; and a being which is being is indeed actual being or actuality; and the change of coming into existence is a transition from possibility to actuality" (PF 91). Existence is the *kinesis* from non-being to being; it is a leap into being. It is why, as we saw, Gadamer speaks of mimetic figuration as a "leap" into the true; something is presented *as* something and hence rendered meaningful, a rendering that marks an increase in its being. This suggests that non-being (possibility and freedom) and not some substance is the depth of self. The self is always in the risk of non-being sustained over pure nihility. Stated differently: the self is ever in the process of coming to be; it is future-directed and rooted in freedom even as it must initiate its existence in response to the force of the present. As Kierkegaard notes, we think backward, but we always live forward. The futural and actualizing thrust of existence stands contrary to the retroactive gaze of thought.

For both Aristotle and Kierkegaard the discussion of motion is related to the problem of time. Each of them sees time as the measure of motion. For Kierkegaard, the movement of coming to be is our experience of time not in consciousness but in existence. Hence the temporal "instant" (*Ojeblikkelig*) of decision and choice is the event of the self coming to be and hence being in time. Robert Widerman has written:

> In the instant, when by a self-relating directed towards the eternal within him the individual "chooses himself," the eternal is present (*er til, naer-vaerende*) concretely, and the self is posited. If, by contrast, the eternal merely is, or is not (for the individual), then we have life in the moment. With the instant begins internal time and history, the moment corresponds to exterior time and history.[51]

Widerman is incorrect to suggest that the eternal is within the individual. This would merely be the idealistic scheme introduced through temporal categories. Kierkegaard rejects this framework. What is important to see is that the "instant" is an existentially decisive moment. Thus we might understand the "moment" as accidental change (*alloiosis*) whereas the *instant* is the increment of time in relation to kinetic existential change. Kierkegaard's point is that the *kinesis* of the self is tensed, and that in its coming-to-be its time and history begin. The self is temporal because the self as kinetic is the measure of time, or at least it is the vantage point from which to understand time existentially. Indeed, the present act of the self relates the past and the future directedness of life into an existential unity.

The coming-to-be of the self is of fundamental importance for Kierkegaard's notion of history and the self's relation to past events, like the event of Christ. We can say that the mimetic character of prefigured existence is rooted in the character of coming-to-be. This lends greater plausibility to Ricoeur's idea of narrative identity since self-identity is rooted in temporal experience. But this temporality of the self, correspondingly, ties Kierkegaard's analytic to textual mimesis. His notion of time is an interpretation of the dynamics of change. The problem then becomes: How does one actualize a possibility? The question of the "how" occupies Kierkegaard throughout the authorship.

"Existence," in its most literal sense means to stand forth, stand out, or to arise. Climacus speaks of existing as a striving. In the *Postscript* he writes:

> Existence itself, the act of existing, is a striving, and is both pathetic and comic in the same degree. It is pathetic because the striving is infinite; that is, it is directed towards the infinite, being and actualization of infinitude, a transformation which involves the highest pathos. It is comic, because such striving involves a self-contradiction. Viewed pathetically, a single second has infinite value; viewed comically, ten thousand years are but a trifle, like yesterday when it is gone. And yet, the time in which the existing individual lives, consists of just parts [CUP 84–85].

Existing is a striving, an emerging, from possibility to actuality. Kierkegaard thus rethinks the relation of beings to Being and the unity of existence in temporal and existential terms. This suggests that the root problem for Kierkegaard is twofold: the actualization of any possible way of existing (the how), and the continuity of the self through its acts of existing.

Climacus answers this twofold problem in the following way:

> An abstract continuity is no continuity, and the very existence of the existing individual is sufficient to prevent his continuity from having essential stability; while passion gives him a momentary continuity, a continuity which at one and the same time is a restraining influence and a moving impulse. The goal of a movement for an existing individual is to arrive at a decision, and to renew it. The eternal is the factor of continuity; but an abstract eternity within the existing individual is the maximum of his passion [CUP 277].

The answer has been set in two terms: *passion* and *telos*. The teleological perspective, again suggestive of Aristotle, relates to the bipolar facticity of the self. Each of the stages of existing relates the eternal pole of the self to the self differently. We should note however that it is the *passion* that the telos invokes that helps give continuity and integrity to the self.

The answer to this problem of actualization is *pathos*. Climacus writes that existence "constitutes the highest interest of the existing individual and his interest in his existence constitutes his reality. Reality is an *inter-esse* between the moments of that hypothetical unity of thought and Being which abstract thought presupposes" (CUP 279). Existence is always *inter-esse*, that is, a leap, a *kinesis*, of the self as a decisive act. The self is a leap into the true of existence; it is a particular figuration of Being. The question then becomes: What form of self is true?

For Kierkegaard, the individual's interest in his or her existence is crucial to constituting that existence. This interest or desire inserts the individual into the world of his texts and thus helps explain their mode of communication. But more important, it is the driving force of existence, and as a result it has import for the rhetoric of the authorship. Throughout his corpus there is, by means of various *pathoi*, an interlocking of modes of existing with the journey to selfhood. Basic to the characterization of these modes of existing, or stages, is the supposition of the paradoxical bipolar structure of human existence. The individual is precisely the dialectical relation of finite/infinite, possibility/ necessity, time/eternity, reality/ideality, body/soul as the self relates to itself. The self is a paradox. The various stages of existing are distinguished not by the formal structure of the self, but by the *pathos* and its object in which these poles are related or fail to relate in the self. To understand each mode of existence and what is demanded for a true self, we must grasp the particular way of relating the self to its formal structure in each stage.

The aesthetic stage is characterized by the *pathos* for the possible, which manifests an immediate form of faith.[52] There is, however, a tension between two forms of aesthetic life: the immediate and the reflective. The immediate aesthete, as the name implies, is lost in immediacy whereas the other loses the self in the endless maze of reflection and projection of possibilities. What these forms of aesthetic life share is a desire for pure possibility freed from the travail of actual life. The determination of the self is posited external to the self. That is, the infinite pole of existence is not brought into relation to the finite pole, and the self does not relate to the relation between them. Hence the immediate aesthete loses the self in the immediacy of sensation; and the reflective aesthete, in the abyss of reflection. To fail to make a decision to actualize any possibility is to defer existing altogether. Thus the aesthete is not in a state of becoming (existing), but is lost in relation to the idea, the possible. Climacus writes: "Aesthetic pathos expresses itself in words, and may in its truth indicate that the individual leaves his real self in order to lose himself in the Idea; while existential pathos is present whenever the Idea is brought into relation with the existence of the individual so as to transform it" (CUP 34). For the aesthete, the self has not related to itself. Reality has become the occasion for the ideality of the possible.

The ethical stage, as Kierkegaard calls it, is the mode of becoming and actuality, and its *pathos* is that of action and decision. Later I shall suggest a different understanding of ethics. But for Kierkegaard the point is that in the "ethical" stage the emphasis is on commitment and faithfulness, even fidelity. The individual makes a decision to relate itself over time to universal principles. Fundamentally, the ethical stage is one of relationship. The ethical person thinks the relationship is to God where the self comes into subjectivity by decisive action. Thus the ethical stage is an expression of will bringing into actuality various possibilities open to it. The ethical self is quite clearly not interested in "world-historical consequences," or any other end for that matter. The thought of acting for particular consequences is contrary, so the ethical person feels, to being ethical. The task is to relate the self to the universal, the absolute good. The ethical is depicted here in a Kantian form complete with an agent legislating its freedom relative to universal principles.[53] Ultimately the ethical *pathos* brings the self into the possibility of a relationship to God, or, as with Kant, the postulating of God based on moral faith. This is why the ethical is closely related to the religious.

There is, of course, a tension in the ethical. Though in the first instance the relation to God is posited as external to the self, which the self appropriates through decision, in the final analysis the self becomes aware of itself exclusively. The transcendence of the Good is captured by the drive of the self. The ethical person exists by willing a relation to the absolute good, but in the end is preoccupied and concerned only with the self and its success or failure. Yet in doing so the supposed disinterestedness of the self-agent is unmasked. As Nietzsche saw, a will-to-power is disclosed at the heart of the ethical so conceived. Thus the preoccupation of the self with itself over against its ostensive moral disinterestedness is the *Anfechtung*, the temptation, of the ethical. It is to assert the particularity of the self over the universality of the good. And yet the universal is supposedly definitive of the ethical.[54]

The tension is redoubled yet again. Unavoidably the *pathos* of the individual for existence is basic to the ethical stage. The eternal is easily related to the temporal, the finite to the infinite, through this *pathos*, because the finite self is related to an absolute goal over time. Finally, the individual comes to the realization that it cannot, as a finite being, fulfill universal moral obligations. The ethical stage, because of its intensity of inwardness, ends in guilt. The polar structure of the self is lost in the ethical concern for the self as such. At this the ethical breaks open to the religious.

The next sphere of existence that Kierkegaard depicts is what he calls "Religiousness A." It is the religious sublimation of the aesthetic. Here the religious life is the apprehension of divine immanence as the ontological ground of the self. The task of this form of religiosity, its *pathos*, is to relate the self to this ground through recollection. This requires the annihilation of the self as an obstacle to the recollection of the divine. The paradox of existence for Religiousness A is that the self in itself is related to the infinite. Given this, the movement toward the infinite is inward, or backward as Kierkegaard is wont to call it, through recollection. Climacus notes that "because God is the basis when every obstacle is cleared away, and first and foremost the individual himself in his finiteness, in his obstinacy against God. Aesthetically, the holy resting place of edification is outside of the individual, who accordingly seeks the place; in the ethico-religious sphere, the individual himself is the place when he has annihilated himself" (CUP 498). The relation of the self to the infinite is the dialectical inward appropriation of the self's relation to its ground. But in the end the self is annihilated, put aside, in order to recollect the infinite. There is a total mediation of the lost immediacy of aesthetic existence, but it one that obliterates the self. This is why, as noted above, language and thought must be transcended in the aesthetic or Religiousness A. The annihilation of the self is through the self's failing to relate itself in freedom to the formal structure of the self.

Thus far three modes of life have been illustrated: the aesthetic, where the infinite is posited as remote from the self; the ethical, where the infinite and finite are brought into relation by decision but so as to end in guilt; and Religiousness A, where the self is annihilated in an act of total mediation to expose its eternal ground. Corresponding to these modes of existing are three different *pathoi* for relating the self to itself: the *pathos* of possibility (imagination); the *pathos* of action (will); and the *pathos* of recollection (memory). The modes of existing are defined by the *pathos* of each sphere as it attempts to relate the self to itself. The struggle of existence is to bring the self into being, and, correspondingly, we can say that the self is a figuration, a mimesis, of the shape and power of existence. Any advance beyond these various stages will demand a new *pathos* as a means of relating the self to itself and to the power that establishes it. Not surprisingly, a new figuration of life will also be required.

Johannes Climacus insists that he is not a Christian, and yet he dares to think Christianity may have something to say about life. He notes that for Christianity "sin is the new existence medium" (CUP 516). The consciousness of sin, or the fact that we are in error, is the decisive breach with all forms of immanence, idealistic or religious. Much as Christianity's paradoxical vision is used to break though cognitive idealism, now it is explored in its ontological depth. The central issue facing Kierkegaard, given this admission of sin, is the way the self comes into relation with the infinite, with the truth. The problem is twofold because the self is in error separated from the truth and is also in time. The answer to this problem is, of course, the paradox of Christ. Christianity is a paradox because the dialectic of finite/infinite is not located in desire (aesthetics), or in the will (ethical), or in thought (speculative philosophy), but in the infinite entering the finite in time: the God–Man, the Absolute Paradox.

> In religiousness B [Christianity] the edifying is something outside of the individual, the individual does not find edification by finding the God-relationship within himself, but relates himself to something outside of himself to find edification. The paradox consists in the fact that this apparently aesthetic relationship . . . is nevertheless the right relationship . . . [CUP 489].

Christian edification begins with something, the divine, external to the self that requires a passionate decision for existence. Kierkegaard puts the matter as strongly as possible by asking whether one can base eternal salvation on an historical event. This edifying strategy is the occasion for scandal and offense.

It asserts that the self is in sin, is estranged from the truth, and also that the infinite is revealed in time in the person Christ. This makes the dialectic absurd because eternal blessedness and existence are related to an external historical reality. The Incarnation is a scandal to the understanding, which grasps abstract universals, and it presents the individual with an awesome choice: either offense or faith.

The *pathos* of Christianity is a specific faith: it is a second immediacy that relates the self to the power that establishes it as well as relating one to the past and a hoped-for future; and it is salvific since it is enabled by grace. This complex faith relates the individual to Christ in coming to be as a Christian. The self, then, is deeply temporal and is paradoxically related to another in time. Though the polar structure of the self is the same as other modes of existing, in the Christian sphere the relation of the poles is posited not in the self, but in the relation of faith. In faith, the self relates to itself and in doing so relates itself, as Anti-Climacus claims, to the power that creates it. "Hence . . . faith is a sphere for itself which, paradoxically distinguished from the aesthetic and the metaphysical, accents existence, and paradoxically distinguished from the ethical, accentuates the existence of another person, not one's existence" (CUP 514). Christianity is, in some sense, a taking up and transforming of the other stages of existence. It is a mediated immediacy. But unlike the Hegelian *Aufhebung*, there is no necessity to this movement, logical or otherwise. Faith holds true to the absurdity of the God–Man and hence is a paradox: it is intense inwardness directed outward. The self comes to be relative to the power that establishes it through faith.

Passionate faith in Christ, the God–Man in time, constitutes the Christian self and thereby relates the believer to the eternal as his or her telos. The paradox of the infinite in time is the condition for the believer's relation to the absolute, according to Kierkegaard. Thus Incarnation is the condition for the advance beyond Socratic and Hegelian accounts since it breaks with all forms of recognition as a way to relate to the truth of one's being. It not only discloses human sin, but provides a different condition for the self to relate to the truth and thereby demands a new strategy of existential communication.

Kierkegaard's thought at this point moves in a circle around sin and the human relation to the truth.[55] At its center is the Incarnation as the condition for the demise of immanence and the possiblity of moving beyond it. However, we should note that although the truth is exposed as not being in us, the human problem remains the same as for Socrates: how to come to the truth, given the shape of existence. Passion and freedom are basic in the coming-to-be of the self, whether its object be internal or external. And in both cases, the *pathos* claims the eternal and relates it to itself for the actualization of the self. For the Christian inwardness is directed outward, but it is still inwardness. The struggle is to live in what is communicated, to bring that truth to existential expression—a truth that, nevertheless, is not *in* the human even though one may be *in* the truth.

Kierkegaard's poetics, as I have called it, is related to arguments about the limits and sphere of thought, the character of Being, and the nature of language. All these cohere in the function of the authorship to communicate indirectly. But the heart and soul of the authorship, its very reason to be, is existence. Because of this, we are pushed beyond literary strategies to explore the concrete shape of coming-to-be as a self, specifically as a Christian. The problematic for Kierkegaard, seen in the light of our previous discussion, is to bring the truth to existence. My contention is that the analytic of Christian existence exposes something about human existence more generally considered. It seems clear that the authorship is, as Gadamer and Ricoeur have helped us see, mimetic. The various "authors" of the pseudonymous authorship present ways of existing, and the authorship as a whole opens possible worlds for the reader as crucial for the edification of the human. Likewise, existing is mimetic in shape: the self is the kinetic transformation of the *pathos* for life into a form of existence. In turning to the Christian life we are, as it were, turning to the strategy of reception and understanding commensurate with the telos of the authorship and the central event of the Incarnation.

The *Training in Christianity*

Training in Christianity is often a neglected text in Kierkegaard's corpus. This is unfortunate, and, indeed, confusing. The text includes themes found throughout the Climacus/Anti-Climacus texts, such as existential communication, the problem of the self, and other issues I have been exploring. Moreover, it presents a complex portrayal of the human relation to the truth beyond recollection and immanence and of the way this should mark the Christian life. Because of this, *Training* provides an important occasion for my reading of Kierkegaard. It neatly configures the problem of the authorship and his analytic of existence that I am attempting to unfold and to understand.

The text is not without its difficulties. Since my concern is with its argument and not these textual problems, I shall note these difficulties and my approach to them. The first of these is the curious relation of Climacus, who claims not to be a Christian, and Anti-Climacus, who embodies a radical form of Christianity. What is the relation between these authors? Is it that they explore similar themes, as just noted? Does the "anti" of Anti-Climacus mean "against" Climacus or something else? Perhaps these are moot questions. My reading assumes that common themes run through the works of these authors even though they present different existential modes of life.

Next, there is a question about the title of the work. *Indovelse*, translated by "training," means most basically "drilling," "as when soldiers or athletes drill in preparation for the real contest."[56] This suggests that "practice," so rich in moral, religious, and pedagogical import, is the best translation for the title of the work. It is clear that the text has edifying concerns. My contention, as noted before, is that the language of mimesis/*imitatio* has always had this pedagogic import; it is certainly fitting, then, that Kierkegaard's text on "practice" in Christianity is a dialectical presentation of existential mimesis vis-à-vis the Christ. At least that is how I shall read the text.

The final problem of the text is that it is a composition of separate pieces. Does this mean that it lacks dialectical structure? I think Gregor Malantschuk is correct when he argues that "*Practice in Christianity* came about through the joining together of some separate pieces, but Anti-Climacus manages to give this work, too, a dialectical, cohesive structure."[57] My reading seeks to unfold this structure within the problematic of "practice" and the general concerns of the Climacus corpus. I am reading the text as it now appears relative to its subject matter and the basic questions uncovered in this chapter.

In *Training*, Anti-Climacus lays out the reasons for the particular shape of the Christian life. "Why then this, why this lowliness and humiliation? It is because He who in the truth is to be the 'pattern' [*Forbillede*] and is concerned only with followers [*Efterfolger*] must in one sense be located behind men, to drive them on, whereas in another sense He stands before them, beckoning them on. This is the relationship of the loftiness and lowliness in 'the pattern.' "[58] Christ as pattern stands behind the follower, as humiliated and as past, and before the follower, as exalted and futural. The life of Christ is the pattern for the Christian retrospectively and prospectively. By faith the self is related to the scandal of the God–Man and lives that encounter out on the pattern of Christ. Only in the offense of the Paradox is the self placed in the possibility of faith. Likewise, the paradox that the exalted is lowly is the model for the *imitatio Christi*. If the Incarnation is the unique condition for the advance on Socratic thought, then the *imitatio* is the corresponding way of edification or practice beyond the flights of idealistic recollection or dialectics.

One's relation to Christ is the occasion for scandal. Christ is the example (*Forbillede*) to be imitated, to be followed, and not admired (TIC 243–44). Admiration is an aesthetic relation to the pattern. The Admirer remains at a distance from what is admired and thus is exempt from the demands of that life. In following the pattern, the believer seeks to express, as Christ did, the truth in her or his own existence. Anti-Climacus states emphatically:

> Truth [*Sandheden*] in its very being is not a simple reduplication [*Fordoblelse*] of being in relation [*Forhold*] to thought, which only yields the thought [*taenkt*] of being. . . . No, truth in its very being is the reduplication in me, in thee, in him, so that my, that thy, that his life, approximately, in the striving to attain it, may express [*udtykker*] the truth, so that my, that thy, that his life, approximately, in striving to attain it, is the very being of truth, is a life, as the truth was in

Christ, for He was the truth. And therefore, Christianly understood, truth is not to know [*vide*] the truth, but to be the truth [TIC 201].

Being a follower means, then, the reduplication of the truth in the self so that the truth is expressed or presented in one's life. Unlike the admirer who holds the self at a distance from what claims it, the follower strives to be a witness to the truth. This act of reduplication in a life is the way of scandal.

The *imitatio Christi* is mimetic in shape because it is a form of interaction with the truth in time so as to present that truth in action. The *imitatio* is a double mimesis: it is an existential fusion of horizons, to recall Gadamer's phrase, and an existential hermeneutic of truth, a refiguration of life through which the truth is presented. Truth is transformed into a "figurative" life. Anti-Climacus states that "Christ is the truth in such a sense that to be the truth [*at vaere Sandheden*] is the only true explanation [*Forklaring*] of what the truth is" (TIC 200). The only adequate interpretation of the truth is the life of Christ and the believer's appropriation of this in faith and life.

Kierkegaard has not abandoned the notion that "truth is subjectivity" regarding the Christian life. On the contrary, the *imitatio Christi* becomes the presentation of the paradox of Christ. The truth is explained or displayed by the self's existing in it. In this sense, the Christian life becomes the hermeneutic and mimetic presentation of Christian claims about Christ. The *imitatio Christi*, as the embodiment of faith, is existential communication in which the believer both receives existence from Christ and presents this existence to others.[59] But what then is the shape of the Christian life?

Training in Christianity presents an account of the process of the individual's coming-to-be as a Christian. My concern is to trace the dialectical character of existence relative to its mimetic configuration in the shape of the argument. *Training*, as we now have the text, is composed of three parts or moments descriptive of this coming-to-be.[60] Each of these parts is a dialectic in itself considered from the vantage point of both Christ and the individual. The internal dialectic of the parts is then a correlate Christological and anthropological study. Moreover, the larger structure of the work is itself a dialectic that we must grasp first before turning to the parts. *Training* forms, therefore, nothing less than a mimetic configuration of Christian existence.

As a configuration of Christian existence, the text dips its roots into prefigured human existence, and calls for a concrete refiguration of life. Kierkegaard's poetic and rhetorical strategy is to confront the reader with the shape of existence by creating a clash between the being of Christ and the human passion for existence. What emerges is the shape of existence and the desire that drives human being and doing. What is refigured, finally, is not only the structure of existence but the *pathos* of selfhood.

There is a three-part movement to the book. Part I is an invitation to discipleship as the grounds for the possibility of the Christian life and salvation. This invitation demands a decision on the part of the individual. The decision is either confession or rejection of Christ as Lord. Part II is the negation of the invitation because the nature of the Truth, the God–Man, is the occasion for an offense, and the corresponding demand for faith itself raises the possibility of scandal. Part III is the negation of the negation in that the Truth is understood graciously to draw the individual to himself. We should note that the way one is drawn to the Truth is the path of self-denial. Part III does not represent an Hegelian mediation of Parts I and II. Rather, the demand and travail of Christian existence is intensified. Yet in Part III we do learn that grace has been operative through the negations of the dialectic and the corresponding demand for decision. Grace operates through the process of coming-to-be actualized in decisive action (*imitatio*). The believer is transformed by the work of grace through the dynamics of faith, a faith, as mentioned before, that is salvific, decisive, and active and hence at once "religious" and "moral." This means that the primary concern is also always with the God–Man, and hence the Pattern, as the sign of the Offense and the object of faith. The God–Man is the sign of Offense precisely in the paradoxical character of his existence. His life renders all testing of his truthfulness beyond the pale of reason; he is the object of faith because only faith relates the individual to the one who is the God–Man. This faith demands nothing less than following the way of the Truth.

Part I of *Training* begins with an invitation to "rest" and an analysis of the human desire for "rest." Thus at the outset the text configures a human desire as its precondition and as what will insert the reader into its argument. This desire is intensified by the "invitation" to rest in the Savior; it stands as the force of the present requiring some response, some initiation, on the part of the reader. In theological terminology, Anti-Climacus begins with a soteriological concern: the problem of salvation and the Savior who comes (TIC 21). Both the invitation and the human desire for salvation set the grounds of the possibility of discipleship. But there is also the possibility for offense as another response to the text and to Christ. Because we so deeply desire to rest in God, as Augustine notes, we may be scandalized by the Savior who comes. The desire for salvation, paradoxically, holds the conditions for its own negation. The "Come hither!" of the Inviter leads to the obstacle: the Inviter himself.

By beginning with the human desire for salvation, Anti-Climacus quickly turns to the Christological issue correlate to that desire. And this sets the problematic for the entire book: the human desire for salvation in collision with the Savior who comes to us, and the required response and relation to *that* Savior. The clash is in the meeting of the supposed immanent grounding of the self in truth with the Christ that exposes our being in error. Anti-Climacus analyses the collision of desire and Savior from the side of the individual and from the side of the paradox, the God–Man. Hence Part I of *Training* is a double mimesis of religious desire and the Christ. It explores the preunderstanding of religious and moral existence in its prefigured condition of desire.

In Part I the immediate negation of the invitation, as the grounds for discipleship, is the Inviter himself. The invitation to eternal rest is given by a man who "insists upon being the definite historical person He was 1800 years ago . . ." (TIC 326). This is the same theme Climacus explored in the *Fragments* and the *Postscript*. That is, can one base eternal salvation on an historical event? Anti-Climacus first addresses the question from the side of what history will tell us about Christ. The answer is, of course, nothing because "all historical communication is communication of 'knowledge'; hence from history we can learn nothing about Christ" (TIC 28). Historical knowledge is made up of objective data and as such is not the transformative truth that marks salvation. Any historical facts about Christ merely reduce him to objective effects of historical causes and allow a cognitive relation to him. Put differently, historical knowledge rests on a form of immanentalism: Christ must be known within the immanent horizon of historical effects. Anti-Climacus' biting satire of various historical approaches to Christ clearly demonstrates that from Christ's historical effects one cannot judge his claim to truth or his claim to divinity. In this Anti-Climacus challenges Gadamer's claims about effective-historical consciousness if and when that consciousness is viewed as a total mediation of our relation to the truth.

The reader is then deprived of any historical account of Christ that might ease the risk of response and is confronted with a crisis of decision about this person. The Obstacle is accented yet again in that the Inviter is also the humiliated one. This is the dialectical knot: the person and the work, the Inviter and the invitation, cannot be separated in order to allow one to accept the invitation and not the Inviter. The obstacle has appeared on two levels. The Savior is not the one whom we desired (he identifies with the outcast in humility and not power) and the human problem he addresses (sin) is not the problem that concerns us. Nonetheless, given the identification of the Invitation and the Inviter, the reader is faced with a decision concerning the Savior stemming from the desire for salvation.

Through the negation of any historical approach to Christ, the realization of the desire for salvation, and the absolute nature of God (who this man claims to be), we are contemporaneous with the scandal of Christ (TIC 67). That is, under the force of the present, as Ricoeur put it, the past (Christ on earth) and the future (hope for eternal salvation) are brought into a tenuous, existential present. This sparks an increase of inwardness. The reader is driven inward, into the self, in relation to the Truth that transcends her or him in order to decide whether to accept or reject the Inviter and the suffering of coming-to-be as a Christian. The individual is driven to contrition and hence to the possibility of entering the narrow way (TIC 72). This contrition marks the movement away from the original problematic of salvation and leads to Part II, the dialectic of faith. Part I moves from the desire for salvation through the Offense to the moment of contrition. And thus it leads to the possibility of faith. Indeed, in reading this text we follow the dialectical path from the preunderstanding and prefigured life to a consideration of the refigured life relative to the Christ. In order for us to do so, the text must explore the person of Christ himself.

Part II of *Training* traces the dialectic of the Offense, and hence faith, in considering the God–Man. It serves as the negation of Part I: when the individual reaches the point of confession (Part I), she or he is confronted with the paradox of the God–Man (Part II). We confront the Christ who seems to negate divinity and humanity. Anti-Climacus is adamant that the "possibility of Offense is not avoided, thou must pass through it, and thou canst be saved from it in one way only—by believing" (TIC 100). The end of the dialectic will be faith as the only proper response to Christ (TIC 143).

Part II begins by noting that the Offense has *essentially* to do with the God–Man. This is because the "God–Man is the paradox, absolutely the paradox; hence it is clear that the understanding must come to a standstill before it" (TIC 85). The offense broadly conceived is threefold: Jesus in collision with the established order; the God–Man as concerns the notion of God; and the God–Man as concerns our usual thoughts about humanity.

Jesus' collision with the established order was that of a Teacher of Inwardness and godly fear (piety) against the external formalism of the established religion. The collision is between faith and the deification of the establishment (TIC 92). The text is, then, a critique of "Christendom" as well as one of culture from the perspective of radical Christian faith. The norms and values that structure the religious and social order are called into question as are preconceptions about duty and humanity.[61] This interrelated social, anthropological, and theological critique is central to the negation Part II works relative to the preunderstanding figured in Part I. The collision, religiously construed, is between a living faith in God and a religion controlled by human passion and fancy. Anti-Climacus finds the depiction of the Pharisees in the Gospel of Matthew ample evidence of this clash. Thus Kierkegaard locates his critique of religion in its political, anthropological, and theological dimensions at the heart of the biblical texts. The Christ witnessed to by the text is one who collides with established religiosity. And his clash, now as then, is ample occasion for offense. There is good reason, as Anti-Climacus avers, to leave this Christ to his own devices.

Beyond the collision between vested interests and Christ, the essential offense is the God–Man himself. He is the offense because the notion of the God–Man either demeans the glory of God or is a blasphemous claim to divinity by a man. Anti-Climacus explores several biblical passages to highlight both the lowliness of Jesus and his claim to divinity. The God–Man is then a "sign of the Offense." He cannot be comprehended cognitively under the concepts "God" or "human being" and so is the object either of faith or of rejection. The limits of reason and the paradoxical structure of orthodox Christian claims about Christ form the arena of the individual's relation to this person.

But what if one does grasp Christ in faith? Is this act free of the possibility of offense? Actually the offense is intensified. When the offense of the God–Man is overcome in faith, a new offense arises to take its place: Christianity is suffering. "The decisive mark of Christian suffering is the fact that it is voluntary, and that it is the possibility of offense for the sufferer" (TIC 111). The struggle to hold onto faith is raised to a new pitch. Interestingly, this Offense, of the God–Man and the suffering of the Christian life, is precisely the "repellent force by which faith comes into existence" (TIC 122). On the grounds of the *incognitio* of God in Christ, the Offense of the God–Man and Christian suffering, and the impossibility of direct communication concerning this Truth—on this the individual is to make a decision about Christ and her or his existence! Hence there is a dialectical transformation of desire for salvation (Part I) into the way of suffering as a form of existence.

"The contradiction puts before him a choice, and while he is choosing, he himself is revealed" (TIC 126). The way Anti-Climacus sees it, the paradoxical situation of the believer, the Offense, grounded in the God–Man, opens onto the possibility of faith. In faith the believer is revealed, and a proper relation to the Truth is expressed. Faith rests on no historical verification, and because it is voluntary suffering it rests on no prudential concern. Finally, because of the nature of the God–Man, this faith is based on no direct evidence or communication. Faith rests solely on the object of faith: the God–Man. Thus, paradoxically, the human desire for "rest," which opened Part I, is revolutionized through the demand for faith in Christ. Through the negation of the Offense one is driven to more radical statements of faith, venturing out over 70,000 fathoms, as Kierkegaard would say, supported only by the object of faith.[62] Much as the self is exposed as rooted in nothingness, so faith is exposed in its nihility. And yet this is not nihilism; it is the affirmation of the depths of existence as non-substantial and the self as a presentation of no-thingness. The question now is the shape and impulse of that faith relation.

We move from Part II, ending with the decision of faith, to Part III and the dialectic of discipleship. Anti-Climacus once again considers the dialectic from the perspective of Christ and the individual. As we have seen, he notes that it is the loftiness and lowliness of Christ as the pattern that is crucial for Christian existence. In Part I we began by approaching the humiliated Christ. Now we see that in faith (Part II) Christ is drawing the self to Himself. The Christian life is lived out precisely between Christ's humiliation (the possibility of offense and faith) and exaltation.

We have yet to explore what Christ's exaltation means for Christian life. But at this point the inner workings of the dialectical structure of the life of faith are exposed. The self is drawn to Christ first by entering the self (the increase of inwardness of Part I) and then by making a choice of obedience in relation to Christ (Parts II and III) who is "external" to the self. "Hence Christ would first and foremost help every man to become himself, would require of him first and foremost that by entering into himself he should become himself, so as then to draw him to Himself. He would draw him only as a free being, and so through a choice" (TIC 160). Divine grace works precisely through the arduous path to selfhood where an individual confronts the relation of the self to the eternal first expressed in the desire for salvation. This faith is salvific since grace "must be present as the condition that enables the subject to believe, but the will must be present to decide whether the individual will believe."[63] Christianity in relating the self to the power that creates it is not the denial of inwardness; Christianity is the perfection of inwardness. Again, the desire at the heart of existence is transformed or revolutionized, and this transformed passion comes to expression in a mode of life.

The struggle for selfhood is lived out through progressive negations of certitude and self and increasing demands for faith. In the seven expositions of Part III of *Training*, Anti-Climacus explores how the individual is drawn to Christ through the dynamics of choice and obedience (TIC 184). The method of exposition is through a passage of Scripture (Jn 12:32). Anti-Climacus is relying on a use of the Scriptures to present a picture of Christ, in his humiliation, contrasted with the imagination's picture of ideality or perfection.

Contrary to Ricoeur, the ideality of the picture of Christ is not of one humanity and one history, but the humiliation and suffering at the heart of existence. Given the clash between human ideality and the picture of Christ, the individual must will a relation to Christ as depicted in Scripture. To follow that Christ is "to will to be and to express perfection (ideality) in everyday reality" (TIC 188).[64] It is the imitation, the following, of Christ that is the only proper relation to him. Following Christ is the working out and appropriation of faith; it is the refiguration of life that itself is the presentation of life. Imitation, we can say, is the reduplication of the Truth in the self. It is an existential appropriation of the Truth and its expression in one's life. In a word, *imitatio* is living the Truth; it is being in Christ. Contrary to the Admirer, who has only an aesthetic relation to Christ, the Follower (*Efterfolger*) strives (*streben*) to be what he or she admires. In that process one's existence is refigured.

The dialectic has moved from Christ drawing the individual to himself to the realization that the drawing works through the demand of obedience. Finally, we come to see that Christ as the Way, Truth, and Life has sustained the journey throughout. This is not the end, however. For Anti-Climacus the Christian life has a further intensification. While the Christian hopes for exaltation, "Christianly understood exaltation is in this world humiliation" (TIC 251). So it is that the Follower in striving to be what is admired must accept the Cross. One must lose the self to gain it. The follower must suffer in the likeness of Christ. The dialectical movement of Part III ends not with a mediation, a synthetic resolution, but with an intensification of the life of faith as the *imitatio Christi*.

The movement of *Training* is from the desire for salvation (Part I) to Christian obedience and self-denial (Part III). One makes this journey only by passing in faith through the offense of the God–Man (Part II). The mimetic narrative journey of *Training* then is from the prefigured desire for salvation to refigured existence in the *imitatio Christi* by the reader. Given this, the *imitatio* is the double mimesis of human desire *and* Christian faith. Anti-Climacus has depicted a process whereby the Christian exists not through self-fulfillment, or humanization, but in the exaltation of humiliation. This is a life of faith and grace as the presentation of Christian existence in the world.

At this point, two questions arise regarding the contribution of *Training* to our reflections. The first and simplest is whether or not Anti-Climacus' portrayal of Christian existence legitimates an asceticism that demeans human life in the world by calling for radical self-denial and suffering. To be sure, Kierkegaard has been read in this way, and there clearly is evidence in the text for such a reading. Yet whatever one's judgment on that question, what I wish to draw from him concerns the mimetic character of the transformation of existence as deepening what Ricoeur called the refiguration of practical life. Put differently: there is no necessary connection between the depiction of the *content* of Christian existence in the text and the mimetic shape of life. Authentic existence may entail self-denial and suffering. Within limits, I would be willing to argue that it does. However, the point concerns the mimetic strategy of *Training* and not what it says about the content of Christian existence. One can conceive of a construal of life that is mimetic while not being marked by radical and complete self-denial. Indeed, in the first chapter I noted this through the work of J. B. Metz and Arthur Cohen. Thus the issue is the mimetic dynamic of existence and not a specific construal of how Christians should live their lives.

The second and related question regarding *Training* and the reconstruction of mimesis is more difficult. Is it possible, we can ask, to draw a general hermeneutic of human existence from Kierkegaard's text, or is it confined to claims about Christian faith? Of course, this question coinheres with the one about the asceticism of the text. But it expands that question into a general hermeneutical problem. Does the configuration of Christian existence in *Training* in all its particularity disclose anything about human life in more general terms? The issue is not between competing claims about how the Christian ought to live, as the first question was. Rather, it is about the contribution of a specific way of life to understanding the human condition.

My reading of Kierkegaard has implicitly answered this question by moving from a prefigured desire through its refiguration in the act of the reader. Yet I have also argued that Kierkegaard's concern was indeed with the irreducible particularity of the task of being a self, specifically a Christian. Any reading of him that attempts to avoid the question of Christianity begs that question. However, his work also unfolds notions of language, thought, and paradox that contribute to understanding the mimetic shape of existence *qua* existence. Put differently: my contention is that *Training* coheres with the analytic of existence isolated earlier in this chapter even as it helps to unfold the mimetic shape of life by exploring a particular form of existence. This is not to reduce Kierkegaard's work to a system. Rather, it is to claim that in the specific demand on the reader to come to be as a self something about the mimetic shape of any authentic life is presented and figured.

With these questions in mind, I want to isolate what Kierkegaard specifically contributes to the rethinking of mimesis. Having done such, it will be possible, in the next chapter, to construe the analogies in understanding, narrativity, and selfhood. These analogies, I contend, are important for the constructive task of theological and ethical reflection in the postmodern context.

KIERKEGAARD AND THE RECONSTRUCTION OF MIMESIS

I argued earlier that Kierkegaard's authorship is the mimetic presentation of the dialectic of existence and the *imitatio Christi*. We have seen how the self, or rather the problem of the self, is implicated in his literary and existential strategies. To grasp this mimetic strategy we must see the way in which these aspects of his thought are related.

The steps of the *imitatio* that I have traced in *Training* were desire, faith, discipleship. The Christological correlates to this existential movement were the Inviter, the Christ, and the Pattern. The interrelation of the believer's existence and Christ is clear enough. But what of the self, and what of the strategy of the authorship? Using notions developed earlier, we can say that existence is passionate interaction, temporal *kinesis* of the self through faith, and the presentation or witness of faith in existence. The self is a double mimesis of the passion for existence and that which is followed. Once we see this formal structure of the dialectic of *Training*, its relation to our study of the self becomes clear.

The *pathos* of a stage of existence relates, or fails to relate, the self to itself and thus, as Anti-Climacus claims, relates the self to that which, as the object of *pathos*, brings it into being. The self, in the *kinesis* of coming-to-be, expresses or presents itself in the world even as it is a specific figuration of life. Kierkegaard explores the passional roots of human existence, and he does so, I have argued, through mimesis, specifically relative to the Christ. For him, Christ is the incarnate God–Man. And even though Kierkegaard does not explore theologically the intelligibility or plausibility of this confession, it is clear that his understanding of Christ requires a different assessment of imitation.

Kierkegaard's critique of the other stages of life is that they fail to allow the self to make this movement, this full standing out (ex-isting) in the world. Existence is communicated in Christianity because Christ's existence is the condition for the self to come to be, to ex-ist, even as that distanciation is mediated through faith and discipleship, allowing the believer to participate in Christ, to be *in* Christ. Yet though he clearly holds that only the Christian through *imitatio* truly exists, the depiction of existence he offers reaches to all human life. All existing is under the demand to stand out in presentation, being deeply temporal, and to be moved by passion and will. Because the self ex-ists through the *imitatio*, Kierkegaard seems to be claiming that all authentic human existence is mimetic in character.

The movement of the self and the movement of the *imitatio* are then formally the same: passion, temporality, and presentation. These are analogous elements of mimesis uncovered earlier in Gadamer's work: interaction, temporality, and figuration. What Kierkegaard has shown us is that human action in, and interaction with, world and others is driven by passion. Likewise, human temporality is tied to the movement of existence and its coming to presentation in selfhood under the force of the present, the hope for the future, and the givenness of the past. We can say this since the self is the figuration of the passion for existence. For Kierkegaard, the only adequate figuration is that of obedient and humble following. Yet this suggests a mimeticism of existence beyond the particularities of Christian faith, as I noted above. The self is a figuration of its *pathos* enacted in life.

Here we meet the next question: How does the authorship relate to this movement of the self? That is, if Kierkegaard's pseudonymous authorship has the character of textual mimesis, how does this relate to existential *imitatio*? Is there anything corresponding to the movement of the self seen in the authorship? If there is, then we shall have discerned something of Kierkegaard's mimetic strategy while relating it to our previous argument.

If the self begins in passion and ends in presentation, the works move in the opposite direction. That is, the authorship is first and foremost a mimetic presentation of possible modes of life. Insofar as the authorship, or a particular text, is understood, if it evokes some passionate decision about existence, then, according to Kierkegaard, it has reached its end. The movement of the authorship is from presentation to passionate decision or lack of decision by the reader. This is precisely why it is indirect communication: it is indirect because it is inversely tied to the movement of the self. This expands on the centrality of reading in the refiguration of life, as Ricoeur argued. To be sure, reading for Kierkegaard is integral to the disclosive power of the text and its ability to refigure life. But that refiguration of life is conceived as an act definitive of the existence of the self vis-à-vis its passion for existence. Thus Kierkegaard confirms Ricoeur's claim that the power to refigure time, and hence practical existence, is not the text *qua* text; it requires the passionate interest of the self. Yet at this point we are pushed beyond both Ricoeur and Kierkegaard to ask about the power that refigures time and establishes the self. I shall return to this in the last chapter. Here it is sufficient to see how Kierkegaard has helped us to grasp the further import of the mimetic refiguration of life.

The arena of the authorship and hence its mode of indirect communication is, as I noted earlier, language. Why? Because in language thought (the presentation of possible modes of life) and time (the measure of the movement of the self) meet, helping to bring existence to figuration even as existence is not *in* language. Thus even though language is the meeting point of the authorship and the self, this does not violate the limitations that Kierkegaard put on thought. The reason is that the works present existence at its end (presentation) and not its movement. The actual process of existing (passion, time, presentation) cannot be realized simply in thought. The authorship, as I take it, does not attempt to think existence in that way. It seeks to display in a depicted mode existence as realized or not.

Kierkegaard's mimetic strategy is the interrelation of the movement of the authorship with the movement of the self. The crossed reference, as Ricoeur called it, occurs when the reader makes a passionate decision in the present to come to be relative to the poeticized existence presented in the works. And this decision then demands a mode of life commensurate with one's object of faith. Decision moves existential enactment. This is the depth of paradox in Kierkegaard's authorship. The authorship, finding its telos in Christian existence, does not seek to expose the reader's *a priori* grounding in the truth. The movement of the authorship is precisely to confront its readers with their being in error, their separation from the truth. It is with this recognition that the self may then move toward a relation to the truth. And that movement is deeply existential, temporal, and mimetic.

Kierkegaard's mimetic strategy seeks to build up the self; it is an edifying, practical mode of reflection. The whole notion of being "formed" by Christ, so central to the Christian tradition, has been cast in a different light. The process of formation, of coming-to-be, is now through the *imitatio Christi* and not prior to it. He retrieves and rethinks the dynamic notion of *imitatio* found in the biblical tradition. It is through the *imitatio* that the being of the human is realized and shown for what it is. And yet for him, the human, as *imago Dei*, does not somehow exist prior to the existential journey of the *imitatio*. We should recall here that Gadamer rethought the relation of *Bild* and *Urbild* by retrieving performative mimesis and thereby overcame classical and modernist theories of imitation. In a similar way, Kierkegaard has rethought the *imago Dei* by reconsidering the existential shape of *imitatio* and in doing so has overcome traditional construals of imitation as a way of life. This understanding of Christian existence shapes his whole authorship. Through the use of language and paradox, Kierkegaard attempts to prompt the reader to follow after the truth and thus to become a self. And in following the truth one's life becomes the working out, appropriation, and presentation of that truth. Existence is the hermeneutic of the truth.

Kierkegaard's mimetic strategy entails rethinking the relation of human existence to the divine in time. The relationship is interpreted through his mimetic hermeneutic of existence: passion, temporal *kinesis*, and presentation. On the level of passion and will, we have seen that the self relates to itself and to the divine who graciously establishes the self. Through passionately willing to be a self relative to the divine, revealed in Christ, there is the *kinesis* of existence.[65] This *kinesis* marks the deep and unique temporality of the self. The movement of the self is a standing out, an ex-isting, and thus the presentation of the self and its faith. As Hidehito Otanti writes, for Kierkegaard the Christian is always coming to be, is never a finished project or substance: "being a Christian means 'becoming a Christian'; in the objective sense there is no Christian."[66] We can now say that being a self means becoming a self. There is in the objective sense no substantial "self." Yet given this, how do we speak of any continuity of existence through the diversity of its action?

The *imitatio Christi*, as the particular mimetic hermeneutic of Christian faith, is the coming-to-be of the Christian. The *imitatio* is helpful for speaking of self because the self is always a following after, always a process and never a substance. We can say that the *imitatio Christi* for Kierkegaard *is* the Christian self. And the other stages of existence are the troubled attempt to present a self relative to some passionately held object of belief. For Kierkegaard, *imitatio* is an enactment of existence; it is how the self stands out, ex-ists, in time. In this sense the self has continuity only through existential mimesis. That is, his radical mimetic notion of self seems to suggest that the human exists *only* in its specific acts of decision and enactment, a movement in and out of presence. Given this, it seems difficult to speak of the self through time in its being and in its accountability. No doubt, it is the case that radical forms of occasionalism and existentialism render talk about perduring selfhood, as well as the continuity between the human and the natural world, problematic. My reading of Kierkegaard seems to imply this since it is through the *imitatio* that the being of the human, the *imago Dei*, comes to be.

At this point we must return to narrativity to speak of the continuity of the self through the diversity of its acts and hence through time. Ricoeur's proposal of narrative identity for speaking of the self in the diversity of its acts reached beyond itself to the problem of existence, as we saw. It took us into our reading of Kierkegaard. And yet at the end of this reading, we are driven back to the idea of narrative identity enriched by our reflections on Kierkegaard's strategy of existential mimesis. Thus by reading him and Ricoeur together this difficulty can be overcome without recourse to an iconic idea of the self.

First, it is clear that for Kierkegaard the fundamental force of human life is the passion or desire for existence. Different modes or stages of existence are various existential figurations of this desire. In this qualified sense, then, desire and passion are perduring realities of all selfhood regardless of one's particular mode of life. The issue then becomes, for Kierkegaard and for much of the Christian tradition, the transformation of that basic passion, or love, for existence. Here I have argued, by reading *Training*, that the *imitatio* works as a refiguration of this passion for life. Thus there is continuity in selfhood at the level of fundamental passions and dispositions even while these are open for transformation, indeed conversion or revolution.

However, these passions did not exist, in any substantial sense, outside of their coming to be, or failure to do so, in concrete forms of life, or stages of existence. "Self" means then, a specific figuration of human *pathos* or interest in active existence, a presentation of life that has identity with others and is genuinely responsible for itself. The being of the human as an agent comes to be through its figuration in self, which is profoundly relational. The agent comes to be in relation to the power that establishes the self, others, and also itself. That act of being a self is the mimesis of possibilities for existence open to the human, whether these are Christian or not. Thus Kierkegaard does provide an analysis of selfhood more general than the specifically Christian way of being. What we see here is that the human passion for existence opens onto the depths and horizon of life. The *imitatio* is a way of coming to be relative to the power that establishes it. Kierkegaard assumes a Christian construal of that "power." We can bracket that construal for the moment to see at the level of passion the condition for the continuity of the self through time and the opening of the human to its depths.

What seems evident is that the passion for existence is the condition for the continuity of the self, the opening of the human to its depths, and the possibility for appropriating narrative configurations of life. Yet while "passion" is a condition for concrete existence in this threefold sense, it still does not explain the unity of the self. We must also grasp how that passion becomes transformed into existence. And here an appeal to "narrative identity" seems appropriate, but one that is dependent on the initiative of the agent, as Ricoeur admitted. This identity entails the practical unity of the self when we interpret our lives narratively. The stories, symbols, and beliefs of a community or tradition provide configurations for life calling for appropriation. Understanding a community's narrative tradition refigures, re-forms, the self. Thus though it is the passion for existence that inserts the self into those narratives, through reading and appropriating them that passion is refigured. Identity is formed and dispositions are engendered and fostered through this process.

Kierkegaard's point is that the refiguration of existence has a mimetic shape. Yet we can grasp the unity of self or communal identity only against the backdrop of a tradition and its beliefs and construals of the world. Given this, the self comes to be as one figuration of a tradition, a coming to be that is open, so it would seem, to infinite variations and that refigures, even revolutionizes, the self.[67] Thus not only is identity engendered by a narrative tradition, it is also another interpretation and presentation of those beliefs and stories. His mimetic strategy allows us to think about the one who can be shaped by a tradition and its narratives.

The intersection of a narratology and Kierkegaard's analytic of the self has a yet more profound depth. We saw how the aporias of temporality opened the question of the paradoxical orientation of the human to death and eternity, an "eternity," we can say, figured by the text, rooted in a desire for "salvation," and lived out in fidelity. Kierkegaard has shown that the self is rooted in possibility, in freedom—and hence in non-being even as the quest for existence is made relative to what confronts the self as transcendent, as other—and in the passion for life. In this sense, his analytic of authentic existence does not see the authentic Being-whole of *Dasein* as rooted only in being-toward-death or an expression of the "I." His understanding of the kinetic and mimetic shape of self exposes the relation of the religious import of narrative to the act of being human.

The mimetic shape of the act of being human means, paradoxically, that to be a self we are first acted upon, we first respond, while that act of response is a standing out into existence. Of course, for Kierkegaard it is Christ who confronts the self seeking to elicit the response of existence. And yet the same claim can be made more generally. The character of the human condition means that we do not start with the introspective gaze of the *cogito*. Understanding is a response to what confronts us and induces action on our part. What confronts us in the affective way is an Other. Human existence, mimetically conceived, is one of response to a world and to others. The self is not a substance, an icon, but a mimetic process within fundamental relations to world, to others, and to the horizon of life.

Kierkegaard provides us, therefore, with a novel understanding of the self. It is a mimetic process. His argument against immanentalism is simultaneously a critique of all forms of idolatry and a substantialist notion of the self. Rather than understanding the *imitatio Christi* as a strategy for (re)forming a self already given, he takes it as part and parcel of the existence of the self. The *imitatio* therefore becomes the way to actualize and present the *imago Dei* as the being of the human. Better yet, the *imitatio* is the *imago Dei* in its coming to be, in act. This dialectical relation between the *imago* and *imitatio* provides a way to accept the current critique of the self and "image." It is in and through religious and moral practice that the self comes to be as self. The moral and religious life is a process of edification, of building up a mode of existence we call a self or a community. And it entails the constant refiguration or revolution of the self. *Imitatio*, as the presentation of faith, far from demeaning human life and capacities for creative action, is a way of authentic existence.

At this point we are driven to think with but also beyond Kierkegaard. We must do so in two ways. First, can we explore the analogies between the mimetic dynamic of existence and the shape of narrative and understanding? If this is possible, then rethinking mimesis may aid in addressing some of the questions raised at the beginning of this study. Second, is it possible to think what remains undeveloped in the works studied? Specifically, is it possible to think about the power of solidarity that is the condition and goal of understanding, the power of speaking that refigures time, and also the power that establishes the self? If this is possible, then we shall have reached both the limits of this study and entered the task of fundamental theological and ethical reflection. I want now to turn to these questions that have emerged by reading Gadamer, Ricoeur, and Kierkegaard.

NOTES

1. For this trend in deconstruction literary criticism and philosophy, see *Deconstruction and Criticism*, edd. Harold Bloom, Paul de Man, Jacques Derrida, Geoffrey Hartmann, and J. Hillis Miller (New York: Seabury, 1979). For a theological use of deconstructionism, see *Deconstruction and Theology*, edd. Thomas J. J. Altizer, M. A. Myers, C. A. Raschke, R. P. Scharlemann, M. C. Taylor, and C. E. Winquist (New York: Crossroad, 1982).

2. See, for example, Taylor's *Erring* and Allan Thiher's *Words in Reflection: Modern Language Theory and Postmodern Fiction* (Chicago: The University of Chicago Press, 1984).

3. See Richard Rorty, "Deconstruction and Circumvention," *Critical Inquiry*, 11 (1984), 1–23.

4. Clifford Geertz has shown that game, drama, and text are central metaphors currently used for interpreting human experience. See his *Local Knowledge: Further Essays in Interpretative Anthropology* (New York: Basic Books, 1983). See also my "Sacrifice, Interpretation, and the Sacred."

5. H. Richard Niebuhr, drawing on the thought of Mead, Dewey, and others, spoke of such a position as "objective relativism." His formulation was specifically concerned with the problem of moral, cognitive, and religious relativism, a perspectivalism that he embraced. However, his "objective relativism" was designed to show that all perspectives are views of something. Though the position I am suggesting has affinities with his work, I am more concerned with the ontological problem of "world" in light of post-Heideggerian hermeneutics, a problem that has arisen after Niebuhr. See his *Responsible Self*. For a recent discussion of relativism in moral philosophy that remains within the confines of different forms of life, see Jeffrey Stout, *Ethics After Babel: The Languages of Morals and Their Discontents* (Boston: Beacon, 1988).

6. Karl Morrison, in *Mimetic Tradition of Reform in the West*, aptly demonstrates this tendency of mimetic thought, but as an historian, he is more concerned than I am to preserve this impulse within mimetic thinking.

7. In this light I should mention that Jürgen Habermas' critical theory is linked to a therapeutic concern through Freudian analysis. Although it is not my concern to trace this connection, it is clear that all critical theories, and the position I am forwarding, attempt to develop procedures to combat distortion, oppression, and false ideology. See Habermas' *Theory and Practice*, trans. John Viertel (Boston: Beacon, 1973) and *Knowledge and Human Interests*, trans. Jeremy J. Shapiro (Boston: Beacon, 1971).

8. Taylor, *Erring*, p. 35.

9. Ibid., p. 48.

10. This point was made by Gadamer, of course. Recently, it has also been made in a forceful way by David Tracy. See his *Plurality and Ambiguity: Hermeneutics, Religion, Hope* (New York: Harper & Row, 1986).

11. *The Logic of Subjectivity: Kierkegaard's Philosophy of Religion* (Tuscaloosa: University of Alabama Press, 1984), p. 23.

12. The difference between my position and that of "textual" thinkers is that I see them perpetuating, albeit in more subtle ways, this same error. All texts become reduced to the problem of reference, and the critical task of thinking is complete when it is shown that a text is an ambiguous thing.

13. See, for example, Niebuhr's *Meaning of Revelation* and Crites' "Narrative Quality of Experience."

14. For a recent study of Kierkegaard's dialectic, see Stephen N. Dunning, *Kierkegaard's Dialectic of Inwardness: A Structural Analysis of the Theory of Signs* (Princeton: Princeton University Press, 1985). For a recent deconstructionist reading of his work, see H. A. Nielsen, *Where the Passion Is: A Reading of Kierkegaard's Philosophical Fragments* (Tallahassee: University Presses of Florida, 1983).

15. *Kierkegaard's Dialectic of Inwardness*, pp. 242–51.

16. Pojman sees in the account of the human as spirit relating itself to itself found in *Sickness unto Death* an argument for the existence of God. He constructs the argument as follows:

1. Man must either be constituted by another (superior to himself) or be self-constituted.
2. If he has been self-constituted, he will not be in despair over trying to attain selfhood.
3. But he *is* in despair over willing to be a self.
4. Therefore (by 2 and 3), man cannot have constituted himself.
5. Therefore (by 1 and 4), man must have been constituted by a superior power.

See his *Logic of Subjectivity*, p. 15. Though this may be a helpful analysis of the structure of Kierkegaard's argument in *Sickness unto Death*, it does not account for its central claim: that through faith one relates to the divine. In my reading of these texts, then, I am concerned less with their logical structure than with the problematic Kierkegaard seeks to address and how he proceeds to do so.

17. Cited in Walter Lowrie, *A Short Life of Kierkegaard* (Princeton: Princeton University Press, 1942), p. 260.

18. Paul Holmer, "On Understanding Kierkegaard," in *A Kierkegaard Critique*, edd. Howard Johnson and Niels Thulstrup (Chicago: Regnery, 1962), pp. 40–53, and "Kierkegaard and Ethical Theory," *Ethics*, 63 (1953), 155–70.

19. This understanding of text has been advanced by Paul Ricoeur; see his *Interpretation Theory*. See also Tracy's *Analogical Imagination*.

20. Edd. P. A. Heiberg, V. Kuhr, and E. Torsten, 2nd ed. (Copenhagen: Glyndendal, 1968), 10, 2, 1, 184.

21. Climacus notes that ordination alters all this since the preacher is ordained in time, making the moment, and the preaching, of eternal significance. This is why Kierkegaard called his works "edifying discourses" rather than sermons; he claimed to be without authority. We must grasp the irony here. Through the pseudonymous works Kierkegaard literally attempted to be without "authorship" since he was keenly aware

of the relation of authority and authorship. As noted earlier, the pseudonyms deny the writer control over the reader or the reader fascination with the author. In some sense, then, it is odd that we speak of Kierkegaard's authorship. See Kierkegaard's *Concluding Unscientific Postscript*, trans. David Swenson (Princeton: Princeton University Press, 1941), pp. 243–45. Henceforth citations will be given in the text as CUP. See also Kierkegaard's *Philosophical Fragments, or, A Fragment of Philosophy*, trans. David Swenson, rev. Howard H. Hong (Princeton: Princeton University Press, 1962). References will be given in the text as PF.

22. See *Journeys to Selfhood: Hegel and Kierkegaard* (Berkeley: University of California Press, 1980), pp. 122–40.

23. This is a contested claim, of course. Dunning, in *Kierkegaard's Dialectic of Inwardness*, does argue that "there is a total of three stages, and they constitute a progression (although without any implication of logical 'necessity'), rather than utterly discrete or diffusely overlapping spheres" (p. 4). I am less concerned than Dunning is with a "structural" analysis of the relation of the stages. Yet it is important to see that the stages are *neither* "utterly discrete" *nor* related by logical necessity.

24. *Reason and Existenz* (New York: Noonday, 1957), p. 27. Mark C. Taylor, *Kierkegaard's Pseudonymous Authorship* (Princeton: Princeton University Press, 1975), points out that the works place the reader on the map of existence.

25. Louis Mackey, *Kierkegaard: A Kind of Poet* (Philadelphia: University of Pennsylvania Press, 1971).

26. For a helpful article on this matter, see Mark C. Taylor, "Language, Truth, and Indirect Communication," *Tijdschrift voor Filosofie*, 37 (1975), 74–88.

27. This is from Kierkegaard's *Johannes Climacus, or De omnibus dubitandum*, cited in ibid., 75.

28. *Journals and Papers*, edd. Howard V. Hong and Edna H. Hong (Bloomington: Indiana University Press, 1970), no. 1590.

29. *Either/Or*, trans. David Swenson, 2 vols. (Princeton: Princeton University Press, 1944), I 88.

30. Regarding the recent attack on pure presence, Kierkegaard is concerned more with what this means for existence than with its implications for language. Nonetheless, he shares the suspicion of immediacy and presence, seeing them as essentially aesthetic. The irony of this is that Kierkegaard does so on Christological grounds whereas deconstructionist theologians see classical Christology as seeking presence.

31. See Paul Sponheim, *Kierkegaard on Christ and Christian Coherence* (London: SCM Press, 1968). Sponheim speaks of the diastatic moment and the synthetic moment in Kierkegaard's thought. His concern is the relation of God and man in Christ, and thus he focuses on Kierkegaard's Christology. I am using the term "diastasis" in a broader sense to refer to the breaking of immediacy between self and world through thought, time, and language.

32. Kierkegaard's understanding of imagination is beyond the scope of this study. It seems clear that he understood it as the power of producing images, and in this sense it is linked with aesthetic existence. The ambiguity of his notion of imagination need not concern us here.

33. *The Journals of Søren Kierkegaard*, ed. Alexander Dru (New York: Oxford University Press, 1938), no. 1002. Henceforth cited as J and followed by the entry number.

34. Pojman, *Logic of Subjectivity*, p. 77.

35. "Some Aspects of Time in Aristotle and Kierkegaard," *Kierkegaardiana* VIII,

ed. Niels Thulstrup (Copenhagen: Munksgaard, 1969), pp. 7–21. Mark C. Taylor also explores time in relation to the self in Kierkegaard's thought. See his *Kierkegaard's Pseudonymous Authorship*.

36. Søren Kierkegaard, *The Concept of Anxiety*, trans. Reidar Thomte (Princeton: Princeton University Press, 1980), p. 15. Henceforth citations given in the text as COA. Langdon Gilkey, in *Naming the Whirlwind: The Renewal of God-Language* (Indianapolis: Bobbs-Merrill, 1969), points out the similarity of Kierkegaard and process philosophy. That is, Kierkegaard shares with process thought an ontological position concerning change and novelty.

37. This is why, I think, Kierkegaard speaks to our situation far better than many others. It is often assumed that the problem of the self is how it is formed. Kierkegaard saw the deeper problem: the crisis of the idea of the self. He did not forsake this issue but actually heightened the problem. That is, his critique of immanentalism can be seen as an attack on simplistic assumptions about the self.

38. The relation between Kant and Kierkegaard too often is overlooked in the preoccupation with Kierkegaard's relation to Hegel. I shall note just one similarity. For both Kierkegaard and Kant the religious question is essentially a practical one. Indeed, for Kierkegaard a notion of God is of little existential import unless it determines life.

39. Jerry H. Gill, "Kant, Kierkegaard, and Religious Knowledge," in *Essays on Kierkegaard*, ed. Jerry H. Gill (Minneapolis: Burgess, 1969), p. 71. Pojman has noted five specific limitations on reason set by Kierkegaard. These are: (*a*) the attempt in Hegelian dialectics to abstract the self from existence; (*b*) the limits of reason to provide final epistemic justification for truth claims due to its internal characteristics; (*c*) reason provides only possibilities while certainty is needed in existence; (*d*) reason through language cannot capture reality; and (*e*) reason is not the essence of the human but a function of the passions. See his *Logic of Subjectivity*, p. 26. In the course of my reading I have noted all these. However, I have also attempted to show how Kierkegaard still holds to the important place and task of reason vis-à-vis existence.

40. Søren Kierkegaard, *On Authority and Revelation: The Book of Adler, or, A Cycle of Ethico-Religious Essays*, trans. Walter Lowrie (Princeton: Princeton University Press, 1955), pp. 105–106.

41. *Where the Passion Is*, p. 2.

42. See Alastair McKinnon, "Kierkegaard: Paradox and Irrationalism," in *Essays on Kierkegaard*, ed. Jerry H. Gill (Minneapolis: Burgess, 1969), pp. 110–22. Kierkegaard insisted on the principle of non-contradiction, following Trendelenberg, against what he took to be Hegel's attempt to overcome it. For Kierkegaard, the principle of non-contradiction has its cogency as an existential category and not as a logical principle. Mediation is a logical possibility, but not an existential one. See Taylor, *Journeys to Selfhood*, pp. 162ff.

43. See Cornelio Fabro, C.P.S., "Faith and Reason in Kierkegaard's Dialectic," in *A Kierkegaard Critique*, edd. Howard Johnson and Niels Thulstrup (Chicago: Regnery, 1962), pp. 156–206.

44. *Where the Passion Is*, p. 7.

45. *Logic of Subjectivity*. p. 39.

46. Mackey claims that there are two questions that back Kierkegaard's authorship: What is it to be a human who raises the question of being a Christian, and how does one become a Christian? I am not happy with this way of formulating Kierkegaard's project. To be sure he was concerned with existence, specifically Christian existence.

Yet I am not certain that Kierkegaard would hold that one is completely human outside of being Christian. His point is precisely that Christianity is existential communication. It is not an accidental modification of our already attained humanity, as Mackey's ordering of questions suggests, but a kinetic change in existence. The more helpful way of formulating the issue, I think, is to say that Kierkegaard's concern is with the human relation to the truth. This concern drove him into considering the human, the truth, the relation between being human and the truth, and the way to communicate all this. This way of formulating Kierkegaard's problem avoids the implications of Mackey's ordering of questions. See his *Kierkegaard: A Kind of Poet*, pp. 133–94.

47. Dunning has noted these forms of dialectic in the pseudonymous corpus. He also argues that contradiction is the dialectic of the aesthetic and the reciprocity of the ethical, and that the religious is marked by the paradoxical dialectic. See his *Dialectic of Inwardness*, pp. 6–12.

48. Trans. Walter Lowrie (Princeton: Princeton University Press, 1941), p. 146. Henceforth cited in text as SUD followed by reference. See also John W. Elrod's *Being and Existence in Kierkegaard's Pseudonymous Works* (Princeton: Princeton University Press, 1975) and "The Self in Kierkegaard's Pseudonyms," *International Journal for the Philosophy of Religion*, 4 (1973), 218–40.

49. *Being and Existence*, p. 30.

50. *Kierkegaard's Existential Ethics* (Tuscaloosa: University of Alabama Press, 1977), p. 47. Stack is one of the few scholars to have noted the importance of the orders of causation in Kierkegaard's understanding of the self. This is, of course, central to my argument. My interpretation differs from Stack's at two points. First, Stack does not seem to accent the notion of *pathos* as the force behind decision and as central to the continuity of the self in time. Second, he does not consider Kierkegaard's understanding of the Christian life. This is a glaring oversight and a major difficulty with his interpretation. I shall suggest that it is the shape of the Christian life, as *imitatio Christi*, that is central to all of Kierkegaard's thought.

51. "Some Aspects of Time in Aristotle and Kierkegaard," p. 14.

52. Pojman has argued that various kinds of "faith" are important to the authorship, and he notes various forms ranging from aesthetic to salvific faith. Although this is an important formulation, my concern is with the various *pathoi* that drive existence and take form in these faiths. See his *Logic of Subjectivity*, pp. 76–86, 126–30.

53. The influence of Kant on Kierkegaard's depiction of the ethical is obvious. Not surprisingly, it is thinkers like Stack, who explore the ethics of Kierkegaard, who see the relation to Kant. See his *Kierkegaard's Existential Ethics*.

54. In *Fear and Trembling* Kierkegaard notes that in the religious dimension the individual is higher than the universal. Thus the religious, at least Religiousness B, accents the individual over the universal. This is the unique paradox of Christianity and Judaism. See *Fear and Trembling*, trans. Walter Lowrie (Garden City: Doubleday, 1954).

55. See J. Sperna Weiland, *Philosophy of Existence and Christianity* (Assen: Van Gorcum, 1951), p. 116.

56. Dunning, *Kierkegaard's Dialectic of Inwardness*, p. 291. Dunning also notes the problem of the relation between the authors and the status of the text.

57. *Kierkegaard's Thought*, ed. and trans. Howard V. Hong and Edna H. Hong (Princeton: Princeton University Press, 1981), p. 339.

58. Trans. Walter Lowrie (Princeton: Princeton University Press, 1944), p. 232.

Henceforth cited in the text as TIC followed by reference. Mackey notes that Christ is first the Savior and secondly the pattern. Yet although this is true it is also the case that these are inseparable. Luther made this point and clearly was an inspiration for Kierkegaard on this matter. Theologically the indicative and the imperative are one and the same. For a helpful discussion of the place of Christ in the moral life see James M. Gustafson, *Christ and the Moral Life* (Chicago: The University of Chicago Press, 1979).

59. These are exalted claims on Kierkegaard's part, claims which would seem open to some empirical investigation. Do Christians evidence a change in existence in their lives? Kierkegaard retreats from answering this question by understanding faith to be related to inwardness. The position I am developing is that Christians are called to evidence their basic love, trust, and loyalty in life. Life is, albeit in distorted and incomplete ways, the presentation of our loyalties and trusts. This means that there are some actions Christians are distinctively called to enact although they share many loyalties with the wider public.

60. I am not concerned here with Kierkegaard's authorial intention in linking the three parts of *Training* into a unified work. I am taking the text as a whole and offering an interpretation of it. My concern is to follow the dialectics of the work as a whole rather than to attempt to discern the reason why he joined these pieces into a whole.

61. On the social and political import of Kierkegaard's work see John W. Elrod, *Kierkegaard and Christendom* (Princeton: Princeton University Press, 1981).

62. Pojman writes about this form of faith that it is "an attitude of living *as if* an important proposition were true — of risking one's life in behalf of an idea even though one's mind has not been made up regarding the truth value of the proposition." See his *Logic of Subjectivity*, p. 130. Pojman is correct to call this "faith as hope." However, the problem here is not belief in a proposition and its truth-value! Faith, for Anti-Climacus, is an existential posture relative to a person, not a proposition, who claims to be the Truth.

63. Ibid. Again, my qualm with Pojman's formulation is that he is interested in propositional belief; I take it that Kierkegaard is concerned with the existential act of faith.

64. I am not able to explore Kierkegaard's notion of perfection relative to other options in the Christian tradition. What is of interest to me is that perfection is linked to the presentation or expression of faith in existence. This presentation is, furthermore, seen as the way of the *imitatio Christi*.

65. In his *Large Catechism* Luther comments, on the First Commandment, that a God is that in which we find our ultimate good. Kierkegaard has deepened this insight: not only is a God that in which we passionately trust, but that trust is what brings the self into being.

66. "The Concept of the Christian in Kierkegaard," *Inquiry*, 8 (1965), 82.

67. H. Richard Niebuhr has made a similar point by noting that what is meant by "revelation" is the ongoing revolution of the natural religion of the self or community to a radically monotheistic faith. See his *Meaning of Revelation*.

5

The Analogies of Mimetic Practices

OVER THE COURSE of the last three chapters I have attempted to explore the import of mimesis for thinking and speaking about understanding, narrative configuration, and the self. I have done so through the study of thinkers who explicitly address the problem of understanding and reflection on experience. What has emerged is a challenge to the assumption that we can find a single right image of the human—be it the *imago Dei*, "thinking reed," or *Homo dialogicus*—unmindful of the problem of image itself. Of course, as human beings we do inherit and construe images to interpret, orient, guide, and give coherence to our lives. To recall Iris Murdoch's point, we need to explore and understand the human as the kind of creature that construes images or pictures of life that it struggles to resemble. And this entails, as Mary Midgley rightly insists, understanding the task of moral philosophy as one of thinking and speaking about the fragile unity of life in all its complexity and richness.[1] The question, finally, is what it means to be human and how to live this out. Beyond the inscription of the human within an imitative logic of the image, I have been exploring how human life and world become meaningful through forms of mimetic praxis. My contention is that this helps us understand the ways we have thought and spoken about the human condition.

The mimetic activities I have explored include understanding, narrative configuration, and the existential task of being a self. These serve as ways to reflect on and talk about the activities through which domains of reality become meaningful in a complex, creative process in which we are participants. By understanding these as *mimetic* practices, I have attempted to show that the self in its humanity is not a ghostly autonomous being freed from its rootedness in nature through passions and loves and with others in community and tradition. The self as agent is a figuration of the passion for life relative to others, and perhaps an Other, in time. In the same way, understanding is not simply the imposition of order on the chaos of sensation or the copying of an external or ideal world; it is an interpretive engagement with texts and others in and through language being shaped by while also shaping those encounters. And even our timeliness is not simply a matter of intentional consciousness or the objective movement of the cosmos. Through mimetic configuration the meaningfulness of human time is the crossing of phenomenological and cosmological times even as it calls for some practical response on our part. In a word, taking understanding, narrated time, and self as mimetic practices means claiming that they are activities in and through which our profound belongingness to the natural and social world comes to some figuration and transformation as crucial for what it means to be human. But it also means that this coming to figuration is always relative to another power or powers elusively deferred in the enactment.

Discourse about mimesis mediates through figuration the domains of ontology and practical philosophy, talk about the meaning of being, and the being of the human. This mediation is found in the very structure of the argument of this study where narrative configuration draws from and relates understanding and its social, historical, and linguistic world to the demand for authentic existence driven by fundamental passions. What is crucial to note is that what is meant by "figuration" is not the expression of the "I" as the unity and power of life, a transcendental act of the imagination constructing experience into a whole, the relation of Being and beings as an imitation of an *eidos* by existents, or simply the artistic representation of reality. Rather, by mimetic figuration the authors we have explored mean various forms of linguistic and existential praxis through which being becomes understandable, time becomes meaningful, and the self is actualized. This notion of mimetic figuration has three things of considerable import for the rest of my argument.

First, this notion of mimetic figuration means that the fragile unity and elusive power of world, our experience of time, and the selfhood of an agent must be thought and spoken about relative to those acts (interpretation, narration, existential imitation) through which they are figured and enacted. These acts, moreover, are not easily reducible to one primal act (Being or the "I") understandable in itself free of figuration. The reconstruction of mimesis we have undertaken means that there is no total mediation. Granting this, we will attempt in this chapter to explore the relation of understanding, temporality, and selfhood through the analogies among the various practices that enact them.

Second, the reason there can be no total mediation of these acts is that they are practices that figure and yet defer the powers that move them. Thus though the analogies of the mimetic practices I shall explore below provide a way to think and speak about the relation of Being becoming meaningful and the structure and transformation of experience, Being and experience must be understood in and through these practices. The analogic relations in the variety of mimetic practices means construing the human as a being who participates in the figuration of Being as world, time as a discordant/concordant whole, and life as a self with others. Likewise, it entails understanding Being, time, and life in and through these figurations (linguistic world, narrative whole, existential self) even as the power of these is deferred, never captured. In a word, our argument has led us to "picturing" the human as a mimetic being who dwells figuratively in world, time, and life. But this notion of the human, I have tried to argue, entails a thinking beyond previous imitative visions of the human, Being, text, and even the divine.

Finally, this suggests that the perplexing question of the being-whole of human being is best considered not relative to one basic mood (being-toward-death). Rather, we can think and speak about the unity and complexity of life through the relation between the various acts of interpretation, narration, and existential imitation and the affective comportments they imply, that is, solidarity, being before death and eternity, and the passion for life. These comportments are, moreover, clues to the meaning of the power of solidarity to manifest a world, of the power of speaking to refigure time, and of the power that establishes the self. Thus the force of our reading has been to prompt us to explore the basic question of the tenuous unity of life, but in a different way from metaphysical, transcendental, and even existential accounts of the unity of Being and being human. That is, given the hermeneutical journey we have charted in the previous chapters, such unity as we can think and speak of is not based on a metaphysical first principle, the transcendental act of the "I," or an existentially authentic being-toward-death, but appears in and through the various practices that structure experience and render domains of reality meaningful. Accordingly, we have spoken of a linguistic world and the "understanding I," the practical ideas of history and identity relative to the inscrutability of time, and the shape of selfhood driven by a passion for life before another in time. The import of these findings will concern us in the next chapter.

On the way to exploring the ethical and theological import of those findings, it is important to ask in this chapter what it means that we have isolated throughout our reading a formal structure present in varieties of mimesis. This does not allow us to grasp the meaning of any actual, concrete activity from some pre-given or *a priori* standpoint. It merely serves to show the analogies between practices, analogies I shall explore in detail below. The structure of a mimetic practice, whether in ritual or understanding, includes (inter)action, temporal *ek-stases*, and figuration through which something is presented. By charting the analogies between different mimetic practices we are attempting to explore both the complexity and the elusive coherence of the human condition and the ways Being is rendered meaningful.

My reading of Gadamer concluded that this general dynamic helps us explore language and also the work of art and historical understanding. His hermeneutic demonstrated that whatever we mean by "Being," it is not a transcendental "x" or the totality of concrete entities. Rather, Gadamer argued that we must understand Being on analogy with the social praxis of self-presentation (*Spiel*) which, through the participation of the human, is the dynamic of a meaningful world. This means that what is presented in the genuine act of understanding is the commonality that humans share, given their participation in the figuration of Being as a world. The medium and horizon of this world is language. Accordingly, Gadamer could claim that Being that can be understood is language. This claim has far-reaching consequences for understanding the human project.

Aside from the substantive claims found in Gadamer's work regarding language and understanding, it was also possible to begin with him in developing a vocabulary for rethinking mimesis. This entailed the threefold dynamic just noted: interpretive interaction between what presents itself for understanding and the one who can understand, the festive character of time in the act of interpretation, and figuration through which what is understood comes to presentation, even as understanding is formed anew. This dynamic was found in the work of art, in historical understanding, and, most importantly, in language as the medium of world. Regarding mimesis, Gadamer's argument hinges on the possibility of reclaiming the performative and social character of mimetic acts by returning to its roots in festival and drama. This primitive meaning of mimesis has long been understood by classics scholars and historians of ideas. Gadamer helpfully deployed it to philosophical ends, and by doing so made an advance on classical and modernist mimeticisms while making possible a reconstruction of mimesis relative to our central concerns.

The advance in thinking made by Gadamer's mimetic strategy is to escape a vision of mind as copying reality or as simply fashioning it. Understanding is a complex interpretive relation shaped by the effects of its world while also shaping that world. Thus understanding, the human participation in the construal and appropriation of its world, is crucial to rendering Being meaningful. Gadamer took as his ontological clue *Spiel*, dance and social festival, in which there is an ephiphany of meaning, of the "god," in and through the activities of the participants. This certainly does not imply a static metaphysics of presence and light because, as we saw, the festive act is always being in becoming, a movement in and out of presence. But it does entail a social vision of reality in which we are actors and one which accents the practical character of understanding. For this reason Gadamer links hermeneutics with practical philosophy. Rendering Being meaningful is an act of practical reason and life vis-à-vis the solidarity of human world. Hence the question of our participation in the world and the shape of human understanding is really a question of the good we share and seek. The central turn of hermeneutical reflection, I have argued, is precisely to the practical shape and task of understanding. I have argued that this turn is crucial for any escape from traditional mimeticisms still able to help us think about understanding, human temporality, and selfhood.

Though Gadamer provided a general vision of mimetic praxis, I have argued that further inquiry is needed regarding text and the task of being human. Of course, Gadamer's hermeneutical philosophy does explore linguistic figuration as well as human life. This is why his mimetic strategy provided the background for further inquiry. Nevertheless, his understanding of mimesis, which is our concern, is not systematically developed relative to narrative time or the act of being a self. Even his claims about solidarity and commonality as the condition for understanding call for further elaboration in terms of what we seek to interpret, the problem of human agency, and the power of solidarity. For these reasons we were compelled to think with and yet beyond Gadamer.

By reading Ricoeur, I explored the textual expression of the mimetic process relative to humans as agents in time. Again, this is not to say that he does not explore the general problem of understanding or the concrete task of personal and social existence. He does. Yet Ricoeur's reading of mimesis centers on narrative and time. His contribution to rethinking mimesis is at this level of reflection. Accordingly, I charted the mimetic arch from the prefigured order of action to the refiguration of life won in response to textual configuration. Within each aspect of the threefold mimesis we found active, temporal, and "symbolic" or figurative elements. Ricoeur's point is that narrative has its roots in the order of action and hence opens language to the field of practical existence even as it helps us understand human temporal experience. Human action is always already symbolically mediated and articulated even as we present our prefigured world through it.

A narratology always implies a more general hermeneutic of human being and understanding. This means that story *qua* story is not sufficient for understanding the human condition. To be sure, we make sense of our lives through narratives, and we identify with the stories of those communities in which we live, act, and have our being. Nevertheless, narrative on its own does not exhaust the power to refigure time or the demands of being agents in community with others. Narrative for its part is an entrance point into the temporality of human life and the timing of being in our existence. It thereby raises the question of the power that refigures our temporality.

The aporias of temporality exposed by interpreting narrative configurations include the commonality one seeks in human world and the question of who can act. Human solidarity, the commonality of "world," must be seen as a task as well as the condition for understanding. As a practical task it is guided by the idea of one history and one humanity, an idea that cannot be known but must be thought and imaginatively configured. It cannot be known since human life is mired in the inscrutability of time. The aporia can be rendered productive only through a practical, imaginatively construed idea. In this sense a narratology renders talk about solidarity problematic and practical: problematic since it cannot be known in the strict sense even though it is the ideal horizon of human world; practical in that the task of moral and political existence can and ought to be guided by this idea. What we see is that the condition for understanding (solidarity) is in itself a practical task as well as a given power that renders possible genuine understanding.

Another aporia of temporality of concern to us is the unity of the self in the diversity of its acts. In thinking about the human condition one constantly seeks to answer the question "Who was acting?" Again, Ricoeur's answer, narrative identity, is a practical one since the human self comes to be within an inscrutable horizon of time. What this aporia brings to the fore is the way in which human life is oriented to death and to an encompassing vision of time, to eternity, as presented in a text or construed by a religious and cultural tradition. Life is a being-toward-death in that we live out in front of ourselves, always being toward a future that seems to return us to the nihility ever present in existence. And yet individuals and communities are also oriented to "eternity" since they make sense of their experience within a symbolic framework that seeks to figure but not master the totality of time. Narrative identity discloses how persons make sense of their condition, even as it calls for reflection on what it means to be a self with others. The character of this narrative identity is rooted in the temporal, symbolic, and active dimensions of the prefigured order of human life. And it is achieved in the practical task of being a particular kind of individual or community in the world relative to the narratives we appropriate and enact. Here too mimesis figures the mediation of ontological claims (the horizon of time) and the practical task of human existence (narrative identity). Narrative mimesis has this mediating power through the imaginative configurative act and the act of reading.

As Ricoeur noted, "imagination," like "representation," has become problematic in current discourse. The criticism centers on grounding reflection on a transcendental act because this seems to determine the world and the other from the standpoint of intentional subjectivity. I have tried to argue that we can reconsider the imagination as a linguistic and practical phenomenon, and thus understand mimetic figuration in narrative relative to the aporias of time and human action. The construals of one history and narrative identity are practical ones and hence cannot claim absolute transcendental foundation. History and identity must be seen against the horizon of the inscrutability of time. Time always remains other, and so too other persons since they figure time in their practical existence even as they are bearers of value. This frank admission of the limits of language and understanding is due to the texture of human temporal existence. A mimetic narratology provokes us to reconsider the human subject beyond the classical self as an image of the divine or the modernist self as an autonomous being actualizing its humanity in freedom. It requires exploring without absolute foundations the complex ways in which human beings participate in their world and struggle to come to be relative to others, or an other power, in time.

The inscrutability of time means that absolute knowledge is not possible; there is no narrative of all narratives. But it also means that the response to the limits of our ability to construe time are practical ones vis-à-vis the demands of a situation. As we saw, the aporias of temporality drive the argument back to the shape of understanding and world and forward to the problem of the being of the self even as the inscrutability of time requires a turn to the practical import of narrative. The claims we make for the veracity of configurations of identity and history are ones that depend on the practical life even as we acknowledge the inscrutability, and hence radical otherness, of the horizon of the human condition.

Finally, I turned to Kierkegaard's dialectic of existence in order to explore the shape of selfhood. We saw how passion is basic to human existence. But we also saw that this passion for life becomes a self, a figuration of life, only through concrete acts of existence, through *imitatio*. There is a paradox in all this: the *imitatio* is at one and the same time an act of my being and yet not my act. Thus Kierkegaard isolated existentially the basic problem we charted in understanding and narrative: How does the self relate to the power that establishes it in and through acts constitutive of its being? How too does understanding relate to its world through interpretation? And how do we relate to the temporal ambiguity of our being and doing in narration and reading? In each case, these relations are practical ones that are best understood as forms of mimetic praxis. They open inquiry into the ontological import of these practices. Through the mimetic praxis of understanding and narrative configuration the horizon of life emerges in the inscrutability of time and in the commonality of human solidarity. This commonality and the ambiguity of time meet in the problem of the self.

Kierkegaard also called for a more adequate account of the passional dimension of human life. He showed that affectivity and passion, too long exiled from much theology and philosophy, are central to understanding human being and doing.[2] Feelings are not only second-order intentional acts that insert one into the world of a text, although they certainly are that. Affectivities and passions also move existence and shape a mode of life. We have seen that the self is a mimetic process of relating or failing to relate to the power that establishes it moved by a passionate interest in existence. Human beings exist in situations of desire. Yet Kierkegaard sees the need to relate the self to a power beyond the domain of human desire. He explores this dynamic in and through the *imitatio*, or what I have called existential mimesis.

The specifically Christian shape of *imitation* that Kierkegaard champions is not unique in its plausibility for speaking about the human self. But it is unique relative to the object of *imitatio*; it is the imitation *of Christ*. This does not detract from the mimetic shape of self. It suggests that we come to be as agents through the dynamic enactment of our passion for life relative to possibilities presented to us and others. Different communities and religious traditions present, or fail to present, ways for humans to live in the world, giving rise to diverse forms of selfhood and community. Agency is really a double mimesis since the enactment shapes the passions and feelings that give rise to it and that it presents. This enactment forms settled dispositions and affections that motivate and guide future actions; it is the root of habits and virtues. The existential task is to disclose the power that establishes life in one's own life. For a Christian, like Kierkegaard, that power is named "God" as revealed in Christ. Our task here is not to enter the problematics of Christological reflection or Kierkegaard's own understanding of Christ. To be sure, Christianity presents a specific way of life, given that the self comes to be relative to another, to Christ, in time. The general point is that mimesis provides a way to think and speak about this process of the self coming-to-be and the existential task that this entails.

Thus the last three chapters have been a rethinking of the import of mimesis for hermeneutical reflection by reading three postmodern thinkers around basic questions confronting current thought. Of course, my reading is not without tensions. There clearly are points of disagreement among the thinkers I have explored. I have noted these along the way. Gadamer's retrieval of dramatic and cultic mimesis begins reflection at a point different from Ricoeur's. Indeed, Ricoeur's reading of mimesis is content to extend Aristotelian insights in order to speak about the figuration of time. Gadamer's task, as we saw, was to explore the primordial belongingness of the human to its world disclosed in the event of truth. Although Ricoeur and Gadamer differ in their retrievals of mimesis, I have tried to show an analogic relation between their readings of it.

Not surprisingly, Kierkegaard has disagreements with both philosophers. His project challenges what must seem like the immanentalism of Gadamer's hermeneutics. The advance on Socrates and Hegel would then also amount to a departure from Gadamer. Overcoming the alienation of the human is not a matter of understanding our participation in world and the event of truth; it is a matter of redemption through the Savior. And on this point Kierkegaard would be suspicious of Ricoeur's talk about the imagination. After all, the imagination too often exalts the humiliated Christ in its rush for salvation and identity. The Christian life is one of the suffering and not an aesthetic relation to the glorified Christ.

Yet we have also uncovered analogies, in Kierkegaard's analysis of existence, the act of understanding as Gadamer details it, and Ricoeur's understanding of narrative as well. These analogies keep us mindful of the tensions among these thinkers while allowing their work to contribute to our argument. Morever, beyond the analogies about the shape of mimetic acts, there is another relation among these thinkers of import for my argument. For each thinker the problem of the human (alienation, being toward the horizon of time, being in sin) is explored and responded to in and through forms of figurative praxis. Thus the tensions among Gadamer, Ricoeur, and Kierkegaard remain, and necessarily so. Nonetheless, given what has been uncovered by reading them, it is possible to think with and beyond them about mimetic practices. The first step in doing so is to clarify the analogies we have already uncovered. Before doing so it is now possible to return to an earlier discussion.

RESPONDING TO CRITICS

Given the results of this detour of interpretation, it is now possible to forward a response to the criticism of mimesis found in the works of Girard, Derrida, and others. At bottom the dispute is over the way mimesis is understood and what it is used to understand. My interest is not in entering into an extended argument with these critics but in taking another step toward ethical and theological thinking. This requires attending to a simple but important maxim: what is closest to us is often most concealed. The task of interpretation is to understand what lies hidden. What is at dispute in the current debate over mimesis is not only the way to understand it and its complex history of effects on Western thought, but also what lies hidden that one is seeking to interpret through it.

Put succinctly: the differences between Girard and Derrida center on their construals of mimesis and the way these cohere with their central concerns, with what they seek to uncover. To recall the first chapter, Girard thinks that mimesis is best understood relative to the dynamics of ritual acts within a trajectory of violence sparked by the triangular structure of desire. Girard's substantive concern is with the primal violent act of culture. The relation between "mimesis" and social violence is religion, the sacred, which has the power to conceal the primal act on which cultural stability is built. It does so through mimetic, ritual practices. Thus Girard seeks an escape from religion, from mimetic practice, in and through what he sees as the anti-mimetic strategy of biblical texts, especially the New Testament. These texts are to help dissipate the fog of the sacred, as he puts it. His task is a critical one: to explain the mechanisms of power and to avert cultural violence.

Given Girard's interest in the structures of power and desire, it is not surprising that he contests Derrida's reading of mimesis and all other poststructuralist ones as well. Yet Derrida is pursuing different questions and does so through another construal of mimesis. He explores the theatrical roots of mimesis in mime. Here is a solitary actor deferring any reference to the real of speech and presence. By concentrating on the play action itself, Derrida seeks to reveal the process of deconstruction that infests all modes of thought claiming to provide a total vision of the world. This is as true of classical metaphysics as it is of the Kantian account of the imagination. Indeed, Derrida argues that the imaginative act of the artist attempts to determine the other in its otherness. Thus any imaginative act of figuring a whole within which to understand experience is an act of totalization. Derrida's task is to undo this perceived tyranny by challenging the ability of the imagination to construe a whole within language. This is because language is an endless mimetic play of figuration that undoes all attempts to find stability or presence.

What lies concealed for Derrida, and what he seeks to understand, is this process of undoing that is, paradoxically, also productive of meaning through

movements of signification. It is a process that is at once destructive of claims
to absolute truth and yet is the economy of meaning. For this reason Derrida is
not a nihilist in any simple sense. Indeed, without the play of figuration,
Derrida avers, we would have a meaningless world. His concern is with the
complex economy of meaning: the mimetic production of meaning in sign
systems. Far from escaping mimetic practices, Derrida wants to concentrate
on its free play. Yet the very productivity of this play is always destructive of
claims to permanent truth.

Derrida's and Girard's readings of mimesis raise profound problems for
previous construals of understanding and its world, the character and status of
texts, and the being of the self. Furthermore, because talk about the divine has
been related to these topics, these criticisms of mimesis render problematic
theological discourse. Any response to them must move on three interrelated
levels: a response to the issues inherent in traditional mimeticism and its breakdown; a reconsideration of understanding, text, and self in and through this
response; and a drawing out of the implication of these arguments for theological and ethical discourse. Such has been the trajectory of my argument,
although I have yet to suggest its import for theology and ethics.

What I have tried to uncover through mimesis is not primarily the mechanisms of the production of meaning within sign-systems and their self-undoing,
nor merely the concealing of the mechanism of power in social reality. These
have been topics of concern, of course. Still, my task has been to explore the
complex shape of those acts through which the power of some reality, its
being, is present as meaningful through figuration, *and* how world, time, and
human agency might be transformed or refigured in these acts that structure
experience. What lies hidden but close to us is twofold: the dynamic of
figuration through various acts that renders meaningful the being of something
while structuring experience; and the power to transform human life and world
by what is presented and yet deferred in these figurative practices. What mimesis helps us to explore is the elusive relation of meaning, practice, and power
in certain fundamental acts.

We have examined how Being becomes figured in and through understanding by the act of interpretation, how time becomes meaningful in the mimetic
shape of narrative, and how the self becomes actual through existential mimesis. And in each case, the question of the power to transform understanding through interpretation, refigure our temporality in narrative, and establish
the self in life remains problematic. Paradoxically, this power is and yet is not
understandable in terms of the immanent dynamic of these acts. On the one
hand, it is human solidarity, the power of speaking in narratives, and the passion for existence that enable and require the refiguration of understanding,
time, and self. On the other, none of the mimetic acts that enact this refiguration (interpretation, narration, and imitation) exhausts those powers but
presents and defers them. Each of the basic mimetic acts I have explored

requires human participation even as each is not simply the presentation of the power of those activities.

Let me make the point by considering what is going on in the practices that we have explored. The refiguration of time requires a reader, and yet the act of reading is not in itself sufficient to understand the refiguration of temporality by the power of speaking. If it were, then narrative would exhaust refiguration and capture the inscrutability of time. The struggle for solidarity as a good of the human requires people who understand. And yet, that solidarity, as condition and goal of understanding, always eludes the grasp of the interpreters. If it did not, such solidarity would not appear as a good beyond the given conditions of life eliciting and empowering our lives. And the self seeks to rest in the power that establishes it through the act of "following." It does so through faith, which escapes reduction to immanent reflexive acts. If it did not, then the problem of becoming a self would be a cognitive and not a moral and religious one. In each of the mimetic acts, the human comes to be as a participant in the enactment of human solidarity, the refiguration of time, and being a self relative to some other power or powers.

However, in the very act of doing so, the power of each eludes us; it withdraws within the act even as it paradoxically, empowers the act. Given this, human life as a self with others, the experience of time, and the character of our sociality is ambiguous. The power of solidarity, of refiguring time, and of establishing the self supports human life even as we participate in it through the mimetic practices I have explored. We live in and through the passion for existence, we move and act in time, and we have our being as ones who understand and dwell in a world. Morever, the elusive power or powers encountered in these human activities are not only supportive of the human project, but also threatening. The self can be lost in oppressive communities or isolated and alienated; the power of speaking ever fails to refigure our response to time even as we seek to master it; the solidarity that sustains life and is one of its goods can sweep up all human activities into a tyrannous, maddening crowd. The human response to that which is encountered in and through mimetic practices raises fundamental religious and moral questions.

I take the ambiguous relation of meaning, power, and practice enacted in any basic mimetic act to be emblematic of the human moral and religious condition. We cannot escape our being as participants in world, time, and selfhood under the conditions and demands of solidarity, facing the horizon of time, and amid a passion for existence. What I have sought to uncover through reclaiming mimesis is the ambiguous relation of meaning and power in and through basic acts definitive of human life that shapes understanding and its world, the temporality of our being agents, and the passion for existence. What this means more specifically for theology and ethics will concern us later.

How does this respond to Girard, Derrida, and the host of critics of mimesis? First and most simply, I have tried to show that mimesis allows us to think about the experience of power and the economy of meaning in a way that is inseparable from basic human practices. Understanding is not a simple drive to encompass all that is within its grasp or a deceptive covering for violent social acts. As mimetic it is the figuring of human world while through that act it is also transformed. Understanding thus raises the question of the power to which we are responding in and through a meaningful world. Texts are not simply webs of signs endlessly productive of other texts and other meanings. Through the participation of the reader, they are also ways of configuring and refiguring a temporality that ironically excludes the reader from any claim to mastery. And the self is not a substance or simply a trick of modern discourse. Under the force of the present and possibilities presented to one, to be a self as an agent is to enact in life the passion for life in a particular way. Yet in doing so, that desire ever escapes one; it withdraws even as it empowers life. Hence to be a self is to encounter but not master the power of existence in one's own life.

Regarding understanding and its world, text, and the self, rethinking mimesis has sought to deconstruct traditional imitative notions of these even as it has sought to reconstruct our ways of speaking and thinking about them. My argument is not content, then, with explaining cultural mechanisms or showing how the economy of meaning undoes metaphysical systems. It has attempted to chart the complex relations of meaning and power that meet and cross in three basic mimetic activities. Against Girard's reduction of religion to social acts of violence, we can understand religions as complex mimetic responses, in texts, rituals, and modes of life, to the power of solidarity to manifest a world found in understanding, to the power to refigure time, and to that power that establishes the self seeking to render life meaningful. Religious traditions differ on all these points relative to the complex matrix of mimetic practices that they embody. Likewise, the responses that religious tradition represents to these powers can take violent expressions, as the history of religious traditions sadly shows. But this does not exhaust the meaning of religious traditions; it merely signals their ambiguous character.

My argument also departs from Derrida's attempt to understand the economy of meaning purely within the mimetic play action of sign systems. By exploring the forms of mimetic *practices*, rather than the structure of sign systems, we see that these practices render something present as meaningful and structure experience even as they defer the elusive power of their subject matter. Most simply this means that texts, the voices of others, ideas place a claim on those who understand them without ever capturing totally that claim. My concern is then not only with the economy of meaning and undoing false attempts to master this economy. It is to explore resources for thinking and speaking about the ways in which human world, time, and selfhood are rendered meaningful and transformed in and through basic acts. It is to raise the question of the power of good, the meaning of our temporality, and what it means to be a self once we have escaped the illusion that we are the measure of the good, sovereigns of time, and masters of life.

Thus my reading of mimesis centers on a turn to praxis without locating it solely in sign systems or social actions. By doing so, the argument has moved toward an interpretation of understanding, narrativity, and the self that overturns traditional ideas even as it reconsiders them. That is, I have traced a shift in discourse about mimesis from using it for theoretical and aesthetic purposes to employing it to think about the practical shape of understanding, human life, and the imaginative configuration of time. By making this shift, mimesis forces on us the question of the human relation to those powers that are the condition for understanding, refigure time through speaking, and establish the self.

Put most sharply: my contention, contrary to Derrida and Girard, is that the power or powers to which human beings respond in and through interpretation, language and time, and existence are not reducible to social processes or the productivity of meaning. On the contrary, social and personal existence is a troubled response to them as they bear on the meaning and shape of life. Beyond the imitative logic of the image, it is still possible to speak of an experience of transcendence. One does so by exploring basic practices and the powers they figure and yet defer. The next chapter expands on this claim.

I have, then, traced the theme of mimetic praxis in Gadamer, Ricoeur, and Kierkegaard against the background of important criticisms of hermeneutical reflection and discourse about mimesis. Given this detour of interpretation, it is now possible to draw some constructive conclusions for the task of hermeneutical reflection. And the first step is to draw out the analogical relations between the forms of mimetic praxis that have emerged from our reading. Following this it will be possible, in the next chapter, to say something about the shape and task of theological and ethical reflection.

MIMETIC CONNECTIONS

Thus far I have made the general claim that mimesis denotes the dynamics of being, time, and self becoming meaningful in and through forms of action in which the human lives, moves, and has its being. In each case, it should be noted, we ended with a series of questions: What is the power of solidarity that enables understanding? What is the power of speaking that refigures time? What is the power that establishes the self? What the reconstruction of mimesis has enabled us to do is to think and speak about understanding, narrative temporality, and the self so that we might approach these more elusive questions.

We might also add that the unique forms of human fault, failure, and even sin are the enactment of a tyrannous world, the denial of our temporality, and living an inauthentic existence that centers on the attempt to master the power of solidarity, speaking, and the passion for life. My task is not to explore these failings although they are assumed and will be noted throughout. Indeed, they form a limit to the present work and call for further reflection.

The task here is a more limited one. It is to delineate the relations between the types of mimetic praxis. Thus far our inquiry has been analytic and reductive in character; the argument separated what must always be related. At this point the task is to discern relations previously separated. Of course, the relations between the kinds of mimetic acts are at best analogies: they are similarities-in-difference. For instance, the mimetic shape of understanding is like and yet unlike narrative or existential mimesis. Yet in order to draw this reconsideration of mimesis together, it is necessary to outline these analogical relations. The complexity of drawing out these analogies of mimetic practices is that I must isolate the three moments of interaction, temporality, and presentation in understanding, text, and self even while realizing that these three moments are internally threefold. The figure below is presented as a guide to the argument.

FORMS OF MIMETIC PRAXIS

THE MEDIUMS OF MIMETIC PRAXIS

	Language	Text	Existence
	Mimetic Activities		
Moments	Interpretation	Narration	Selfhood
inter- action:	1. prejudgment 2. dialogue 3. *Bildung*	action acts "in" plot reading	passion decision obedience
time:	1. effective history 2. contemporaneity 3. fusion of horizons	death/eternity shape of plot practical ideas	*alloiosis* *kinesis* instant
figure:	1. self-presentation 2. *Gebilde* 3. understanding	norms and rules plot itself refigured life	possibility stages of life "*imitatio*"

Regions of Being and of Experience
Enacted in Mimetic Praxis

world	time	life

What we see is that mimesis connotes forms of praxis that present a meaningful world, a configuration of time, and human life, thereby structuring and transforming experience. These are presented in the mediums of language, narrative text, and existence through the mimetic acts of interpretation, narration, and selfhood. We can also discern the interactive, temporal, and figural "moments" of each form of mimetic praxis even as they vary between different practices. Of course, these "moments" are not sequentially related. One does not act and then experience time and only then bring that action to presentation. The moments are interpretive distinctions to help us grasp the texture of any mimetic act. By exploring them I shall unfold the analogies between the forms of mimetic praxis. But the difficulty that remains is to understand the mutual infusion of the active, temporal, and figurative moments or elements of any specific mimetic praxis.

As the above figure suggests, imaginative configuration in narrative plays a mediating role. It does so on three levels. (*a*) Configuration mediates through reading the prefigured order of meaningful experience and the refiguration of life. (*b*) Because of this mediation, imaginative configuration mediates between a received social world of symbols, norms, and rules, and the coming-to-be of the self. (*c*) Configuration mediates meaningfulness and personal existence through the figuration of the order of intelligibility. Intelligibility is rooted in the shape of human action that emerges in the mimetic act of understanding and concrete human existence. Configuration has this mediating rule because it is fully dependent on understanding and the act of being human.

Narrative as a specific form of imaginative configuration interests us because of its mimetic dramatic character. Narrative in itself lacks the necessary power to render meaningful human world even though people obviously tell stories in order to make sense of their lives. As Ricoeur noted, narrative only refigures time through the act of reading and thus points to a power of speaking that exceeds narrative. My suggestion has been that this power emerges from our inherited world and the passion for existence even as these raise further moral and religious questions. But the claim to truth of narrative is grounded in its mimetic character linking language, time, and action. As will become clear, the split reference of narrative draws on the doubly mimetic character of understanding and self. It is because of this that narrative lends meaning to our lives.

With these remarks in hand, I want to turn to the analogies of mimetic practices that have been uncovered by reading Gadamer, Kierkegaard, and Ricoeur. With this the argument moves beyond any of their individual contributions. The task now is to attempt to rethink mimesis in relation to the questions that face us and what we have learned from these thinkers.

Mimetic Interaction

Understanding is an interaction, in the medium of language, between an interpreter and her or his world. It is so in three ways. In the prefigured order of experience our interaction with the world is one of prejudgment, or, we might say, settled dispositions, habits, and virtues formed through acquiring a language and culture. Obviously these prejudices are forms of prethematic interaction with the world that nonetheless inform our being, doing, and thinking.

Our lives are formed by the language, symbols, norms, and rules of our culture in ways that often escape us. In this sense our language is the horizon of understanding. Of course, this prethematic horizon can be oppressive. In an ironic sense we do live in an "imitative" world insofar as different cultural systems assign to individuals and groups their stations in life. The task is, of course, to transform oppressive structures and the desires that drive them. Still, the first thing to see is the way in which we interact with our world through prejudices. Though they are not rigid but open to revision, our prejudgments mark our thrownness into the world. Prejudgments are the self-presentation of our historicity, our belongingness to a world.

The move to genuine understanding, and hence to the possibility of transforming our received world, entails another form of interaction. In the act of interpretation we are ever projecting and revising our guesses about the meaning of a whole. The activity of interpretation is carried on vis-à-vis the artifacts of a tradition. At this level of interaction, there is simply self-presentation (*Selbstdarstellung*) that will become a presentation for another at the level of figuration, as Gadamer argued. What is transformed and presented in dialogic interpretation is our belonging in the world relative to the subject matter we are interpreting.

Through interpretation there is another level of interaction, and this time it is a leap into the true. In the formation of understanding there is a corresponding increase of Being and meaning marking yet a different interaction with what is interpreted. We should note immediately that the formation of *Bildung*, personally and socially, is through the action of interpretation. This means that all understanding, even our pre-understanding, is the product of interpretative interaction, which restructures the field of experience with others.[3] Human belonging to the world, first expressed in prejudgments, is formed and transformed anew through interpretation, while those pre-understandings are, in themselves, expressions of past acts of interpretation. *Bildung* is, in a word, the refiguration of human understanding through the dynamics of our dialogic response to what presents itself for interpretation. Our cultural world is figured in the act of understanding.

If we turn to consider explicitly "text" as what is interpreted, we can discern an analogous dynamic to that of understanding. "Text" here is not limited to literature. It means any matrix of meaning that has become autonomous in relation to the intentions of those who enacted, pronounced, or professed it; a "text" is "independent with regard to the social conditions of its production," even as it provides a way to understand and critique those conditions through this distanciation.[4] The specific prefigured world narrative texts dip into is the order of human action in all its social embeddedness. Human belongingness to world includes not only formed judgments but also its rootedness in action. Human action is informed by the norms, rules, and symbols of a community and its traditions. This "informing" is carried out precisely through prejudgments even while our actions express them. Not surprisingly, different communities understand and judge human actions differently. And their actions provide insight into what a community uses to interpret and guide human activity. Social action expresses and realizes the pre-understanding and meaningfulness of human world that guides and informs it. Yet action is the medium through which those symbols and norms are activated and presented. This happens most obviously in highly formalized types of social practice, like rites of passage or worship. Yet all human action expresses and realizes to a greater or lesser degree the cultural matrix that supports it.

The configuration of human action in narrative has its own active dimension. It is found in the actions, events, and episodes *in* the plot. And here too the same dialectic holds. That is, the actions of characters and the episodes in the plot give us insight into how the human dilemma is understood. This is why Aristotle claimed that dramatic poetry provides moral insight. By reasoning out a drama we learn something about human life as actualized. And this gives us insight into the way particular kinds of characters can and should act. Thus in plot the action reveals the prejudgments that inform, guide, and evaluate human being and doing. Through configuration there is an increase of meaning and Being: human action is seen as an intelligible whole of discordant concordance even as it brings to presentation the human dilemma and the symbols and norms that inform our lives. By interpreting narratives we attempt to grasp the intelligibility of human action in such a way as to refigure our practical existence. That is, through the power of speaking, we attempt to render our lives meaningful.

Understanding itself is won through a unique form of praxis. In reading, or interpreting, we interact with others, a narrative, or an event. Through that interaction understanding is formed. This is why I noted above that understanding at this level is a *Bild-ung*. It is informed by an interaction with others, whether that other is a person or a "text," in and through figurations or images (*Bilder*) about the subject matter under question. In the act of reading we reason out a plot that, when grasped and understood, refigures our own lived experience. This happens through the formation of settled dispositions to act in particular ways and the cultivation of practical judgment. What is presented at this level of interaction is not a world behind the text. Through reading there is a disclosure of a world in front of the text, a possible way of life, as Ricoeur put it. Given this, what is "imitated" in the act of reading is the order of human action configured narratively, even as the praxis of reading helps form dispositions and judgments and thus transforms life.

Prejudgments and actions of various forms are not the only way we interact with our world. There is also the domain of human affections, passions, and desires. "Feelings" insert us into our world and its linguistic presentations. These feelings are second-order intentional modes of appropriation and motives for existence. Thus at the prethematic level, we must speak first of affections evoked by the action of the world on us and of passions and desires that motivate our being and doing. These passions and affections are primal ways of being in the world; prejudgments and actions are themselves driven by affections and desires. Thus though the order of action opens onto the question of the human orientation to the horizon of time, the domain of affectivity and passion reveals that their orientation is a matter of concern to us. What comes to presentation in human passion for existence is our way of being in the world as one of concern and anxiety about existence.[5] Anxiety and concern are evoked by our affective interaction with the world. This was an insight of Kierkegaard's that shifted hermeneutical reflection away from concentrating on consciousness to exploring the various moods of the human condition.

Our passionate interaction with texts, traditions, and persons, while carried on through dialogic interpretation, confronts the reader with the crisis of decision. This is particularly true of religious and moral narratives and symbols. The confrontation evokes feelings that insert us into the world of the event or text. How am I to understand this happening? What am I to be and what am I to do relative to the world presented by this work of art? How am I to respond to the needs of this person in this situation? Such decisions are the configuration of human passion for existence. They require an act in the present, an initiative that renders one an agent in the company of others. Much as the character's decisions in a narrative are revealed in the course of the plot, so too the world and others confront us with a host of decisions. And our responses disclose the affections and passions, indeed the character, not only of the persons in the narrative but of ourselves as well. Thus in our decisive interaction with a text we have both the configuration of our fundamental passions and affections in the decision, and the formation of feelings and settled dispositions.

A decision about our being with others involves a refiguration of life. Not only do interpreting and reading inform understanding, they also call for concrete modes of action. Kierkegaard spoke about this as "obedience." Perhaps we cannot remove all the heteronomous connotations from this term in order to show that there is an element of obedience in all genuine understanding and action, but the refiguration of life follows from a conformity in action to some principle, impulse, or reality. If we realize that what is *minimally* confronted in the acts of interpretation and decision is a presentation of human being as the passion for life, then what is conformed to is the being of the human in these acts. And if what is *maximally* presented is configured by various traditions as the being and activity of "God," an encounter with the sacred or nature, then what is conformed to in action is the ultimate. Such conformity *in* action is, to use Robert Sokolowski's phrase, the "being-at-work of human nature."[6] Paradoxically, the being of the human, the claims of an other, and the activity of the ultimate potentially confront one in an obligatory way requiring one to enact one's life. To be sure, there are heteronomous claims. It is crucial, nevertheless, to see that human nature is achieved and shown for what it is in praxis. In its authentic forms this is not a heteronomous obedience since it is a conformity to the being of those acts that constitute the human in relation to others. The deeply moral character of our lives is that through relations and actions we come to be or fail to be with others and our world.

The first moment of mimetic praxis is, then, the complex structure of human interaction with its world and the various forms that this takes. Human understanding and action draw from and return to our prethematized, affective, temporal, active, and passionate interaction with our world. At this point we should note a curious insight whose significance will build through my argument. Imaginative configuration of human temporal action mediates understanding and its world and the self with others. This suggests that it is through our encounter with and interpretation of figurations of our world that we come to be and understand life vis-à-vis the commonality that is human world. Here again the human condition is marked by unique forms of distortion and fault through tyrannous ideologies and distorted self-understandings that configure forms of life that destroy human solidarity and identity. The importance of imaginal configuration, then, is that it is also a clue to the forms of distortion in our world and to the ways we attempt to enact a just and peaceable life. Throughout the rest of our analysis we shall see that the relation and mediation of agency and world continue to include imaginative configuration. At this point we can say that coming-to-be a self is standing out, existing, from commonality even as selfhood is a presentation, a specific figuration, of human solidarity. In a word, we realize in our very selfhood the world that forms us, even as we seek to stand out from and transform that world.

Mimetic Temporality

The first analogical relation between mimetic practices is, then, their interactive character, with all the complexity of this in each specific kind of praxis. The full import of this analogy will not be seen until the next chapter, but at this point it is important to note how the interactive shape of a mimetic practice figures the way in which the human condition is shaped by and yet shapes its environing world. This is also the case with the temporal character of any mimetic practice. And this forms another analogical relation among understanding, narrative, and selfhood. Again, I want to move through their temporal shape exploring their analogical relations.

Understanding is deeply temporal. This is true not only in our projection of a world, but also in that we are always thrown into a world, into tradition. This thrownness is our being in the effects of history, as Gadamer put it. These effects are not simply the traces of the past in cultural artifacts; they are the effects of the past on understanding in prejudgments and consciousness. In this respect it is proper to speak of the human as being *in* history even as we project an historical horizon. And again, the medium of this historicity is language since it etches the effects of history into human consciousness. Thus what is brought into meaningfulness in the mimetic act of understanding is not simply our belonging to world. Rather, it is our belonging to an historical world, to tradition and its effects. This temporal belongingness is the condition of the possibility for our ability to understand the past in all its alienness. The historical distance between us and what is interpreted is not an ugly ditch we must leap over in order to understand. We already belong to tradition and its effects on us. In this sense it is correct to say that we are more acted upon than acting. The formation of our prejudgments through the effects of history signals the radical historicity of human life. Ironically, it is precisely this thrownness that is the condition for understanding.

When we consider dialogical interaction with the past, our own or a culture's, there is a new mark of human temporality. We find that through the drama of interpretation we become contemporaneous with what was past. The contemporaneity between interpreter and text signals a paradox in human temporality: we are able to relate to the past in the act of being different from the past. To understand at all is to understand differently, as Gadamer said. And yet each act of understanding is equally originary since it marks the contemporaneity of interpreter and the past. Thus what is "imitated" in the dialogical act of understanding includes the temporality of our belonging to world and the paradoxical shape of human time.

Finally, in a genuine event of understanding there is a fusion of horizons between our world and the world that confronts us from the past. This fusion entails an expansion of our horizon; it is a transformation of understanding itself. We can escape the provincialism of our horizon through the infusion of our view of the world by what meets us as alien. No doubt, this is the temporal expression of *Bildung* since to be formed, to be cultured, is to expand one's understanding and accordingly one's world. And given that human world is deeply historical, any formation is itself part of the historical process called tradition. The radically temporal character of human life is that its being is in becoming. Yet what is disclosed or presented in the fusion of horizons marking the temporal structure of understanding is our belonging to the past even as we enact the future.

Human temporality finds expression in history and fictive plots. I am not interested here in exploring the complex and ambiguous relation between writing history and construing a plot. I can say, however, that the analogous structure of historical and fictive narratives cohere in the temporal character of life. Narratives are the configuration not only of human action but of our experience of time. Dramatic plots mediate our understanding of a shared world with the self. They do so since they present a world while calling for an act of interpretation and understanding on our part. The power of narrative configurations to mediate "world" and understanding is due to the fact that in them language, as the medium of human world, meets the act of coming to be a self.

The prefigured order of experience is marked by the paradoxical orientation of the human to death and "eternity" as the world presented by a text. Stated more generally, life is oriented to death since as finite beings who stand out of possibility we also reach toward the limits of our finitude, toward nihility. This is the recognition of the finite freedom that is our existence. And yet given our rootedness in tradition our experience is always shaped symbolically. For the West temporal experience has been informed by Greek visions of time and Jewish and Christian theologies of history, as Ricoeur noted. Accordingly, our experience of time is always informed by these different construals of eternity.

The significance of various construals of eternity for our reflection is not in their competing claims to truth. That is a question beyond the scope of this study. What is crucial is that in the symbolic construal of time we see two things. We see (a) the marks of effective history on our consciousness even as we acknowledge the projective character of existence. That is, the projective character of life is marked by the prejudices, the cultural appropriations, that inform it. And this includes configurations of the horizon of time. We also see (b) that the orientation of human existence to death and eternity evokes the passionate concern for life that Kierkegaard announced, and raises a fundamentally practical question about the shape and quality of our relation to life and to the world as marked by good and evil. This question is basic to theological and ethical reflection. As H. Richard Niebuhr has noted, the "revelation with which [humans] therefore begin is not the revelation of God as infinite being in the finite, but of his goodness in evil."[7] We construe the world as a whole, and we read it in order to make sense of the ambiguity of our experience. Our construals are always in part interpretations of received configurations of the horizon of existence, even as they seek to meet the ambiguities of good and evil in present practical experience.

When we reflect on narrative itself, this temporal quality of experience is transformed into figuration. What is crucial here is the synthetic act of making a plot, the act of ordering episodes into a coherent whole. The temporal dynamic is shown not simply through the action of the characters in the plot, but also through the curious structure of plot itself. Plot is a discordant concordance in which the disjunctive shape of lived experience is rendered into a whole. What is disclosed in the structure of plot is the ambiguous character of human lived time. Because the structure of plot is grounded in the order of lived experience, it is possible for us to experience contemporaneity with it. And yet, as we shall see shortly, it also evokes movement, *kinesis*, in the self. More important, the experience of contemporaneity manifests itself in discordant concordance: through the act of interpretation we achieve a concordance with what is presented in the text even as our act of understanding is itself originary and hence discordant with the historical origin of the work.

As Ricoeur argued, plot does not solve the aporias of human temporality but renders them productive while calling for some response on our part. What is required is an act of reason, the imaginative figuration of practical ideas. These ideas, such as narrative identity and human solidarity, do not resolve the aporias of temporality. In these practical ideas we have the meeting of language, time, and action that mediates human world and human self. Much as understanding is dependent on prior mythic and poetic construals of time and hence can never escape these symbols, so too in these practical ideas we are contributing to the construal of our world that forms the context for more specific claims to knowledge.

The practical idea of one humanity and one world draws on a commonality, or solidarity, with others and the earth. And yet it also suggests that such solidarity is a task, a moral and political project that has fallen to us. It is both a task for our interpretation of what it means to be human and a guide, an ideal, for those forms of action seeking to enact a just and peaceable world. This suggests, moreover, that human world is pervaded by the same aporia of temporality that we find in figured order of action. The practical idea of one humanity and history is our contribution to the construal of the world since it forms the imaginative matrix in which particular acts are understood.

If the practical idea of one humanity entails a task, then it confronts us as agents and demands some initiation of action in the present. One way to speak of this is through the idea of narrative identity. However, we must also consider the dynamics of the self consistent with "narrative identity." This refigured identity won through interpretation helps us understand the continuity of the self and its belongingness to world. Identity is engendered through the interpretation and appropriation of narratives. Kierkegaard, for his part, explored the self relative to one specific set of narratives (the New Testament Gospels) and one specific event (Jesus Christ). Drawing on his work, I argue that the act of being a self has a mimetic structure that specifies the existential shape of narrative identity. I shall return to this in a moment.

"Imitated" on the level of practical ideas are, then, the aporias of temporality as found within self, tradition, and world. These practical ideas, we can surmise, are imaginal transformations into figures of the aporias of time calling for a refiguration of life. It is in this respect that they mediate, again by coupling language and action, world and human agency.

If we turn to the problem of the self, we isolate an analogous temporal structure to text and understanding. The prefigured order of existence entails qualitative changes in life (*alloiosis*). The effects of history on us imitate moves in our given existence; they form fundamental patterns of consciousness and disposition. These basic settled dispositions are "virtues" when they are excellences of character enabling us to enact the basic practices that sustain and enhance human life and community. Thus our very ability to act in our world and to sense our interdependence with others is a clue to the qualitative effect of historic change on us. Human being is within the effects of history. It is also moved by the passion for life crucial to confronting the problem or task of being a self relative to others. In confronting the event of Christ, Kierkegaard claimed that the self in the act of decision moves in a more radical sense. There is a kinetic realization of the self. Through decision in response to what encounters the self, the self comes to be relative to what moves it. And as we saw, Kierkegaard claimed that this is nothing less than coming-to-be relative to the power that establishes the self. At this point I can generalize on his insight, given the rest of my argument. Coming to be a self is always a response to what and who confronts us and the struggle to enact the self with others in that encounter.

The temporality that marks this standing out as self Kierkegaard called the "instant." It exposes the existential dimension of the fusion of horizons in understanding since we see that this fusion means to ex-ist as a self in a particular way, in a specific way of being human. This helps us deepen the practical idea of narrative identity since to be a self is not simply to respond to a narrative. It is to come to be in a specific way, as a particular human being with others. Narrative identity provides a way to understand the continuities in human affections and passions by forming them into settled dispositions, character, and understanding. Of course, that narrative identity must also be understood in its full existential import and demand. What is disclosed in the existential mimesis is the temporal shape of coming to be as a self.

The second moment of mimetic praxis is, then, the complex and ambiguous character of temporality in understanding, action, and selfhood. This level of temporality inheres differently within mimetic interaction and figuration. It is a mark of all forms of interaction that they are deeply temporal in the sense we have uncovered. In mimetic configuration this temporal character is inscribed in the text or the work of art and becomes activated again through reading, interpretation, and decision. Given this, the narrative inscription of time mediates historicity and the temporality of the self. I have isolated this mediation under the practical ideas of history and narrative identity. Those construals derive their ontological import from human being in the world and the kinetic shape of the self. And yet, we must also claim that those ideas seek to guide, inform, and present in figured form, world and human agency. They form a poetic matrix within which to grasp the meaningfulness of our lives because they link language, as the medium of human world, and the act of becoming a self in the company of others.

Mimetic Figuration

Another moment or dimension of any mimetic praxis is that of "figuration." As with the other aspects of mimetic praxis, I want to consider the figurative shape of understanding, narrative, and self to isolate their interrelation and threefold character. No doubt the element of figuration is what has classically been understood as "representation" or even "re-presentation." By retrieving mimesis as I have, we now can see that figuration is a presentation in structured form of the being of a reality. My concern is to isolate this figuration in understanding, narrative, and self.

Not only is the mode of being of *Spiel*, as an ontological clue, interactive and temporal; it includes self-presentation. This suggests that the play of Being is always one of self-disclosure and withdrawal behind appearances. The presentative character of Being (disclosure/withdrawal) includes a realization for others insofar as someone participates in that event. The true import of the *theoros* is this dialectic of participation and distanciation. Our most primitive forms of participation in our world are again prejudgments, the prethematic order of action, and our passions even as they distance us from sheer immediacy. Participation is refined and deepened through our acts of interpretation and understanding which mediate temporal and other forms of distance. The significance of *Spiel* as an ontological clue is that it announces the social character of human life and being. Hence meaningful Being won through our participation is best called "world," itself a structure of experience.

The disclosure of world is not initially found at the primal depths of *Spiel*-action itself. It emerges only through the transformation into figure of that play within which "world" is a figuration of environment (*Umwelt*). Gadamer explicitly linked mimesis to this transformation, which he called a leap into the true. Being becomes meaningful through its figuration: in the act of interpretation Being is presented as understanding and as world. In concrete terms this means that in every act of understanding what we do is construe and configure reality as a meaningful world. This is why a completely meaningless world cannot be articulated, let alone understood. Of course, any human world is deeply broken and scarred by violence; experience is fractured. And a fundamental religious and moral question has to do with goodness amid this evil. Still, in the configurational act of understanding, "world" comes to some meaningfulness, whether good or evil. This is not a creation *ex nihilo* since the fundamental fact of our existence is that we find ourselves in a world to which we respond. The struggle of understanding is to enact a meaningful world; we are responders to our world and participants in its enactment. Accordingly, every genuine act of understanding forces upon us a dilemma: What kind of world should we seek to present? This question too is at the limits of the present study. It signals the direction of thought we will consider in the next chapter.

The *Gebilde*, whether in understanding or the work of art, is structured activity through which the character of being as self-presentation is revealed. Given this, it is incorrect to understand the figuration, the "image" or artifact, as a representation of some prior non-figurative reality. This was the move first made by Plato in the *Republic* and elsewhere, and it has marked much of the

subsequent history of reflection on mimesis. Yet through our dialogic participation the figure is the presentation of a world. In a moment we shall see how
narrative configuration helps specify this claim.

Understanding is also a figuration, one won through the interpretation of
other figures. Not surprisingly, understanding is formed through the appropriation of the images and "pictures" that we interpret. Through the fusion of
horizons in interpretation, understanding is formed and raised to a more comprehensive perspective. Yet because understanding itself is a figured activity
through which something presents itself, we can ask what presents itself in
understanding. In the medium of language, what presents itself is Being as
meaningful, as world. This world is the condition for understanding and is
deeply historical, impressing its effects on consciousness. Understanding is
our way of being in the world in that through the act of understanding we come
to be in the presentation of a world. The emergent power of Being realizes
itself in the specific structurations of world and understanding, a theme I shall
return to shortly. Yet if understanding comes to be through the interpretation of
works of art, texts, cultural artifacts, and our natural environment, then we
must consider more carefully the phenomenon of configuration itself. And
here narrative emplotment is again important.

In prefigured experience, what marks out action from simple movement is
precisely that it is informed by norms, rules, and cultural symbols or figures.
These are, in a sense, the figurative self-presentation of any culture that shapes
action. Action is both the presentation of a cultural matrix, its norms and
symbols, and the being-at-work of the human. We can say, then, that what
most obviously distinguishes mimetic praxis from any kind of movement is
precisely this figurative dimension. On its most primitive level what is presented is the action itself.

In plot we meet the explicit imaginal configuration of human action. Narrative reference is split: it dips into the prefigured order of action even as it
opens up a possible way of life. In the configurational act of narration, human
action and the cultural world that structures action move beyond self-presentation
into presentation for another. That other may be the self, a distant reader, or
even another culture. But through narrative emplotment the order of action is
presented as figured. Of course, such configuration, as noted above, attempts
to render productive the discordant elements of human temporality into a concordant whole. In this sense mimetic plot is a productive act of the imagination rendering into a meaningful whole lived experience. Whereas understanding metaphoric utterance is the emergence of a new semantic pertinence from
the clash of literal claims at the level of the sentence, in narrative it is this
grasping together of all the elements of human action into a unified whole. In
this act of understanding won through the interpretation of plot, what is disclosed is a world of action opened for us.

In opening a world, narrative configuration calls for reading and the refiguration of life. Understanding entails the potential restructuring of human experience and action. We can say that although any work potentially calls for some radical adjustment in our lives, those texts that elicit radical transformation or conversion in our character and conduct are best called classics. As David Tracy has noted, classic here designates our response to a work, and not some supposed quality of the work.[8] That response is one of refiguring our lives relative to what is presented by the text through our interaction with it. This refiguration is the work of the reader, even as the power to refigure time is not exhausted by her or his act; the power of reading relative to time enacts and yet defers another power, that of speaking. Religious classics, in this light, are those texts, events, persons, or activities that empower and demand a transformation of our existence vis-à-vis the worshipful power of reality that manifests itself in and through our engagement with them.

At this point it is clear that what narrative configurations of human action open up is the possibility for the refiguration of practical existence. Yet because narrative specifically configures human temporality, the refiguration of life must also touch on our experience of time. I have argued for the practical ideas of one history and humanity along with narrative identity to shape and guide that refiguration. Such practical construals of life are the work of the imagination seeking to bring into a whole history and human agency. Yet they do so not on the level of the given self or the given world, but in projecting a possible mode of existence. Hence here too these practical ideas disclose and inform human action.

Insofar as a text elicits some refiguration of life through the act of the reader, we must also consider the self as a specific figuration of life and structuring of experience. On its most simple level, we have isolated the imaginative presentation of possibilities for life. Thus whereas a narratology moves toward disclosures of possible ways of life through the narrative act of configuration and reading, the existential concern is different: How do I come to be as an agent with others? We saw that for Kierkegaard the point of Christianity is not the possibility of existence inherent in the being of the human, but the actuality of Jesus Christ as the God–Man in time. This shatters all immanental modes of thought, including the tradition of hermeneutical reflection. At the prefigured order of the self, what we confront are possible ways of being human. The existential dilemma is to actualize one of these possibilities here and now.

The actual realization of a mode of life sets up Kierkegaard's intricate stages of existence. The aesthete was the one who could not actualize the self either because of a loss of self in sensual delight or the reflective projection of infinite possibilities for life. The "ethical" stage of existence, as Kierkegaard defines it, fails precisely because the self becomes stricken with the demands of the duties it is to enact. We find that we are simply unable to fulfill the law in its perfection. The religious mode of existence expresses itself, it would seem, in aesthetic and ethical ways.[9] Religiousness A entails the mystical loss of the self in the sublimation of the aesthetic. Christianity, or Religiousness B, confronts the self with the task of coming to be as a self before the event of Christ through faithful discipleship.

My point in rehearsing Kierkegaard's stages is that it is in confronting and actualizing given possibilities for life that the self comes to be. We can say that in encountering configurative presentations of ways of being human the reader faces a crisis of understanding. Will I come to be a self, will we become an authentic community, relative to what meets us in this text, this event, this person, the cries of the poor? The self or a community is realized and displayed in its response to just these kinds of encounters. Therefore, the stages of existence are configurations of possible ways of existing. Indeed, different modes of existence are themselves configurations of life through which human life is presented.

Kierkegaard's more radical point was that to come to be as a genuine, authentic self is to live out a specific mode of life. For the Christian that mode is the *imitatio Christi*. Again I have tried to suggest that *imitatio* as existential mimesis reveals something about all human existence. It shows that human life becomes refigured and truthful when one takes on a mode of being that presents life structured in such a way as to be a presentation of those passions and beliefs that form the self. To recall my earlier remarks: we are confronted in action by what elicits our fundamental devotion and we thereby enact it in our own lives even while struggling to present that devotion.

The history of reflection on the *imitatio* has been to concentrate on this level of concrete action and obedience. Yet if we recall Buber's insight noted in the first chapter, we can see that *imitatio* connotes more the act of being human than simple prescriptions and moralistic modes of action. Of course, what is conformed to in action and how the human comes to be in its acts are of considerable importance. Yet at this level of analysis we are simply trying to interpret the shape of the act of being a self. And it seems clear, not only from the biblical tradition and Kierkegaard but from Ricoeur and Gadamer as well, that human being, in understanding and action, is the figuration of life through appropriation and enactment. *Imitatio* is a double mimesis: the self is actualized in a specific mode of life, and human existence comes to presentation in a concrete self. Thus the *imitatio*, as all forms of mimetic praxis, is both symbolic or figurative action and a way of effectively transforming life and world.[10]

The final dynamic of mimetic praxis, realizing that these are interpretive distinctions, is that of figuration. I have charted how understanding, a particular mode of life, and imaginal mimesis are diverse figurations. Obviously they structure different aspects of reality and experience: understanding is the human appropriation of its being-in-the-world; imaginal configurations of the order of action figure human temporality; the self is a specific figuration of the human passion for life relative to others in time. I have also tried to show how these three different forms of mimetic figuration mutually inform and draw on each other. World comes to a unique presentation through its artistic configuration even as narratives draw their intelligibility from the symbolical character of human world. The self comes to be relative to possibilities presented to it, whether in texts, or imagination, or the ordinary affairs of life. Yet the self in coming to be is a presentation of what elicits its passion and devotion. The complexity of any mimetic activity is that the three moments of action, temporality, and figuration mutually inhere in each other even as each has a threefold character.

Mimetic Praxis

The force of my argument has been to rethink mimesis as a form of figurative praxis and thereby to move beyond imitative notions of art, questions of denotative referentiality in language, and a mirror image of mind. More specifically, I have explored fundamental acts or practices of being human in a temporal world. The argument has resisted the temptation, so obvious in the history of theology and philosophy, to isolate *the* fundamental *actus* of being and being human, whether this is the act of being *qua* being, the free, reflexive act of consciousness, or communicative interaction. I have explored three forms of mimetic praxis crucial for depicting what is meant by Being and being human, acts that have complex analogical relations. Obviously there are many kinds of mimetic practices, particularly in ritual and social actions, that require further investigation. Certainly there are manifold ways of understanding, diverse narratives with wildly complex plots and claims, and a host of ways of being a human agent. Hence the analogies of mimetic practices isolated above do not allow any *a priori* determination of the power and import of particular mimetic acts. Still, in the face of the criticism of "imitation" on the level of text, understanding, and self it seems fitting to attend to these basic acts.

The complexity, even mystery, is that Being and experience are the relation and figuration of these basic acts in and through language, configured time, and selfhood under the powers of manifesting a world, refiguring time, and establishing the self. Thus "world," "text," and "self" cannot be understood simply as imitative representations of God, author, or the *imago Dei*. As forms of mimetic praxis, they are dramatic enactments in which being becomes meaningful and experience structured and unified through figural acts. What is disclosed, presented, or "imitated" in each form of praxis differs even as each mutually informs the others.

In the dynamic activity of understanding, human participation and distanciation in its world are brought to presentation. Yet "world" itself is mimetic of the commonality and solidarity that are the condition for the possibility of all human being, doing, and understanding; it is a structuring of the field of experience. This solidarity, in other words, is the power that enables and transforms understanding even as it escapes our total grasp. Narrative mimesis is the presentation of human action and time as meaningful. That temporality, of course, marks the shape of human world even as the world is etched with the effects of past human acts. Through the act of reading, the power of speaking refigures time even as this act does not exhaust this power. Finally, the self is a mimesis of the human passion for life. Different kinds of selves are, accordingly, different presentations of human life. The power that establishes the self, whether called freedom or God, also escapes our control. World, self, and text are ways that being is enacted and experience structured and transformed. They are "mimetic" since they all are dramatic figurative activities through which something is presented and deferred.

Understanding and its world are mediated by narrative mimesis with self and passion. This mediation is due to the confluence of action, language, and time in narrative mimesis. Again, it is not simply "narrative" that is crucial for this mediation; but the imaginal, linguistic act understood as mimetic and hence dramatic.[11] This means that the split reference of mimetic works draws its intelligibility from the double mimesis of world/understanding and passion/self. Understanding and human agency are doubly mimetic because in the acts of interpretation and existential imitation the world and passion for life are figured and enacted as understanding and self. Imaginal mimesis draws on and refers to this shared world and the problem of human identity. This is why it reaches the aporias that it does, and why they can be rendered productive only through practical act, through understanding and our concrete lives. Given this, the power to refigure time, to trans-form world and self, emerges not from narrative but in understanding and the coming to be of the self, or it does not emerge at all. Ironically, this suggests that the powers of speaking, of solidarity, and of our passion for life enact but do not capture an elusive other power that also structures and transforms experience.

A mimetic praxis is, then, any form of action through which the being of something becomes meaningfully presented and deferred in a figurative way while allowing a transformative appropriation of it by structuring experience. This notion of mimesis allows us to consider old questions in a new light: the shape of human understanding and its world, how texts make a claim to truth and refigure life, and what it means to be an agent. And it does so relative to those powers that transform understanding, our temporality, and existence.

INCONCLUSIVE RESULTS

The results of this chapter are suggestive but inconclusive. They suggest a mode of reflection that seeks to understand the import of these basic mimetic practices for what is going on in the world, what is the possible measure of our lives, and what we are to be and to do. That is, they suggest a direction of thought for moral reflection. And insofar as these mimetic activities raise the question of that power or powers which they present and yet defer, they open the space for religious reflection, as I understand it.

The results achieved in this chapter remain inconclusive and importantly so. We have found that it is not possible to interpret Being as world, time as narrated, or life as self from the vantage point of one fundamental *act*, either of being or of consciousness.[12] Rather, we have had to trace analogies between a plurality of mimetic acts as a way to speak about world, text, and self. This too has implications for theology and ethics, as we shall see. We must explore what it means to live, move, and have our being within a plurality of these practices. But initially the results achieved mean that subsequent explorations and reflection will always remain inconclusive. Lacking a single vantage point, a view from nowhere, we can no longer claim to be the masters of life, sovereigns of time, or the measure of goodness. And such a condition raises questions about our being and doing and also about that to which we are ultimately responding. These questions form the context for the next chapter, itself an inconclusive one.

NOTES

1. See Murdoch's "Metaphysics and Ethics" and Midgley's *Heart and Mind: The Varieties of Moral Experience* (New York: St. Martin's, 1981).

2. For a study of this question which draws on Kierkegaard, see John D. Caputo, "A Phenomenology of Moral Sensibility: Moral Emotion," in *Act and Agent: Philosophical Foundations for Moral Education and Character Development*, edd. George F. McLean et al. (Lanham, Md.: University Press of America, 1986), p. 199–222. For a recent use of affectivity in theology, see Gustafson's *Ethics from a Theocentric Perspective*.

3. The notion that understanding is a reconstruction of fields of experience is found in pragmatism. See John Dewey, *Reconstruction in Philosophy*, enl. ed. (Boston: Beacon, 1948) and William James, *Pragmatism and the Meaning of Truth* (New York: Longmans, Green, 1910). See also Robert Johann, *Building the Human* (New York: Herder and Herder, 1968); Richard J. Bernstein, *Philosophical Profiles* (Philadelphia: University of Pennsylvania Press, 1986), John E. Smith, *Purpose and Thought: The Meaning of Pragmatism* (New Haven: Yale University Press, 1978), and my "Iconoclasts, Builders, and Dramatists."

4. Ricoeur, *Political and Social Essays*, p. 260.

5. On the importance of care (*Sorge*) for our way of being in the world, see Martin Heidegger, *Being and Time*, trans. John Macquarrie and Edward Robinson (New York: Harper & Row, 1962). See also Paul Tillich, *The Courage to Be* (New Haven: Yale University Press, 1952).

6. *Moral Action*, pp. 41–76. Sokolowski takes moral existence to be grounded in and oriented to the being of the human. My concern is to show not only that human being is oriented to self, others, and world, and hence is moral, but also that it is open to the divine. In this sense the religious and moral dimensions of existence intertwine.

7. "Review of Paul Tillich's *Systematic Theology* vol. I," *Union Seminary Quarterly*, 7 (1951), 45–49.

8. See his *Analogical Imagination*. At this point Tracy is borrowing from Gadamer. For a helpful essay by Gadamer tracing the difference between religious and poetic texts, see his "Religious and Poetical Speaking," in *Myth, Symbol, and Reality*, ed. Alan M. Olson, Boston University Studies in Philosophy and Religion 1 (Notre Dame: University of Notre Dame Press, 1980), pp. 86–98.

9. This is a point that Friedrich Schleiermacher and others made in the nineteenth century. Against "mystical" forms of religion they saw Christianity as a form of ethical monotheism, along with Judaism and Islam. See his *The Christian Faith*, trans. H. R. Mackintosh and J. S. Stewart (Philadelphia: Fortress, 1976), pp. 3–93.

10. Schleiermacher argued that human action, and particularly Christian action, has two aspects: effective, or corrective, action, which orders and transforms life and the public world; and presentative (*Darstellung*) or symbolic action, which presents the character of the agent or community. In this I am following him. Yet I am doing so in and through a new hermeneutic of mimetic action, one not grounded, as Schleiermacher's, in the dynamics of consciousness. See his *Christliche Sittenlehre: Einleitung*, ed. Hermann Peiter (Stuttgart: Kohlhammer, 1983). See also my "From Cultural Synthesis to Communicative Action: The Kingdom of God and Ethical Theology," *Modern Theology*, 6 (1989), 367–88.

11. My difficulty with recent "narrative" theology is with its understanding of narrative. Too often the concern is to speak about the formation of the self through the appropriation of narrative, or of the status of religious texts as "realistic fictions," rendering an agent (e.g., God) present through the plot without grappling with the conceptual problems that inhere in these formulations. My rethinking of mimesis is undertaken not to rehabilitate narrative theology, but to see mimetic narrative as one element in a more general theological task. For examples of narrative theology, see Stanley Hauerwas, *Truthfulness and Tragedy: Further Investigations into Christian Ethics* (Notre Dame: University of Notre Dame Press, 1981) and Frei's *Eclipse of Biblical Narrative*. See also Gary Comstock, "Truth and Meaning: Ricoeur and Frei on Biblical Narrative," *Journal of Religion*, 66 (1986), 117–40, and William C. Placher, "Paul Ricoeur and Postliberal Theology: A Conflict of Interpretations?" *Modern Theology*, 4 (1987), 35–52.

12. For a discussion of the problem of "act" as a basic notion for theological reflection, see Burrell's *Aquinas*. Burrell is concerned with the grammar of this act and thereby shifts the discussion of Thomas' metaphysics to language and not simply to that of the act of being (*esse*) or the transcendental act of consciousness. I am also arguing for the importance, even centrality, of the notion of act beyond previous ontological or transcendental paradigms, but I am exploring several complex acts and the analogies between them.

6

Mimetic Reflections:
Toward a Theology and Ethics

THE PREVIOUS CHAPTER ended in a suggestive, albeit inconclusive, manner. It attempted to show analogies between understanding and its world, narrative configuration, and the self that have emerged from our reading of central postmodern thinkers. These are, of course, analogies; they are relations of similarity-in-difference. The shape of understanding is different from a narrative text, and both differ from the radical demand of personal existence here and now. Who could doubt this? Yet the force of my argument has been to show that these mimetic practices have an analogical character. They provide a way to speak and to think about the coherence and richness of life in response to our constant search to understand the human condition and to render the dynamics of Being, time, and life meaningful and actual.

We have seen, however, that the search for a single substantive image of the human grounded in the act of Being, the transcendental act of consciousness, or even communicative praxis, may well be impossible, given the critique of "image." The preceding chapters, and especially the last one, have attempted to understand the human within forms of mimetic praxis in and through which world, temporality, and the self are figured, presented, and transformed, and their power elusively deferred. Beyond the desire for a total knowledge and control of Being and the human, we can say that the human is a mimetic being dwelling figuratively in a temporal world with others and responding to powers that escape our control. The task of this chapter is to show that the forms of mimetic praxis already explored raise questions that religious and moral reflection attempts to understand, articulate, and address. In doing so we return to a theme announced at the outset of these reflections: the way in which the ontological, textual, and existential dimensions of the problem of imitation meet in discourse about the divine and the moral life.

The very need to show the religious and moral dimensions of mimetic thinking is a mark of the modern and postmodern critique of classical imitation. An imitative mindset allowed classical Christian theologians to talk about the divine relative to the structure, value, and purpose of the world, the self, and the biblical texts as these were taken as images or signs of what transcended them. Yet to an age scarred by massive suffering and nuclear madness, the very idea that the world is the theater of God's glory seems untenable and even dangerous. The claim that sacred texts disclose the world and divine purposes is suspect to all who have felt the wrath of religiously legitimated oppression. And the notion that the self is the image of God seems naïve for a culture aware of the manifold forces that shape the psyche and its world. In the name of intellectual honesty, critical self-understanding, and freedom from oppression, the imitative and theistic universe is one we must escape. Yet its lure remains.

The lure of the imitative universe is its promise of unity and coherence in life and our world. The postmodern experience is one of fragmentation and gaming, a constant overturning of all claims to supremacy and permanency.[1] Not suprisingly, "God," "world," and "self" have become extraordinarily problematic notions since they seem to imply a unified context of meaning, a center of value, or a tyrannous hierarchy. Cultural critics turn to Yeats to express the loss of this center:

> Turning and turning in the widening gyre
> The falcon cannot hear the falconer;
> Things fall apart; the centre cannot hold;
> Mere anarchy is loosed upon the world. . . .[2]

When "mere anarchy is loosed upon the world" "God" becomes problematic as do the self and the natural and social worlds — and for the same reason: the divine seems to dissipate within the play of language and to retreat whenever one attempts to understand who is acting. Whirl has becoming king.

Faced with such perplexities thinkers often divide the questions of life into manageable bits and pieces. The job of moral philosophy, to recall Mary Midgley's insight, is to put the pieces back together again in the attempt to understand the fragile unity of human life in its widest and most complex sense.[3] The same holds for critical and constructive theological reflection since its task is to speak of the divine and to examine life. And yet in our time such thinking seems confounded. The grand vision of onto-theology that once sustained Western culture has dimmed and with it a theistic unity of life. That vision was built on a notion of imitation and an imitative mindset, and when these crumbled so too did its theological expression. Why?

We should recall that traditional imitation theory held that the meaning of ideas, works of art, language, and even the human inhere in a relation to what transcends them — a concept, the artist's idea, the world, or the *Logos*. What imitation articulated was a theory of analogy and transcendence embodied religiously and morally in a certain way of thought and life. The religious and moral purpose of human existence was to relate to the transcendent in such a way as to become godlike (Plato), or to actualize the divine image in the self and community, whether that image be a reflection of the divine Trinity in the structure of the soul (Augustine) or a following in the ways of God as given in divine commandments and precepts. The myriad forms of religious, ascetic, and moral practices were all ways to carry out this journey of transforming the human before the ultimately real. As an aid in the venture, one interpreted imitative symbols or texts to discern that transcendent reality and its purposes. The human inhabited a symbolic universe that, for those graciously bestowed with eyes to see, reflected its divine purpose and unity.

This understanding of religious discourse and life has fallen to the modern and postmodern criticisms of imitation, as I noted in the first chapter. The question now is whether the reconstruction of mimesis with its many analogies carried out in the previous chapters of this study has provided any means for reconsidering the tasks and questions of religious and moral reflection.

POSSIBILITIES AND PROBLEMS FOR REFLECTION

Rethinking mimesis means three things for religious and moral reflection. First, a turn to mimetic praxis in understanding has meant that Being becomes meaningful in and through the act of interpretation; meaning is dependent on and interrelated with certain practical activities of individuals or communities that structure experience. Hence a figure is not so much a re-presentation of prior, more originary reality (*Urbild*) as a presentation through the interpretive act in which there is a leap into the true, an increase of being. This act is also a transformation of the one who understands. For instance, the world configured in understanding means that we live, move, and have our being in figural patterns of language and tradition that draw their import from interpretive practices even as they shape human life. An environment (*Umwelt*) becomes "world" for individuals and communities through the figurative act of under-standing. Ironically, this means seeing the human again in a mimetic universe open to various modes of interpretation. And not surprisingly, different com-munities develop complex interpretive, narrative, and existential practices that shape life. Human life, whatever else it is, is a dwelling among complex lin-guistic and figural patterns. Yet because we cannot escape the modern critical turn of thought, this mimetic universe is in part one of our own making; it is not simply given to us to be discovered by us as ancient mimeticism implied. For all of that, it is a world not understandable simply as the expression of the intentional or transcendental act of the "I."

An awareness of our figural world confronts us with the problem of how we are to live. How can and ought we to seek to transform our world toward one of justice and peace? Here too the lure of traditional mimeticism remains: to see this world as a distorted but analogical representation of a truer order provides motive, measure, and guidance to the quest to overcome and trans-form present conditions of life. Yet the realm of action, the context of the human condition, is one marked by past human acts signaling the tragedy and the task of our situation. It is tragic in that the tyrannies of our social and personal existence are the consequences of human purposes and actions, consequences often not foreseen or intended. This sparks the abiding concern and passion to change the world that grips us all. Utopian and messianic visions of various sorts can be seen as political forms of mimetic thinking. And yet in spite of the power of human acts to shape our "world" and to imagine a transformed one, we too often seem powerless to transform it even as we must live with the scars of past action. Imaginative utopias, as Ricoeur too must admit, too quickly fail to inspire and guide us, or they do so to detrimental ends.

One problem that inheres in the mimetic shape of world is simply that its reality is a human one, whatever else it is. This challenges capacities for transforming the human situation since we cannot escape our humanity. This is a painful realization. It follows on the footsteps of the failure of modernist faith in the capacity of freedom to determine and change itself. We face the question of what impedes the human project and of what can empower transformative action as the being-at-work of genuine human existence.[4] More profoundly, we confront the question of the possibility and presence of goodness amid the travail of our world. How are we to relate to and enact the power of solidarity between persons and the natural world as a way to transform this situation? How too might we consider and speak of that power or powers? And last we ask, who can save us when the gods are silent? The human moral and religious world is a world of the ambiguity of meaning and power within practical existence.

We have confronted these issues of meaning and power throughout our investigations. Mimesis, I have argued, helps us to understand those activities through which the emergent power of Being becomes meaningful even as it is finally deferred. That power is never captured within systems of meaning — language or existence. Given this, mimetic practices provide a way to speak of what constitutes a world, meaningful time, or a self and of the quest for transformation that inheres in the basic acts of being human, a quest for good amid evil and the power to transform life and world. These are the terms, it would seem, within which we must understand the longing for and experience of "transcendence" and hence the import of much religious and moral discourse. That is, within the complex web of experience enacted in the basic mimetic practices there are direct, if mediated by interpretation, experiences of another power or powers through which "world," meaningful time, and existence are constituted, transformed, and determined anew. One task of religious reflection, as I shall note below, is to think and speak about what humans encounter in the ambiguity of time, action, and the travail of their figural world. It is to interpret and configure the experience of transcendence and the possibility of that experience in another power. Such reflection seeks to ask about that to which we are ultimately responding. The hermeneutic developed throughout this study provides a way to understand the task of such reflection since it enables us to speak of the activities in which these questions and experiences arise.

The second contribution mimesis makes to our reflection on moral and religious discourse is found in narrative. The shape of a figural universe is a temporal one. Part of the human quest for meaning and empowerment expresses itself in the imaginative configuration of our temporal experience. I have charted the double problematic in our temporal experience of the inscrutability of time. These find a practical answer in narrative identity and the construal of history and human solidarity. Yet our being in the inscrutability of time raises a religious and moral problem that prompts further reflection.

Confronted with the ambiguity of human world and the duality of our orientation to the horizon of time, persons face possible despair. Since time bears existence and yet sweeps it into nothingness, one is driven to ask "What's the use?" The problem of the temporality of being human poses the question of the meaning, power, and value of life. Is life meaningful if it sinks into nihility? Is solidarity with others and the natural world powerful enough to transform our world, or are these attempts destined to failure? These questions express the cynicism, skepticism, and even nihilism of the age. Following Ricoeur, I have tried to argue that narrative configuration renders meaningful the intelligible order of action. And understanding these configurations helps direct life toward the transformation of world and self. Mimetic narrative, in and through its practical response to the aporias of temporality, opens onto the question of our comportment to the horizon of time even as it provides a critical perspective of present conditions of life. Religious and moral reflection must address this quest vis-à-vis the ambiguities of our temporal being and doing as agents and the narratives that inform and configure life. Narrative figuration is one way to speak and think about religious and moral experience even as it finally cannot answer the question of the power to refigure time and avert despair or nihilism.

Finally, the reconstruction of mimesis helps us understand religious and moral discourse relative to personal and communal existence. After all, it is *we* who confront the ambiguities of time and our world, and *we* who seek to come to be within this reality of action. By reading Kierkegaard, I have explored this problem. For him the matter came to focus in sin, where the human is separated from the power that establishes it, and from a relation to Christ, the redeemer in time. "Sin" was his answer to the final impediment to the realization and transformation of the human, and, for him, Christ was the definitive answer to it. Existential mimesis, more generally, was a response to the problem of being a self relative to the power that establishes it.

Religious discourse not only presents or discloses something about our existence and about what constitutes and transforms "world" and human life. Kierkegaard argued that Christianity challenges all forms of immanence in which the self simply *is* in the truth. He argued that the mark of genuine faith and its symbols is that the self is confronted with what is other, an other power. In this encounter what is sought is existential communication demanding and empowering the self to come to be relative to what is presented to it. Kierkegaard's whole strategy of reflection, I argued, seeks to be a mimesis of this existential communication found definitively, for him, in Christ. The *imitatio* is that praxis that forms and transforms the human by enacting the power that establishes the self.

When we reflect on the self, or on a specific community, within the context of our mimetic world and the ambiguities of time, another religious and moral problematic emerges. Within the question of how to relate to and transform world and what is the meaning and purpose of human timeliness, we also ask "Who am I, and what am I to be and to do?" "Who are we, and what are we to be and to do?" These questions arise within social and temporal experience under the force of the present. The self is not an isolated monad; it is deeply formed by its world and by time. Exalted claims have been made for the centrality of the *cogito* or the existential self intentionally constituting the meaning and value of its world. Such arguments champion radical freedom removed from our sociality, historicality, and continuity with the natural world. And they imply a form of immanence that Kierkegaard, a supposed proponent of such thought, consistently challenged.

The postmodern *ethos* announces the end of this "self," the end of "man." I have added to these criticisms by exploring our participation in the world and solidarity with others through prejudgments and feelings as well as the interactive element in any mimetic act. Yet for all this, we still must ask about what we are to be and to do, and about the communities of which we are a part. This is a question of the relation of the self and community to what establishes them as bearers of identity and value amid all that distorts and destroys authentic agency; it is a question that moral and religious reflection must explore.

The reconstruction of mimesis helps us understand both religious and moral discourse beyond a simple imitative understanding of symbol or sign and modernist understandings of language, imagination, and the self. It also implies basic questions for theological and ethical reflection. These are questions about the desire for transformation, the struggle to face the horizons of time, and the travail of authentic identity relative to what constitutes, transforms, and determines life in and through the basic acts that structure experience. This means that any mode of reflection that seeks to be at once theological and ethical must attempt to speak of the human relation to the power or powers that generate a world of meaning, that establish and transform agency within the ambiguities of life, and have the capacity to refigure lived time in and through the power of speaking. More simply, religious discourse has to do with the question of power and meaning presented and yet deferred within a community's manifold forms of figurative praxis as well as the basic mimetic acts of interpretation, narration, and existential imitation that structure and transform experience.[5] And moral discourse seeks to understand what is going on in the world in its widest and most complex sense, the measure for human being and doing, and what we are to be and to do in the struggle for critical understanding and truthful life. Both these modes of thinking and speaking seek to respond to the questions I have isolated.

Despite the failings of traditional and modern thought we are still faced with the dilemma of thinking about the tenuous unity and richness of life. The mimetic analogies discerned in the last chapter are one step in that direction. The task now is to explore the questions implied in those practices and their analogies. Given this, the following remarks are an ending and a beginning. As an ending they draw together in brief fashion some of the strands of my argument as they bear on the shape and task of theology and ethics. They are a beginning since they are manifestly a prologue to substantive constructive reflection. The task here is a modest one: to unfold the moral and religious questions noted above within critical religious and moral reflection. To do so, it is important to situate the discussion within current debates in theology and ethics with greater specificity than was attempted in the first chapter.

TOWARD A THEOLOGY AND ETHICS

Modernity is characterized by the critique of religious discourse. And it is marked by an ironic concentration, and yet dispersion, of ethics, or moral philosophy. Postmodern thought attempts to counter these tendencies in ethics and to think in and through the critique of religion.

By a "concentration" of ethics I mean that much modern moral philosophy saw its task as needing to establish absolute moral principles for the sake of rational choice by autonomous agents or showing the final impossibility of such a venture. Ethics became concentrated around the problem of moral norms, the meaning of moral discourse, and the possibility of human autonomy. This meant curtailing traditional concerns in ethics, like the question of the meaning and value of being human, the interpretation and assessment of social mores and customs, character formation, the practical guidance of life, and the like.

This modern development in ethics was genuinely novel. With Aristotle and others, moral philosophy was seen as a basic arena of thought, along with logic and physics, even if it was not a "science" in the strict sense of establishing timeless principles. After all, the human condition is a deeply temporal one, and reflection on the human and its good must account for its variable and contextual character. In fact, for Aristotle it was precisely because of its non-scientific character that ethics could not be reduced to establishing norms for choice or questions about the meaning of moral terms. In the court of modernity there were protesters as well to developments in post-Kantian ethics. Schleiermacher, in his *Die Grundriß der philosophischen Ethik* and elsewhere, saw ethics as the discipline for inquiry into the human and history even as the moral was a dimension in all aspects of thought and life. Given this, ethics had to explore not only norms, but also the power of action, and the good. Indeed, the subject matter of moral philosophy, for Schleiermacher, was the action of reason on nature. What was at stake in the constriction of ethics was a picture of human life. And though other thinkers could be noted here, it is clear that there were disagreements about the project of modern ethics, its concentration on rational, moral autonomy, and the meaning of moral terms.

The constriction of ethics rested on a narrow vision of the human. It was one picturing the human as an autonomous agent realizing its freedom in self-legislative acts or contracting with others to form civil society, as Hobbes and others argued. Given this, much modern moral and political thought had to figure out both how to relate such an autonomous agent to its political community and to history, and how to do this without impeding moral freedom while establishing means for judging and evaluating personal and communal goods.

The concentration within ethics on normative questions and discourse led, ironically, to its dispersion. The interpretive and practical concerns of ethics were taken over by other fields, ranging from history and sociology to psychology. And these disciplines, so the story went, were thereby free of normative concerns and could pursue their development in and through value-neutral modes of inquiry. As we have seen, Gadamer's hermeneutics counters this development in and through the critique of method.

The apotheosis of this movement in ethics came earlier in this century when moral philosophy took as its sole task the analysis of the logical status and meaning of moral discourse. This meant that many of the former questions of ethics were lost, ignored, or bequeathed to other fields of thought. Here too the picture of the human as an autonomous self actualizing its humanity in free acts beyond its relation to others or its dependency on the nature system expressed itself in philosophy and culture. Ethics became an enterprise of specifying the status of "moral" claims over against non-moral ones or of showing how all moral discourse is finally expressivist in nature. In this moral philosophers merely reflected their culture rather than critically examining it, a culture marked by emotivism and often unable to carry on sustained moral argument about what makes human life human.

Our situation is marked by a concern to overcome the dispersion and concentration of modern ethics.[6] The critique of modernism has been carried on along two broad and diverse lines that form the context for the specific developments in ethics germane to my argument. First, there has been the challenge to the possibility of universal normative claims because of cultural pluralism. Human life is social and linguistically shaped; different languages, histories, and experiences, not surprisingly, give rise to different forms of life. But this does not mean a turn to emotivism in ethics. Acknowledging that we dwell in linguistic communities disallows an atomism of moral discourse, as Ricoeur and Gadamer showed. Moral language is a shared, if fragmented, one; living in a community means in part learning its moral language. The real contention for this line of argument is that human moral life is so irreducibly contextual that universal normative claims are not possible, compelling, or needed. As Bernard Williams has noted, any account of ethical reflection must meet "the obvious fact that the repertory of substantive ethical concepts differs between cultures, changes over time and is open to criticism."[7] Given this, what is needed is the retrieval of traditions of discourse about the life well lived, along with the critical assessment of these traditions relative to the needs of the day. Claims about universal norms and metaphysical foundations of morality simply do not meet these needs.

This type of criticism of modernist ethics coheres with the general attack on epistemological foundationalism I have noted throughout this study. Absolute norms founded transcendentally on the reflexive act of consciousness, metaphysically in first principles, or historically in the realization of the Absolute seem difficult to sustain for beings who are mired in time and language and who have abandoned the search for absolute knowledge. There is, as Ricoeur put it, no total mediation. Reason is plainly limited in its capacity to determine and guide the moral life simply because of its complex shape and vulnerability to moral luck, as Martha Nussbaum calls it.[8] And the experience of this century, noted in the first chapter, dispels confidence in any progressive realization of the Absolute in the domain of freedom. These arguments challenge the modernist, autonomous self by placing human life within the fragility of human community, history, language, and the winds of fortune not ruled by a rational, if cunning, spirit.

One strategy of postmodern moral discourse is to challenge the specific concentration on normativity and autonomy found in modern ethics. The other way of overcoming modernist ethics concerns its dispersion. The turn to hermeneutical reflection, rhetorical inquiry, and the various forms of archaeological and genealogical studies by thinkers in various disciplines has highlighted the irreduciblity of values in culture and thought. It has also meant an expansion in ethical reflection. As Agnes Heller puts it, "ethics is a condition of the world."[9] That is, a domain of meaning enacted in and through cultural, economic, political, and dialogic interactions, a "world," is always and already a moral one, shaped by values and goods. The possibility and demand of criticizing and understanding the moral "worlds" within which human life takes place have therefore come to the forefront of inquiry.[10]

The realization that understanding is shaped by the effects of history and related to the prefigured shape of human action renders problematic the disengagement of the one seeking to understand from what is being interpreted. This insight was signaled by Kierkegaard and taken as central by Gadamer and Ricoeur. Human interests and purposes inhere in all modes of inquiry. The question of what is normative about human being and doing cannot be isolated from inquiry. Thus inquiry must be critical regarding the status of its own discourse, and must seek, to some extent, both to understand what is under study and to change it. This is particularly the case for moral and political thought. The second strategy of overcoming modernist moral philosophy seeks, then, to show the problems of norms, interests, and values in all domains of life with implications for courses of action.

These are broad and exceedingly diverse responses to the modernist project in ethics, and thinkers articulate them in different, even conflicting, ways. But within these developments there are specific currents in moral theology and philosophy important for my argument. First, there are thinkers who try to shift the discussion of the status and binding character of moral norms from a concentration on the act of autonomous subjectivity to the generic features of free, purposive action or communicative praxis. Their task is to show that the structure of a specific act, communicative or otherwise, entails normative claims binding on all beings engaged in those activities. The norms are specified differently, such as undistorted communication or the generic rights of freedom and well-being. They are taken, nevertheless, as universally valid, or at least ideally so.[11] Thus the problem of normativity is bound not to autonomous subjectivity, but to communicative intersubjectivity or the features of any act.

Next, there are theologians and philosophers concerned with the shape of human character in community beyond the pale of the modernist, existential self who seek to reclaim discourse about the virtues and practical wisdom. For instance, Alasdair MacIntyre argues that the emotivism and fragmentation of our moral world can be countered only by reclaiming our place in traditions of moral reflection. These traditions, and the communities that embody them, are extended arguments over what the good of the human is. As arguments tradition represents diverse accounts of justice and practical rationality; they are scenes of conflict over the human good.[12] Against the seeming timelessness of modernist in-principled ethics, the turn here is to the historicality and sociality of human life. In this way, "Neo-Aristotelian" and narrative ethics, in theology and philosophy, reconsiders the character of human agency and the shape of practical reasoning as a response to the excessive claims for autonomy and the existentialist contention that authentic subjectivity is constituted by an act of radical choice. By attending to the context and shape of the moral life, these positions seek to situate the human within the context of its historically formed natural and social world.

Finally, there have been developments within phenomenological and hermeneutical reflection. Thinkers like Gibson Winter and John D. Caputo explore the shape of human dwelling, the originary *ethos* of the human condition. Their concern is to overcome classical and modernist modes of ethical reflection and theories of value by reconsidering the ways in which humans participate in the being of their world.[13] This participation is a condition and motive for human existence. As we have seen, the inscrutable horizon of human dwelling is its being-in-time. Given the possible end of history and earth through the capabilities of technological culture, the demand for a future takes on obligatory force. In facing that future, as Werner Marx and Hans Jonas argue in different ways, there is the possibility of rethinking the motives and measure of moral existence.[14] Despite their differences, each of these thinkers has reclaimed moral reflection as a fundamental hermeneutic of human dwelling.

In a moment we shall see that the kind of reflection undertaken in this study draws on and contributes to each of these options in ethics. The construal of selfhood and the historical shape of understanding mean that the human dwells as a participant in a world of natural, affective, temporal, social, political, and economic relations as varying spheres of goods. The turn to mimetic praxis provides a way to account for the binding force of measures on those who participate in the acts of interpretation, narration, and the struggle to be a self. And the temporality of world and human agency provides motive and measure in the moral life even as the inscrutability of time disallows the human as *the* measure of good. However, before we turn to these matters it is'important to locate the reconstruction of mimesis within the current debates in theology.

Perhaps the most pervasive mark of modernity is its vehement critique of religion and of the possibility and desirability of doing theology. The suspicion is that theological discourse always grasps at domination or simply has nothing to talk about, and that religious traditions are nothing but trails of innocent blood, as Girard might put it. This forces a basic question: Why should theologians, or anyone, speak of the divine, and how can they speak and think of the divine relative to where "God" is manifest for thinking and speaking? Such thinking and speaking will always be a reflective consideration of those texts, events, and persons taken by a community as decisive disclosures of the divine's way with the world and human life. Moreover, since theology, as an activity of practical reason, dovetails with the examination of human being and doing, or ethics, its dilemma is compounded. A basic question in ethics is how one is to speak of the human since this entails reflecting on life relative to where the human condition manifests itself for thinking and speaking. Thus one problem facing anyone seeking to think theologically and ethically is this: Where are the divine and the human manifest so that we can speak and think of our religious and moral existence and of the divine? The principal task of this study has been to explore the practices within which the human is disclosed and transformed in order to address our search for critical understanding. But what does this have to say about theological reflection? Does it help us address the sensitive question of why one would think and speak in this way at all?

As I noted in the first chapter, some theologians argue that all we have is the process of fragmentation and gaming that marks our linguistic practices. The task of theology, as a way of writing, is constantly to undo its own claims and thereby to combat its idolatrous and tyrannous tendencies. Yet in this very process of undoing, so the argument goes, space is created for theological reflection on the margins or limits of language and desire. At these margins there is the possibility of what Charles Winquist calls an "epiphany of darkness."[15] There is the disclosure of a space, a negativity, in which our thinking might take place. The reason one carries on the deconstruction of theology is, then, to open the space where another beginning, another possibility, for theology might manifest itself. But is this all that can be said? Are we simply left with the overturning of theological thinking awaiting an epiphany of the gods or God? How could we even think of the power of this "epiphany" in theological terms?

There are also theologians who see their task as exploring the metaphysical claims entailed in theism and post-theistic thinking. Theology in this mode becomes an interpretation of the world and its divine ground and goal.[16] In the grand style of metaphysics, these thinkers attempt to understand the divine relative to our cosmos and the manifold religious responses to it. They do so in decidedly neoclassical ways, rejecting previous mono-polar construals of the divine that defined transcendence as sheer externality in relations. These thinkers understand the divine as the supremely worshipful reality internally related to all and the power of possibility, of the future. The reason for such discourse is to help us make sense of our experience to the widest and most comprehensive extent.

Others scorn this speculative route. The concern of these theologians is practical and edifying. They want to explore the character of Christian praxis and the demand on the Christian community in a world of strife. The idea of God, accordingly, is a practical one relative to the domain of action and history. The Christian message subverts the logic of developmental, progressive history with an apocalyptic, political message of liberation. The reason for engaging in theological discourse is to guide and inspire those who struggle for that liberation in solidarity with the oppressed.[17] Religious discourse in this mode is the interpretation and presentation of the faith of a community amid the misery and joy of life.

Finally, there are thinkers who take the task of theology to be the imaginative construal of the symbol "God." Theological reflection is to bring coherence to our construals of the world while challenging all forms of idolatry.[18] The image, concept, or metaphor "God" is an imaginative construct relative to the human participation in the world. Theologians differ on the reason for offering such a construct, to help humanize life, to aid us in being responsible for our world, or to guide us in a quest for a meaningful existence. But theological reflection in this vein entails some understanding of the dilemmas of moral and political existence relative to an interpretation of a religious tradition and the construal of God, self, and world. Here theology is an imaginative, constructive act, one that requires the ability to metaphorize well.

There are many ways of doing theology, more than I have noted. Given this wild plurality, the suspicion arises that perhaps in the final analysis theological discourse is groping for a subject matter. The reconstruction of mimesis will not settle all disputes about the task of theology or its subject matter. Nor do I have any desire to do so. Nevertheless, the hermeneutic unfolded throughout this study does provide some resources for understanding the task of theology that draws on the options just noted. It is not the only way, but it is one that meets the problems of imitation and addresses the religious and moral questions we have uncovered.

Theological reflection begins in affective and interpretive encounters with the world, the question of personal existence, and the narrative construals of time, life, and the divine within a religious community and its traditions.[19] As reflection on these experiences, actions, and traditions, it must be self-critical regarding its criteria of validity and the meaning and possibility of its own discourse. In a critical mode, basic questions about understanding, religious narratives and symbols, and the dilemmas of existence give rise to different types of thinking such as fundamental and dogmatic theology. Similarly, ethics also begins with experience and questions. It examines human being and the life worth living, what human beings are to be and to do, our relations to a social and natural world shaped by beliefs and practices of communities, and some measure of good relative to life and action. It too must be self-critical regarding its criteria and the meaning and possibility of its discourse. Yet in doing so, it remains tied to basic concerns that require ethical discourse to be interpretive, normative, and practical in character.

The hermeneutic developed through the course of this book allows us to think anew about these modes of reflection in and through the criticism of their classical and modern expressions. Substantively it provides a way to consider the performative dynamics of understanding, self, and texts as a way to explore what is enacted in and yet deferred through these performances in order to think about human life and its relation to the ultimate. The question then becomes whether or not one can speak of "God" relative to what is presented and deferred in these mimetic acts crucial to the moral shape of the human condition. In addressing this question we shall turn first to theological discourse which will then lead us back to ethics.

Theological Reflection

What is presented in the mimetic praxis of interpretation is the human belongingness to the world. But the power of this solidarity to constitute and transform understanding is never captured definitively in our figurations. Such belongingness is both the condition for understanding and action and a task to be undertaken. In the act of interpretation what is understood is the emergent power of the human, its *physis*, figured in various ways. This does not imply strong metaphysical claims where individuals are imitations of a singular substance; nor does it mean that cultural configurations are simply mirrors of a community's *Geist*. Rather, it is a claim about the shape of understanding. As we have seen, understanding enacted through interpretation is the mode of human dwelling in time and with others. It is because of the profound participation and distanciation of understanding in its world that the manifold affections and feelings that move life arise and are sustained. But this raises the question, as noted above, of how one is to relate to that power or powers encountered in a figural world of meaning, given a longing for goodness and transformation. This is all the more problematic since the experience of these powers is direct but not immediately comprehended; they must be understood through interpreting various figurations.

The vantage point of classical "natural theology" was the attempt to speak and think of God relative to what is disclosed as worthy of worship in nature, experience, and thought. The divine was understood by analogies of negation and perfection from the power of Being and the orderliness and value of the natural world as this becomes intelligible in human reason and directly sensed as sacred in fundamental affectivities.[20] The critique of imitation undoes the *analogia entis*—the analogy of Being—and thus natural theology, as I noted in the first chapter. It is not at all clear that the natural world is a sign, image, or shadow of divine things. What should lead us to believe or sense that the world is a sign signifying something else? There is little evidence that that one can or must speak of God to make sense of natural processes. The emergent power or powers of solidarity present themselves figuratively and in fragmented ways in our social, historical, political, and personal worlds. This power can be thought and interpreted without appeal to any notion of the being and activity of the divine.

If one grants the plausibility of the reconstruction of mimesis attempted in this study, the problem is merely heightened. The figurative character of any "world" overturns all attempts to grasp definitively this power or powers within the mimetic play of language. While there is, perhaps, a mimetic dynamic to Being in language, the emergent power of Being rendered meaningful in and through language is not in any obvious sense the "divine." Furthermore, theological thinking, if it is to be genuine, protests any simple identification of the divine and these processes; it must avoid "reducing" God to the power immanent in these acts and thus return, in modified form, to a type of natural theology.

Once we understand the mimetic character of language, that our linguistic world is a mimesis of an emergent power, then we can at least ask: How do we stand before this emergent power, and what does this have to do with the final purpose and quality of our existence? Such questions are religious and moral ones. They ask about the meaning of the human condition relative to our being totally affected by an environing world of power when it gives rise to awe, fear, reverence, and even love and thus demanding and empowering some response in a mode of life.[21] Indeed, we have seen that the various mimetic practices are moved by and yet figure various affective comportments, like Care in being-toward-death and the passion for existence. The issue here, then, is not what is inherent in mimetic practices such as interpretation, but how the power or powers not definitively captured by those acts constitute, determine, and refigure existence, evoking affective comportments to life. This is a moral question too since it asks about what is presented in and through human being and doing such that human existence is achieved and shown for what it is. All this rests on understanding the mimetic shape of language as being that can be understood enacted in interpretation and narration.

Here we should recall Charles Taylor's remark cited in the first chapter: "What comes about through the development of language in its broadest sense is the coming to be of expressive power, the power to make things manifest. It is not unambiguously clear that this ought to be considered as self-expression/realization. What is made manifest is not exclusively, not even mainly, the self, but a world."[22] There is a paradox in this. It is through human activity that the "power to make things manifest" is enacted, and yet our activity does not exhaust that power. It is also not reducible to self-expression. What the paradox discloses is the good of language since by acting with it our acting is good: a world is rendered present.[23] Indeed, Arthur Cohen, as we saw earlier, understood this paradox theologically. "The life of man through God, both as imitation and as real presentation, is not surety enough unless enacted within community, where . . . collective language makes audible the silent speech of creation."[24] In and through language we stand before the power to manifest a world, to let creation speak, seeking to enact it on the stage of the world.

The various mimetic practices and their analogies charted in the previous chapters raise the question of the ultimate since each is characterized by the same paradox as that found in interpretation. They do not answer this question, even though part of theological and ethical discourse is always talk about the emergent power of what is when this evokes feelings that insert agents and communities in the world and becomes a question of the purpose and quality of existence. The mimetic shape of understanding and its world, as figurations of the emergent power of what is, creates the space for the question of the human relation to what is ultimate. A world comes to presentation through language; language is the figuration of *physis*. We can ask about this power and a response to it in and through world. This opens the domain of fundamental theology as inquiry into the relation of religious discourse to the shape of human being in the world and the criteria for such reflection. Constructive theological reflection, I shall claim, is best understood as the attempt to provide a mimetic configuration of that power and human responses and thereby to refigure our existence by providing a mediated understanding of what is directly experienced.

Thus a mimetic hermeneutic challenges natural theology even as it opens the space for fundamental reflection;[25] it also entails a criticism of reflexive forms of theological reflection. That kind of theology attempts to grasp the unifying principle of the self. This unifying principle, the "I," relates itself to itself in acts of consciousness. The "I" is always the unity and power of its acts.[26] Yet in reflecting on these acts, in carrying out reflexive thinking, the "I" is never captured. It withdraws into the activity of reflexive thinking, providing what indeed seems like a final ground of freedom for all knowing. The "I" thus transcends in freedom the world of natural relations and causes that it helps constitute as meaningful. And yet the reflexive act also raises the question of the relation of the "I" to the power that creates it. Does the "I" ground and determine itself and thus constitute its world and others? If it does determine itself, then, as Kant argued, "God" can be postulated relative to its free act, or the "I" can be seen as the repetition of the infinite I AM in the finite, as Coleridge put it.

Throughout this study I have charted both the critique and the acknowledgment of reflexivity in consciousness and in language. Regarding consciousness, we have seen that it must be understood with language and the effects of history, the traces of past acts of understanding on it through interpretation. Language is the development of expressive power, as Taylor puts it, and yet this power withdraws in linguistic acts. The reflexive structure of human consciousness and language cannot be avoided even while their seductive claim to finality must be resisted. Hermeneutical reflection questions any simple reflexive philosophy in which the self is transparently immediate to itself, determining its being in and through itself, and others are understood solely through the intentionality of the transcendental *ego*.

Reflexive claims to absolute self-determination are really theological ones. They announce the identity of the "I" and the absolute, an identity which, in the course of our argument, Kierkegaard was quick to disallow.[27] Such claims of immanence are broken by the distortions in existence and by our encounter with what and who are genuinely other when they determine or transform life. This means that the acts determinative of the self are always relative to another in time, be it Christ, the configured horizon of time, or language and the effects of history. The human becomes a self, an "understanding I" as Gadamer called it, relative to others through the acts we have called "mimetic": interpretation, narration, and existential imitation. These acts have a reflexive character since they figuratively present and yet defer the power they enact, the powers of solidarity, speaking, and establishing the self. But these powers, we have seen, are not understandable simply in terms of the "I."

Thus the mimetic structure of the self, its reflexive relation to another, raises the question of the power or powers that establish it experienced directly as other in and through others and understood through various figures, a crucial one for modernity being the "I." Much as world is the linguistic figuration of *physis* through understanding, so the self is an existential figuration of life. Neither natural theology as traditionally practiced is possible, nor reflexive arguments for God. Since reflexivity is always a mimetic relation to other powers, the relation of "God" to the human is always mediated through encounters with others in time. The passion for existence and encounters with others raises the question of the ultimate orientation of life and the power to come to be as a self. As we have seen, this is configured in narrative texts even while they expose the aporias of human commonality and the problem of identity relative to our orientation to the horizon of time. Thus the self creates a space where the question of our response to an environing world of power arises; it opens the possibility for an existential dimension to theology beyond the critique of reflexivity and the analogy of the self for speaking of the divine.

We have seen, then, that the argument of the preceding chapters entails a criticism of natural and reflexive theologies without denying the possibility of fundamental and existential forms of reflection. But what of dogmatic theology? Clearly, traditional imitative understandings of text and Scripture have become problematic. The text is not in any obvious sense the imitation of the author's genius, the world to which it "refers," the structure of the soul, or the divine *Logos*. As a mimetic process texts undo themselves even while being figurations of interpretive praxis. Given this, revealed or dogmatic theology based on revelation, a scriptural principle, and an *analogia fidei* — an analogy of faith — seems impossible because of the performative character of language.

Theologians have long wrestled with the problem of the referential power of language when speaking of God. Karl Barth, for instance, argued that God's being-in-act is the Word of God. "God's Word is God Himself in His revelation. For God reveals Himself as the Lord and according to Scripture this signifies for the concept of revelation that God Himself in unimpaired unity yet also unimpaired distinction is Revealer, Revelation, and Revealedness."[28] Hence the being of God in revelation is the possibility, norm, and subject matter of dogmatic theology. Much earlier St. Augustine argued that the ability of images and signs to take on a double reference to the world and to the divine rests on the quality of the being of the interpreter. Specifically, it rests on love (*caritas*), which is both the ultimate meaning of the biblical texts and a gift of grace from God transforming the interpreter, the reader, enabling her or him to understand that meaning through the text's double reference.[29] Thus the revelatory power of scriptural texts rests, finally, on the being and action of God transforming the reader. Augustine was not alone in these claims. Yet despite this, the critique of classical and Romantic imitation requires a reconsideration of text and expression or "revelation" in theological reflection.

We have seen that narratives, through the power of speaking, are the configuration of the prefigured order of action and the refiguration of the practical field of life. They open the question of the horizon of human time and action by disclosing a world in front of them that is a mimetic configuration of the temporal order of human being and doing. A critical interpretation of narrative construals of human time and action raises the question of the human orientation to death and "eternity." Here again we confront a religious question: How does one stand before the inscrutable horizon of time, and what is our affective comportment in and to time amid our mimetic acts of figuration and reading? This is a religious question because it entails the search for meaning within various comportments and responses, such as love, courage, hope, or fear, to the powers human beings are contending with in basic practices—in this case experienced as the threat of death and the promise of life.[30] And it is a moral one too since it has to do with the shape of life, action, and being relative to basic affective comportments and relations with others.

The question hardly answers itself, however. Reflection on time always takes place within mythic construals. And though the refiguring of time is worked by the reader, the power to do so is neither identifiable with her or his act nor exhausted by it. Therefore, a narratology leads us to the edge of critically retrieving dogmatic theology and the basic myths of a community, but no further. The narrative configuration of human time and action raises the question of the ultimate, thereby creating the space for religious reflection.

The importance of a mimetic narratology for theological reflection is that in narration, language, human action, and time meet in a configuration through which theological reflection seeks to understand the human condition and orientation toward the horizon of life. As Ricoeur insisted, pure reflexive introspection trying to grasp the determinative act of the self and pure ontology attempting to discern the act of being are not possible. The detour of interpretation must be taken in order to understand ourselves and our world. Yet this means that in and through the interpretive act the self and world are determined, transformed, by what is presented and deferred in that act. Hence the interpretive practices of a community regarding its basic symbols and myths attempt to configure and refigure the profoundest reaches of experience by presenting the ultimate's way with the world and human life. And by taking on these interpretive practices, the members of a community understand themselves and their community to live, move, and have their being within this ultimate power or powers.[31] Accordingly, those modes of religious reflection that center on the interpretation of sacred texts, like dogmatic theology, provide the means for members of that community to understand and refigure a vision of the world and human life relative to the ultimate reality of the divine's being and activity.

Yet while this is the case, narrative cannot stand alone, as we have seen. Nor can a dogmatic theology encompass all theological reflection. Narrative dips into the character of human linguistic world and the shape and texture of human action for its power to refigure time relative to what it presents or communicates. Though theological discourse is and ought to be informed by the narratives of a religious and cultural tradition, talk about the divine must also be understood vis-à-vis the character of world and agency and their transformative refiguration. What this means is that any narrative theology is always open to the critical testing and transformation by other ways of understanding and figuring world and human life.

The mimetic structure of understanding and its world, the self, and the narrative figuration of time all raise religious questions. This is because theological thinking seeks to reflect on and speak about affective responses to the powers with which persons and communities are contending. How does one stand before the emergent power of what is as this raises the question of the ultimate purpose and good of existence? How is the self related to the power that establishes it and sweeps it out of being? What is an authentic orientation to death and eternity and the power to refigure affective comportments in and to them? And although natural, reflexive, and revealed forms of theology fall under the critique of imitation in its classical or modernist forms, the reconstruction of mimesis enables us to understand the task of theological thinking with and yet beyond them. What does this mean?

Theological discourse is carried on relative to the powers mimetically figured in world, the self, and narrated time and the various affective responses to them. There is a constant deferral of these powers within this discourse because thinking and speaking arise within the mimetic play and praxis of understanding, imaginative narration, and the existential act of being a self. Nevertheless, theology itself is a mimetic praxis carried on in particular communities and contexts. And it attempts to understand and configure the ultimate within the play of language, the ambiguities of time, and the travail of existence since these are the places in which it is experienced and yet deferred. Given this, theological thinking and speaking entail interpretation, imaginative configuration, and judgment. The interpretive moment in theology seeks to explore talk about the divine relative to understanding and its world, the self, and the symbols and narratives (scriptures) of a religious community. As an act of imaginative figuration, such thinking attempts to construe the being and action of God relative to world, human existence, and time for the guidance of life. And theological judgment seeks to refigure and reconstruct understanding and action as a response to the divine.

The theologian seeks, then, to offer an imaginative figuration of God relative to the emergent power of solidarity, speaking, and what establishes the human within the horizon of time as these evoke basic moods and refigure life. In this regard it is correct to say that theology is critical reflection on the divine and the praxis of faith, what is believed (*fides quae creditur*) and the act of faith itself (*fides qua creditur*). Indeed, the act of faith, as Kierkegaard noted, is the relation of the human to the power that establishes it, and, we might add, to the power to manifest "world" and refigure time as well. Thus the theological task is to offer a figuration of "God" and all things in performative relation to the divine in and through the interpretive and imaginative task of construing world, time, and selfhood under their emergent powers and human responses to them. It seeks to provide meaning and guidance for life. Such reflection works within religious and cultural traditions interpreting symbols and narratives, but it does so relative to the shape and texture of understanding, the self, and the prefigured order of human action.

To offer a figuration of "God," therefore, is to speak of the divine relative to those powers experienced and configured in and through mimetic acts that constitute and refigure world and human life. The theologian cannot speak of the divine outside of such figurations. Indeed, "God" is a figure for the powers experienced directly, but understood by interpreting mediating figures, in and through our encounters with world, time, and self when their powers constitute, determine, and transform existence and evoke faithful or broken responses. Given this, we can say that the figure "God" is a construal of the powers and feelings figured in mimetic analogies that structure and transform experience and render being meaningful.

Although the experience of the divine is always mediated by mimetic practices and rendered meaningful through the figure "God" when it is understood, it is, nonetheless, a direct experience. The experience of the divine entails inference and interpretation because experience is understood only through interpretation and drawing inferences about its ground and horizon. By this I mean, in accordance with the argument of the previous chapter, that experience is the interaction between what is there and a language-user able to appreciate and take account of the interaction. Though always linguistically mediated, it is, for all of that "direct," an encounter with what is there in some sense. As John E. Smith puts it, experience "is a many-sided interaction between man, the symbolic or language-using animal, and all that is to be encountered."[32] The figure "God" in mimetic theological reflection is, then, an interpretation and construal relative to the powers experienced in basic acts when these evoke direct responses such as reverence, trust, hope, and even fear.

The hermeneutic developed here implies something about the way we are to understand thinking and speaking of God. The figure "God" is not a noun that names a being, a verb for the dynamics of Being, a logical claim about the ground of states of affair or ideas to explain their ultimate goal, an adjective marking the quality of the relation between the human and what is ultimate, or a character rendered forth in biblical narratives. Properly understood, "God" is a mimetic configuration of the emergent powers of world, life, and time when these constitute, transform, and determine communities and the human condition. "God" is, then, the mimetic figure for the determinative relation between life and the powers to which human beings are responding and with which they are contending. To speak of God is to offer a figuration, informed by a religious tradition, of those powers as one, as the tenuous unity of all, experienced directly and figuratively understood. And this unity is spoken of through "faith," that is, a relation to the power to manifest a world, refigure time, and establish the self that transforms life, enabling and requiring that one enact solidarity, possibilities for flourishing, and authentic selfhood.

Figurations of "God" may take personal or non-personal forms. Personal construals of God tend to unify the powers of thought, will, and love into a center, a personality. We have seen this in reflexive forms of theology and in dogmatic ones as well. Our explorations of understanding, the shape of temporal action, and the passion for life provide means for understanding theological construals of the divine as personal. Non-personal construals, which avoid unifying these diverse powers in a personal, purposive center, hold that the "ultimate" escape all such construals. Former natural theologies often, but not always, provided non-personal construals of the divine. Within our argument, the need to overturn all figures of the divine provides a way to understand this insight into thinking and speaking of the divine. As a mimetic figuration, "God" is also deferred in the very act of thinking and speaking; experience and discourse do not exhaust the ineffable mystery encountered in the power of solidarity, the power of speaking to refigure time, and the power of that which establishes life.

A mimetic hermeneutics provides a way to understand thinking and speaking of the divine in fundamental, narrative, existential theology taking either personal or non-personal forms. More generally, the suggestion made here means that it is possible to say with St. Paul and the ancient poets that "God" is that in which humans live, move, and have their being (Acts 17:27–28). It is in the drama of language that we have our being in the world as one of understanding. Human beings and communities act and move in time rendered meaningful through narrative configuration. And it is within the passion for existence that one lives out one's life with others. Theological discourse is the attempt to understand and speak about the divine acting on the world and human life in and through our performative, figurative, participation in language, time, and life.

Thus theology seeks to be a mimesis of the divine, to present figuratively the ways of God and thereby to refigure human life. Genuine theology is a mimetic practice because in the theological act its generative power is transformed into figuration even as it withdraws from the practice. Because of this, theological reflection always fails to grasp the divine since in the very act of interpretation, configuration, and transformation there is the constant generation of new figures of the ultimate. The constant temptation of theology is idolatry. It is to take as ultimate its own imaginative construals, forgetting the dilemma of our figural being in the world, or to reduce the divine to the human response to its world. Mimetic reflection seeks to counter these tendencies by deconstructing all images of the divine and showing that our figurative practices do not exhaust the powers they manifest, including the practice of theology. The divine remains inscrutable and ineffable. We are not the masters of life, the sovereigns of time, or the measure of the good. And yet even with this, through the practices of interpretation, narration, and selfhood we can understand experiences of a power or powers theologically configured as "God." Indeed, theological discourse attains its significance when it contributes to the meaningfulness and transformation of world, time, and our social and individual existence.

Ethical Reflection

With this conclusion we have reached the theological limits of the present study. Yet these limits return us to the import of mimesis for moral reflection. We must ask about human being and how we can and ought to live, since we are not the masters of life, the sovereigns of time, or the measure of the good. Like theology, moral thinking begins with experience and questions—about the meaning and value of the world and particularly about goodness amid evil; about the measure of what is good and fitting in human community, character, and conduct—and with perplexity over what we are to be and to do. In a word, ethical reflection is interpretive, normative, and practical in shape, as I noted before. It is critical reflection on human being and the moral life. And it is carried on relative to where the human is presented for thinking and speaking within complex activities and relations. I want to draw out the implications of my argument for these tasks. Proposing an ethic forms the limit of the present work, however.

One of the basic questions in moral theology and philosophy is simply "What is going on?"[33] In many respects this question is the primary one for theology and ethics since it brings into focus the shape and problematic of moral and religious lives, and founds the hermeneutical task of ethics. The concern in such thinking is to examine human life as an interaction and response to what encounters us in and through complex engagements with world and others.

As we have seen, the basic practices of interpretation, narration, and selfhood are complex, temporal, and figurative forms of interaction with others, ourselves, and a world. Thus the question "What is going on?" springs from the shape of these activities even as it focuses attention on their moral and religious import. It forces consideration of what human life is interacting with, and how one distinguishes the marks of our moral and religious lives.

The forms of mimetic praxis we have charted suggest that human life is an interaction with others in several ways: within traditions that shape consciousness; through basic passions and feelings that drive human life; and with the manifold narratives that configure human being and doing as historical agents. Ethical reflection seeks to transform and give direction to natural, given existence; it has to do with the human participation in reality. But the wild complexity of that condition means that it is not possible to give a single answer to the question of what is going on. As Ricoeur put it, there is no narrative of all narratives that would definitively answer this question. This is true of theological claims as well. The radically theocentric affirmation that "God is acting in all actions on you" demands an imaginative and interpretive act to make sense of the symbol "God" amid the buzzing confusion of experiential interactions.[34] Likewise, classic theistic claims that the divine is the unity of all perfections and that whatever is is good because God is Being Itself rested on imitative assumptions that are now problematic, as we have seen. Thus the answer to what is going on cannot appeal simply to sacred narratives or the idea of God; it must be a hermeneutical one about what is encountered directly but understood in a mediated way through language and other practices.

But that is not all. The most obvious surd for total answers to the question of what is going on is the problem of tragedy and evil. Before these, thought is rendered silent. Thus although a fundamental religious and moral question concerns the quest for transformation and the possibility and fact of the presence of goodness and good people in the midst of evil, these cannot be answered in any unrevised theistic or philosophical manner. Total answers escape those whose understanding is mired in time and language. Yet while a total answer to the question of what is going on is not possible, we must still make sense of our lives and our world if we are to interact with others and understand ourselves. We must think about what is going on even if we cannot grasp a definitive answer to this question.

What is going on is in part the complex, historical, and tradition-bound shape of human culture and world. In and through these the condition and task of solidarity are instanciated in understanding through the act of interpretation. Of course, this raises the question of the inscrutable power of this solidarity and how humans are to enact this commonality so as to transform their world. Part of what is going on is the risk and struggle for a common good with others and with the earth amid the misery of life. At this level what humans are interacting with is a world of diversity and commonality. This interaction is a moral one since humans are seeking fitting, responsible ways to present that solidarity with others in the world. Enhancing this solidarity requires the interpretation and critique of the traditions, norms, symbols, and customs that form a world. That is the task for ethics. But it also demands concrete action here and now seeking to transform the world. That is the venture of the moral life.

Yet what is going on also entails complex encounters with time through narrative configuration. I have already noted the dual problematics of identity and human solidarity as practical, moral responses to the aporias of temporality. Yet in the mimetic acts of configuration and refiguration something more is going on that helps form the shape of a moral world and has considerable import for ethics.

Through the power of speaking, narrated time is a response to the mutual implication of cosmological and phenomenological approaches to time. What this means is that in and through the mimetic praxis of narration and reading what one is interacting with in time is the world of natural processes over which human beings exercise a perilous power but under whose sovereignty we finally dwell. Likewise, through imaginative configurations and the act of reading one attempts to understand the elusive power and shape of human life amid time. Thus in and through these mimetic acts what we are interacting with is nothing less than the temporal confluence of consciousness and the natural world on which life depends. Given this, ethical reflection informed by a mimetic hermeneutic must explore the relation of human being and doing to the natural world and its flourishing. What this means morally is that to respond fittingly to others is to struggle to refigure human timeliness for the sake of others and the earth. And yet this struggle, as noted above, raises the question of that power of speaking that escapes one's grasp and can confront possible moral despair with courage, hope, and perseverance.

The questions of solidarity and encounters in time place individuals and communities under the force of the present. They must make a decision to respond to these forms of interaction. At this level what is going on is the question of moral identity and selfhood as a complex interaction with communites that shape us, the gifts and needs of others, and the ambiguities of our being in time before powers we do not control. Ethics seeks to think and speak about this dimension of being human.

What the force of the present challenges one with is the task of responding fittingly to others, seeking to come to be as selves or a community. This struggle is not one attainable by simple introspection, as we have seen; it requires critical reflection relative to the traditions that shape prejudgments, the narratives of those communities that figure one's timeliness, and the possible ways of life presented to one. It also requires undertaking specific courses of action relative to the needs and demands of a situation. These mark out the moral life. Thus in undertaking the task of self-understanding in response to the question "What is going on" moral reflection returns to the cultural world with all its diverse forms and figures and thus to the condition and task of solidarity. The question of moral identity is tied to that of others and their well-being.

I am suggesting that a mimetic hermeneutic provides direction for understanding how an ethic explores the basic question about what is going on and the quests for transformation, facing time, and the identity that it implies. This hermeneutic does so not by supplying a narrative of all narratives or a system of absolute knowledge, but by providing a way to interpret the basic acts within which this question arises, acts, as we have seen, that mark the human condition. Yet the force of the present always confronts one with the demand of responsibility, to respond fittingly to others. And that is the problem. How do we know what is a fitting response?

At one level any response to this question is a matter of practical reasoning, of *phronesis*, as Aristotle put it, since the moral life is contextual and temporal in character. But the question of what constitutes an appropriate response moves our reflection on ethical thinking from inquiry into what is going on to another question and a different level of moral reflection. In a word, by showing how the question about what is going on arises in basic acts, we encounter the normative level of moral reflection in the form of a question.[35] And ethics must ask: Is there a measure for fitting responses to others, our world, and ourselves, and if so, what is it? This question founds the normative task of ethics.

What do we mean by measure? Werner Marx has succinctly stated its meaning for onto-theological, metaphysical thought.

> A measure is a "normative standard" that as such contains the demand of an "ought." As something already valid prior to any derivation of measure, its mode of Being is one of "transcendence." At the same time, it has the "power" to determine man "immanently," and here lies the decisive significance of a measure, its "binding obligation." It also has the power to endure as "selfsame" in various situations and thus has the traits of being "manifest" and "univocal."[36]

A measure is a transcendent, binding standard with the power to determine human life immanently while remaining univocal in all situations. Not surprisingly, this idea of measure has often been linked both to the concept of duty and thus to a commander, whether God or not, and also to an ideal, "transcendent" observer able to judge actions impartially.[37]

With the decay of traditional theism and metaphysically construed norms, the task of much modernist moral philosophy after Kant was to provide some such measure by exploring the free act of self-determination. The contention was that the measure for the moral life must be found within an autonomous human act of self-legislation. The self must measure itself, be the measure of good, since any other measure is heteronomous and thus destructive of a genuine moral existence, that is, what makes human life human.

This kind of position found a unique theological inversion in Neo-Orthodox divine command ethics. In the act of God being God in Jesus Christ as the Word of God, there are given the possibility and command for life. This command determines life immanently though not being identified with self-legislating freedom. And the command or Word of God remains selfsame even as it speaks uniquely to each person in specific, concrete life-situations. Any other ethic, Karl Barth averred, denied the freedom and sovereignty of God; it was sin. Even for more existentialist theologians the point held. Rudolf Bultmann argued that it was precisely in the crisis of faith, in an act of decision determinative of existence, that we must speak of God being God. God is that which determines existence irreducibly tied to an existentially decisive act.[38] Thus in both these cases, and others as well, divine "transcendence" is reconceived beyond traditional theism even as the marks of the traditional notion of measure remain.

The current critique of the modernist self and its anthropocentrism as well as highly personalistic construals of the divine challenge such grounding of moral measures, not to mention the perennial debate about the relation of religion and morals. And yet the question of measure remains. As noted above, current theologians and philosophers have attempted to address it by exploring the norms implied in free, purposive actions, communicative praxis, or the shape of human dwelling. They seek to escape a concentration on the autonomous, existential self while not reducing the question of measure to personal preference or cultural mores. In so doing, they seek to retrieve the marks of measure without embedding it in traditional metaphysical, transcendental, or theistic claims.[39]

Yet if there is no narrative of all narratives, can there be a measure of all measures in the traditional sense? The quest for a definitive meta-narrative rests on a construal of thought that is now problematic. And it would seem that the quest for a single measure relies on isolating *the* act, whether dialogic or existential, in which all human agents *qua* agents engage. But is there one "act" definitive of the human condition that can measure the moral life, that can measure what makes human life human? The argument forwarded in these pages would suggest not.

This problem has theological import as well. Indeed, as we saw in the first chapter, the divine has been understood as the *summum bonum* in metaphysical theism, as the ultimate standard postulated by practical reason in transcendental theism, and as the free Lord who commands and saves in kerygmatic theology. Theologically what is at stake here is the relation of the divine to the moral life, once it becomes difficult to speak of a single ultimate measure. My contention is that the problem of measure, and the possibility of conflicting measures, must be answered in any ethical reflection beyond imitation relative to the basic acts we have explored. In doing so, we shall see that the measures for fitting responses to others in a mimetic ethic must be characterized not by sheer univocity but as relative to understanding, refiguring time, and selfhood.

I have argued that the condition and task of interpretation is solidarity. This means that the measure of any interpretive act, and hence of understanding as its transformation into a figurative structure, is forging and disclosing solidarity with whom or what is understood. It requires that in the interpretive encounter one must seek to present what is in question in an understandable way. Any interpretive act is thus suspect, as Gadamer argued, when it does not begin in listening to what another presents, when it seeks to impose on another one's own meaning, is deceptive, or is distorted through systematic impediments to understanding. Thus measure here is not a sheer external norm; it is the power of transformation figured in understanding. In this sense it is a measure in the traditional sense; it has normative, binding power, even as it is now the measure of linguistic praxis. To override this measure would require appealing to other measures seeking a critical balance between them and that of solidarity.

But under the measure of solidarity one is not compelled simply to succumb to the position of another. Solidarity is not brute unanimity; it is enacted in critical understanding open to transformation. In a word, the measure of understanding through interpretive praxis is its figuration of that solidarity which is a good of human life and the power to manifest a world. And since all who seek to understand must engage in the act of interpretation, this measure emerges within praxis and is binding upon those who enact it. Of course, one paradox of human life is that there are those who do not seek to understand and thus rebuff any measure implied in interpretation action. Yet this does not mean that those who do seek to understand can forgo the measure of solidarity, the common good. They cannot. This measure entails an affirmation of the power of solidarity within understanding.

The measure of solidarity gives rise to other norms for thought and action, ones concerned with the common good like utility and justice. These cannot be specified here. What is more important to see is that this measure is also a motive to prefer and pursue the good over evil. That is, because this measure concerns the transformative power of the act of interpretation, the motive for the moral life is the quest for a meaningful world figured by that act. This is the case even when the demands of solidarity may require limiting, even sacrificing, my perceived individual goods. Here too I cannot explore the specifics of these issues. The point is that the measure of solidarity also gives a motive for life, even as it arises in the basic practices of our condition.

A more perplexing problem than the irrationalist who chooses not to understand and thus is not moved by the measure of solidarity is the question whether or not there is a measure for the transformation that occurs through understanding. After all, the common good can be used to override the needs of the minority or individuals, and any "solidarity" that is not critically measured can become tyrannous. Since understanding, as the determination or transformation of life and social existence, is won through language, this measure must emerge within language. The paradigmatic examples of the mimetic power of language are metaphor and narrative. Within these we have actually discerned a measure for understanding and community in a non-imitative ethic.

Any act of understanding, as a transformation of life, must take place relative to what is presented as a possible way of life. This implies a temporal measure of human being and doing rather than a timeless norm. That is, any solidarity and understanding as well as the practices that enact them that do not open up possibilities for these implies a negation of the temporal horizon of the human and natural world. Insofar as authentic human life requires some posture in and to time, as we have seen, the coercive negation of time destroys the possibility of authentic life. It is the negation of the power of speaking to refigure time. The same applies to the natural world. Solidarity with the earth empowers and demands modes of understanding and action that open possibilities for the flourishing of that environment. These possibilities might be as minimal as that of allowing inquiry to continue about how we are to live or as grave as limiting consumption for the sake of future generations of people and wildlife. But the point is that from within the mediation of narrative between cosmologic and phenomenological approaches to time emerges a measure for acts of solidarity with others and world.[40] Ethics beyond imitation must attempt to think and speak about this measure.

The measure in question concerns the power of speaking to refigure time, a power, as we have seen, not exhausted by the reader or speaker even as it is enacted through reading. A narrative configuration, whether by a community or an individual, which fails to provide genuine possibilities constricts the temporal character of the human condition and the natural world. This failure can issue from the impotence or death of basic narratives or symbols to open up ways of life, a condition that characterizes much of the current Western situation. But it can also and more dangerously issue from the attempt by an individual or community to claim that their speaking exhausts the elusive power to refigure time. In so doing, such figurations attempt to negate the inscrutability of time and hence possibility itself.

Here again we find basic motives for pursuing the good over evil that inhere in the measure for this form of ethic. And we also see that this measure gives rise to other ones as well. Specifically it gives rise to norms of personal and distributive justice since it is concerned with rendering due to individuals and communities possibilities for life. Again, I cannot explore these derivative norms in detail. What is more important is the relation of measure and motive. Most simply put, the motive to pursue the good over evil implied in this measure is that of the hope and longing for the transformation of self, community, and world into a just and peaceful condition. These desires drive and are figured by the practices that possibility measures. Not surprisingly, insofar as one participates in the practices explored in this study, individuals or communites are bound to that measure even as it is a motive for the moral life.

The measure found in the power of speaking can be overridden only by compelling claims from other measures and their goods, like that of solidarity or the transformation of the self through understanding. For instance, the generations of technological possibilities for human life are overridden when they destroy the fundamental solidarity and common good between us and the earth. One seeks a critical balance between various goods and measures relative to the particular and concrete situations within which life takes place. But this balance is not simply a subjective judgment. It is enacted relative to the actual measures and goods of life. That is, the question of the good arises relative to that solidarity which is the condition and task of life as well as to the way one is to respond to the force of the present entailed in the human temporal condition.

The demand for a critical balance between goods and their measures means that a specific measure does not emerge from the self. The moral agent, for a mimetic ethic, is not a measure, but a measurer. One comes to be as an agent precisely in the struggle to respond to the measures of solidarity and possibility driven by the motives they entail. Yet this does not mean that there is no measure for acts of measuring, such that moral judgment becomes an expression of preference or a simple, brute act of choice. There is a measure for the act of measuring. It entails the demand for the recognition of others, their claims and needs, and mercy because of limitations in actualizing those possibilities presented to them or to oneself. Recognition and mercy arise in the act of measuring precisely because they cohere with solidarity (recognition) and possibility (mercy), with what we are seeking to measure and balance. Thus within solidarity, and the norms of the common good, and possibility, with the norms of justice, arises the measure for measuring. And such a measuring of these measures, we can now say, is the act of practical reason, of *phronesis*, that we explored in Gadamer's thought. Hence the ethic implied in this hermeneutic is one that retrieves the importance of practical wisdom.

This measure of practical reasoning also entails a motive for pursuing the good over evil. Put in traditional terms: it is to do unto others what you would have done unto you and to love others as you love yourself. In the act of measuring, one instanciates a desire for recognition against the horizon of the good and measure of solidarity, and a desire for mercy regarding actions and intentions within the scope of the measure and good of possibility. This measure of measuring also implies derivative norms, like consistency of judgment, limits of responsibility, the demands of conscience, and so on. But more important than these for understanding ethical thinking and a possible mimetic ethic is the relation of this measure to motives for the moral life that arise in response to the force of the present. Reflection on this leads to practical moral discourse.

As a measurer, the agent is co-implicated in the practical moral question that arises under the force of the present: What are we to be and to do? Just as the normative and interpretive dimensions of moral reflection co-implicate each other, they cohere with practical reflection. The acts of interpretation and narration help us to think about basic questions in moral theology and philosophy: What is going on? What is the measure for human responsibility? And yet we must also understand the practical moral question of what we are to be and to do. The final answer to this is the task of the moral life itself. It requires measuring and seeking to enact solidarity, the refiguration of life and world, and presenting in one's own existence the passion for life. And ethics seeks to reflect on the praxis of the moral life. The hermeneutic developed here provides resources for that task.

The practical question about action and identity illuminates basic options in moral theology and philosophy. Is the power of one's community what estab-

lishes the self such that moral existence is best seen as the adoption and fur-
therance of the life of that community? Is the force of the present under the
power of the future what establishes the self such that my decision here and
now constitutes my authentic being as an absolute good? These positions represent the extremes of collectivism and existential individualism contrary to
the image of the human condition suggested by our reading. Indeed, we might
say that the task of being a self is to discern and enact life in the world with
others while avoiding these failed options. To do so, one must reject a simple
social or existential immanentalism. It is to claim that human practical existence is the coming-to-be relative to others and an other power in time.

Based on the argument in the previous chapters, we can say that for a mimetic
ethic being a moral agent requires the development of the habits and virtues
that shape and guide desires and freedom, and formation (*Bildung*) of life in
and through the critical appropriation of a tradition within a community. It also
requires developing the capacities of discernment and judgment that character-
ize practical reasoning in order to be a measurer of the various goods implied
in the practices that mark human life and its world. These virtues and practical
wisdom are traits of character that develop and are transformed relative to
others in time. They entail the disciplined shaping of given capacities. Yet
more than that, these virtues and wisdom do not exhaust the power of practical
life to transform one's existence. The identity of an agent is forged in being a
measurer of solidarity and possibility dependent on others and even an Other.
Given this, practical moral reflection, as the quest for critical self-understanding
amid life, bears within itself a relation to discourse about this other power
encountered in and through others.

Thus just as thinking about theological reflection led us into ethical discourse, so moral inquiry leads us back to theology, to thinking and speaking
about experiences of this other power configured as "God." Indeed, I have
suggested that the basic questions that theological discourse addresses, those
of transformation, the human posture in time, and identity, arise within moral
existence. "God" is figured as one amid the diversity of goods and measures.
But this means that theological reflection itself is a figuration of the moral life.
It understands the human condition as with others but also as one of living,
moving, and having its being in "God." This transforms the horizon of solidarity and the scope of possibility as well as the quest for recognition and
mercy that measure and motivate the moral life. Indeed, it is to claim that
"God" is the final measure and motive of life experienced in and through
those practices that enact human natural existence. To understand the divine
simply as a means for the advancement of human ends is to forget that we are
not the masters of life, the sovereigns of time, or the measure of goodness.

The task of the moral life interpreted theologically is the struggle to understand and enact the divine purposes by transforming world into solidarity,
seeking to create the conditions for its future flourishing, and developing selves

and communities that can recognize and respond in mercy to these needs and goods. But this also means that theological discourse draws its significance from its ability to inform human being and doing relative to experiences and questions that arise in the context of the moral life. Hence the argument of this text is to suggest a mode of reflection that seeks to be truly theological and truly ethical. Elucidating such a position is beyond the scope of this study.

Limits on Reflection

Though developing an ethics and theology is not the task of this book, one issue remains that must be noted. It concerns the plurality of goods and measures that unfold within the mimetic acts, goods like solidarity and authentic selfhood, measures like the disclosure of possibilities for life and the refiguration of time. This problem coheres with the question, noted in the last chapter, about isolating *the* image, principle, act, or perspective for grasping the unity of Being, time, and life.

The task of much theological and ethical reflection has been to isolate the *summum bonum* and the single measure that cohered with and structured the motive for religious and moral existence. This found expression in the relation of the "I" to a personal God as well as the divine as that toward which all things strive. The position suggested here acknowledges both the plurality of goods and of measures in our various figurative acts, and the limitation on reflection to unify all these goods and measures in our moral and religious existence.

What this limitation means is that there is the possibility of genuine tragedy, the conflict between goods, or of goods and measures, of duties with duties, motives with motives, or relative evils with unclear measures. It is because of these conflicts and tragedies that theologians and philosophers sought the definitive norm or good for life. Such a measure was to provide a way to resolve tragedy and help secure our tenuous grasp of goodness. But as noted above, the surd for all such thinking is tragedy and evil and the limits of understanding. In saying, as I did, that these form the limit of my inquiry, I meant that they limit all systematic thinking in theology and ethics, and also that exploring the ways of facing tragedy is beyond the scope of this work. Even so, something is gained in this limit.

What is gained by this limit, what emerges within the ambiguous shape of our condition, is of considerable import. Mimetic reflection, as I have unfolded it, disallows a total mediation of goods and measures. And yet in understanding the human condition as a mimetic one, this limitation is rendered productive, if practically so. It means that the postmodern dispersion of the self, world, and text is not the negation of a moral universe, of what makes human life human. Indeed, the mimetic and practical shape of understanding and its world, the narrative configuration of time, and the task of selfhood, far from heralding the triumph of nihilism, present the deeply moral and religious character of the human condition. It is an ambiguous character, of course. Yet amid this tragic ambiguity we discern something surprising as the very possibility and transformation of that tragedy. In every act of understanding, the goodness of solidarity to manifest a world is enacted amid forces of misunderstanding and distortion. This empowers and demands a way of life marked by the recognition of others and seeking of the common good. Despite the tyrannies of the past and present, in every opening of possibilities for life through narration, the power of speaking refigures time. Such experiences enable and require a mode of existence that seeks justice and loves mercy. And in every act of authentic selfhood the power that establishes life is presented in the world amid its misery. Encountering this other power demands and empowers a life of reflection and judgment about what we are to be and to do, the fruit of which is the examined life that explores the life worth living. The limits on our reflection mark out the tasks that shape the human condition. Thought gives way to life.

What we have seen throughout these reflections is that there is goodness amid evil. It is this "revelation" and its power to transform life that we have sought to explore in hermeneutical reflection on the way to theology and ethics. It empowers and demands seeking not only to understand world, time, and self, but to critique and transform them and the myriad conditions within which they are enacted. Understanding and exploring this "revelation" as it bears on life is the task for religious and moral reflection. Enacting it in the world is the adventure of the life well lived.

CONCLUSION

With these reflections on the divine and on human life the limits of this study have been reached. Further theological thinking would have to begin with an extended interpretation of the symbols and narratives of a community. And in ethics, as reflection on the human, the same would be true. But that is not the task of this study. The concern here has been to take stock of ways of thinking and speaking about the human and its world that might help in the task of religious and moral reflection. I have done so by offering a reading of Kierkegaard, Gadamer, and Ricoeur while attempting to rethink the import of mimesis for hermeneutical reflection.

Most generally, I have tried to isolate and articulate a position that interrelates ontological, textual, and existential approaches to the problem of "image" in its various facets. I have done so by turning to basic practices in which the problems of meaning and power meet. By exploring mimetic practices, I have tried to show how the powers of solidarity, speaking, and life come to presentation through their figuration as world, narrated time, and selfhood even as these powers elusively escape our control. The acts that present these powers as figured—the acts of interpretation, narration, and existential imitation —have their full import and significance when they are conditions for rendering Being understandable, figuring time as meaningful, and constituting selfhood as actual. The experience of these powers is not reducible, then, to the immanent dynamics of these practices even as one must think and speak of those powers as they are figured in these acts. I have argued that this helps us escape an imitative mindset and the logic of the image while enabling us to attend to the questions they attempted to answer, questions that ranged from aesthetics to the experience of the divine.

In reconstructing mimesis I have argued that it has a formal structure present in various types of practices while recognizing that particular forms have their own unique character. The structure of a mimetic practice, whether in ritual or understanding, includes (inter)action, a temporal dimension, and figuration through which something is presented. My reading of Gadamer concluded that this general dynamic helps us explore not only language but also the work of art and historical understanding. In fact, it was a way to speak about the meaning of Being. Thus Gadamer provided the first impulse to reconstruct mimesis by reclaiming its performative roots as a way to think beyond metaphysical and transcendental accounts of imitation and the philosophical stances they represent. He took as his ontological clue *Spiel*, dance and social festival, where there is an epiphany of meaning in and through the activities of the participants. This means that what is presented in the genuine act of understanding is the commonality that humans share, given their participation in the figuration of Being as a world. Thus Gadamer could claim that Being that can be understood is language. The central turn of hermeneutical reflection is to language and the practical shape and task of understanding. I have argued that this turn is crucial for any escape from traditional mimeticisms still able to help us think about understanding, human temporality, and selfhood.

I developed the textual expression of the mimetic process relative to our being agents in time by exploring Ricoeur's thought. There I charted the mimetic arch from the prefigured order of action to the refiguration of life won in response to textual configuration. Within each aspect of the threefold mimesis I found active, temporal, and "symbolic" or figurative elements. Though Ricoeur did not explore the performative roots of mimesis, as Gadamer had, he did allow us to reconstruct mimesis relative to text and action. Narrative is an entrance point into the temporality of human life and the timing of being in our existence. Here too mimesis figures the mediation of ontological claims (the horizon of time) and the practical task of human existence (narrative identity and humanity). In fact, the aporias of temporality drove the argument back to the shape of understanding and world and forward to the problem of the being of the self even as the inscrutability of time required a turn to the practical import of narrative.

Finally, I turned to Kierkegaard's dialectic of existence in order to explore the shape of selfhood. The contribution he made to our project was to rethink *imitatio* and the self beyond the inscription of the human within the logic of the "image." We saw that the passion for life becomes a self, a figuration of life, only through concrete acts of existence, through *imitatio*. Our affectivities and passions move existence and shape a mode of life within basic practices. The self is a process of relating or failing to relate to the power that establishes it moved by a passionate interest in existence. It is really a double mimesis since the enactment shapes the passions and feelings which gave rise to it and which it presents. This enactment forms settled dispositions and affections that motivate and guide future actions; it is the root of habits and virtues. The existential task is to disclose the power that establishes life in one's own life. Existential mimesis provides a way to think and speak about this process of the self coming to be and the task that this entails.

What I have tried to uncover through this reconstruction of mimesis are not only the mechanisms of the production of meaning within sign-systems and their self-undoing, not only the concealing of the mechanism of power in social reality. My task has been to examine the complex shape of those acts that structure experience and how through them the power of some reality, its being, is present as meaningful through figuration in such as way as to transform world, time, and human agency. What mimesis helps us to explore is the elusive relation of meaning, practice, and power in certain fundamental acts.

I have explored how Being becomes figured in and through understanding by the act of interpretation, how time becomes meaningful in the mimetic shape of narrative, and the self becomes actual through existential mimesis. And in each case, the power to transform understanding, refigure our temporality, and reform the self in life remains elusive. On the one hand, it is human solidarity, the power of speaking, and the passion for existence that enable and require the refiguration of understanding, time, and self. On the other, none of the mimetic acts that enact this refiguration (interpretation, narration, and praxis) exhausts their power but each presents and defers it. Each of the basic mimetic acts I have explored required human participation even as none was simply the presentation of the power of our acts.

The paradox of mimetic acts called for theological and ethical reflection, a mode of thinking that limits the present study. Indeed, the ambiguous relation of meaning, power, and practice enacted in any basic mimetic act is emblematic of our moral and religious situation. We cannot escape our being as participants in world, time, and selfhood under the conditions and demands of solidarity, facing the horizon of time, and a passion for existence. The concern of this study has been to uncover resources for thinking and speaking about the ways in which human world, time, and selfhood are rendered meaningful and transformed in and through basic acts. It has been to raise the question of the power of good, the meaning of our temporality, and what it means to be a self once we have escaped the illusion that we are the measure of the good, sovereigns of time, and masters of life.

I began this study with challenges to the way we understand our lives and our world. I have argued that exploring imitation provides a means to understand the import and coherence of those criticisms. While accepting them I have also argued that the reconstruction of mimesis is both necessary and possible. The praxis of figuration provides a way to think and speak about our world and the human condition beyond previous ways of picturing life. What emerges from these reflections is something abut the character of human life, the conditions of our being in language, time, and the passion of life, and the purposes that elicit and empower thought and action. Beyond that my reflections remain open since they have figured the human condition as an ongoing linguistic, imaginal, and existential praxis. Thus while ancient mimeticism dreamed of transcending the image in order to grasp the real, such an escape is not possible for us. Our condition, tragically or not, is to be participants in the figuration of our world and our lives.

NOTES

1. See Lyotard's *Postmodern Condition*.

2. "The Second Coming," *The Collected Works of W. B. Yeats* (New York: Macmillan, 1956), p. 184.

3. See her *Heart and Mind*.

4. For the theme of transformation and revolution as crucial to moral and political thought, see Brian Fay, *Critical Social Sciences: Liberation and Its Limits* (Ithaca: Cornell University Press, 1987) and Bernard Yack, *The Longing for Total Revolution: Philosophical Sources of Social Discontent from Rousseau to Marx and Nietzsche* (Princeton: Princeton University Press, 1986). For an account of the "deep structure" of religion as a transformative process, see Ronald M. Green, *Religion and Moral Reason* (Oxford: Oxford University Press, 1988).

5. I have explored these issues elsewhere. See my "Iconoclasts, Builders, and Dramatists"; "Beyond Imitation: The Mimetic Praxis of Gadamer, Ricoeur, and Derrida," *The Journal of Religion*, 68 (1988), 21–38; and "Sacrifice, Interpretation, and the Sacred."

6. For differing examples of this general development in moral philosophy, see Albert R. Jonsen and Stephen Toulmin, *The Abuse of Casuistry: A History of Moral Reasoning* (Berkeley: University of California Press, 1988); John Rawls, *A Theory of Justice* (Cambridge: The Belknap Press of Harvard University Press, 1971); MacIntyre's *After Virtue*; and Jonas' *Imperative of Responsibility*.

7. *Ethics and the Limits of Philosophy* (Cambridge: Harvard University Press, 1985), p. 96. For the development of accounts of rationality in moral philosophy, see Alasdair MacIntyre, *Whose Justice? Which Rationality?* (Notre Dame: University of Notre Dame Press, 1988). And for a recent attempt to sustain the viability of moral thought centered on linguistic communities against charges of relativism, see Stout's *Ethics After Babel*.

8. See her *Fragility of Goodness*. See also Bernard Williams' *Moral Luck: Philo-*

sophical Papers, 1973–1980 (Cambridge: Cambridge University Press, 1981), and Thomas Nagel, *Mortal Questions* (New York: Cambridge University Press, 1979).

9. *General Ethics* (Oxford: Blackwell, 1988), p. 31.

10. There are numerous studies of the moral worlds of cultures and historical periods. For examples of these in theology and ethics see Wayne A. Meeks, *The Moral World of the First Christians* (Philadelphia: Westminster, 1988); Fiorenza's *In Memory of Her*; Peter J. Parish, *The Social Teachings of the Black Churches* (Philadelphia: Fortress, 1985); and H. Richard Niebuhr, *Christ and Culture* (New York: Harper & Row, 1951). For the classic example in this kind of work, see Ernst Troeltsch, *The Social Teachings of the Christian Churches*, trans. Olive Wyon, 2 vols. (Chicago: The University of Chicago Press/Midway, 1979).

11. John Rawls, in his *Theory of Justice*, works within the contractarian tradition and develops his theory of justice relative to an "original position" of free debate about the criteria of justice. Alan Gewirth, in his *Reason and Morality* (Chicago: The University of Chicago Press, 1978), explores the features of action (freedom and purposiveness) as the foundation for an absolute moral principle of generic consistency. Jürgen Habermas has developed a communication ethics employed by theologians as well. He is concerned with the norms implied in any free, uncoerced communicative act. See his *Communication and the Evolution of Society*. For theological examples of communication ethics, see Jens Glebe-Möller, *A Political Dogmatics*, trans. T. Hall (Philadelphia: Fortress, 1987), and Helmut Peukert, *Science, Action, and Fundamental Theology: Towards a Theology of Communicative Action*, trans. John Bohman (Cambridge: MIT Press, 1984).

12. MacIntyre gives a fuller account of the development of moral rationality in his *Whose Justice? Which Rationality?* On this see also Jonsen and Toulmin, *Abuse of Casuistry* and John Mahoney, s.J., *The Making of Moral Theology* (Oxford: Oxford University Press, 1987).

13. See Winter's *Liberating Creation: Foundations of Religious Social Ethics* (New York: Crossroad: 1981), and Caputo's *Radical Hermeneutics: Repetition, Deconstruction, and the Hermeneutic Project* (Bloomington: Indiana University Press, 1987). See also my "To Dwell on the Earth: Authority and Ecumenical Theology," in *Worldviews and Warrants: Plurality and Authority in Theology*, edd. William Schweiker and Per M. Anderson (Lanham, Md.: University Press of America, 1987), pp. 89–112.

14. On this see Jonas' *Imperative of Responsibility* and Marx's *Is There a Measure on Earth: Foundations for a Nonmetaphysical Ethics*, trans. T. J. Nenon and R. Lilly (Chicago: The University of Chicago Press, 1987).

15. *Epiphanies of Darkness: Deconstruction in Theology* (Philadelphia: Fortress, 1986). On the problem of authentic theological thinking, see Robert P. Scharlemann, "The No to Nothing and the Nothing to Know: Barth and Tillich and the Possibility of Theological Science," *The Journal of the American Academy of Religion*, 55 (1987), 75–106.

16. In the United States the best examples of this kind of theology are those thinkers influenced by process philosophy. For an example, see John Cobb, Jr., *God and World* (Philadelphia: Westminster, 1969) and Charles Hartshorne, *A Natural Theology for Our Time* (LaSalle, Ill.: Open Court, 1967). European thinkers with these concerns are often influenced by Hegel. See Wolfhart Pannenberg, *Jesus—God and Man*, trans. L. Wilkins and D. Priebe, 2nd ed. (Philadelphia: Westminster, 1977).

17. For examples of this position, see Metz's *Faith in History and Society*. See also Jürgen Moltmann, *God in Creation: An Ecological Doctrine of Creation*, trans. M. Kohln (London: SCM Press, 1985) and *On Human Dignity: Political Theology and Ethics*, trans. M. D. Meeks (Philadelphia: Fortress, 1984). And see Gustavo Gutierrez, *A Theology of Liberation: History, Politics and Salvation*, trans. C. Inda and J. Eagleson (Maryknoll, N.Y.: Orbis, 1973) and *The Power of the Poor in History*, trans. R. Barr (Maryknoll, N.Y.: Orbis, 1983).

18. See Gordon D. Kaufman's *Theology for a Nuclear Age* (Philadelphia: Westminster, 1985), *An Essay on Theological Method*, rev. ed. (Chico, Calif.: Scholars Press, 1979), and *Theological Imagination*. See also Sallie McFague's *Metaphorical Theology* and *Models of God: A Theology for an Ecological, Nuclear Age* (Philadelphia: Fortress, 1987). See likewise Gustafson's *Ethics from a Theocentric Perspective*. For positions less "constructivist" in character, see Ruether's *Sexism and God-Talk* and Tracy's *Plurality and Ambiguity*. See also Jüngel's *God as Mystery of the World*.

19. My argument here is that theology critically explores and interprets human experience and the beliefs of a religious tradition in undertaking an examination of world and the human condition. Against other options in current theology, I contend that theological reflection does not attempt to derive knowledge of the human condition solely from the "revelation" of the divine, whether in sacred narratives or sui generis experiences, or to postulate or to construe "God" from the conditions of our being in the world. Rather, theological reflection explores how the configurative acts of communities and traditions mediate understanding and its world with passion and existence. Theology is a transformative hermeneutic, if I may call it that, of what is directly experienced but not immediately known as this bears on life. The means three things for theological reflection. First, the theologian explores the figurative practices of a religious and cultural tradition to see how they mediate world and human agency vis-à-vis their construal(s) of that in which we live, move, and have our being. Second, one offers a critical and constructive figuration of "God," world, and human agency in response to basic questions of meaning, power, and the direction of life. Finally, the narratives of a community and any constructive theological configuration are open, by the nature of the case, to criticism and even revision from other ways of interpreting and knowing the world and human agency. This method of thought requires that theological and ethical reflection continually inform and transform each other. I would trace this concern and mode of thought back to John Calvin, who argued that true and sound wisdom consists in knowledge of God and knowledge of ourselves but that the relation between these is difficult to discern. See his *Institutes of the Christian Religion*. What this means is that discourse about the divine entails a transformative hermeneutic of the human condition. Natural modes of being in the world are transformed and redirected when figured theologically. For similar, but different, arguments see Niebuhr's *Meaning of Revelation*, and Paul Tillich's *Systematic Theology*, 3 vols. in 1 (Chicago: The University of Chicago Press, 1967).

20. For a classic discussion of analogy in theological discourse, see Thomas Aquinas, *Summa theologica*, trans. Fathers of the English Dominican Province, 5 vols. (Westminster, Md.: Christian Classics, 1981), Ia, qq. 1–13. For a recent consideration of analogy in theology, see Tracy's *Analogical Imagination*.

21. In describing the religious in this way, I am drawing on Gadamer's notion of effective-historical consciousness, Kierkegaard's existential analysis, and H. Richard

Niebuhr's understanding of experiential religion. See Niebuhr's *Experiential Religion* (New York: Harper & Row, 1972). That is, I am claiming that religion has to do with the ultimate meaning, value, and purpose of existence within our being affected by an environing world of power as this world evokes responses of awe, reverence, love, and even terror. A religion is more than a system of belief; it is a way of life. However, an understanding of "religion" is not yet a doctrine of God.

22. *Human Agency and Language*, p. 238.

23. I am here drawing again on Robert Sokolowski's work. See his *Moral Action*.

24. *Tremendum*, pp. 92, 94.

25. For issues in fundamental theology see Francis Schüssler Fiorenza, *Foundational Theology: Jesus and the Church* (New York: Crossroad, 1984); David Tracy, *Blessed Rage for Order: The New Pluralism in Theology* (New York: Seabury/Crossroad, 1975); Schubert Ogden, *On Theology* (New York: Harper & Row, 1986); and Metz, *Faith in History and Society*.

26. For a classic expression of this form of reflexive, idealist thinking, see Johann Gottlieb Fichte, *The Vocation of Man*, ed. R. M. Chisholm (Indianapolis: Bobbs-Merrill, 1956). For a hermeneutical retrieval of reflexivity in theology, see Robert P. Scharlemann, *The Being of God: Theology and the Experience of Truth* (New York: Seabury, 1981).

27. See Lawson, *Reflexivity*, and Theunissen, *The Other*. It is unfortunate that the last chapter of Theunissen's study, the one on theology, was omitted from the translation!

28. *Church Dogmatics* I/1, p. 295.

29. *On Christian Doctrine*, trans. D. W. Robertson, Jr., Library of Liberal Arts (Indianapolis: Bobbs-Merrill, 1958).

30. For a helpful study on this, see Arthur C. McGill, *Death and Life: An American Theology*, ed. Charles A. Wilson and Per M. Anderson (Philadelphia: Fortress, 1987).

31. Currently there are theologians who argue that for believers the narratives of their community are the "primary reality" that incorporates the world. Hence it is an error theologically, these thinkers argue, to undertake a hermeneutic of the human condition. To remain faithful to the Bible one must see life within its story, specifically the story of God's actions. For an example of this, see Lindbeck, *Nature of Doctrine*, and Frei, *Eclipse of Biblical Narrative*. My points of agreement with this position should be obvious. My disagreements, profound ones at that, are found at two points. First, I have argued for the importance and yet limits of narrative, limits these thinkers often fail to acknowledge. I need not repeat that argument here. Second, there is a disagreement about what is meant by "experience." I understand experience as the complex web of relations within which we live, move, and have our being, whereas *an* experience is the determination or formation of one's existence by what is understood or undergone. I have tried to argue for the importance of both senses of experience in understanding the import of religious texts and symbols. It remains unclear to me what these "narrative" thinkers mean by experience, other than that it is opposed to a Bible-based theology. Hence their challenge to hermeneutical reflection remains ambiguous. My point has been that without some account of experience (first sense) we cannot understand experiences (second sense) determinative of existence. But this does not mean, as we know from Kierkegaard, that the immanent character of our being in the world (experience in the first sense) is solely determinative of life (experience in the second sense). What determines, or, better, what transforms, existence is encountered

in and through mimetic practices, though it is not reducible to them. When one speaks of "God," one is speaking of that in which we live, move, and have our being as well as that which determines and transforms world and human life in and through the practices that structure experience and render being and time meaningful. In this sense, there is an experiential knowledge of God in both senses of experience. However, the knowledge of God as that in which we live, move, and have our being is mediated by those experiences that transform world and life. This is why theological reflection entails a transformative hermeneutic of human experience relative to claims about the divine.

32. *The Analogy of Experience: An Approach to Understanding Religious Truth* (New York: Harper & Row, 1973), p. 24. See also his *Experience and God* (Oxford: Oxford University Press, 1968).

33. H. Richard Niebuhr made this question central to his moral philosophy. See his *Responsible Self*. It actually is found in Stoic moralists as well as in Aristotle's concern for the particularities of moral situations. For a recent expression of cathecontic ethics, see Calvin O. Schrag, *Communicative Praxis and the Space of Subjectivity* (Bloomington: Indiana University Press, 1986).

34. This is Niebuhr's formulation. His answer is: "So respond to all actions upon you as to respond to his action." See *Responsible Self*, p. 126. A constant criticism of this form of moral thinking is its seeming inability to specify critiera for judgment. I attempt to do this through the temporal character of our configurative acts. By doing so, I am providing, not timeless norms of choice, but a measure for our timely actions and thus retaining the concern for what is "fitting" in responsibility. For a different position see Trutz Rendtorff, *Ethics*. I. *Basic Elements and Methodology in an Ethical Theology* (Philadelphia: Fortress, 1986).

35. This way of phrasing the issue is of considerable importance. That is, I am avoiding the is/ought problem in two ways. First, I am not putting the matter in terms of the validity of deriving moral oughts from non-moral states of affairs and goods, a division in ethical discourse I find troublesome. Rather, I am trying to show that the forms of activities within which questions about states of affairs arise also imply "normative" questions. These activities are moral ones in that they have to do with human interactions with others, self, and world, and at the same time they enact human being and its relation to what "is." Second, I have suggested that the *question* of an ought arises within these activities even if this ought does not exhaust them or their "measure." Thus what must be established is the content of that ought vis-à-vis the basic acts of human moral existence, as the question puts it, and not its relation to non-moral goods or states of affairs. Thus while I am avoiding the problem of is/ought, I am arguing that interpretations of states of affairs and their goods and the question of the measure for human being and doing are related. Furthermore, I am claiming that they are so related in and through the basic activities (interpretation, narration, and selfhood) that make up the human condition and its goods.

36. *Is There a Measure on Earth?* p. 20.

37. For a clear statement of this problem see G. E. M. Anscombe, "Modern Moral Philosophy," *Philosophy*, 33 (1958), 1–19. See also the essays collected in *Divine Commands and Morality*, ed. Paul Helm (Oxford: Oxford University Press, 1981).

38. Barth was the most consistent advocate of a divine command ethics in this century. For his general ethics see *Church Dogmatics* II/2. See also Rudolf Bultmann,

"Welchen Sinn hat es, von Gott zu reden?" *Glauben und Verstehen* I (Tübingen: Mohr, 1954), pp. 26–37.

39. It seems to me that of the authors mentioned, Marx, Caputo, and Jonas, among the philosophers, have tried to rethink the notion of measure, whereas Rawls, Gewirth, and, perhaps, Habermas remain with the traditional notion. Theologians have been less attentive to this issue. Winter addresses the matter relative to our participation in the created order. Gustafson's contribution has been to challenge the anthropocentrism of most religious and moral "measures." Yet neither of these theologians, nor the others mentioned, explore in depth the problem of measure *qua* measure.

40. The moral status of the natural world is a complex question and cannot be considered here. For different approaches to this question, see Jonas, *Imperative of Responsibility*; Kohák, *The Embers and the Stars*; and Paul Taylor, *Respect for Nature* (Princeton: Princeton University Press, 1986).

BIBLIOGRAPHY

Anscombe, G. E. M. "Modern Moral Philosophy." *Philosophy*, 33 (1958), 1–19.

Aquinas, Thomas. *Summa contra Gentiles*. Rome: Marietti, 1925.

——. *Summa theologica*. Trans. Fathers of the English Dominican Province. 5 vols. Westminster, Md.: Christian Classics, 1981.

Aristotle. *The Basic Works of Aristotle*. Ed. Richard McKeon. New York: Random House, 1941.

——. *On Poetry and Style*. Trans. G. M. A. Grube. Library of Liberal Arts. Indianapolis: Bobbs-Merrill, 1958.

Auerbach, Eric. *Mimesis: The Representation of Reality in Western Literature*. Trans. Willard R. Trask. Princeton: Princeton University Press, 1959.

Augustine. *Confessions*. Trans. R. S. Pine-Coffin. New York: Penguin, 1961.

——. *On Christian Doctrine*. Trans. D. W. Robertson, Jr. Library of Liberal Arts. Indianapolis: Bobbs-Merrill, 1958.

——. *On the Morals of the Catholic Church*. Nicene and Post-Nicene Fathers of the Christian Church 4. Ed. Philip Schaff. Grand Rapids: Eerdmans, 1979. Pp. 41–63.

——. *On the Holy Trinity*. Nicene and Post-Nicene Fathers of the Christian Church 3. Ed. Philip Schaff. Grand Rapids: Eerdmans, 1980.

Barth, Karl. *Church Dogmatics*. Edd. G. W. Bromiley and T. F. Torrance. 12 vols. Edinburgh: Clark, 1956–1969.

Bernstein, Richard J., *Beyond Objectivism and Relativism: Science, Hermeneutics, and Praxis*. Philadelphia: University of Pennsylvania Press, 1983.

——. *Philosophical Profiles*. Philadelphia: University of Pennsylvania Press, 1986.

Betz, Hans Dieter. *Nachfolge und Nachahmung Jesu Christi im Neuen Testament*. Ed. Gerhard Ebeling. Beiträge zur historischen Theologie 37. Tübingen: Mohr, 1967.

Bloom, Harold. *Kabbalah and Criticism*. New York: Seabury, 1975.

Boyd, John D., s.j. *The Function of Mimesis and Its Decline*. Cambridge: Harvard University Press, 1968. Repr. New York: Fordham University Press, 1980.

Buber, Martin. *Mamre: Essays in Religion*. Trans. Greta Hort. London: Melbourne University Press, 1946.

Bultmann, Rudolf. "Welchen Sinn hat es, von Gott zu reden?" *Glauben und Verstehen* I. Tübingen: Mohr, 1954. Pp. 26–37.

Burrell, David B. *Aquinas: God and Action*. Notre Dame: University of Notre Dame Press, 1979.

Calvin, John. *Institutes of the Christian Faith*. Trans. Ford Lewis Battles. Ed. John T. McNeill. 2 vols. Library of Christian Classics 20–21. Philadelphia: Westminster, 1960.

Caputo, John D. "Being, Ground, and Play in Heidegger." *Man and World*, 3 (1970), 26–48.

———. "A Phenomenology of Moral Sensibility: Moral Emotion." In *Act and Agent: Philosophical Foundations for Moral Education and Character Development*. Edd. George F. McLean et al. Lanham, Md.: University Press of America, 1986. Pp. 199–222.

———. *Radical Hermeneutics: Repetition, Deconstruction, and the Hermeneutic Project*. Bloomington: Indiana University Press, 1987.

Casey, Edward S. "Truth in Art." *Man and World*, 3 (1970), 351–69.

Cobb, John B., Jr. *God and World*. Philadelphia: Westminster, 1969.

Cohen, Arthur. *The Tremendum: A Theological Interpretation of the Holocaust*. New York: Crossroad, 1981.

Coleridge, Samuel Taylor. *Bibliographia Literaria*. Ed. George Watson. New York: Dutton, 1965.

Collingwood, R. G. *An Autobiography*. Oxford: Oxford University Press, 1970.

Comstock, Gary. "Truth and Meaning: Ricoeur and Frei on Biblical Narrative." *The Journal of Religion*, 66 (1986), 117–40.

Crites, Steven. "The Narrative Quality of Experience." *The Journal of the American Academy of Religion*, 39 (1971), 291–311.

Critics and Criticism: Essays in Method. Ed. R. S. Crane. Abr. ed. Chicago: The University of Chicago Press, 1957.

Deconstruction and Criticism. Edd. Harold Bloom, Paul de Man, Jacques Derrida, Geoffrey Hartmann, and J. Hillis Miller. New York: Seabury, 1979.

Deconstruction and Theology. Edd. Thomas J. J. Altizer, M. A. Myers, C. A. Raschke, R. P. Scharlemann, M. C. Taylor, and C. E. Winquist. New York: Crossroad, 1982.

Derrida, Jacques. *Dissemination*. Trans. Barbara Johnson. Chicago: The University of Chicago Press, 1981.

———. "Economimesis." *Mimesis des articulations*. Paris: Aubier–Flammarion, 1975. Pp. 57–93.

———. "Economimesis." Trans. R. Klein. *Diacritics*, 11 (1981), 3–25.

———. *Margins of Philosophy*. Trans. Alan Bass. Chicago: The University of Chicago Press, 1982.

Dewey, John. *Reconstruction in Philosophy*. Enl. ed. Boston: Beacon, 1948.

Divine Commands and Morality. Ed. Paul Helm. Oxford: Oxford University Press, 1981.

Dumochel, Paul. "Différences et paradoxes: Réflexions sur l'amour et la violence dans l'oeuvre de Girard." In *René Girard et le problème du mal.* Edd. M. Deguy and J-P. Dupuy. Paris: Grasset, 1982. Pp. 216–18.

Dunning, Stephen N. *Kierkegaard's Dialectic of Inwardness: A Structural Analysis of the Theory of Signs.* Princeton: Princeton University Press, 1985.

Eliade, Mircea. *The Sacred and the Profane: The Nature of Religion.* Trans. Willard R. Trask. New York: Harcourt Brace Jovanovich/Harvest, 1959.

Elrod, John W. *Being and Existence in Kierkegaard's Pseudonymous Works.* Princeton: Princeton University Press, 1975.

——. *Kierkegaard and Christendom.* Princeton: Princeton University Press, 1981.

——. "The Self in Kierkegaard's Pseudonyms." *International Journal for the Philosophy of Religion*, 4 (1973), 218–40.

Else, Gerald F. "'Imitation' in the Fifth Century." *Classical Philology*, 53 (1958), 73–99.

——. *The Structure and Date of Book 10 of Plato's* REPUBLIC. Heidelberg: Winter, 1972.

Essays on Kant's Aesthetics. Edd. Ted Cohen and Paul Guyer. Chicago: The University of Chicago Press, 1982.

Fabro, Cornelio, C.P.S. "Faith and Reason in Kierkegaard's Dialectic." In *A Kierkegaard Critique.* Edd. Howard Johnson and Niels Thulstrup. Chicago: Regnery, 1962. Pp. 156–206.

Fay, Brian. *Critical Social Sciences: Liberation and Its Limits.* Ithaca: Cornell University Press, 1987.

Feminist Interpretations of the Bible. Ed. Letty M. Russell. Philadelphia: Westminster, 1985.

Fichte, Johann Gottlieb. *The Vocation of Man.* Ed. R. M. Chisholm. Indianapolis: Bobbs-Merrill, 1956.

Fiorenza, Elisabeth Schüssler. *Bread Not Stone: The Challenge of Feminist Biblical Interpretation.* Boston: Beacon, 1984.

——. *In Memory of Her: A Feminist Theological Reconstruction of Christian Origins.* New York: Crossroad, 1983.

Fiorenza, Francis Schüssler. *Foundational Theology: Jesus and the Church.* New York: Crossroad, 1984.

Frei, Hans. *The Eclipse of Biblical Narrative: A Study in Eighteenth- and Nineteenth-Century Hermeneutics.* New Haven: Yale University Press, 1974.

Gadamer, Hans-Georg. *Die Aktualität des Schönen: Kunst als Spiel, Symbol, und Fest.* Stuttgart: Reclam, 1977.

——. *Dialogue and Dialectic: Eight Hermeneutical Studies on Plato.* Trans. P. Christopher Smith. New Haven: Yale University Press, 1980.

——. "Dichtung und Mimesis." *Kleine Schriften. IV. Variationen.* Tübingen: Mohr, 1977. Pp. 228–33.

——. *Hegel's Dialectic: Five Hermeneutical Studies.* Trans. P. Christopher Smith. New Haven: Yale University Press, 1976.

——. *The Idea of the Good in Platonic–Aristotelian Philosophy.* Trans.

P. Christopher Smith. New Haven: Yale University Press, 1986.

——. *Kleine Schriften. IV. Variationen.* Tübingen: Mohr, 1977.

——. "On the Problem of Self-Understanding." *Philosophical Hermeneutics.* Trans. and ed. David E. Linge. Berkeley: University of California Press, 1976. Pp. 44–58.

——. "On the Problematic Character of Aesthetic Consciousness." Trans. E. Kelly. *Graduate Faculty Philosophical Journal,* 9 (1982), 31–40.

——. "Practical Philosophy as Model of the Human Sciences." *Research in Phenomenology,* 9 (1979), 74–86.

——. "The Problem of Language in Schleiermacher's Hermeneutics." Trans. David E. Linge. In *Schleiermacher as Contemporary.* Ed. Robert W. Funk. Journal of Theology in the Church 7. New York: Herder and Herder, 1970. Pp. 85–95.

——. *Reason in the Age of Science.* Trans. Frederick G. Lawrence. Cambridge: MIT Press, 1981.

——. *The Relevance of the Beautiful and Other Essays.* Trans. Nicholas Walker. Ed. Robert Bernasconi. Cambridge: Cambridge University Press, 1986.

——. "Religious and Poetical Speaking." In *Myth, Symbol, and Reality.* Ed. Alan M. Olson. Boston University Studies in Religion and Philosophy 1. Notre Dame: University of Notre Dame Press, 1980. Pp. 86–98.

——. "Das Spiel der Kunst." *Kleine Schriften. IV. Variationen.* Tübingen: Mohr, 1977. Pp. 234–40.

——. "Theory, Technology, Practice: The Task of the Science of Man." *Social Research,* 44 (1977), 529–61.

——. *Truth and Method.* Trans. Garrett Barden and John Cumming. New York: Seabury/Continuum, 1975.

——. *Wahrheit und Methode: Grundzüge einer philosophischen Hermeneutik.* 2nd ed. Tübingen: Mohr, 1965.

Garceau, Benoît. "La violence et le vrai savior de l'homme." *Sciences Religieuses/Studies in Religion,* 10 (1981), 5–14.

Gasché, Rodolphe. "Joining the Text: From Heidegger to Derrida." In *The Yale Critics: Deconstruction in America.* Edd. Jonathan Arac, Wald Godzich, and Wallach Martine. Theory and History of Literature 6. Minneapolis: University of Minnesota Press, 1983. Pp. 172–73.

Geertz, Clifford. *The Interpretation of Cultures.* New York: Basic Books, 1973.

——. *Local Knowledge: Further Essays in Interpretive Anthropology.* New York: Basic Books, 1983.

Gewirth, Alan. *Reason and Morality.* Chicago: The University of Chicago Press, 1978.

Gilkey, Langdon. *Naming the Whirlwind: The Renewal of God-Language.* Indianapolis: Bobbs-Merrill, 1969.

——. *Reaping the Whirlwind: A Christian Interpretation of History.* New York: Crossroad, 1981.

Gill, Jerry H. "Kant, Kierkegaard, and Religious Knowledge." In *Essays on Kierkegaard*. Ed. Jerry H. Gill. Minneapolis: Burgess, 1969. Pp. 58–73.

Girard, René. *Deceit, Desire, and the Novel: Self and Other in Literary Structure*. Trans. Yvonne Freccero. Baltimore: The Johns Hopkins University Press, 1965.

——. "Mimesis and Violence: Perspectives in Cultural Criticism." *Berkshire Review*, 14 (1979), 9–19.

——. *The Scapegoat*. Trans. Yvonne Freccero. Baltimore: The Johns Hopkins University Press, 1986.

——. *To Double Business Bound: Essays on Literature, Mimesis, and Anthropology*. Baltimore: The Johns Hopkins University Press, 1978.

——. *Violence and the Sacred*. Trans. Patrick Gregory. Baltimore: The Johns Hopkins University Press, 1977.

Glebe-Möller, Jens. *A Political Dogmatics*. Trans. T. Hall. Philadelphia: Fortress, 1987.

Golden, Leon. "Mimesis and Katharsis." *Classical Philology*, 54 (1969), 145–53.

——. "Plato's Concept of Mimesis." *British Journal of Aesthetics*, 15 (1975), 118–31.

Goldstein, Harvey D. "Mimesis and Catharsis Reexamined." *Journal of Aesthetics and Art Criticism*, 24 (1966), 567–77.

Green, Ronald M. *Religion and Moral Reason*. Oxford: Oxford University Press, 1988.

Grondin, Jean. *Hermeneutische Wahrheit? Zum Wahrheitsbegriff Hans-Georg Gadamers*. Monographien zur philosophischen Forschung 215. Tübingen: Athenäum, 1982.

Gutierrez, Gustavo. *The Power of the Poor in History*. Trans. R. Barr. Maryknoll, N.Y.: Orbis, 1983.

——. *A Theology of Liberation: History, Politics, and Salvation*. Trans. C. Inda and J. Eagleson. Maryknoll, N.Y.: Orbis, 1973.

Gustafson, James M. *Christ and the Moral Life*. Chicago: The University of Chicago Press, 1979.

——. *Ethics from a Theocentric Perspective*. 2 vols. Chicago: The University of Chicago Press, 1981, 1984.

——. *Protestant and Roman Catholic Ethics: Prospects for Rapprochement*. Chicago: The University of Chicago Press, 1978.

——. *Treasure in Earthen Vessels: The Church as Human Community*. Chicago: The University of Chicago Press/Midway, 1976.

Habermas, Jürgen. *Communication and the Evolution of Society*. Trans. Thomas McCarthy. Boston: Beacon, 1979.

——. *Knowledge and Human Interests*. Trans. Jeremy J. Shapiro. Boston: Beacon, 1971.

——. *Theory and Practice*. Trans. John Viertel. Boston: Beacon, 1973.

Handelmann, Susan. *The Slayers of Moses: The Emergence of Rabbinic Inter-pretation in Modern Literary Theory*. Albany: State University of New York Press, 1982.

Hartshorne, Charles. *A Natural Theology for Our Time*. La Salle, Ill.: Open Court, 1967.

Hauerwas, Stanley. *A Community of Character: Toward a Constructive Chris-tian Social Ethic*. Notre Dame: University of Notre Dame Press, 1981.

———. *Truthfulness and Tragedy: Further Investigations into Christian Ethics*. Notre Dame: University of Notre Dame Press, 1977.

Hegel, G. W. F. *Phenomenology of Spirit*. Trans. A. V. Miller. Oxford: Clarendon, 1977.

Heidegger, Martin. *Being and Time*. Trans. John Macquarrie and Edward Rob-inson. New York: Harper & Row, 1962.

———. *Essays in Metaphysics: Identity and Difference*. Trans. Kurt F. Leidecher. New York: Harper & Row, 1962.

———. *An Introduction to Metaphysics*. Trans. Ralph Manheim. Garden City: Doubleday Anchor, 1961.

———. "Letter on Humanism." *Basic Writings from* BEING AND TIME *(1927) to* THE TASK OF THINKING *(1964)*. Ed. David Farrell Krell. New York: Harper & Row, 1977. Pp. 189–242.

———. *Der Satz vom Grund*. Pfullingen: Neske, 1975.

———. *Sein und Zeit*. Tübingen: Neimer, 1963.

Heller, Agnes. *General Ethics*. Oxford: Blackwell, 1988.

Hermeneutik und Dialektik: Hans-Georg Gadamer z. 70. Geburtstag. Edd. Rüdinger Bubner, Konrad Cramer, and Reiner Wahl. 2 vols. Tübingen: Mohr, 1970.

Hirsch, E. D., Jr. *Validity in Interpretation*. New Haven: Yale University Press, 1967.

Holmer, Paul. "Kierkegaard and Ethical Theory." *Ethics*, 63 (1953), 155–70.

———. "On Understanding Kierkegaard." In *A Kierkegaard Critique*. Edd. Howard Johnson and Niels Thulstrup. Chicago: Regnery, 1962. Pp. 40–53.

Hoy, David Couzens. *The Critical Circle: Literature, History, and Philosophy*. Berkeley: University of California Press, 1978.

Huizinga, Johann. *Homo Ludens: A Study of the Play Element in Culture*. Boston: Beacon, 1955.

Huyssen, Andreas. "Mapping the Postmodern." *New German Critique*, 33 (1984), 5–52.

Idhe, Don. *Hermeneutic Phenomenology: The Philosophy of Paul Ricoeur*. Evanston: Northwestern University Press, 1971.

James, William. *Pragmatism and the Meaning of Truth*. New York: Longmans, Green, 1910.

Jaspers, Karl. *Reason and Existenz*. New York: Noonday, 1957.

Jennings, Theodore W. "On Ritual Knowledge." *The Journal of Religion*, 62 (1982), 111–27.

Johann, Robert. *Building the Human*. New York: Herder and Herder, 1968.

Jonas, Hans. *The Imperative of Responsibility: In Search of an Ethic for the Technological Age*. Trans. Hans Jonas and D. Herr. Chicago: The University of Chicago Press, 1984.

Jonsen, Albert R., and Toulmin, Stephen. *The Abuse of Casuistry: A History of Moral Reasoning*. Berkeley: University of California Press, 1988.

Jüngel, Eberhard. *God as the Mystery of the World*. Trans. Darrell L. Gruder. Grand Rapids: Eerdmans, 1983.

Kant, Immanuel. *Critique of Judgment*. Trans. J. H. Bernhard. New York: Hafner, 1951.

———. *Fundamental Principles of the Metaphysics of Morals*. Trans. T. K. Abbot. New York: Liberal Arts, 1949.

———. "Ideas for a Universal History from a Cosmopolitan Point of View." In *Immanuel Kant: On History*. Ed. Lewis White Beck. Indianapolis: Bobbs-Merrill, 1963.

———. *Lectures on Philosophical Theology*. Trans. Allen W. Wood and Gertrude M. Clark. Ithaca: Cornell University Press, 1978.

———. "Perpetual Peace." In *Immanuel Kant: On History*. Trans. Lewis White Beck. Indianapolis: Bobbs-Merrill, 1963.

Kaufman, Gordon D. "Constructing the Concept of God." *Neue Zeitschrift für systematische Theologie und Religionsphilosophie*, 23 (1981), 29–56.

———. *An Essay on Theological Method*. Rev. ed. Chico, Calif.: Scholars Press, 1979.

———. *The Theological Imagination: Constructing the Concept of God*. Philadelphia: Westminster, 1981.

———. *Theology for a Nuclear Age*. Philadelphia: Westminster, 1985.

Kermode, Frank. *The Genesis of Secrecy: On the Interpretation of Narrative*. Cambridge: Harvard University Press, 1979.

A Kierkegaard Critique. Edd. Howard Johnson and Niels Thulstrup. Chicago: Regnery, 1962.

Kierkegaard, Søren. *The Concept of Anxiety*. Trans. Reidar Thomte. Princeton: Princeton University Press, 1980.

———. *Concluding Unscientific Postscript*. Trans. David Swenson. Princeton: Princeton University Press, 1941.

———. *Either/Or*. Trans. David Swenson. 2 vols. Princeton: Princeton University Press, 1944.

———. *Fear and Trembling*. Trans. Walter Lowrie. Garden City: Doubleday, 1954.

———. *Journals and Papers*. Edd. Howard V. Hong and Edna J. Hong. Bloomington: Indiana University Press, 1970.

———. *The Journals of Søren Kierkegaard*. Ed. Alexander Dru. New York: Oxford University Press, 1938.

——. *On Authority and Revelation: The Book of Adler, or, A Cycle of Ethico-Religious Essays*. Trans. Walter Lowrie. Princeton: Princeton University Press, 1955.

——. *Papirer*. Edd. P. H. Heiberg, V. Kuhr, and E. Torsten. 2nd ed. Copenhagen: Glyndendal, 1968.

——. *Philosophical Fragments, or, A Fragment of Philosophy*. Trans. David Swenson. Rev. Howard H. Hong. Princeton: Princeton University Press, 1962.

——. *Sickness unto Death*. Trans. Walter Lowrie. Princeton: Princeton University Press, 1941.

——. *Training in Christianity*. Trans. Walter Lowrie. Princeton: Princeton University Press, 1944.

——. *Works of Love*. Trans. Lillian Swenson. Princeton: Princeton University Press, 1946.

Klemke, E. D. *Studies in the Philosophy of Kierkegaard*. The Hague: Nijhoff, 1976.

Klemm, David E. *The Hermeneutical Theory of Paul Ricoeur: A Constructive Analysis*. Lewisburg: Bucknell University Press, 1983.

Köller, Herman. *Die Mimesis in der Antike: Nachahmung, Darstellung, Ausdruck*. Bern: Francke, 1954.

Kohák, Erazim. *The Embers and the Stars: A Philosophical Inquiry into the Moral Sense of Nature*. Chicago: The University of Chicago Press, 1984.

The Kristeva Reader. Ed. Toril Moi. New York: Columbia University Press, 1986.

Kühn, Helmut. "Die Ontogenese der Kunst." In *Festschrift für Hans Sedlmayr*. Ed. Karl Oettinger. Munich: Beck, 1962. Pp. 13–55.

LaCapra, Dominick. *Rethinking Intellectual History: Texts, Contexts, and Language*. Ithaca: Cornell University Press, 1983.

Lawson, Hilary. *Reflexivity: The Post-Modern Predicament*. La Salle, Ill.: Open Court, 1985.

Levinas, Emmanuel. *Totality and Infinity*. Trans. Alphonso Lingus. Pittsburgh: Duquesne University Press, 1969.

Lindbeck, George. *The Nature of Doctrine: Religion and Theology in a Postliberal Age*. Philadelphia: Westminster, 1984.

Lowrie, Walter. *A Short Life of Kierkegaard*. Princeton: Princeton University Press, 1942.

Lyotard, Jean-François. *The Postmodern Condition: A Report on Knowledge*. Trans. Geoff Bennington and Brian Massumi. Theory and History of Literature 10. Minneapolis: University of Minnesota Press, 1984.

McFague, Sallie. *Metaphorical Theology: Models of God in Religious Language*. Philadelphia: Fortress, 1982.

——. *Models of God: A Theology for an Ecological, Nuclear Age*. Philadelphia: Fortress, 1987.

McGill, Arthur C. *Death and Life: An American Theology*. Edd. Charles A. Wilson and Per M. Anderson. Philadelphia: Fortress, 1987.

MacIntyre, Alasdair. *After Virtue: A Theory in Moral Philosophy*. Notre Dame: University of Notre Dame Press, 1981.

———. *Whose Justice? Which Rationality?* Notre Dame: University of Notre Dame Press, 1988.

McKeon, Richard. *Thought, Action, and Passion*. Chicago: The University of Chicago Press, 1954.

Mackey, Louis. *Kierkegaard: A Kind of a Poet*. Philadelphia: University of Pennsylvania Press, 1971.

———. "Slouching Towards Bethlehem: Deconstructive Strategies in Theology." *Anglican Theological Review*, 65 (1983), 255–72.

McKinnon, Alastair. "Kierkegaard: Paradox and Irrationalism." In *Essays on Kierkegaard*. Ed. Jerry H. Gill. Minneapolis: Burgess, 1969. Pp. 110–22.

Mahoney, John, S.J. *The Making of Moral Theology*. Oxford: Oxford University Press, 1987.

Malantschuk, Gregor. *Kierkegaard's Thought*. Edd. and trans. Howard V. Hong and Edna H. Hong. Princeton: Princeton University Press, 1971.

Maraux, Paul. " 'La mimesis' dans les théories anciennes de la danse, de la musique, et de la poésie." *Les Etudes Classiques*, 23 (1955), 3–13.

Marsh, James L. "The Post-Modern Interpretation of History: A Phenomenological and Hermeneutical Critique." *Journal of the British Society of Phenomenology*, 19 (1988), 112–27.

Martin, Ralph P. "Salvation and Discipleship in Luke's Gospel." In *Interpreting the Gospel*. Ed. James Luther Mays. Philadelphia: Fortress, 1981. Pp. 214–30.

Marx, Werner. *Is There a Measure on Earth: Foundations for a Nonmetaphysical Ethics*. Trans. T. J. Nenon and R. Lilly. Chicago: The University of Chicago Press, 1987.

Meeks, Wayne A. *The Moral World of the First Christians*. Philadelphia: Westminster, 1988.

Metz, Johann Baptist. *Faith in History and Society: Toward a Practical Fundamental Theology*. Trans. David Smith. New York: Crossroad/Seabury, 1980.

Midgley, Mary. *Heart and Mind: The Varieties of Moral Experience*. New York: St. Martin's, 1981.

Miller, J. Hillis. *Deconstruction and Criticism*. New York: Seabury, 1979.

Moltmann, Jürgen. *God in Creation: An Ecological Doctrine of Creation*. Trans. M. Kohln. London: SCM Press, 1985.

———. *On Human Dignity: Political Theology and Ethics*. Trans. M. D. Meeks. Philadelphia: Fortress, 1984.

Morrison, Karl F. *The Mimetic Tradition of Reform in the West*. Princeton: Princeton University Press, 1982.

Murdoch, Iris. "Metaphysics and Ethics." In *The Nature of Metaphysics*. Ed. D. F. Pears. London: Macmillan; New York; St. Martin's, 1957. Pp. 99–123.

——. *The Sovereignty of Good*. London: Routledge & Kegan Paul, 1970.

Nagel, Thomas. *Mortal Questions*. New York: Cambridge University Press, 1979.

Nelson, Paul. *Narrative and Morality: A Theological Inquiry*. University Park: The Pennsylvania State University Press, 1987.

Niebuhr, H. Richard. *Christ and Culture*. New York: Harper & Row, 1951.

——. *Experiential Religion*. New York: Harper & Row, 1972.

——. *The Meaning of Revelation*. New York: Macmillan, 1941.

——. *The Responsible Self: An Essay in Christian Moral Philosophy*. New York: Harper & Row, 1963.

——. "Review of Paul Tillich's *Systematic Theology*, vol. 1." *Union Seminary Quarterly*, 7 (1951), 45–49.

Nielsen, H. A. *Where the Passion Is: A Reading of Kierkegaard's* PHILOSOPHICAL FRAGMENTS. Tallahassee: University Presses of Florida, 1983.

Nietzsche, Friedrich. *The Birth of Tragedy and the Genealogy of Morals*. Trans. Francis Gilffing. New York: Doubleday Anchor, 1956.

Norris, Christopher. *Deconstruction: Theory and Practice*. New York: Methuen, 1981.

North, Robert, S.J. "Violence and the Bible: The Girard Connection." *Catholic Biblical Quarterly*, 47 (1985), 1–27.

Nussbaum, Martha C. *The Fragility of Goodness: Luck and Ethics in Greek Tragedy and Philosophy*. Cambridge: Cambridge University Press, 1986.

Ogden, Schubert. *On Theology*. New York: Harper & Row, 1986.

O'Leary, Joseph S. *Questioning Back: The Overcoming of Metaphysics in the Christian Tradition*. Minneapolis: Winston, 1985.

Origen. *On First Principles*. Trans. G. W. Butterworth. Gloucester, Mass.: Smith, 1973.

Otanti, Hidehito. "The Concept of the Christian in Kierkegaard." *Inquiry*, 8 (1965), 74–83.

Palmer, Richard E. *Hermeneutics*. Northwestern University Studies in Phenomenology and Existential Philosophy. Evanston: Northwestern University Press, 1969.

Pannenberg, Wolfhart. *Jesus—God and Man*. Trans. L. Wilkins and D. Priebe. 2nd ed. Philadelphia: Westminster, 1977.

Parish, Peter J. *The Social Teachings of the Black Churches*. Philadelphia: Fortress, 1985.

Pellauer, David. "*Time and Narrative* and Theological Reflection." *Philosophy Today*, 31 (1987), 262–86.

Peukert, Helmut. *Science, Action, and Fundamental Theology: Towards a Theology of Communicative Action*. Trans. John Bohman. Cambridge: MIT Press, 1984.

Placher, William C. "Paul Ricoeur and Postliberal Theology: A Conflict of Interpretations?" *Modern Theology*, 4 (1987), 35–52.

Plato. *Plato: The Collected Dialogues*. Edd. Edith Hamilton and H. Cairns. Bollingen Series 81. Princeton: Princeton University Press, 1961.

Pojman, Louis P. *The Logic of Subjectivity: Kierkegaard's Philosophy of Religion*. Tuscaloosa: University of Alabama Press, 1984.

Rawls, John. *A Theory of Justice*. Cambridge: The Belknap Press of Harvard University Press, 1971.

Redfield, James M. *Nature and Culture in the* ILIAD: *The Tragedy of Hector*. Chicago: The University of Chicago Press, 1975.

Rendtorff, Trutz. *Ethics*. I. *Basic Elements and Methodology in an Ethical Theology*. Philadelphia: Fortress, 1986.

Ricoeur, Paul. "Appropriation." *Hermeneutics and the Human Sciences: Essays on Language, Action, and Interpretation*. Ed. and trans. John B. Thompson. Cambridge: Cambridge University Press, 1981. Pp. 182–96.

——. "Can Fictional Narrative Be True?" *Analecta Husserliana*, 14 (1983), 3–19.

——. "Erzählung, Metapher, und Interpretationstheorie." *Zeitschrift für Theologie und Kirche*, 84 (1987), 231–53.

——. *Essays on Biblical Interpretation*. Ed. Lewis S. Mudge. Philadelphia: Fortress, 1981.

——. "Ethics and Culture: Habermas and Gadamer in Dialogue." *Philosophy Today*, 17 (1973), 153–65.

——. "The Fragility of Political Language." *Philosophy Today*, 31 (1987), 35–44.

——. "From Existentialism to the Philosophy of Language." In *The Philosophy of Paul Ricoeur*. Edd. C. Regan and D. Stewart. Boston: Beacon, 1978. Pp. 86–94.

——. "The Hermeneutical Function of Distanciation." *Hermeneutics and the Human Sciences: Essays on Language, Action, and Interpretation*. Ed. and trans. John B. Thompson. Cambridge: Cambridge University Press, 1981. Pp. 131–44.

——. "Ideology and Utopia as Cultural Imagination." *Philosophical Exchange*, 2 (1976), 17–30.

——. "Imagination in Discourse and in Action." *Analecta Husserliana*, 7 (1978), 3–22.

——. *Interpretation Theory: Discourse and the Surplus of Meaning*. Fort Worth: Texas Christian University Press, 1976.

——. "Metaphor and the Central Problem of Hermeneutics." *Hermeneutics and the Human Sciences: Essays on Language, Action, and Interpretation*. Ed. and trans. John B. Thompson. Cambridge: Cambridge University Press, 1981. Pp. 165–81.

——. "The Metaphorical Process of Cognition, Imagination, and Feeling."

In *On Metaphor*. Ed. Sheldon Sacks. Chicago: The University of Chicago Press, 1978. Pp. 141–57.

——. "Mimesis et Représentation." *Actes du Congrès des Sociétés de Philosophie de Langue Française*, 18 (1980), 51–61.

——. "Narrated Time." *Philosophy Today*, 29 (1985), 259–71.

——. "Narrative and Time." *Critical Inquiry*, 7 (1980), 169–90.

——. *Political and Social Essays*. Edd. David Stewart and Joseph Bein. Athens: Ohio University Press, 1974.

——. *The Rule of Metaphor: Multi-Disciplinary Studies in the Creation of Meaning in Language*. Trans. Robert Czerny, Kathleen McLaughlin, and John Costello. Toronto: University of Toronto Press, 1977.

——. "The Status of *Vorstellung* in Hegel's Philosophy of Religion." In *Meaning, Truth, and God*. Ed. Leroy S. Rouner. Notre Dame: University of Notre Dame Press, 1982. Pp. 70–90.

——. *Temps et récit*. 3 vols. Paris: Editions du Seuil, 1983–1985.

——. *Time and Narrative*. 3 vols. Trans. Kathleen McLaughlin and David Pellauer. Chicago: The University of Chicago Press, 1984, 1986, 1988.

Rorty, Richard. *The Consequences of Pragmatism: Essays, 1972–1980*. Minneapolis: University of Minnesota Press, 1982.

——. "Deconstruction and Circumvention." *Critical Inquiry*, 11 (1984), 1–23.

——. *Philosophy and the Mirror of Nature*. Princeton: Princeton University Press, 1979.

Ruether, Rosemary Radford. *Sexism and God-Talk: Toward a Feminist Theology*. Boston: Beacon, 1983.

Scharlemann, Robert P. *The Being of God: Theology and the Experience of Truth*. New York: Seabury, 1981.

——. "The No to Nothing and the Nothing to Know: Barth and Tillich and the Possibility of Theological Science." *The Journal of the American Academy of Religion*, 55 (1987), 75–106.

Schleiermacher, F. D. E. *The Christian Faith*. Trans. H. R. Mackintosh and J. S. Stewart. Philadelphia: Fortress, 1976.

——. *Christliche Sittenlehre: Einleitung*. Ed. Herman Peiter. Stuttgart: Kohlhammer, 1983.

——. *Hermeneutics: The Handwritten Manuscripts*. Ed. Heinz Kimmerle. Trans. James Duke and Jack Forstman. American Academy of Religion Texts and Translations 1. Missoula, Mont.: Scholars Press, 1977.

Schrag, Calvin O. *Communicative Praxis and the Space of Subjectivity*. Bloomington: Indiana University Press, 1986.

Schulz, Anselm. *Nachfolge und Nachahmung: Studien über das Verhältnis der neutestamentlichen Jüngerschaft zur urchristlichen Vorbildethik*. Edd. V. Harp and J. Schmid. Studien zum Alten und Neuen Testament 4. Munich: Kösel, 1962.

Schweiker, William. "Beyond Imitation: The Mimetic Praxis of Gadamer, Ricoeur, and Derrida." *The Journal of Religion*, 68 (1988), 21–38.

——. "From Cultural Synthesis to Communicative Action: The Kingdom of God and Ethical Theology." *Modern Theology*, 6 (1989), 367–88.

——. "Iconoclasts, Builders, and Dramatists: The Use of Scripture in Theological Ethics." *The Annual of the Society of Christian Ethics*. Washington, D.C.: Georgetown University Press, 1986. Pp. 129–62.

——. "Sacrifice, Interpretation, and the Sacred: The Import of Gadamer and Girard for Religious Studies." *The Journal of the American Academy of Religion*, 55 (1987), 791–810.

——. "To Dwell on the Earth: Authority and Ecumenical Theology." In *Worldviews and Warrants: Plurality and Authority in Theology*. Edd. William Schweiker and Per M. Anderson. Lanham, Md.: University Press of America, 1987. Pp. 89–112.

Shapiro, David S. "The Doctrine of the Image of God and the *Imitatio Dei*." *Judaism*, 12 (1963), 57–77.

Sheehan, Thomas. "On Movement and the Deconstruction of Ontology." *Monist*, 64 (1981), 534–42.

Smith, John E. *The Analogy of Experience: An Approach to Understanding Truth*. New York: Harper & Row, 1973.

——. *Experience and God*. Oxford: Oxford University Press, 1968.

——. *Purpose and Thought: The Meaning of Pragmatism*. New Haven: Yale University Press, 1978.

Sörböm, Göran. *Mimesis and Art: Studies in the Origin and Early Development of an Aesthetic Vocabulary*. Uppsala: Svenska, 1966.

Sokolowski, Robert. *Moral Action: A Phenomenological Study*. Bloomington: Indiana University Press, 1985.

Sponheim, Paul. *Kierkegaard on Christ and Christian Coherence*. London: SCM Press, 1968.

Stack, George. *Kierkegaard's Existential Ethics*. Tuscaloosa: University of Alabama Press, 1977.

Stout, Jeffrey. *Ethics After Babel: The Languages of Morals and Their Discontents*. Boston: Beacon, 1988.

Strasser, Stephan. "Zeit und Erzählung bei Paul Ricoeur." *Philosophische Rundschau*, 34 (1987), 1–14.

Taylor, Charles. *Philosophical Papers*. I. *Human Agency and Language*. Cambridge: Cambridge University Press, 1985.

Taylor, Mark C. *Erring: A Postmodern A-Theology*. Chicago: The University of Chicago Press, 1984.

——. *Journeys to Selfhood: Hegel and Kierkegaard*. Berkeley: University of California Press, 1980.

——. *Kierkegaard's Pseudonymous Authorship*. Princeton: Princeton University Press, 1975.

———. "Language, Truth, and Indirect Communication." *Tijdschrift voor Filosofie*, 37 (1975), 74–88.

Taylor, Paul. *Respect for Nature*. Princeton, N.J.: Princeton University Press, 1986.

Theunissen, Michael. *The Other: Studies in the Social Ontology of Husserl, Heidegger, Sartre, and Buber*. Trans. Christopher Macann. Cambridge: MIT Press, 1986.

Thiher, Allen. *Words in Reflection: Modern Language Theory and Postmodern Fiction*. Chicago: The University of Chicago Press, 1984.

Thulstrup, Niels. *Søren Kierkegaard's Relation to Hegel*. Trans. George Stengren. Princeton: Princeton University Press, 1980.

Tillich, Paul. *The Courage to Be*. New Haven: Yale University Press, 1952.

———. *Systematic Theology*. 3 vols. in 1. Chicago: The University of Chicago Press, 1967.

Tinsley, E. J. *The Imitation of God in Christ: An Essay on the Biblical Basis of Christian Spirituality*. The Library of History and Doctrine. London: SCM Press, 1960.

Tracy, David. *The Analogical Imagination: Christian Theology and the Culture of Pluralism*. New York: Crossroad, 1981.

———. *Blessed Rage for Order: The New Pluralism in Theology*. New York: Seabury/Crossroad, 1975.

———. *Plurality and Ambiguity: Hermeneutics, Religion, Hope*. New York: Harper & Row, 1986.

Troeltsch, Ernst. *The Social Teachings of the Christian Churches*. Trans. Olive Wyon. 2 vols. Chicago: The University of Chicago Press/Midway, 1979.

Troisfontaines, Claude. "L'identité du social et du religieux selon René Girard." *Revue Philosophique de Louvain*, 78 (1980), 71–90.

Turner, Victor. *From Ritual to Theatre: The Human Seriousness of Play*. New York: Performing Arts Journal, 1982.

Valadier, Paul. "Bouc émissaire et révélation chrétienne selon René Girard." *Etudes*, 357 (1982), 251–60.

Verdenius, W. J. *Mimesis: Plato's Doctrine of Artistic Imitation and Its Meaning to Us*. Philosophia Antiqua 3. Leiden: Brill, 1962.

Wallulis, Jerald. "Philosophical Hermeneutics and the Conflicts of Ontologies." *International Philosophical Quarterly*, 24 (1984), 283–302.

Warnke, Georgia. *Gadamer: Hermeneutics, Tradition, and Reason*. Stanford: Stanford University Press, 1987.

Weidle, Wladamir. "Vom Sinn der Mimesis." *Eranos*, 31 (1962), 249–73.

Weiland, J. Sperna. *Philosophy of Existence and Christianity*. Assen: Van Gorcum, 1951.

Weinsheimer, Joel C. *Gadamer's Hermeneutics: A Reading of* TRUTH AND METHOD. New Haven: Yale University Press, 1985.

Wheelwright, Philip. *Metaphor and Reality*. Bloomington: University of Indiana Press, 1962.

Widerman, Robert, "Some Aspects of Time in Aristotle and Kierkegaard." *Kierkegaardiana* VIII. Ed. Niels Thulstrup. Copenhagen: Munskgaard, 1971. Pp. 7–21.

Williams, Bernard. *Ethics and the Limits of Philosophy*. Cambridge: Harvard University Press, 1985.

——. *Moral Luck: Philosophical Papers, 1973–1980*. Cambridge: Cambridge University Press, 1981.

Winquist, Charles E. *Epiphanies of Darkness: Deconstruction in Theology*. Philadelphia: Fortress, 1986.

Winter, Gibson. *Liberating Creation: Foundations of Religious Social Ethics*. New York: Crossroad, 1981.

Yack, Bernard. *The Longing for Total Revolution: Philosophical Sources of Social Discontent from Rousseau to Marx and Nietzsche*. Princeton: Princeton University Press, 1986.

Yeats, William Butler. "The Second Coming." *The Collected Works of W. B. Yeats*. New York: Macmillan, 1956. P. 184.

Yoder, John Howard. *The Politics of Jesus: Vicit Agnus Noster*. Grand Rapids: Eerdmans, 1972.

INDEX